CONTINGENT
WORK

CONTINGENT

WORK

AMERICAN EMPLOYMENT RELATIONS IN TRANSITION

*Edited by Kathleen Barker
and Kathleen Christensen*

ILR Press
an imprint of
Cornell University Press
Ithaca and London

First published 1998 by Cornell University Press
First printing, Cornell Paperbacks, 1998

Printed in the United States of America

Library of Congress Cataloging-in-Publication Data

Contingent work : American employment relations in transition /
    Kathleen Barker and Kathleen Christensen, editors.
            p.   cm.
        Includes bibliographical references and index.
        ISBN 0-8014-3369-X (cloth : alk. paper). —
    ISBN 0-8014-8405-7 (pbk. : alk. paper)
        1. Temporary employment—United States. 2. Part-time
    employment—United States. 3. Seasonal labor—United
    States. 4. Piece-work—United States. 5. Contract system
    (Labor)—United States. 6. Employee fringe benefits—Law
    and legislation—United States. 7. Labor laws and legisla-
    tion—United States. I. Barker, Kathleen, 1951–   .
    II. Christensen, K. (Kathleen)
    HD5854.2.U6C66   1998
    331.25'72—dc21   98-11445

Cloth printing   10 9 8 7 6 5 4 3 2 1
Paperback printing   10 9 8 7 6 5 4 3 2

Contents

Acknowledgments

This book grew out of a series of informal conversations that the two editors initiated in 1993. These conversations led to a broader dialogue with the contributors to this volume and eventually to the plans for a collection on contingent work.

We would like to acknowledge many individuals for their contribution to this project. To begin, we especially thank our contributors, who thoughtfully responded to suggestions for revision and deadlines during a very long project. We also appreciate the efforts of librarian Jane Hyrshko, who deserves special thanks for her skill and good humor in providing numerous articles, chapters, books, and government documents during the early stages of the collection's development.

The staff and reviewers employed by Cornell University Press/ILR were a tremendous asset in the development of the volume, giving us prescient insights, comments, and recommendations. We want to thank Fran Benson, Editor-in-Chief of Cornell University Press, and her staff. Through stops and starts, Fran's unflagging support and guidance were critical in the early stages through to the final development of the volume. The efforts of Cornell's Teresa Jesionowski and Kay Scheuer were critical to the final shaping of the project, as was John LeRoy's astute sense of language. Others who provided help at various points included Manasi Tirodkar and Lilian Barria.

Finally, our family members lived through the best and worst moments of this project. Kathleen Barker thanks her husband, Gary Holden, for his diplomatic and *almost* unerringly correct solutions to problems of text and data presentation. The combination of his high tolerance for ambiguity, his affection, and his love of merriment made the development and completion of this collection an easier task. Family members Agnes and Russell deserve special thanks for believing that each corner turned on this topic represented a significant achievement. Kathleen Christensen wants to thank her husband, Jack Murray, for his thoughtful editorial suggestions and his good humor and her daughters, Clare and Grace, for their patience.

During this project, we moved a number of times and each of us experienced significant changes in job responsibilities. Through it all, our families were steadfast in their support and nurturance. We thank them and hope that their nurturance, our contributors' insights, and our perseverance result in a compelling portrait of one aspect of the transition in American employment relations at the beginning of the twenty-first century.

K. B. and K. C.

CONTINGENT

WORK

Controversy and Challenges Raised by Contingent Work Arrangements

Kathleen Barker
Kathleen Christensen

Contingent work constitutes one of the most controversial labor issues. In this era of corporate downsizing and a general sense of job insecurity, the notion that American workers have become "disposable" has pervaded the American consciousness (*New York Times,* 1996). Perhaps this is illustrated nowhere as clearly as in the fact that the largest U.S. employer is now Manpower, the temporary help agency. Within this economic climate, many argue that what once were lifetime jobs have increasingly become contingent ones and that what once were solid links between employers and workers have become tenuous ones.

The term "contingent work" was coined initially by labor economist Audrey Freedman (1985:35) to refer to those "conditional and transitory employment arrangements as initiated by a need for labor—usually because a company has an increased demand for a particular service or a product or technology, at a particular place, at a specific time." For many, contingent work represents the human resources equivalent to a just-in-time inventory system, constituting a just-in-time workforce. Contingent work has generally been thought to include those jobs that are done on temporary, self-employed contract, or involuntary part-time bases (Belous, 1989; Christensen & Murphree, 1988). The public debates on the pros and cons of contingent work have become vociferous (U.S. House of Representatives, 1988).

Advocates for contingent staffing argue that it offers multiple benefits for the firm—it increases staffing flexibility, cuts direct labor costs, as well as reducing or eliminating benefit costs, and it can, in addition to benefiting the firm, enhance workers' leverage in the marketplace, particularly for those workers whose skills are in demand. Critics, on the other hand, maintain that contingent work can hurt firms by increasing turnover, limiting the development of firm-specific knowledge, and weakening worker loyalty, and it can undercut organized labor's ability to represent workers, leaving an increasingly large number of workers with no safety net of federal protections or health and pension coverage.

Despite this public concern about contingent work, the number of contingent workers appears quite small. According to the U.S. Bureau of Labor Statistics (BLS), the maximum number of contingent workers in the United States, as of February 1995, was six million, representing only 4.9 percent of the workforce (Polivka, 1996a)—hardly a significant share of American workers. Why has such a small fraction of workers been able to attract such a large proportion of U.S. political, economic, and social attention?

Are the numbers simply wrong, and are there more contingent workers than have been counted by the government? Some might argue this point on the grounds that with a different definition of contingent work than that used by BLS, the percent of the U.S. workforce increases to 25 to 33 percent (Belous, 1989). Are the media hypersensitive to these issues, providing more coverage than this phenomenon warrants? Others could argue this point, as it is quite clear that both the electronic and print media have experienced a proliferation of contracting-out arrangements. Or are people sensing that something much more profound is happening to the basic contract between employer and employee that has defined, at least in principle, the fundamental obligations and responsibilities between the firm and the worker? We are convinced that this last supposition rings truest.

We believe that contingent work, despite the lack of consensus on size and demographics, represents a profound deviation from the employment relations model that has dominated most of this century's labor relations. Although a secondary workforce is certainly not new to our economy—one has existed in this country since at least the mid-1800s—the emergence of a highly skilled, technical or white-collar secondary workforce is new. Until recently this relatively privileged set of workers has worked under a very different model of employment relations.

Hierarchical Control: The Dominant Model of Twentieth-Century Employment Relations

When the history of twentieth-century labor relations is written, it will essentially be the history of the transformation of the small craft-based firms of the late 1800s into the large hierarchically controlled corporations of the 1900s. The defining characteristics of a hierarchically controlled organization include the following (Pfeffer & Baron, 1988):

- strong administrative control through explicit personnel rules
- encouragement of long-term employment

- creation of internal career ladders
- high premium placed on firm-specific knowledge
- physical concentration of workers

Under this model, employees are firmly entrenched inside the corporation. In effect, the corporation substitutes hierarchy and internal promotion for the open labor market as a way of securing and controlling workers.

Personnel rules provide a formal set of rules and procedures which determine how workers are to be compensated, disciplined, trained, and promoted; these rules serve as an explicit statement of the employees' rights and obligations within the firm and, for white-collar workers, substitute for an explicit employment contract.

Long-term employment relations can heighten and intensify the identification of the worker with the firm and the firm with its workers, yielding a powerful loyalty of one to the other. Such intense worker-firm loyalty was perhaps nowhere articulated as forcefully as in William Whyte's 1956 book, *The Organization Man*. Long-term employment also creates the possibility for internal career ladders, which have redefined *jobs* into *careers*, as well as opportunities for training, skill upgrading, and promotion.

The cumulative effect of long-term employment, strong worker loyalty, and internal career paths has been that firms develop and refine a large body of firm-specific knowledge. This knowledge can be developed and shared through casual, informal ways, as well as through formal on-site training programs, because of the emphasis on the physical concentration of workers in the workplace. This emphasis on keeping workers on site and highly visible has led to visibility, often referred to as "face-time," becoming a critical indicator of worker commitment, loyalty, and productivity.

As we approach the end of the twentieth century, however, many of the tenets highly valued by the traditional hierarchical firms are being challenged. As firms have gone through successive waves of downsizing, it appears that highly centralized administrative control has been weakened, job tenure has been shortened, at least for the one in fourteen workers involuntarily terminated between 1993 and 1995 (Uchitelle, 1996), firms appear to be placing less importance on firm-specific knowledge, and many workers have found themselves not working in centralized work sites. With these changes has come a sense that the history of twentieth-century employment relations is in the process of being rewritten. But many questions remain: How is it being rewritten?

Is it affecting all workers? Where are we heading? What will be the new model of employment relations?

Transition in Employment Relations

Many workers today work in organizations that differ considerably from traditional hierarchically controlled organizations. Perhaps the central difference has to do with the employer-employee relationship and the control that the firm exercises over the workers. Many firms now operate with variable administrative control, exercising tight control over some workers and minimal or no control over others. This variable administrative control leads to many questions: Are there shorter terms of employment? Is long-term employment, along with a career ladder and training opportunity, still valued, and if so, by whom? How important is firm-specific knowledge and the physical concentration of workers?

The critical change in employment relations in many firms is the introduction of variable administrative control over workers. Increasingly complex hiring relationships are supplanting what has been a simple direct relationship between employee and corporate employer. Workers are being hired in larger numbers on a variety of different bases: temporary hires made directly by the firm; temporary hires made through an agency (who technically remain employees of the agency not the firm); and self-employed independent contractors who are hired on a project basis. In addition, entire functions of organizations, ranging from data analyses to janitorial, cafeteria, and security services, are being outsourced, that is, subcontracted out to other companies. The amount of control the firm exercises over this range of workers can vary greatly.

Temporary workers can be hired directly by the firm or as employees of the temporary help service. Direct-hire temps remain employees of the firm and are hired for multiple purposes, including to cover employees who are out sick or on leave, to staff for high-demand periods that are seasonal, cyclical, or unanticipated, or to serve in a floating pool to cover needs as they occur across the firm. As employees of the firm, direct-hire temps are supervised on site and are potentially eligible for firm-based benefits. Actual eligibility is typically a function of annual hours worked.

Temporary agency hires find themselves in a more complicated co-employment situation: they are technically employees of the temporary agency, which is responsible for setting compensation and for providing training, yet they are supervised, and at times disciplined, by the client firm to which they are assigned. The handling of issues such as sexual harassment and worker safety becomes more complicated because of this co-employer relationship. Case law in the United States has only begun to address some of these complications regarding liability. For example, if a worker files a complaint that he or she is a victim of sexual harassment at a client site, who is legally responsible: the on-site firm or the off-site employer?

In the case of independent contractors, the firm minimizes or avoids control over the worker because the worker is legally hired as a self-employed worker. The firm pays for the job that is contracted for but typically bears no responsibility for providing training or benefits. As a self-employed worker, the worker has no rights under federal or state law to be eligible for unemployment insurance or workers compensation. Such workers also fall outside protective legislation such as the Family Medical Leave Act. In the case of outsourcing of entire functions, the worker becomes an employee of the subcontracting firm, and the original organization abdicates any direct responsibility for compensation, training, benefits, or liability.

In these cases involving temporary, contract, or outsourced workers, the employer has willingly abdicated some responsibility for the workers—the amount varies according to the conditions of hiring. The firm's control over such workers is exchanged for the newfound flexibility these new relationships or "attachments" can provide (Barker, 1995). Explicit personnel rules governing the firms' permanent full-time employees have little relevance for these contract and temp workers.

This mix of hiring practices has resulted in a complex network of employer-worker relations within any one firm. Some employees remain firmly entrenched in the organization, others are being taken outside of it. This complex set of hiring practices of workers has raised questions about its differential effects on commitment, on the importance of firm-specific knowledge, and on having workers work on site. Many of the questions are not yet answerable, either because contradictory evidence exists or minimal information is available.

With regard to job tenure, current research reveals that there has been little to no change, thus far, in workers' overall job tenure (Diebold, Neumark, & Polsky, 1994; Farber, 1995). Yet the evidence of corporate downsizing and the rise in the use of temporary hires have led many workers to question their own job security and their employers' commitment to long-term employment (Bennett, 1989; Uchitelle, 1996). Furthermore, how tenure is defined and understood may need to be revisited in light of the rapid rate of growth of the temporary help service industry. The conventional notion of tenure, which has to do with length of job with one employer, does not and cannot take into account the complicated co-employment relationship experienced by agency temporaries. An agency temporary might be employed for a number of years by that agency but work on short-term assignments at many different client companies. Does job tenure mean the same for an agency temporary who works ten years for an agency at multiple client sites as it does for an employee who works for one employer for ten years?

The hiring of contingent workers also raises questions about the significance that firms place on having workers with firm-specific knowledge. Temps and contractors are hired for the skills they already can bring to the firm. This specialized knowledge is a commodity that the firms can purchase. This is a quite different approach from the traditional model in which firms invest in employees and keep the skills and skill development in-house. There would be little incentive to a firm to provide technical training to workers who are not expected to have a long shelf life at the organization.

Developing in parallel with the notion of contingent work has been a public and corporate interest in telecommuting, involving the physical dispersal of *employees* from the centralized work site to off-site workplaces, typically involving the home or satellite neighborhood work centers (Christensen, 1988a, 1988b; Nilles, 1994). A critical feature of telecommuting, until recently at least, has been the *voluntary* nature of this physical dispersion of employees. Employees have self-selected to work at home or elsewhere off-site because of their performance records and the congruence between their work and lifestyle. But we are now entering an era of much more involuntary telecommuting, in which employees are given no choice but to work somewhere other than their offices. Although usually targeted to certain departments of an organization, such as sales or service, the involuntary nature of the arrangements signal a real change in employee relations. Employees are being physically dispersed on a permanent basis from a centralized workplace.

Promoted as the new "virtual office," these involuntary telecommuting programs keep employees from daily contact with one another and minimize the amount of firm-specific knowledge that can be developed and shared in informal, casual ways. The introduction of a facilities management technique called hoteling, whereby employees dock at an available cubicle when they come into the office, has met with mixed reactions by workers. Furthermore, recent research indicates that client service may actually decrease when the new "involuntary" telecommuters live far away from the centralized site and are reluctant to leave their home offices and commute into the city to meet with a client on what appears to be a minor concern (Paul Attewell, personal communication, May 1996). Involuntary telecommuting results in a physical dispersion of employees.

Many of the changes occurring in today's workplace are often thought to be independent of one another. We contend that as firms seek to loosen their control over growing numbers of workers by hiring increasing numbers on a contingent basis, we are witnessing the beginning of a profound change in labor relations. But actually how new are these changes?

Casting a Broad Net: Framing the Transition

In his historical analysis of labor market patterns from the mid-nineteenth century to when he was writing in 1969, labor economist Dean Morse concluded that

> the structure of the modern labor force . . . consists of a large nucleus of full-time, full-year workers, generally but not always employed by large scale organizations. This nucleus possess a considerable amount of "status" and is protected by a host of private and public institutions. Surrounding it are groups of "peripheral workers," numbering many millions, who do not have the status and protection taken for granted by workers who from one year to the next are likely to have continuous full-time employment. (Morse, 1969:68)

Morse maintains that by the late nineteenth and into the early twentieth century, American society had developed deep-seated negative attitudes toward the kind of people who did the irregular, intermittent, part-time jobs that made up the bulk of the peripheral economy. These persons were seen as outsiders and inferiors to those who worked in the central core of the economy at full-time/full-year jobs. Since the late nineteenth century, these outsiders have included blacks, newly arrived European and Asian immigrants, and women—members of groups marginalized by race, gender, and ethnicity. He further contends that the biases and stereotypes toward these workers were so firmly entrenched in our society that as subsequent groups have taken on these irregular, intermittent, or part-time jobs they also have been subject to the same negative attitudes.

The composition of the peripheral workforce began to shift dramatically during the 1980s, during which time observers began commenting on the implications of the acquisitions, mergers, downsizing, and expansion with nonpermanent personnel. As a result of corporate processes that intended to achieve efficiency through streamlining human resources, workers who had historically dominated the central core (for example, professionals, technical workers, and managers) began to be shifted into the secondary workforce, taking jobs that were intermittent, irregular, or part-time. When this shift of white and middle-class male and female skilled workers into the secondary workforce began to occur, we failed to recognize that this was but a new turn in a long-standing labor market trend. Our historical amnesia was, in part, fueled by the fact that these workers were now being referenced by a new term—contingent workers.

Although the contingent workforce appears to continue to include large numbers of people who have traditionally been in the secondary labor force (for example, semi- and unskilled women, young and older workers, and members of minority races and ethnic groups), the increasing membership of white male and female professionals and managers has gained the attention of the media and the politicians. No longer can this contingent workforce be ignored, for its size has grown and its membership now includes workers who have historically experienced the status, privilege, and protections accorded the core group of workers. What do we know about contingent work from the perspective of the workers?

The Individual Perspective

From the worker's perspective, there is much to be learned about what it is like to work conditionally. It would seem that from the individual perspective, contingent work may be experienced in a variety of ways:

- Varying degrees of opportunity: For some professional and highly skilled workers, it may be argued, the opportunity to move from site to site assists in the development of knowledge, skills, and abilities associated with their occupation or the industry or industries in which they work. When highly educated/skilled workers are in abundance, however, a tight labor market will limit the leverage that these workers can exercise in selecting opportunities and setting rates.

- Variable control over work and variable reliability of work: By the nature of its temporary or contract conditions, most contingent work arrangements carry little to no commitment beyond a limited or ambiguous amount of time. Consequently, contingent work carries with it little to no financial or career security.
- Loss of career ladders, promotion, and training: Most contingent arrangement do not allow the worker to further develop current skills or gain new ones on the job. The contingent worker is considered a commodity, and this commodity is seen as a fixed, nonrenewable resource in which there is little, if any, investment by the firm. Organizations are replenished with new workers as needed, and hence there is no need to replenish the worker.

There remains much to be learned about the workers who constitute the contingent workforce, what kinds of jobs they engage in, and how they experience work on a contingent basis.

About This Book

Part of the controversy surrounding contingent work rests on the fact that fundamental aspects of this phenomenon are not understood. We do not, for example, have precise numbers on the size of this workforce, much less its demographic characteristics. Part of the variation in numbers is due to variation in definitions. We also have little dispassionate understanding of the human face of contingent work: how do workers fare economically, socially, and psychologically as a function of being part of this contingent workforce? And we know even less about how corporations have utilized contingent work in the midst of what are often countervailing staffing and human resource strategies. Finally, the role of government in both fueling the development of contingent work and providing mechanisms to protect workers who increasingly fall outside of the safety net of health and welfare provisions is only beginning to be discerned and clearly understood. The purpose of this book is to provide answers to these unresolved questions.

In framing these questions, we have drawn on the work of a multidisciplinary set of authors. We believe that the ultimate strength of this volume will rest on pulling together thinkers from fields as diverse as sociology, anthropology, social psychology, labor economics, and business administration. Our overall goals for this volume are multiple: to provide an understanding of contingent work from the perspectives of several disciplines; to stimulate our colleagues in the social sciences who are concerned with public interest and corporate vitality; and to promote policies that are deemed fair, just, and feasible for both the worker and the organization.

Chapters in this book are organized into four parts: The Workers: Numbers and Patterns; The Workplace: Tensions and Trends; The Human Face of Contingent Workers; and Policy and Research: Future Directions.

The Workers: Numbers and Patterns

The chapters in this part describe the historical and economic frameworks within which contingent work is defined, enumerated, and contested. The potential for linking the historical "peripheral" workforce with the contemporary "contingent" one is provided by Dean Morse in Chapter 1. In this excerpt from his 1969 monograph, *The Peripheral Worker*, Morse describes a historically rooted workplace hierarchy in which blacks, immigrants, and women were assigned or accepted secondary or "disposable" roles due to sociocultural exclusions based on race, ethnicity, and gender. In his view, such exclusions produced the subsequent waves of contingent or disposable workers and facilitated the successful bifurcation of the American workplace: "In a sense the basic drama continued to be enacted, the only change being in the cast. Other demographic groups upon whom society could ascribe a label of innate inferiority simply took the place of the immigrant. . . . It remained proper that irregular, casual, part-time, intermittent work should be performed by the 'outsider' [who is] by definition biologically inferior" (see p. 29 below).

Morse reasoned that tax policies and corporate flexibility requirements were responsible, in part, for the rise of the peripheral workforce, an argument that foreshadows contemporary reasoning regarding the role of government in the rise of contingent employment (Gonos, Chapter 7) and in underwriting a cheap source of female labor as a form of social welfare (Spalter-Roth & Hartmann, Chapter 3), in which women supplement low and intermittent wages with means-tested benefits.

If flexibility, whether for corporations or the individual, has been one of the hallmarks in discussions of contingent work, conceptualization and enumeration represent its most contested terrain. In the late 1980s, the number of contingent workers in the United States was roughly estimated to range from 29.9 to 36.6 million or 25 to 30 percent of the workforce (Belous, 1989), but this estimate was quickly challenged by economists at the U.S. Department of Labor's Bureau of Labor Statistics (BLS) (Polivka & Nardone, 1989). Their new BLS definition stated that a set of characteristics such as variable hours and job insecurity must be present to designate the job as contingent, in effect ruling out most part-time jobs and many of the self-employed. In an effort to provide a coherent definition of contingent work, Anne Polivka and Thomas Nardone offered the following: "any job in which an individual does not have an explicit or implicit contract for long-term employment or one in which the minimum hours worked can vary in a nonsystematic manner" (Polivka & Nardone, 1989:11).

In Chapter 2, economists at the Bureau of Labor Statistics (BLS) present their most recent research on contingent work. They have developed three estimates of the size of the contingent workforce based on the definition that contingent workers are "individuals who do not perceive themselves as having an explicit or implicit contract for ongoing employment." The BLS estimates, were developed from a special supplement to the Current Population Survey (CPS) and were released to the press in August 1995. Their numbers are much lower than the widely cited Belous figures. Moreover, the CPS figures are also much lower than longitudinal estimates based on panel data, the U.S. Bureau of the Census's Survey of Income and Program Participation (SIPP), analyzed by sociologist Roberta Spalter-Roth and economist Heidi Hartmann (Chapter 3). The least conservative estimate provided by the BLS is that 4.9 percent of the American workforce is contingent, while Spalter-Roth and Hartmann argue that at least 16 percent of all workers are working contingently. The discrepancy is due in part to different definitions and data sets that each research group utilizes (the CPS is cross-sectional while the SIPP data is longitudinal).

Controversy continues to plague the conceptualization and enumeration of contingent work, especially in regard to the categories of the self-employed, independent contractors working for one employer, and part-time/part-year arrangements. Chapters 2 and 3 reflect the difficulties in defining and enumerating contingent work arrangements in the United States. Chapter 3 also examines the gendering of contingent work.

Women are represented disproportionately in contingent work, even as many indicators show that they are increasing their commitment to full-time and full-year work. Spalter-Roth and Hartmann dispel earlier notions regarding the attractiveness of contingent arrangements to women as they show that women's hourly wages are lowest in contingent and permanent part-time jobs with a correlated decrease in the ability to support a family on such earnings. Women working contingently are also most likely to have young children *and* to live without the support of a full-time/full-year breadwinner.

These authors argue that women, still stereotyped as secondary workers, tend to perform the jobs that are less valued in our society and that women and their families are at a special risk from these contingent arrangements. As contingent workers, they are typically ineligible for any employer-provided work-family benefits, such as referrals or vouchers for child care, or for paid parental leave (Christensen, Chapter 4). Yet they do not have the resources from their jobs to meet all of their family needs. Spalter-Roth and Hartmann's analysis shows that one out of seven women employed in contingent arrangements relies on means-tested welfare benefits. Institutions and organizations are providing "employment" that fails to provide a living wage, and the result is a hidden cost to society and taxpayers. At exactly the point that "tough love" (a kind of term limit for welfare benefits) has been adopted as a solution to women's dependence on the state for aid for themselves and their children, large numbers of women find themselves in jobs that provide inadequate support.

The Workplace: Tensions and Trends

The purpose of the four chapters in this part is to illustrate ways in which contingent staffing is being rolled out within corporations, specifically examining how it relates to other organizational strategies.

In Chapter 4, Kathleen Christensen considers the human resource contradictions raised by a firm's dual pursuit of contingent staffing arrangements and progressive work-family policies. The first pursuit treats workers as commodities which are entirely fungible and often expendable, while the second views employees as assets which are to be mined and in which investments should be made. Her findings, based on survey and interview data, reveal that even in forward-thinking and progressive firms, contingent workers are typically ineligible for the firm's work-family benefits that support permanent workers and that many human resource managers are troubled by what appears to be an increasing bifurcation of their internal labor markets into the "haves" and "have-nots." Christensen considers whether legal considerations and current labor law, as well as a limited sense of corporate responsibility, rationalize and institutionalize the liminal status of contingent workers, a theme that is also developed by Stanley Nollen and Helen Axel (Chapter 5), George Gonos (Chapter 7), and James Rebitzer (Chapter 10). But the urgency of the work-family conflicts facing contingent workers is dramatic, as Christensen's study confirms that many of the surveyed firms plan an increase in contingent arrangements over the next three years.

Are such workers cost effective? Are there instances in which contingent arrangements are dubious cost-control and cost-effective mechanisms? As companies shed responsibilities for both core and contingent workers and establish distant relationships with those who are contingent, do the firms accomplish all they expect to when restructuring work for different status workers? In Chapter 5, Nollen and Axel address the issue of tangible and intangible benefits of employing contingent workers and address a range of human resources deployment strategies. Wages and benefits are only one factor in the cost equation; productivity, training, and length of service are predictive factors in the effectiveness of contingent workers. Nollen and Axel describe methods for estimating the utility of using contingent work arrangements and suggest approaches for raising worker productivity through the design of specific programs with appeal to these workers.

Running parallel to the increased popularity of contingent staffing in the United States has been the comparably increasing popularity of the high-performance workplace where high employee involvement (EI) is valued. Yet, no research has been done to determine if there are patterns within firms as to their use of contingent staffing and high EI. Using one of the few data sets available, the Australian Workplace Industrial Relations Survey (AWIRS), economist Robert Drago (Chapter 6) addresses whether contingent arrangements and high-performance workplaces are linked. He argues that there are two paths to high performance—through "workplace transformation" and through the "disposable workplace." Expanding on some of the ideas found in Nollen and Axel, Drago finds that contingent work arrangements are, as suspected, related to job insecurity. His results suggest that contingent work signals "job insecurity for all employees, and [does] not generally serve as a buffer for core employee job security." Furthermore, Australian government initiatives that facilitate the development of employee involvement are suspected of encouraging employers to expand contingent arrangements in a disposable workplace model. Drago concludes his analysis with some comments on the pertinence of the findings to conditions found in the United States.

To consider contingent work as solely an institutional or organizational solution to cost-effectiveness is to continue to perpetrate the *economic* framework for contingent work, according to sociologist George Gonos (Chapter 7). Furthermore, it disregards the direct role government plays, and likely will continue to play, in maintaining a labor and policy environment that facilitates the increasing use of certain forms of contingent employment. According to Gonos, contingent employment is first of all a social arrangement. A socio-legal framework for understanding how particular forms of contingent work have been transformed over the past twenty-five years uncovers not only the interactive role of government and business in the transformation of temporary employment but also the web of relationships from which this category emerged. Gonos maintains that the transition to a new model of employment relations began not in the 1980s, as conventionally believed, but in the 1950s. Gonos argues that evidence from the temporary help industry's legal and political maneuvering, so as to create alternative employment relationships, locates the industrial relations U-turn as early as the 1950s. The securing of legal status for temporary help service firms within states and the establishment of a legal, if not entirely legitimate, relationship among temporary agencies, workers, and work sites were long and costly battles for the temporary help industry. Other industries and institutions may not have faced such a long struggle as they attempted to displace permanent workers with less costly contract or temporary workers (Barker, Chapter 8; Rebitzer, Chapter 10). Yet the notion that the temporary help industry may have provided a subtle legal context for other industries—those experimenting with contingent work—is intriguing. The conversion of employment itself from a relationship to a commodity has significant consequences for the worker. In the next part, contributors provide a framework for understanding the human experience of contingent employment.

The Human Face of Contingent Workers

The chapters in this part address contingent work as a social process entailing human reactions and social costs. The part starts with a social psychological exploration of the psychological and career consequences experienced by temporary professional workers of higher education— adjunct professors—and the value ascribed to them by potential employers (Barker, Chapter 8). Next, a sociocultural analysis of temporary workers in a small southern city—Greenville, South Carolina—documents the realities of living on the periphery and the struggle of workers to maintain themselves in contingent, highly disposable arrangements (McAllister, Chapter 9). The third chapter of this part describes institutional features of the contract employment relationship and health and safety issues in the petrochemical industry (Rebitzer, Chapter 10). Returning to a theme which Morse emphasized, all contributions in this part are concerned with the moral and human costs associated with systematic exclusion.

Social psychologist Kathleen Barker explores how difference is constructed in alternative work arrangements and utilizes a *difference-as-deficit* model to explore contingent work. Such a model specifies that difference itself is constructed from the viewers' perspective and is also filtered by evaluators and institutional expectations concerning what is "typical" and what is not. When individuals do not meet such a standard they are ascribed a deficient identity and are thus rationalized as falling outside the moral community, a community in which rules of justice and fairness are understood to prevail. She then proceeds to explore one particular industry, higher education. As a site for workplace transformation, higher education is interesting mainly because it a institution that utilizes uniquely educated contingent workers in a setting that appeals to the ideal of the collegium but which is layered with institutionally mediated identities that are not necessarily equivalent in worth or value. As the workplace becomes a site that replenishes itself on an as-needed basis with new skilled workers without replenishing these workers with investments such as training and career development, individual adjunct professors absorb the risks and the stigma associated with contingent work. These adjunct professors discuss their plight as one in which they accumulate the deficits associated with contingent work, a view which is then tested on a national survey of department heads in four-year colleges and research institutions.

The contingent workers of higher education and those working in the warehouses of Greenville, South Carolina, share a certain sense of marginality, vulnerability, and uncertainty due to their working conditions. But if a failure to land a permanent job for a Ph.D. results in a bitter revision of expectations and scrutiny of the concept of meritocracy, for other workers who are already challenged by their education, geographic location, race, gender, or age, contingent work may result in especially problematic if not cruel day-to-day realities.

An anthropologist, Jean McAllister crosses the borders of race and community in one of the first studies of industrial temp workers (Chapter 9). McAllister provides multiple portraits of temporary workers that expand on many of the themes developed earlier in the volume. These are temporary workers who experience exclusion in the workplace (see

Morse, Chapter 1); they accumulate deficits as they are passed over for training (see Barker, Chapter 8); however, they also struggle to maintain a family household while working contingently and so are not provided with many family-work initiatives (see Christensen, Chapter 4) and become, sometimes, an unwilling recipient of means-tested benefits (see Spalter-Roth & Hartmann, Chapter 3). McAllister draws a portrait of workers in a community in which the permanent, full-time job—the "killer job"—becomes a necessary, almost centripetal, force for maintaining a family constellation. That the individual appears to be assuming increasing amounts of risk—getting a raw deal instead of a New Deal—needs to be carefully weighed with the corporate benefits accrued from greater certainty and flexibility.

Organizations that use temporary or contract workers disavow health and safety responsibilities for such workers by assigning the primary responsibility for their safety training and supervision of contract employees to individual contractors. James Rebitzer (Chapter 10) provides one of the few analyses of health and safety issues raised by contingent work arrangements, particularly for one of the least protected classes, the contract workers. Of eleven major workplace accidents in the U.S. petrochemical industry in the six months from January to June 1991, nine involved contract workers. Prior to this period, the Phillips 66 explosion in October 1989, in which contract workers were implicated, brought the issue of contract workers to a crisis. Rebitzer's analysis, based in part on the data collected for the John Gray Institute study that followed the Phillips 66 explosion, suggests that host plants offer more effective safety training and supervision to their employees than to contractors. But the legal aspects of liability play a role in this discrepancy. If host plants are not penalized for failing to supervise contract workers adequately, then making the plants equally liable for these workers and for their own employees might provide greater incentive for taking primary responsibility for safety training and supervision. The proposed likelihood would then be that accident rates would be reduced.

Policy and Research: Future Directions

The picture that emerges from the chapters in Part III is one in which borderless loyalties appear as rational choices for workers to pursue. Self-loyalty appears the most rational response to a workplace environment that emphasizes the fungibility of workers. Yet, contingent work, as developed by different authors throughout the volume, erodes an ideology of self-sufficiency. As a number of authors point out, even when workers want to protect themselves, their ability to do so is eroded in a work environment that limits their wage, fails to provide basic protections for health and safety, renders them ineligible for employer-provided work-family benefits, and undercuts their ability to accumulate intellectual assets necessary to improve their working condition. Such erosion raises important questions that are addressed in Part IV. Chapters 11 and 12 address how contingent work challenges current labor and employment law, as well as the organizing strategies used by the unions. The final task of this part is to chart future research needs. Chapter 13 identifies the issues that must inform the next generation of research on contingent work.

Virginia duRivage, Françoise Carré, and Chris Tilly maintain in Chapter 11 that U.S. labor law has become increasingly out of date in its ability to serve the needs of contingent workers. These laws, crafted in the 1930s and 1940s, were designed to regulate labor-management relations and to guarantee a worker's right to choose union representation. Yet they were premised on the traditional permanent, full-time employment relationship. These laws are inadequate to serve the needs of the contingent workers, some of whom are not employees at all (self-employed contractors), others of whom work in complicated co-employment conditions (agency temps), and others who do not work on full-time bases (part-time employees). As a result, duRivage and her colleagues argue that contingent workers suffer from a series of problems, including few to no benefits, low wages, reduced employment security, and barriers to advancement. The authors detail the flaws in existing labor laws and identify the changes necessary to remedy these flaws. They also argue that changing labor laws will not be enough and that the unions, slow to respond to workplace change, must develop more effective organizing strategies for this contingent workforce. To illustrate their points regarding the necessary changes to labor laws and unions strategies, they draw on examples from two industries, construction and garment, where alternative union structures and legal provisions for a contingent workforce have had a long history.

Just as labor law and union strategies regarding contingent work require change, Anthony Carnevale, Lynn Jennings, and James Eisenmann argue in Chapter 12 that employment law and entitlement coverage is eroded for many workers who work contingently. Demonstrating an employment relationship is required for workers to qualify for coverage under the Fair Labor Standards Act, the Equal Pay Act, Title VII of the

Civil Rights Act of 1964, the Age Discrimination in Employment Act, the Employee Retirement Income Security Act, the Occupational Safety and Health Act, and other legislation. The chapter focuses on why the establishment of an employment relationship for contingent workers is at best a jurisdictional hurdle and often an impossibility given the way employment law is currently written and practiced. Of the tests available to the courts for establishing an employment relationship, only a minority use the "economic realities" test that would provide greater protections for the greater number of workers. As Carnevale and his colleagues note, however, in the emergence of a two-tier employment system the contingently employed face a second set of barriers that the permanently employed do not. When job security is minimal, fear of retaliation for having initiated a course of action is potentially great. These authors conclude their chapter with comments on the issues analysts and policy makers face in accommodating contingent workers.

Chapter 13 surveys the contributions to this collection. In this chapter, the editors cull the issues and questions that investigators will face in the next generation of research in the twenty-first century. The definition of contingent work remains contentious. Even as this volume was going to press, a reanalysis of BLS data provided new estimates of the number of contingent workers in the United States. We briefly highlight this new research in the context of definitional concerns before turning our attention to the research needed on contingent work as an employment strategy and the questions that emerge from the workers' perspectives.

In preparing this volume, a workplace scholar commented to one of the editors, "Aren't we all contingent?" This question strikes a resonant chord regarding the insecurity of our jobs in our society. It misses the point, however, that contingent workers are robbed to a large extent of the privileges still held by most full-time "permanent" employees, no matter how insecure those employees might be. In the wisdom that comes from hindsight, we may eventually recognize these contingent workers as the canaries in the mine shaft—they may reveal whether we can live with a model of employment relations that differs radically from the model that has dominated most of this century.

Part I

The Workers:
Numbers and Patterns

CHAPTER ONE

Historical Perspective: The Peripheral Worker (1969)

Dean Morse

*T*wenty-nine years ago a publication of the Conservation of Human Resources Project of Columbia University,[1] The Peripheral Worker, was issued by the Columbia University Press. Its proximate genesis was a series of studies made by the Conservation of Human Resources which were focused on career paths and what was then termed, "the process of work establishment."[2] But the Conservation of Human Resources had long been concerned with the major subgroups of the population who constitute the largest proportion of those workers we included in the term "the peripheral worker."

Moreover, the director of the Conservation of Human Resources Project, Eli Ginzberg, and other members of its research staff had become increasingly concerned that the very nature of global employment statistics and investigations of what were termed labor force participation rates were unwittingly giving credence to a sense that attachment to work was an either/or status and that "the process of work establishment" was both easy and inevitable.

It was a time, it may be recalled, when the Japanese economy was supposedly able to give employees what amounted to lifetime tenure. It was also just after the publication of John Kenneth Galbraith's The Industrial State, *which seemed to imply that the American economy was to a significant extent made up of large corporations, large trade unions, and large government in a complex symbiotic relationship which was supposed to provide stability for its corporate and trade union members.*

Related to the importance of large corporations and large trade unions as mediators of the work experience of corporate employees was an emerging interest in what was called "the internal labor market." If employees

1. The Conservation of Human Resources Project is now the Eisenhower Center for the Conservation of Human Resources at Columbia University.
2. See Eli Ginzberg's *Career guidance: Who needs it, who provides it, who can improve it* (1971) and Marcia Friedman's *The process of work establishment* (1969), among other publications by authors of the Eisenhower Center.

tended increasingly to enter into stable and long-lasting relationships with large corporations, then inevitably the personnel practices, career paths, and promotion patterns of these corporations would increasingly determine the lifetime work experiences of the American labor force. It was recognized by economists interested in what they termed the internal labor market[3] that not all workers could expect to become employees of large corporations. Those who did were considered to be members of the "primary labor market," protected by corporate personnel practices, contracts between their unions and their employers, and government policies. The rest of the labor force were members of the "secondary labor market," unsheltered from the vicissitudes of the market by unions or government.

The relationship between the concept of the "secondary labor market" and the concept of the "peripheral worker" is evident but not exact. Members of the "secondary labor market" as conceived by Peter Doeringer and others are often full-time and full-year employees, even though not employed by large corporations. Our concept centered instead upon work experience. If an individual's work experience was part-time or intermittent, he or she was considered to be a "peripheral worker." We recognized the crudeness of the statistical data available and the transitoriness of the peripheral status for many individuals. What we were interested in were the broad correlations between peripheral work experience and significant subcategories of the population.

As a working set of hypotheses, we felt that the basic forces that tended to sort the labor force into those who clearly enjoyed stable and predictable work experiences and career patterns and those who, however temporarily, were not related to the world of work in such a way were not confined to purely economic or what could be termed market forces. Subtle historical and social factors played, we believed, important if not easily disentangled roles in such a sorting process. We recognized that government policies, particularly tax policies, played a role and that changing technologies along with changing consumer tastes and the inherent requirements for flexibility in a modern market economy also made for some degree of peripheral status, that is, part-time and intermittent work experience.

We also recognized that a peripheral status from the worker's point of view might very well be voluntary and that some peripheral work experience might therefore be primarily a response of the economy to the sup-

---

3. Among others, Peter Doeringer and Michael Piore played prominent roles in investigating internal labor markets and in developing the concept of "the primary labor market" and the "secondary labor market."

ply of such individuals. The entry of very large numbers of women into the labor force in the post–World War II era, many of whom confronted severe limitations on the hours they could work because of family responsibilities, undoubtedly led some employers, including very large corporations such as AT&T, to provide flexible schedules for some of them. On the other hand, the emergence of fast-food chains like McDonald's undoubtedly induced some young high-school and college students to enter the labor force.

The following excerpts from The Peripheral Worker *enlarge upon some of these issues and touch upon others. A rereading of a book after twenty-five years is a bit of a shock to its author. But it is impossible to see very clearly into the future, and those twenty-five years were of course the future we faced in 1969. One of the purposes of this chapter is to provide the reader with a perspective from the past and therefore a sense of the changing view of the nature and importance of peripherality.*

Dean Morse, 1998

The Peripheral Worker in America: A Historical Hypothesis

The substance of the following pages consists of a general framework within which it may be possible to find an explanation for a number of the characteristics of peripheral workers over a substantial period of time. This framework, or theory, will attempt to draw together elements from history, economics, and sociology. One of the virtues of such an approach, from the point of view of our present concerns, is that it treats the question as one involving primarily the process of forming increasingly firm commitments, on the part of both the firm and the individual, to the provision and performance of labor services. Another virtue of this approach is its emphasis on the fact that, in a highly differentiated society with an advanced economy, there are powerful societal forces tending to create a high degree of stability in a large fraction of the labor force, forces which operate both from the side of the employer and from the side of the employee. The implication of this is that in such a society a very large proportion of the work force should, in the absence of counteracting factors, follow a pattern of increasing socialization as far as commitment to work is concerned. The major institutions of society, particularly the family, will exert very powerful influences to lead the child in an orderly way to the development of attitudes toward work which assume an eventual full commitment to work. If, then, there is a considerable proportion of the population whose work experience is irregular, it is necessary to examine the interaction of the major subsystems of the total society to see how it comes about that a portion of the population is not fully integrated into the economy.

Among the important aspects of the differentiation of the working population into *(a)* a stable group of full-time, full-year workers and *(b)* a fluctuating group of part-time and intermittent workers are the characteristic attitudes that each group comes to hold about itself and about the other group. Individuals from the two groups develop pervasive expectations that tend to confirm their status. The central institutions of the labor markets will also be shaped in part by these expectations and so tend to confirm them. Eventually it will come about that the widely differing patterns of work experience displayed by individuals from these two groups seem inevitable and "natural," a rationalization serving to justify and perpetuate the patterns. What from the point of view of other societies or other times might seem inexplicable and "wrong" becomes the usual state of affairs.

* * *

The circumstances of the United States in the last decades of the nineteenth century encouraged whatever tendency may have existed in earlier American experience for individuals from distinct groups of the population to find themselves in a subordinate position in the labor markets. Sudden increases in the numbers of immigrants, and radical changes in their national origin, in their social, religious, and educational background, combined to create two distinct groups of workers. One group considered itself to be the true possessor of America, really "American" by virtue of its connection with a semi-mythical revolutionary and pioneering past, possessing some degree of education and skill, occupying positions of authority and influence, or tied by family to individuals who did.

The new immigrants were strange in tongue, in dress, in manner, and above all in religion to the dominant Protestant population of the northern cities. They were largely peasant in background, uneducated and equipped with skills more or less irrelevant to the urban industrial and commercial environment into which they were poured by the channels of immigration. Forced by their initial lack of capital into the most disorganized parts of the cities, they were impelled to accept whatever employment an economy engaged in a tremendous expansion of activity might offer them.

And employment this boisterous economy did offer them, but on its own terms. Their employment experience was fitful, casual, rough, and demoralizing. In boom years it was connected with the sudden expansion of construction activity, the building of cities and roads, mining, and lumbering. The flow of immigrants was, during these decades, a very sensitive register of the ups and downs of the economy. Even when there were sufficient employment opportunities to make immigration seem attractive to the European peasant, the kinds of work experience available to him often tended to lack continuity. He was still confined to those tasks at the bottom of the occupational and industrial hierarchy which were most peripheral, which lacked status. The recent immigrant was apt to have very little proprietorial interest in his job, he was not welcome in the craft unions, his relation to labor markets was in many cases mediated by the *padrone*, he was frequently part of a labor gang, anonymous himself, subject to arbitrary hiring and firing.

* * *

Politically the immigrant was "accepted" according to the fundamental law of the land, the idealized Constitution itself. Although a growing movement might advocate the prevention of more immigrants landing on American shores, no serious political movement advocated the denial of citizenship to immigrants as a matter of principle. It was expected that the immigrant would make some effort to Americanize himself by learning the rudiments of English and by mastering the elements of American history and showing acquaintance with the forms of American political processes. Socially, however, the immigrant was "unacceptable" unless his national background conformed to that of the dominant white Protestant group; unless he was a member of one of the numerous acceptable Protestant sects; unless his economic and educational achievements placed him within the middle class.

The consequences of this double view were bound to be very ramified. On the one hand, the dominant white Protestant group could feel, with a satisfactory degree of self-righteousness, that they had done all that could be expected of them, that the "new immigrant" was free to take his place in American life, that indeed the "new immigrant" had been treated with matchless generosity. In a political sense the illusion of community, of a shared political life, could be maintained. The ballot box made no distinctions. Any man could become president, except for the immigrant, and even the immigrant's son could aspire that high. On the other hand, the "new immigrant" did not and could not, except in the rarest cases, really belong socially to the central core of the traditional American society. In a striking way, the political and social situation of the "new immigrant" in the United States represented a reversal of his age-old position in Europe. In Europe, he had been a socially full-fledged member of a highly organized community, the peasant village.

Unfortunately for the "new immigrant," a precedent for exclusion of a major portion of the society had long existed in American life. The Negro had been almost totally excluded, politically and socially, until the Civil War. During the very time that the "new immigrant" was arriving in ever increasing numbers, the Negro in the South was being systematically stripped of whatever formal political equality he had received as a result of that war. It was not difficult to find a rationale for the *de facto* subjection of the Negro. The Negro, and along with him the American Indian, and for good measure the Chinese and Japanese, were, it was asserted, racially inferior, morally and intellectually below the standards of American life. The proof of this inferiority was their poverty, their different standards of living, and their ignorance.

* * *

For the Negro, exclusion meant an almost absolute lack of access to any of the protections offered by federal or state governments, protections which in any case were apt to be particularly weak in the area of economic hazards. In a profound sense the nation learned "to look the other way," learned how "not to see" the Negro. It was all too easy to generalize this mental trait. For Negro one could partially substitute Southern European. If it was difficult to exclude the immigrant directly from the political community, it was all the more important that the immigrant not be included within the social community. His poverty, his place of residence, above all his lack of status within the occupational and industrial hierarchy made it almost certain that the average member of the white Protestant community would not think of him as one of "us" when it came to the question of the nature of his employment experience. Peripheral socially in a society where occupational status was of ever increasing importance, where it was expected that the full-fledged member of society would rise in the occupational hierarchy and have increasingly strong proprietorial interest in his job as he progressed through life, those immigrants who lacked any special attributes of cultural background, intellect, skill, capital, or just plain luck were forced to accept a most uncertain relationship to the world of work. They constituted the bulk of the peripheral labor force of the late nineteenth and early twentieth centuries. More important for the long run, the mainstream of American society developed deep-seated attitudes towards the kind of person who carried out the peripheral tasks of the economy, the casual day laborer, the intermittent worker, the part-time worker, attitudes which were destined to be carried over to those groups who succeeded the immigrant once the major flows of European and Asiatic immigration had ceased.

Basically such attitudes asserted, first, that it was right and proper that the peripheral work that the economy needed to have performed should be done by those demographic groups who occupied, in one critical sense or another, a subordinate position. Second, these attitudes made it possible for government to neglect to give the peripheral workers, drawn from these "inferior" groups, the same protection that a highly elaborate public and private apparatus, developing over these same years, came to afford the full-time, full-year nucleus of the American labor force.

* * *

The history of nineteenth- and early twentieth-century American trade unions is filled with numberless incidents of exclusionary acts by the skilled craft unions, sometimes aimed at the skilled or semiskilled Negro worker, more generally aimed at the unskilled European and Asiatic immigrant. Indeed, the movement to end immigration found some of its strongest supporters among trade unionists. For several generations the American skilled worker was systematically taught by the majority of craft unions that the unskilled worker, flowing into the great urban centers in great numbers, was his enemy, a threat to his wage standards and his working conditions.

When in the course of time the children and grandchildren of immigrants entered the labor markets, no longer carrying with them the stigma of foreign tongue, foreign dress, foreign manners, now equal or superior to the average American in educational attainment, the barriers that their fathers and grandfathers had met at the entryway to the trade union were significantly lower for them. This was true even in the case of the old craft unions, many of which indeed were to become captives of particular ethnic groups. With the growth of the industrial trade unions, particularly since their period of most rapid growth came at a time of enormous crisis in the 1930s when unemployment was so universal that the traditional groups that comprised the American labor force tended to break down before a sense of common danger and shared disaster, many of the native-born descendants of the "new immigrants" found a strong shelter.

The lesson that their fathers' experience passed on to them was starkly simple. The fundamental function of a workers' institution must be to provide status. It must define the boundary between those who have a stake in the society and the outsider. Wages are important, it is true, but the measure of the success of a trade union can never be simply its ability to raise wages. Above all, a trade union exists to try to prevent its members from being treated as if they are peripheral.

* * *

It is something of a curiosity in the intellectual history of modern times that, in order to convict the trade movement in general of ineffectiveness, it was enough for some economists whose interests have centered upon the price system to show that it was impossible for the trade union movement as a whole to have had any very large effect upon general wage levels. But this is to impose middle-class values upon working-class institutions. To the average university professor it may indeed be true that the test of the success of an institution representing him would be its power to raise his income, particularly if his status is defined by academic tenure. But the very thing which the professors' institutions need do very little about, tenure and status, the working class institutions may be in a position to affect in highly significant ways. An employer may be quite unwilling to raise wages, particularly above the industry level, but he may be quite willing to change hiring and firing practices to provide greater security to the worker, particularly if the union can provide him with workers whose average productivity is higher than what an unstructured labor market could provide him and if the provision of security has a favorable effect upon the morale of his workers. Until we are quite clear in our minds about what it is that the worker wants, it seems fruitless to test the success of an institution by what might be an irrelevant goal. A proper test of the efficacy of aspirin is not how well it takes care of our stomach aches!

Soon after the rise of the powerful industrial unions the American economy entered a period of unprecedented expansion and low levels of unemployment. From the beginning of World War II until the present it has been possible for the nucleus of the labor force, the white married males, to expect something very close to full-time, full-year employment experience. Workers in particular industries and occupations have on occasion been an exception to this generalization, but it fits the year-in, year-out employment experience of the vast majority of white married males. This does not mean that there have not been episodes of interrupted employment in the lives of the typical members of this demographic group. Workers continue to shift from job to job and to experience occasional layoffs. Some occupational groups, such as construction workers and sales workers, continue to have markedly intermittent employment experience. The generalization does not assert the absence of occupational and industrial mobility. Rather it says that the typical white married male has achieved a considerable degree of status which provides him with the expectation of continuity of employment if he so desires. In some cases the status is derived from the power of his union. In other cases, particularly for the white-collar worker, it is derived from the character of the large-scale industrial and commercial bureaucracy which demands continuity of office (and personnel) where possible.

But the total functioning of the economic system also demands that work be performed at odd times, that a certain degree of flexibility in production and distribution be maintained. Indeed, flexibility in market output tends to increase if the share of personal services does.[4] Part-time and intermittent employment on a significant scale are inherent characteristics of dynamic economies and economies in which personal services constitute an important part of final demand. Where the climate imposes a strong seasonal character on production and demand, part-time and intermittent employment are even more an inherent characteristic.

* * *

When in the 1920s the great flow of white immigrants from Europe came to an abrupt end and the overwhelming majority of white married males became full-time and full-year workers, the source of peripheral workers underwent a major change. With the European and Asiatic immigrant no longer available, other demographic groups filled the gap. Women, youth, older workers, and minority groups such as the non-white, the Puerto Rican, and the Mexican increasingly came to constitute the bulk of the peripheral labor force. It goes without saying that members of each of these groups are easily identified and carry with them socially defined marks of their "inferior" status.

In a sense the basic drama continued to be enacted, the only change being in the cast. Other demographic groups upon whom society could ascribe a label of innate inferiority simply took the place of the immigrant. The basic attitudes of society toward the peripheral worker did not need to be altered. It remained proper that irregular, casual, part-time, intermittent work should be performed by the "outsider." The "outsider" was by definition biologically inferior (note that each group—youth, women,

4. I am indebted to Arnold Katz for this observation.

older workers, Negroes, Puerto Ricans, Mexicans—can be considered to labor under physical or racial handicaps). Since the peripheral work of society was still being performed by those who were not considered full-fledged members of the labor force, it was not necessary to ask, as it had not been necessary to ask in the case of the immigrant, whether the peripheral worker was bearing too large a share of the cost of the flexibility in work schedules that the economy required.

As a result of this historical process the American labor force became radically bifurcated. The boundaries of this bifurcation between full-time, full-year workers and peripheral workers came to be lines of profound social cleavages where primarily age, sex, and race characteristics (related to national origin in the case of the Puerto Rican and Mexican) were used as the markers for membership in one social category or the other. Other markers, such as alcoholism, homosexuality, or criminal record, were used on occasion. It is important to note that the boundaries thus set up are not absolute barriers to movement between the peripheral labor force and the central nucleus of full-time, full-year workers. The barriers do not receive any legal sanction, nor does our explicit ideology support them. Rather they are like a tangle of thickets which can be traversed only by a combination of perseverance, favorable circumstances, and knowledge of the hidden paths. In the case of two groups, youth and the elderly, the barriers, being a function of age, will change with changing age. But the fact that the typical white male youth can, for example, expect in time to become a member of the full-time, full-year labor force does not lessen his peripheral status while he is still a youth. And our thesis maintains, essentially, that his status in the American economy is in several profound respects different from the status of youth in other highly developed economies, such as the European and Japanese.

* * *

If we abandon the view that part-time and intermittent employment experience is more or less randomly distributed among the working population, then we are forced to come to grips with several distinct but closely related questions. First of all, we must ask what the influences are which, singly or together, lead to a particular demographic or social group contributing a more than proportionate share of either part-time or intermittent work experience.

Related to the question of whether particular demographic groups and social classes tend to constitute the bulk of the peripheral labor force is the question of whether particular industries and occupations tend to use a conspicuously higher proportion of peripheral workers than other industries and occupations. If so, do these industries and occupations share common features, such as size of the typical firm or degree of training and education which the employee is expected to have and extent of training and education which the firm usually supplies? Where is peripheral work usually located? Is it found more often in rural environments? Does it cluster in the older large cities?

The Sociology of Peripheral Work Experience

The first part of this chapter has presented a thesis about the peripheral worker in American society which is explicitly historical and partly sociological in character. In essence, the thesis asserts several interrelated propositions:

1. It is possible to rank demographic groups in American society by social status.
2. It is possible to rank occupations (and, to some extent, industries) by status.
3. In general, low status occupations (and industries, to some extent) have been and at present are associated with demographic groups who possess low social status. Indeed, the link between the status of a demographic group and an occupation may be much more intimate than this statement indicates. If an occupation has traditionally been one of low status, then it confers low status upon the individuals or groups who are involved in it. Conversely, the presence of social groups of low status in a particular occupation tends to confer low status on that occupation. The resistance presented by individuals of groups of high social status to the entry of individuals of low status into previously high status occupations is undoubtedly in large part due to the fear that low status will be transferred from the social group to the occupation. This seems to be a very general anxiety, felt most strongly perhaps by just those groups which have most recently achieved some degree of status.
4. The status of an occupation (and of industries) is in part a function of the continuity of employment it affords.
5. Occupations (and industries) which have least continuity of employment will therefore be filled, in general, by those demographic groups possessing least social status.

6. Social status in American life is conferred by, among many other attributes, *(a)* sex, *(b)* age, *(c)* color, and *(d)* national origin. When immigration was on a large scale, date of arrival in America was an important determinant of status. Other things being equal, social status was determined by the number of generations of American-born ancestors an individual possessed. A marked decrease in social status occurred when both parents were foreign-born, particularly when the country of origin was itself associated with low status. When an individual was actually an immigrant from countries of low status, he was ranked at the bottom of the status scale.

The conclusion that follows from these propositions is that peripheral work experience, inherently less continuous than other types of work experience, is therefore a characteristic of demographic groups whose sex, age, or color assign to them low status. In contemporary America these groups are (1) females, (2) younger and older workers, and (3) the non-white.

* * *

Our distinction between the full-time, full-year nucleus of the labor force and the peripheral worker emphasizes the fact that differing sectors of the economy use very different proportions of peripheral workers. Agriculture has always relied heavily upon intermittent and part-time workers, perhaps as much or more today than in the past. Many of the industries in the service sector also are characterized by a relatively high proportion of peripheral workers in their work forces. A number of occupations, as well as industries, have high proportions of peripheral workers.

On the other hand, it is likely that the oligopolistic firm does have a stable work force and that therefore what we have called the nucleus of the labor force, the full-time, full-year workers, is located disproportionately in such firms and therefore in the industries where such firms are typically found. However, it is also important to take account of the fact that total employment in firms which can properly be classified as oligopolistic industrial firms is not as large a fraction of total employment in the economy as one might think.

* * *

Large firms, particularly multi-plant firms, can be expected to be pioneers in the introduction of continuous flow processes. If continuous flow is unobtainable over the whole range of the productive process, it is often possible to attain continuous flow operation in subsectors. For a number of reasons the large firm is in a particularly favorable position to introduce such technology. Even if total output is somewhat variable, the firm may find that it is possible to utilize at least one continuous flow plant because total demand for its product can seldom be expected to fall below the capacity of the continuous flow installation. If it is desirable to attain higher levels of output, the firm can utilize obsolescent facilities in its possession or, as frequently happens, subcontract with satellite firms. In addition, large firms can obtain capital on relatively favorable terms. Finally, the large firm is able to maintain a technical staff to keep it abreast of the latest technological possibilities and frequently to develop the requisite technology.

If the labor force necessary to operate intricate and costly continuous flow process plants must receive intensive, expensive, and specialized training, there is an additional incentive on the part of the firm to offer continuity of employment. Any layoff contains a considerable risk that a labor force assembled at great expense, with great difficulty, and over a long period of time will be dissipated to rivals, as a number of defense firms specializing in aviation and space technology have found to their very great cost.

Around large manufacturing firms a host of smaller firms will swarm, each offering to supply goods and services which are needed either in such small quantities that continuous flow operations are uneconomical or at uncertain times or in uncertain quantities. These small firms must use a technology which permits them to vary their output both in kind and in quantity. They in turn will rely heavily upon variable inputs of labor.

In this scheme of industrial organization, the large firm specializes in continuity of output and offers concomitant continuity of employment. Flexibility of output, an unavoidable necessity in a world of uncertainty, seasonality, catastrophe, and change of taste and technology, is to a disproportionate extent provided by smaller firms which specialize in meeting the costs of uncertainty and changing levels and types of output.

A question of very great interest (and of increasing importance) is whether intermittent and part-time employment is by and large imposed on a labor force whose members for the most part are desirous of working full-year, full-time schedules or whether, on the other hand, intermittent and part-time employment is largely the natural result of the desire of a considerable number of individuals to avoid what they may regard as an overcommitment to the world of work. It is possible to find copious illustrations of both situations. Intermittent layoffs, more or less as an accepted pattern, characterize some industries, and it would be difficult to maintain in many of these cases that the variability of income and the uncertainty that result are preferred by the great bulk of the employees. But it may very well be true that the intermittent employment found in the construction industry, to take one example, does represent a preferred pattern of activity for many of its members.

If, moreover, we think of occupations, rather than of firms or industries, it is possible to find several occupations where the preferred work experience of many individuals seems to be intermittent employment. Sales workers are a fairly conspicuous example, a more exotic example being the professional athlete. And it is probable that for a sizable fraction of the teaching profession one of the most attractive characteristics of their work experience is the pattern of vacations it offers.

Ideally, the desirable state of affairs would be one where the flexibility of the labor market and the variability of employment patterns among firms, industries, and occupations would provide sufficient scope both for those workers who desired continuity of employment and for those who desired intermittent employment. Indeed, a labor market characterized by a high degree of mobility and a high degree of knowledge of options would be expected to adjust the supply of those workers desiring intermittent employment of a particular type to the demand for such workers in large part through the agency of wage differentials between full-year and intermittent employment.

* * *

Our hypothesis, then, is that one of the characteristics of intermittency of employment experience is a relative decrease in the amount of investment in specific on-the-job training. If this is correct, two or three consequences can be expected to flow from the situation that is created by this relative training deprivation of the individual worker. First of all, he is unable to share that part of the gains of specific training that accrues to employees. The second consequence is perhaps even more important. The very fact that the intermittent worker does not receive specific training is at the same time one of the reasons why his tie to the employer is weak and why he is more subject to intermittent employment. The employer has no capital sunk in the training of such a worker and therefore cannot lose any of this capital if the intermittent worker does not return to him after a spell of interrupted employment.

It seems probable that there is a further consequence, more indirect but more pervasive. Let us take a firm which has experienced considerable fluctuations of its total labor inputs over a number of years. According to our analysis, such a firm will be reluctant to make any investment in specific on-the-job training of those workers whose employment experience is expected to be intermittent. However, such a firm, it seems reasonable to suppose, must maintain a certain level of total skill in its labor force in order to carry out its operations. To the extent that the fluctuating component of its labor force is underskilled because it does not pay the firm to make any investment in the training of such workers, the firm may be forced to attempt to raise the skill level of that component of its labor force which has continuity of employment in order to compensate for the relatively unskilled character of the rest of its employees.

If this is the case, we can expect to find that there is a tendency for the labor force of such a firm to be strongly and permanently bifurcated. One branch will have a relatively high degree of continuity of employment and high wages since it has relatively a high degree of specific training. The remainder of the labor force of the firm will bear the entire burden of fluctuations of the firm's total inputs of labor over the course of time, but at the same time it will have to accept relatively low wages because the very fact of the intermittency of its employment experience has prevented any investment of capital in specific on-the-job training for this kind of employee. What has been said here about intermittent workers seems to be more or less applicable to workers whose employment experience is part time in character and is the more applicable to that large fraction of the peripheral labor force whose employment experience is at one and the same time intermittent and part time.

* * *

Any adequate concept of human behavior recognizes that basic patterns of life tend to become habits. This is particularly true of work experience. At a very early age, a child, for example, is characterized by his "work habits," and it has long been recognized that for many individuals the abrupt breaking of lifetime patterns of work at retirement age produces profound and dangerous physical and psychic disorder and damage. In terms of the income-leisure choice facing an individual, this means that habituation tends to transform the factors that determine the choice over time and to narrow the range of choice. For at least some individuals who have worked an unvarying pattern of hours for many years, one of the requirements of any new job would be that it conform closely to this pattern. If such a worker, particularly an "older" worker, finds his full-time employment terminated, any intermittent or part-time employment may be profoundly disturbing to him. He finds it difficult to accept the fact that he can no longer command the wages of a full-time, full-year employee or that in the type of employment open to

him there are constraints upon his work schedule. He finds it profoundly disquieting and humiliating to discover that he is no longer
given the responsibilities that he used to have, that he is no longer a full-
fledged member of a work group. He becomes a supernumerary. He dis-
covers, if he never knew it before, the meaning of peripheral work.

Some Policy Implications

What are some of the fundamental policy implications which emerge
from an overall consideration of peripheral work experience? Several
seem to stand out. First of all, since peripheral work experience covers
immensely broad and varied fields of human activity, it is essential that
a general manpower policy take into account as thoroughly as possible
the spill-over effects of any particular measure. To be more specific, a
measure intended to stabilize work experience in general might have the
unintended effect of drying up sources of peripheral work experience
which are an essential element in the total lifetime work experience of
individuals. Part-time or intermittent employment is a desirable option
for many people, for teen-agers, for college students, for postgraduate
students, for married women, for mothers with young children, for
older workers, for individuals whose life style is not patterned around
family and total commitment to work. A healthy economy should provide an adequate supply of peripheral work experience opportunities to
match the demand for such work on the part of individuals whose circumstances differ from those of the typical full-time, full-year married
male worker.

* * *

Up to this point we have been emphasizing the importance of an adequate supply of constructive peripheral work experience for specific
groups, particularly teen-agers, older workers, and mothers who desire
to supplement their income with earnings from part-time work. But it is
important to keep in mind that there is another side to peripheral work.
The peripheral worker is concentrated very heavily in occupations
which require little skill and he is often employed by small firms that
offer little training to part-time or intermittent employees. Large, heavily capitalized firms generally employ full-time, full-year workers. Such
large firms are more apt to be strongly unionized and to operate with
very formal hiring and firing procedures. It is hard for workers with little
education, little training, and a history of irregular and casual employment to surmount the barriers raised by these procedures.

* * *

Several important consequences follow from this general situation. A worker who is 30 years old and whose employment experience has been largely peripheral up to that age is quite possibly on a dead-end road as far as a work career is concerned. He is much less apt than a full-time, full-year worker to have received any training, much more apt to be a victim of seasonal ebbs and flows of production, much more apt to find himself superfluous in a recession, much more apt to be employed by small firms subject to wide variations in output and short lifetimes. He is much less protected by public policy designed to maintain income or shield him from the consequences of illness, accident, or old age. He is less often able to count upon a strong union to interpose itself between him and arbitrary and abrupt termination of employment. He is much more dependent upon casual sources for information about job opportunities.

* * *

It seems likely, however, that many of the recent migrants from the South to the great urban centers of the North, already highly peripheral in the work experience which follows their having been pushed off the land by technological change, may finally drop out of the labor market entirely if their work experience in the city falls below a minimum level. In the South, particularly in the smaller communities, they have been part of a labor pool which depended upon an informal network of information to provide its members with occasional work. In the large northern cities, these recent migrants may have no access to this kind of information and no experience in making use of more formal types of information about job opportunities.

What, then, can public and private policy do for those individuals, all too frequently nonwhite, all too frequently the most defenseless members of society because of age or marital status, whose peripheral work experience places them in such disadvantageous positions? Can anything be done to break the chain of circumstances which fastens casual and irregular employment upon those individuals whose lives are in many other respects also subject to great hazards?

* * *

Since peripheral work status is apt to be associated with low levels of skills, low educational attainment, and the absence of any significant amount of formal or on-the-job training, since it is associated frequently with low wage rates and even lower yearly income, manpower policies designed to improve the situation of the peripheral worker must be both broad in range and deep in effect. Like most specific manpower policies, successful action will depend in the last analysis upon the maintenance of very low rates of unemployment in the nation as a whole. Indeed, the problem of the peripheral worker does not really exist as a specific problem until low rates of unemployment in general are attained. It is only in such a tight labor market that it is possible to see clearly what groups in the population do not have access to sufficient peripheral work experience and to distinguish those groups who seem to be enmeshed in peripheral work experience unwillingly and at the cost of a fuller commitment to more productive work.

* * *

The available evidence seems to indicate that high levels of employment in the country as a whole are not likely to alleviate to a tolerable extent the employment problems of the peripheral workers in the central cores of large cities. To some extent it may be possible for some nonwhite peripheral workers to relocate themselves in the suburbs where more stable employment opportunities may exist for them, but it is hardly likely that the flow of nonwhites out of the central cities can be sufficiently rapid to bring down the very high rates of peripheral employment in the ghetto areas.

If present rates of unemployment, underemployment, and nonparticipation in the labor force of the nonwhite worker in the great city ghettoes continue much longer, they threaten to increase the sense of despair and the sense of alienation and demoralization to truly dangerous degrees. Rather than place all our trust in the long-run beneficent effects of high nation-wide employment rates on the situation of the nonwhite urban worker, it seems better to begin to plan and carry out programs to create more stable employment opportunities for the nonwhite urban worker *where he presently lives.* Public and private manpower policy might properly be directed toward locating those types of public and private enterprises whose employment practices are highly stable in areas where the peripheral worker now lives. It might prove more sensible in the long run to put as much effort and financial support into the provision of stable employment opportunities in slum areas as into public housing in those areas. It is of particular importance that workers who are trapped in a sequence of peripheral work experiences should finally be offered employment which contains a considerable component of on-the-job training to make up for their relative deprivation in this respect.

Conclusion

What has been said up to now has in an important sense been too general, too much a matter of percentages and categories. A more sensitive, a deeper way of examining this whole matter would call upon a very different kind of evidence. We are beginning to amass a body of material produced by the participant-observer, by studies in depth of critically important groups, such as those conducted by Robert Coles among Boston slum residents. A study of a very peripheral group of workers, the work of Elliot Liebow on the street-corner Negro, carried out in Washington, is a necessary complement to these remarks.[5] The informal shape-up of Negro men on a Washington street corner is one part of the reality behind the peripheral worker as we have used the term, and this type of labor market can be found in any city. It is far from a world of union contract, seniority, unemployment insurance, social security, and minimum wages. But so desperate is the situation of those who utilize this type of unregulated shape-up that they hope there will be no attempt to regulate it. To them, regulation of peripheral work of this type seems to threaten total exclusion from the world of work. To them, it is easier to move from peripheral work to no work at all than it is to move toward a stable employment experience. To them, the world of work has become completely bifurcated.

The question this book is concerned with is whether such bifurcation is a very general phenomenon. Do powerful, persuasive, though largely obscure barriers stand between the world of peripheral work and the status of full-time, full-year employment for many individuals? Do we take it for granted that peripheral work in general, and the most peripheral work in particular, should be performed by members of demographic groups whose status is lower than that of the adult white male group that provides the nucleus of the full-time, full-year work force? Will the full-time, full-year worker be increasingly found in those sectors of the economy where large-scale, bureaucratic, usually heavily capitalized firms are the rule? Do we make an overinvestment in human capital in those workers who possess full-time, full-year status and an underinvestment in human capital in peripheral workers? If so, does this in itself constitute one of the important barriers between the peripheral worker and employment in those sectors of the economy that can provide continuity of employment?

5. Elliot Liebow, *Tally's corner: A study of Negro street-corner men* (Boston: Little, Brown, 1968).

To some extent peripheral work experience is unquestionably a manifestation of increasing options available to many individuals. To the extent that it does represent an enlargement of the area of choice of work experience, it is a positive aspect of the economy. On the other hand, to the extent that the peripheral worker is treated as if he were a second-class worker, peripheral work experience cannot but lead to waste, frustration, and angry despair.

The peripheral worker in our society provides the economy with a very important part of the flexibility which it must have if it is to be efficient and dynamic. Recognizing this function, we should try to ensure that an undue share of the cost of this flexibility does not fall upon the peripheral workers themselves, many of whom are among the least able in our society to bear such costs. In the past, the immigrant provided much of the flexibility that a growing economy required and he often paid too much of the costs. We should ask ourselves today whether new groups have taken the immigrant's place. If the answer is "Yes" even in part, we should develop policies which will ensure that the costs of flexibility are not shifted onto the peripheral workers and—in the long run this is much more important—that the social and economic barriers to movement from peripheral work status to full-time, full-year status are reduced to the point where we can truly affirm that part-time and intermittent work experience represents an enlargement of option and opportunity, not a contraction of life's possibilities

CHAPTER TWO

Counting the Workers:
Results of a First Survey

Sharon R. Cohany
Steven F. Hipple
Thomas J. Nardone
Anne E. Polivka
Jay C. Stewart

*T*he considerable flexibility inherent in the United States labor market has produced a variety of employment arrangements. In recent years, there has been a perception that the nature of the employment relationship is changing and that jobs are becoming less secure. Anecdotal evidence of a trend toward more flexible arrangements is fairly extensive; gauging the extent of such employment in the labor force as a whole, however, has been more problematic, as ongoing surveys of employment do not measure the "permanence" of the employment relationship.

To meet the growing demand for such information, the Bureau of Labor Statistics (BLS) sponsored a special survey in 1995 to estimate the number of contingent workers, that is, *individuals who do not perceive themselves as having an explicit or implicit contract for continuing employment.* Also gathered in the survey was information on workers in several alternative employment arrangements, namely those working as independent contractors and on call, and those working through temporary help agencies and contract companies. This chapter provides an overview of the conceptual issues surrounding the measurement of both contingent and alternative employment and presents a demographic and economic profile of workers in these arrangements based on the special survey.

The authors are economists in the Office of Employment and Unemployment Statistics, Bureau of Labor Statistics. The views expressed in this chapter do not necessarily reflect official policy of BLS or the federal government. The authors wish to thank their colleagues at BLS, particularly Robert McIntire for invaluable computer programming services and James Esposito for important contributions regarding the development of the questionnaire. Gratitude is also extended to the staff of the Data Services Division of the Bureau of the Census, especially Maria Reed and Francia McDaniel.

Definition and Measurement

In the late 1980s, well before the collection of any data, economists at BLS devoted considerable effort to crafting a definition of contingent work. There was no official government definition of the term. Researchers had used it to refer to a variety of work arrangements, including part-time schedules, work in the business services industry, and self-employment— in fact, almost any work arrangement that might be considered to differ from the commonly perceived norm of a full-time wage and salary job (Belous, 1989). These conceptualizations of contingent work were unsatisfactory to BLS analysts, in that they overshot as well as undershot the mark. Part-time jobs, self-employment, or jobs in certain industries did not automatically qualify as "contingent," since they were not necessarily jobs which lacked permanence.[1] Also, because these categories are not mutually exclusive, double- and even triple-counting the same people can occur. On the other hand, some jobs that are clearly temporary do not fit into any of these categories, such as when workers are hired directly by a firm to fill a temporary position.

Defining Contingent Work

In the approach adopted by BLS, contingent work is defined primarily in terms of job security (Polivka & Nardone, 1989). Several factors were identified from which the existence of a contingent employment arrangement could be discerned: whether the job was perceived as temporary or was not expected to continue, how long the worker expected to be able to hold the job, and how long the worker had held the job.

The key factor used to determine if a job fit the conceptual definition of contingent was whether the job was temporary or was not expected to continue. The first question of the survey was: "Some people are in temporary jobs that last only for a limited time or until the completion of a project. Is your job temporary?" People who answered no to this question were asked: "Provided the economy does not change and your job performance is adequate, can you continue to work for your current employer as long as you wish?"

Respondents who answered yes to the first question, or no to the second, were then asked a series of questions to distinguish persons who

1. Many part-time jobs are, in fact, quite stable. Data from a 1991 supplement to the Current Population Survey showed that nearly 30 percent of all part-time workers aged twenty-five and older had been with their current employer for more than five years. The comparable figure for full-time workers was 47 percent.

were in temporary jobs from those who, for personal reasons, were temporarily holding jobs that offered the opportunity of ongoing employment. For example, students holding part-time jobs in fast-food restaurants might view those jobs as temporary, since they may intend to leave them at the end of the school year. The jobs themselves, however, would be filled by other workers once the students leave and, hence, would not be contingent.

Workers also were asked how long they expected to stay in their current job and how long they had been with their current employer. The rationale for asking how long an individual expects to remain in his or her current job was that being able to hold a job for a year or more could be taken as evidence of at least an implicit contract for ongoing employment. In other words, the employer's need for the worker's services is not likely to evaporate tomorrow. By the same token, the information on how long a worker has been with the employer shows whether a job has been ongoing. Having remained with an employer for more than a year may be taken as evidence that, at least in the past, there was an explicit or implicit contract for continuing employment.

Rather than adopting a single measure of contingency, three measures were devised to assess the impact of different assumptions about the factors that constitute contingent employment. Since an understanding of the three alternative measures (summarized in Table 2.1) is essential for an accurate interpretation of the findings, they are described in some detail.

The narrowest estimate (estimate 1) includes only wage and salary workers who had been in their jobs for one year or less and expected their jobs to last for an additional year or less. Self-employed workers, both incorporated and unincorporated (and independent contractors), are excluded from the count of contingent workers under estimate 1. The rationale was that people who work for themselves, by definition, have ongoing employment arrangements, even though they may face financial risks. Individuals who worked for temporary help agencies or contract companies are considered contingent under estimate 1 only if they expect their employment arrangement with *the temporary help or contract company* to last for one year or less and they had worked for that company for one year or less. Thus, workers employed by temporary help firms are not counted as contingent under estimate 1 if they expect to be able to stay with the firm for more than a year or have been with the firm for one year, even if the places they are assigned to work by the firms change frequently.

The middle estimate (estimate 2) adds the self-employed (both the incorporated and unincorporated) and independent contractors who expect to be, and had been, in their present arrangement for one year or less. In addition, temporary help and contract company workers were classified as contingent under estimate 2 if they had worked and expected to work for *the customers to whom they were assigned* for one year or less. For example, a "temp" secretary who is sent to a different customer each week but has worked for the same temporary help agency for more than a year and expects to be able to continue with that firm indefinitely is contingent under estimate 2 but not under estimate 1. In contrast, a temp who is assigned to a single client for more than a year and expects to be able to stay with that client for more than a year is not counted as contingent under either estimate.

In the broadest estimate (estimate 3), the one-year limitation on how long workers had held their jobs and expected to remain in them is dropped for wage and salary workers. Thus, this estimate effectively includes *all the wage and salary workers who do not expect their employment to last* (except for those who, for personal reasons, expect to leave jobs that they would otherwise be able to keep) *plus the self-employed from estimate 2*. A wage and salary worker who had held a job for five years (or longer) could be considered contingent under estimate 3 if he or she now viewed the job as temporary. (The conditions on expected and current tenure were not relaxed for the self-employed because they were asked a different set of questions from wage and salary workers.)

Source of the Data

The special survey of workers in contingent and alternative arrangements was conducted as a supplement to the February 1995 Current Population Survey (CPS), a survey of households that is a primary source of information on the American workforce. In addition to the national unemployment rate, probably the best known product from the survey, the CPS provides comprehensive data each month on the employed, unemployed, and persons not in the labor force. Supplements, such as the one on contingent and alternative arrangements, are questions added to the basic monthly CPS to provide in-depth information on specific aspects of the labor force and other topics.

Conducted by the Bureau of the Census for BLS, the CPS had a sample of 56,000 households (containing about 112,000 people) at the time of the contingent work supplement. The CPS uses a state-based, complex probability sample located in approximately 790 geographic areas that reflect the social and economic diversity of the nation as a whole.

Trained Census Bureau interviewers conduct the CPS interview primarily through personal visits and telephone calls using laptop computers on which the questionnaire has been programmed. (A portion of the interviews are conducted from centralized phone centers.) The survey respondent is usually one of the individuals in whose name the home is owned or rented, but can be any member of the household (age fifteen and older) who is knowledgeable about the labor market activities of the other members. Typically, about half of the individuals surveyed answer the questions on their own behalf, and half have responses provided for them by another member of the household, referred to as proxy responses. The overall nonresponse rate ranges between 6 and 7 percent. (Detailed information about the concepts and methods of the CPS can be found in U.S. Bureau of Labor Statistics, 1995a, "Explanatory Notes and Estimates of Error.")

In the February 1995 survey, all employed individuals (except unpaid family workers, a very small category numerically) were eligible for the supplemental questions. For persons holding more than one job, the questions referred to the characteristics of their main job, that is, the job in which they worked the most hours. Several additional points concerning the data should be noted. First, as a survey of households, the CPS captured individuals' perceptions of their job situation, not how their employers would perceive or classify their jobs. Likewise, no attempt was made to identify the legal aspects of persons' employment arrangements. Since the February 1995 supplement was the first survey of its kind, it was not possible to determine trends in the various employment relationships as defined in this survey. (Material in this chapter appeared previously in Cohany, 1996; Hipple & Stewart, 1996a, 1996b; Polivka, 1996a, 1996b, 1996c. Initial findings from the survey were released in U.S. Bureau of Labor Statistics, 1995b. The nature of employment relationships, based on this survey and other sources, was examined in U.S. Department of Labor, 1995, chap. 1.)

A Profile of Contingent Workers

In February 1995, between 2.7 and 6.0 million workers were in contingent jobs, depending on the estimate used. These estimates ranged from 2.2 percent of the total employed at the narrowest level that covers only wage and salary workers who expect to be with their current employer for a relatively short time (as defined above), to 2.8 percent when the self-employed were added in, and finally to 4.9 percent of the total when tenure restrictions were relaxed (Table 2.1).

Characteristics

Contingent workers differed from other workers in several important respects. Under all three estimates, contingent workers were more than twice as likely as noncontingent workers (those who are not contingent even under the broadest estimate) to be young, that is, sixteen to

Table 2.1 Contingent workers as a percent of total employment, February 1995

Definition and alternative estimates of contingent workers	*Percent of total employed*
Contingent workers are those who do not have an implicit or explicit contract for ongoing employment. Persons who do not expect to continue in their jobs for personal reasons such as retirement or returning to school are not considered contingent workers, provided that they would have the option of continuing in the job were it not for these personal reasons.	
Estimate 1	
Wage and salary workers who expect their jobs will last for an additional year or less and who had worked at their jobs for 1 year or less. Self-employed workers and independent contractors are excluded from this estimate. For temporary help and contract workers, contingency is based on the expected duration and tenure of their employment with the temporary help or contract firm, not with the specific client to whom they are assigned.	2.2
Estimate 2	
Workers including the self-employed and independent contractors who expect their employment to last for an additional year or less and who had worked at their jobs (or been self-employed) for 1 year or less. For temporary help and contract workers, contingency is determined on the basis of the expected duration and tenure with the client to whom they are assigned, instead of their tenure with the temporary help or contract firm.	2.8
Estimate 3	
Workers who do not expect their jobs to last. Wage and salary workers are included even if they already had held the job for more than 1 year and expect to hold the job for at least an additional year. The self-employed and independent contractors are included if they expect their employment to last for an additional year or less and they had been self-employed or independent contractors for 1 year or less.	4.9

twenty-four years of age (Table 2.2). In fact, under the broadest estimate, this group accounted for almost one-third of all contingent workers. Contingent workers in this age group were more likely than
noncontingent workers to be enrolled in school. Among young people
not enrolled in school, a larger proportion of contingent than noncontingent workers were high school dropouts. This pattern was also true
for persons aged twenty-five to sixty-four. At the same time, contingent
workers were more likely to have a college degree than traditional
workers. Contingent workers also were slightly more likely than noncontingent workers to be female and black.[2]

Despite an overrepresentation of contingency among some worker
groups, the incidence of contingent work within these groups was quite
small. Even under the broadest definition, just about 5 percent of
women, 6 percent of blacks, and 10 percent of those 16–24 years old
were in contingent jobs. Among those 25–64 years old, only 3.9 percent
were contingent.

Part-time workers—persons who usually work less than thirty-five
hours a week—made up a disproportionately large share of contingent
workers—43 to 47 percent, depending on the estimate used, compared
with only 18 percent of noncontingent workers (Table 2.2). However,
the vast majority of part-time workers (about nine out of ten under the
broadest estimate) were not contingent. Thus, to count all part-time
workers as contingent, as some researchers have done, would appear to
greatly overstate the extent to which these workers perceive their jobs
to be temporary.

Employees of the services and construction industries were overrepresented among contingent workers. The services industry alone employed more than half of contingent workers (but about a third of
noncontingent workers). The construction industry also accounted for
a disproportionate share of contingent workers. This concentration not-
withstanding, the proportion of workers within the services industry

2. Estimates of contingency were quite similar regardless of the type of respondent
involved. The incidence of contingency under the broadest measure (4.9 percent overall)
was 4.7 percent when only self-responses were considered, compared with 5.0 percent for
proxy responses. It should not be inferred that the difference of 0.3 percent indicates inac-
curacies on the part of proxies. Rather, there are worker characteristics that are related
both to the probability that an individual is contingent and is reported for by a proxy. For
example, young workers are more likely to be both contingent and have a proxy responding for them. Similarly, the difference in the incidence of independent contracting (7.4
percent for self-respondents versus 6.1 percent for proxy respondents) reflects the fact
that independent contractors are more likely to be self-respondents, due both to their
older age profile and the nature of their work arrangement.

Table 2.2 Percent distribution of employed contingent and noncontingent workers by selected characteristics, February 1995 (Percent distribution)

Characteristic	Contingent workers			Noncontingent workers
	Estimate 1	Estimate 2	Estimate 3	
Age and sex				
Total, 16 years and over	2,739	3,422	6,034	117,174
Percent	100.0	100.0	100.0	100.0
16 to 19 years	16.6	15.2	10.7	4.3
20 to 24 years	25.0	22.2	19.8	9.6
25 to 34 years	26.0	27.5	26.3	26.1
35 to 44 years	18.5	19.8	21.0	28.0
45 to 54 years	8.2	9.5	12.6	19.8
55 to 64 years	3.8	3.7	5.9	9.4
65 years and over	1.8	2.1	3.7	2.8
Men, 16 years and over	49.3	49.4	49.6	54.0
16 to 19 years	7.2	6.8	4.8	2.2
20 to 24 years	12.0	10.7	9.7	5.2
25 to 34 years	12.9	13.6	13.8	14.3
35 to 44 years	10.0	10.3	10.2	15.1
45 to 54 years	3.3	4.2	5.7	10.5
55 to 64 years	2.6	2.4	3.6	5.1
65 years and over	1.2	1.3	1.9	1.7
Women, 16 years and over	50.7	50.6	50.4	46.0
16 to 19 years	9.5	8.4	5.9	2.1
20 to 24 years	13.0	11.5	10.1	4.4
25 to 34 years	13.1	13.9	12.5	11.8
35 to 44 years	8.5	9.5	10.8	12.9
45 to 54 years	4.9	5.3	6.9	9.3
55 to 64 years	1.2	1.3	2.3	4.3
65 years and over	.6	.8	1.8	1.2
Race and Hispanic origin				
White	80.0	80.1	80.9	85.6
Black	13.9	13.6	13.3	10.5
Hispanic origin	13.6	12.9	11.3	8.3
Full- or part-time status				
Full-time workers	52.9	53.6	57.1	81.8
Part-time workers	47.1	46.4	42.9	18.2
Educational attainment				
Total, 25 to 64 years (thousands)	1,547	2,070	3,968	97,633
Percent	100.0	100.0	100.0	100.0
Less than a high-school diploma	14.0	13.6	12.0	9.6
High-school graduates, no college	27.9	27.5	27.3	32.4
Less than a bachelor's degree	31.2	31.3	27.5	29.0
College graduates	27.0	27.7	33.2	28.9

Note: Noncontingent workers are those who do not fall into any estimate of contingent workers. Entries under race and Hispanic origin will not sum to 100 percent because data for the "other races" group are not presented and Hispanics are included in both the white and black population groups. Details for other characteristics may not sum to totals due to rounding.

that was contingent was small, ranging from about 3 to 8 percent. Similarly, little more than 8 percent of construction workers were contingent. Several large industries, including manufacturing, transportation and public utilities, and trade, had few contingent workers relative to their share of overall employment. Contingent workers were concentrated in the professional, administrative support, service, and operator, fabricator, and laborer occupations. In contrast, managerial and sales occupations had relatively few contingent workers (Table 2.3).

Table 2.3. Contingent and noncontingent workers by occupation and industry, February 1995 (Percent distribution)

Characteristic	Contingent workers			Noncontingent workers
	Estimate 1	*Estimate 2*	*Estimate 3*	
Occupation				
Total, 16 years and over (thousands)	2,739	3,422	6,034	117,174
Percent	100.0	100.0	100.0	100.0
Executive, administrative, and managerial	4.9	5.5	7.6	14.0
Professional specialty	17.2	16.6	20.7	14.6
Technicians and related support	1.8	2.2	2.7	3.2
Sales occupations	6.2	6.9	6.4	12.2
Administrative support, including clerical	20.9	18.7	17.8	15.0
Service occupations	17.9	19.8	16.0	13.4
Precision production, craft, and repair	11.0	11.3	10.0	10.8
Operators, fabricators, and laborers	17.4	16.1	15.8	14.2
Farming, forestry, and fishing	2.6	3.0	3.0	2.6
Industry				
Total, 16 years and over (thousands)	2,739	3,422	6,034	117,174
Percent	100.0	100.0	100.0	100.0
Agriculture	2.8	3.0	2.6	2.6
Mining	.3	.2	.3	.6
Construction	11.5	11.8	9.8	5.5
Manufacturing	10.0	9.5	10.8	17.1
Transportation and public utilities	3.8	3.2	4.2	7.2
Wholesale and retail trade	13.4	13.4	12.0	20.9
Finance, insurance, and real estate	2.0	1.9	2.6	6.7
Services	53.5	54.8	54.0	34.5
Public administration	2.7	2.2	3.6	5.0

Note: Noncontingent workers are those who do not fall into any estimate of contingent workers. The industry classification for temporary help agency workers and workers provided by contract firms is that of the place to which they were assigned. Details may not sum to totals due to rounding.

Table 2.4 Contingent workers by preference for contingent or noncontingent job and reason for working in contingent job, February 1995 (Percent distribution)

Preference	Estimate 1	Estimate 2	Estimate 3
Type of job preferred			
Total, 16 years and over (thousands)	2,739	3,422	6,034
Percent	100.0	100.0	100.0
Prefer noncontingent arrangement	64.1	61.2	55.8
Prefer contingent arrangement	29.9	32.6	30.5
It depends	2.4	2.5	3.1
Not available	3.6	3.7	10.7
Reason for contingent work			
Total, 16 years and over (thousands)	2,739	2,867	5,479
Percent	100.0	100.0	100.0
Economic reasons	44.0	44.3	36.1
Only type of work could find	28.5	29.2	22.4
Hope job leads to permanent employment	7.6	7.4	6.3
Other economic reason	7.8	7.7	7.4
Personal reasons	44.1	44.4	41.0
Flexibility of schedule	7.4	8.2	8.5
In school or training	18.3	17.5	15.6
Other personal reason	18.5	18.7	16.9
Reason not available	11.9	11.3	22.8

Note: Details may not sum to 100 percent due to rounding.

The majority of contingent workers would have preferred to hold permanent rather than temporary jobs; less than one-third were satisfied with their contingent arrangement (Table 2.4). Among nonstudents, the proportion of contingent workers who were satisfied with their arrangement dropped as low as 27 percent. Of all contingent workers with a preference for noncontingent work, about one-third were searching for another job.

Workers gave a variety of reasons for being in a contingent position. Overall, the reasons were about evenly divided between economic ones (for example, the job was the only type of work the person could find) and personal ones (for example, the flexibility of the schedule, or family or school commitments) (Table 2.4).[3] Adult men (age twenty and

3. The questions asking about individuals' preferences and reasons for being in a contingent job had unusually high nonresponse rates (nearly 11 percent for preferences and 23 percent for reasons under estimate 3). This was primarily due to the structure of the

older) were somewhat more likely than adult women to provide an economic reason. One-half of the teenagers gave a school-related reason.

Compensation

Perhaps the most widely accepted measure of the quality of a job is its earnings, followed by benefits, especially health insurance and pensions. Information on these subjects also was collected in the 1995 survey. Under the broadest estimate of contingency (estimate 3), median weekly earnings of contingent workers who worked full-time averaged about 80 percent of the earnings of other full-time workers (Table 2.5).[4] This ratio held for all of the major worker groups—men, women, whites, blacks, and Hispanics. Generally, younger and older contingent workers fared better relative to their noncontingent counterparts, with some age groups (teenagers and 45–64-year-olds) actually earning more than their noncontingent peers. The median usual weekly earnings of all contingent workers under estimate 3 was $385, compared with $479 for noncontingent workers. Estimate 3 had the highest earnings of the three measures of contingency, reflecting in part the longer tenure of the workers in this estimate, as well as the highest representation of managerial and professional positions, which typically pay more than other occupations.

The proportion of contingent workers who had health insurance from any source ranged from 57 to 65 percent, depending on the estimate chosen (Table 2.6). This was 17 to 25 percentage points lower than the proportion of noncontingent workers with health insurance. Moreover, contingent workers with insurance were substantially less likely to have received it from their employer. Under estimate 3, only 31 percent of contingent workers with health insurance coverage received it at work, compared with 66 percent of workers in noncontingent jobs. Sources of health insurance other than their current employer were similar for both contingent and noncontingent workers. The most common source by far was another family member, followed by coverage that workers had purchased on their own. While women in

---

questionnaire: not all workers who were classified as contingent in estimate 3 received these questions.

4. In the main CPS questionnaire, earnings data are collected only for wage and salary workers, not the self-employed. As part of the February 1995 supplement, earnings data were collected for the self-employed (both incorporated and unincorporated) as well as wage and salary workers. However, due to complications processing the data, all earnings estimates for *contingent workers* exclude the self-employed and independent contractors.

Table 2.5 Median weekly earnings of wage and salary workers by contingent employment status, sex, age, race, Hispanic origin, and full- and part-time status, February 1995

| Characteristic | Total | Contingent workers | | Noncontingent workers | Ratio of contingent to noncontingent earnings |
		Definition 1	Definition 3		
Full time					
Total, 16 years and over	$477	$317	$385	$479	0.80
Men	537	360	444	541	0.82
Women	407	281	322	409	0.79
White	495	334	420	497	0.85
Black	360	281	288	364	0.79
Hispanic	335	274	275	341	0.81
Total, 25 years and over	505	368	467	506	0.92
Men	589	478	546	590	0.93
Women	423	300	369	424	0.87
Part time					
Total, 16 years and over	134	102	109	138	0.79
Men	127	109	112	130	0.86
Women	137	98	107	141	0.76
White	137	102	108	140	0.77
Black	120	110	115	121	0.95
Hispanic	130	121	126	130	0.97
Total, 25 years and over	166	142	148	167	0.89
Men	191	153	158	196	0.81
Women	160	134	144	161	0.89

Note: Noncontingent workers are those who do not fall into any estimate of contingent workers. The earnings ratio is based on contingent estimate 3. Estimates exclude the incorporated self employed and independent contractors. The major difference between contingent worker estimate 1 and estimate 2 is the inclusion of the self-employed in definition 2. However, earnings estimates do not include the self-employed; hence, earnings for estimates 1 and 2 are virtually identical. That is why only estimate 1 is shown.

contingent jobs were somewhat more likely than men to have health insurance at all, men were more likely to have obtained their insurance through their employer.

Employer-sponsored pension plans were less commonly offered by contingent workers' employers, and only half of the contingent workers

Table 2.6 Contingent and noncontingent workers and those in alternative and traditional work arrangements by health insurance coverage, February 1995

Characteristic	Total employed (thousands)	Percent with health insurance coverage	
		Total	Provided by employer
Contingent workers:			
Estimate 1	2,739	57.2	10.2
Estimate 2	3,422	58.1	8.6
Estimate 3	6,034	64.9	20.4
Noncontingent workers	117,174	82.2	53.9
In alternative arrangements:			
Independent contractors	8,309	72.6	NA
On-call workers	1,968	66.1	17.2
Temporary help agency workers	1,181	44.9	5.7
Workers provided by contract firms	652	69.9	42.5
With traditional arrangements	111,052	82.7	57.2

Note: Noncontingent workers are those who do not fall into any estimate of contingent workers. Workers in traditional arrangements are those who do not fall into any of the "alternative arrangements" categories. Figures for contingent and noncontingent workers with health insurance coverage provided by an employer exclude the self-employed (incorporated and unincorporated) and all independent contractors.

whose employers offered pensions were eligible to participate. As shown in Table 2.7, about 15 percent of contingent workers participated in a pension plan at work, compared with about half of noncontingent workers.

Table 2.7 Participation in pension plans at work (percent distribution)

	Contingent workers	Noncontingent workers
All workers	100.0	100.0
Employer offered pension	44.5	62.0
Worker participated	15.4	49.5
Worker did not participate	28.5	11.5
Worker not eligible	22.5	7.4
Information not available	0.6	1.0
Employer did not offer pension	42.3	28.4
Information not available	13.2	9.6

A Profile of Workers in Alternative Employment Arrangements

Also of considerable interest to researchers in the area of employment relationships is the prevalence of alternative work arrangements. The February 1995 supplement examined workers in four such arrangements: independent contractors, on-call workers, workers paid by temporary help agencies, and workers paid by contract firms. The four groups varied a great deal in their demographic and economic characteristics. Furthermore, these worker groups differed in important ways from workers in so-called "traditional" arrangements.

It should be noted that employment arrangements were defined separately from contingency; a worker in an alternative employment arrangement may or may not be contingent. For instance, some contract company employees may have perceived their job as temporary and consequently were classified as contingent; on the other hand, many of the workers in that arrangement had an expectation of ongoing employment and were classified as noncontingent.

In February 1995, 8.3 million workers (6.7 percent of the total employed) said they were independent contractors, 2.0 million (1.6 percent) worked on call, 1.2 million (1.0 percent) worked for temporary help agencies, and 652,000 (0.5 percent) worked for contract firms. Table 2.8 provides a summary of the survey questions used to identify these four groups.

Independent Contractors

Independent contractors include all those who identified themselves as independent contractors, consultants, and freelance workers in the survey (and referred to here, for the sake of brevity, as independent contractors). Unlike workers in the other arrangements, independent contractors are not employees in the traditional sense, but rather work for themselves (or their own company), bearing the responsibility for obtaining clients, seeing that work assignments are executed, and otherwise running the business. No conditions were placed on the size or scope of their operation. Independent contractors may have one client or many, may have employees or work alone, and may or may not have businesses that were incorporated. Workers who frequently are independent contractors include computer consultants, freelance writers, insurance and real estate agents, and home builders.

Table 2.8 Workers in alternative employment arrangements as a percent of total employment, February 1995

Type of alternative arrangement	Percent of total employed
Independent contractors	
These are workers identified as wage and salary workers in the basic CPS who answered the following question affirmatively: "Last week, were you working as an independent contractor, independent consultant, or a freelance worker—that is, someone who obtains customers on their own to provide a product or service?" Also included are workers identified as self-employed in the basic CPS who answered the following question affirmatively: "Are you self-employed as an independent contractor, independent consultant, freelance worker, or something else (such as a shop or restaurant owner)?" in order to distinguish those who consider themselves to be independent contractors, consultants, or freelance workers from those who were business operators such as shop owners or restaurateurs.	6.7
On-call workers	
These are workers who answered the following question affirmatively: "Some people are in a pool of workers who are ONLY called to work as needed, although they can be scheduled to work for several days or weeks in a row, for example, substitute teachers and construction workers supplied by a union hiring hall. These people are sometimes referred to as ON-CALL workers. Were you an ON-CALL worker last week?"	1.6
Temporary help agency workers	
These are workers who said their job was temporary and answered affirmatively the following question "Are you paid by a temporary help agency?" Also included are workers who said their job was not temporary and answered affirmatively the question "Even though you told me your job was not temporary, are you paid by a temporary help agency?"	1.0
Workers provided by contract firms	
These are workers who answered the following question affirmatively: "Some companies provide employees or their services to others under contract. A few examples of services that can be contracted out include security, landscaping, or computer programming. Did you work for a company that contracts out either you or your services last week?" These workers also had to respond negatively to the question "Are you usually assigned to more than one customer?" and affirmatively to the question "Do you usually work at the customer's worksite?"	.5

The CPS has obtained information on the self-employed for many years; what was new in the 1995 survey was that they were asked whether they would consider themselves to be an independent contractor as opposed to another kind of business operator such as a shop owner or a restaurateur. About half of the self-employed were independent contractors. Persons who were classified as wage and salary workers in the basic CPS questionnaire also had the opportunity to be classified as independent contractors.[5] Table 2.8 provides the questions asked of each group.

Characteristics

Independent contractors differed sharply from other workers. They were considerably more likely than traditional workers to be male, white, at least twenty-five years old, and a college graduate (Table 2.9). About one in four had at least one employee, a smaller proportion than that for self-employed persons who were not independent contractors (40 percent). Independent contractors were somewhat more likely than traditional workers to work part-time and to hold managerial, professional, sales, or precision production jobs. They also were more likely to work in construction; in finance, insurance, and real estate; and in services. They were less likely to work in manufacturing or wholesale and retail trade (Table 2.10).

In stark contrast to the other arrangements, a large majority of independent contractors (more than four out of five) preferred their arrangement to a traditional job. Only 10 percent gave an economic reason for working as an independent contractor; most cited a personal motivation such as the flexibility of the schedule or the opportunity to be one's own boss (Table 2.11). They had been in the arrangement an average of nearly seven years, the longest tenure of any arrangement.

5. Among those identified as independent contractors, 85 percent were classified as self-employed in the main questionnaire, the remainder as wage and salary workers. Analysts may be tempted to classify independent contractors who were identified as wage and salary workers in the main questionnaire as workers who otherwise would have been employees of the company where they are working or individuals who were "converted" to independent contractors to avoid legal requirements. The basic CPS questionnaire does not permit this distinction, however. Two individuals who are in exactly the same work arrangement may answer the question from the main questionnaire—"Were you employed by government, by a private company, by a nonprofit organization, or were you self-employed?"—differently depending on their interpretation of the words "employed" and "self-employed."

Table 2.9 Employed persons in alternative and traditional work arrangements by selected characteristics, February 1995 (Percent distribution)

Characteristic	Workers in alternative arrangements				Workers in traditional arrange-ments
	Independent contractors	On-call workers	Temporary help agency workers	Workers provided by contract firms	
Age and sex					
Total, 16 years and (in thousands)	8,309	1,968	1,181	652	111,052
Percent	100.0	100.0	100.0	100.0	100.0
16 to 19 years	1.5	7.8	5.2	2.5	4.7
20 to 24 years	2.4	11.5	19.7	12.7	10.5
25 to 34 years	19.7	25.4	34.1	39.0	26.4
35 to 44 years	30.8	23.2	21.3	23.3	27.6
45 to 54 years	25.3	15.9	12.1	11.8	19.2
55 to 64 years	13.6	9.6	5.8	6.7	8.9
65 years and over	6.7	6.7	1.8	4.1	2.5
Men, 16 years and over	67.3	48.4	47.2	71.5	52.8
16 to 19 years	.9	3.9	3.0	1.4	2.4
20 to 24 years	1.6	6.7	11.4	6.4	5.6
25 to 34 years	12.6	13.1	16.8	29.8	14.3
35 to 44 years	21.0	10.8	7.7	19.0	14.5
45 to 54 years	16.7	6.7	4.4	5.7	10.0
55 to 64 years	9.6	3.7	2.8	5.2	4.7
65 years and over	4.9	3.6	1.1	4.1	1.4
Women, 16 years and over	32.7	51.6	52.8	28.5	47.2
16 to 19 years	.6	3.9	2.3	1.1	2.4
20 to 24 years	.8	4.8	8.3	6.1	4.9
25 to 34 years	7.1	12.3	17.4	9.2	12.1
35 to 44 years	9.8	12.4	13.5	4.3	13.1
45 to 54 years	8.5	9.1	7.7	6.3	9.2
55 to 64 years	4.0	5.8	2.9	1.5	4.2
65 years and over	1.8	3.2	.8	–	1.1
Race and Hispanic origin					
White	92.3	84.9	72.7	83.0	85.1
Black	5.0	10.4	21.8	11.7	10.9
Hispanic origin	5.2	9.6	11.3	8.4	8.6
Full- or part-time status					
Full-time workers	74.4	44.1	79.4	84.0	81.7
Part-time workers	25.6	55.9	20.5	16.0	18.3
Educational attainment					
Total, 25 to 64 years (thousands)	7,428	1,456	864	527	91,318
Percent	100.0	100.0	100.0	100.0	100.0
Less than a high-school diploma	8.7	11.3	14.2	9.5	9.7
High-school graduates, no college	29.1	35.6	33.4	29.8	32.5
Less than a bachelor's degree	27.9	31.5	32.1	30.2	29.0
College graduates	34.4	21.7	20.3	30.6	28.9

Note: Workers in traditional arrangements are those who do not fall into any of the alternative arrangement categories. Entries under race and Hispanic origin will not sum to 100 percent because data for the "other races" group are not presented and Hispanics are included in both the white and black population groups. Details for other characteristics may not sum to totals due to rounding. Dash indicates less than 0.05 percent.

Table 2.10 Employed persons in alternative and traditional work arrangements by occupation and industry, February 1995 (Percent distribution)

| Characteristic | Workers in alternative arrangements | | | | Workers in traditional arrange-ments |
	Independent contractors	On-call workers	Temporary help agency workers	Workers provided by contract firms	
Occupation					
Total, 16 years and over (thousands)	8,309	1,968	1,181	652	111,052
Percent	100.0	100.0	100.0	100.0	100.0
Executive, administrative, and managerial	18.6	3.0	6.5	5.7	13.6
Professional specialty	16.3	22.1	8.3	25.6	14.7
Technicians and related support	1.1	1.6	3.7	6.9	3.4
Sales occupations	18.8	6.2	2.6	3.2	11.7
Administrative support, including clerical	3.8	9.9	30.1	·4.8	16.0
Service occupations	10.6	20.0	9.0	27.8	13.6
Precision production, craft, and repair	19.2	13.3	5.6	14.6	10.1
Operators, fabricators, and laborers	6.5	20.1	33.2	10.4	14.6
Farming, forestry, and fishing	5.1	3.8	1.0	.9	2.4
Industry					
Total, 16 years and over (thousands)	8,309	1,968	1,181	652	111,052
Percent	100.0	100.0	100.0	100.0	100.0
Agriculture	5.0	3.7	.4	.3	2.4
Mining	.2	.5	.2	2.4	.6
Construction	21.2	13.1	2.8	8.4	4.4
Manufacturing	5.0	6.3	33.5	17.6	17.9
Transportation and public utilities	5.0	9.0	7.7	13.4	7.2
Wholesale and retail trade	13.2	14.5	8.1	6.0	21.4
Finance, insurance, and real estate	9.6	1.9	7.5	6.9	6.4
Services	40.6	47.4	38.7	32.3	34.4
Public administration	.3	3.5	1.2	12.6	5.4

Note: Workers in traditional arrangements are those who do not fall into any of the alternative arrangement categories. The industry classification for temporary help agency workers and workers provided by contract firms is that of the place to which they were assigned. Details may not sum to totals due to rounding.

Table 2.11 Employed persons in alternative work arrangements by their preferred arrangement and reason for working in their current arrangement, February 1995 (Percent distribution)

Preference	Independent contractors	On-call workers	Temporary help agency workers
Type of job preferred			
Total, 16 years and over (thousands)	8,309	1,968	1,181
Percent	100.0	100.0	100.0
Prefer traditional arrangement	9.8	56.7	63.3
Prefer indirect or alternative arrangement	82.5	36.6	26.6
It depends	5.1	4.2	8.1
Not available	2.6	2.5	1.9
Reason for alternative work arrangement			
Total, 16 years and over (thousands)	8,309	1,968	1,181
Percent	100.0	100.0	100.0
Economic reasons	10.0	47.4	64.7
Only type of work could find	4.0	32.4	39.4
Hope job leads to traditional employment	.6	8.5	17.9
Other economic reason	5.4	6.6	7.5
Personal reasons	87.0	49.7	33.3
Flexibility of schedule	.19.2	23.5	13.5
In school or training	.5	5.6	2.5
Other personal reason	67.3	20.6	17.3
Reason not available	3.1	2.9	1.9

Note: Details may not sum to 100 percent due to rounding. Information on preference and reason for alternative arrangement is not available for workers employed by contract companies.

Compensation

Among full-time workers, independent contractors had the highest median earnings of the four alternative groups ($518) and, in fact, outearned traditional workers (Table 2.12).[6] This pattern held for most demographic groups. In two industries—finance, insurance, and real estate; and agriculture—independent contractors outearned traditional workers by nearly 50 percent. Nearly three-quarters had health insurance, the highest proportion of any alternative arrangement (Table 2.6).

6. Estimates for earnings of independent contractors include the self-employed as well as wage and salary workers.

Table 2.12 Median weekly earnings of workers in alternative and traditional work arrangements by sex, age, race, Hispanic origin, and full- and part-time status, February 1995

Characteristic	Total	Temporary help agency workers	Workers provided by contract companies	On-call workers	Independent contractors	Workers in traditional arrangements
Full time						
Total, 16 years and over	$477	$290	$512	$386	$518	$480
Men	537	277	562	433	590	543
Women	407	297	399	267	361	410
White	495	298	530	416	527	498
Black	360	261	476	280	375	364
Hispanic	335	237	—	281	370	343
Total, 25 years and over	505	299	557	424	524	507
Men	589	297	598	491	597	591
Women	423	300	393	271	365	426
Part time						
Total, 16 years and over	134	147	187	112	180	135
Men	127	147	—	120	252	126
Women	137	147	—	108	146	138
White	137	163	209	110	182	138
Black	120	—	—	117	182	120
Hispanic	130	—	—	119	185	129
Total, 25 years and over	166	150	209	123	196	168
Men	191	127	—	153	272	195
Women	160	163	—	116	158	163

Note: Workers in traditional arrangements are those who do not fall into any of the alternative arrangement categories. Data are not shown where base is less than 75,000.

They were very likely to receive their health insurance from a source not related to employment, typically purchasing it on their own or obtaining it through a family member.

On-Call Workers

An integral aspect of the job for most workers is reporting to work according to a fairly regular schedule. There are exceptions, however. Some workers report to work only when they specifically are asked to do so. These individuals are referred to in this study as on-call workers. Once called to work, they may stay in the assignment for just a day or for several days or weeks in a row. Examples of workers who can be on call are substitute teachers, nurses, and construction workers. Persons with regularly scheduled work that might include periods of being "on call" to perform work at unusual hours, such as medical residents, were not included in this category.

Characteristics

The demographics of on-call workers were fairly similar to those of workers in traditional arrangements; however, on-call workers were somewhat more likely to be women, under the age of twenty-five, and over the age of sixty-four. On-call workers had less education, on average; of the 25–64-year-olds, 22 percent had a college degree, seven percentage points less than the share of traditional workers (Table 2.9). There was an unusually large gender gap with respect to education—only 11 percent of the men had a college degree, compared with 31 percent of the women. This disparity was reflected in the occupational profiles of men and women in this arrangement, discussed below.

On-call workers were much more likely than traditional workers to work part-time (Table 2.9). Women had an extremely high incidence of part-time work (71 percent among adults), much higher than either their male counterparts (33 percent) or women working in traditional arrangements (24 percent). Part-timers constituted the majority of on-call workers in every major occupational group except precision production, craft, and repair. When compared with traditional workers, an unusually large share of those on-call worked part-time involuntarily and would have preferred full-time work.

While found in a variety of occupations, as shown on Table 2.10, on-call workers were concentrated in several categories, with the men tending toward blue-collar work and the women toward selected white-collar and service jobs. Some of the most common occupations for the men were truck drivers, freight and stock handlers, skilled craftspeople, laborers, substitute teachers, and farm workers. For the women, some of the most common fields were food preparation, nursing aides, child care workers, substitute teachers, registered nurses, sales clerks, and cashiers. Clearly, on-call work has quite different meanings for men and women.

While the length of time on-call workers spent in a particular assignment typically was very short, their tenure in the arrangement was relatively long—a median of 2.1 years. As shown on Table 2.11, a majority of on-call workers would have preferred a traditional arrangement, although women were somewhat more satisfied with being on-call than men. About one-quarter of those with a preference for a new job were actively looking for one. Nearly 60 percent of the men gave an economic reason for working on call, while a similar share of the women gave a personal reason.

Compensation

The median earnings of on-call workers who worked full-time were $386 per week, 80 percent of the earnings of traditional workers (Table 2.12). The earnings ratio for men was higher than that for women, but there was very little variation by age. Two-thirds had health insurance from any source, compared with 83 percent of traditional workers (Table 2.6). A total of 17 percent obtained health insurance through the job, much less than the share of traditional workers (57 percent). Less than one-fifth of on-call workers were included in a pension plan at work, compared with about half of traditional workers.

Workers Who Are Paid by Temporary Help Agencies

Perhaps the most well-known employment intermediary is the temporary help agency, which provides workers to client companies, typically on a short-term basis. Since the end of World War II, a variety of social, economic, and demographic changes—including heightened international competition, greater fluctuations in demand, increased costs of fringe benefits, a decline in unionization, and shifts in labor force composition—have resulted in explosive growth among providers of temporary help (see, for instance, Golden and Appelbaum, 1992; Laird and Williams, 1996; Segal and Sullivan, 1997). Today, companies in the industry such as Kelly Services, Manpower, and Olsten are among the most familiar names on the corporate landscape, and temporaries have become a permanent fixture in many workplaces.

Temporary help firms recruit, check references, test, and sometimes train workers. They also issue paychecks, withhold payrolls taxes, and make required employer contributions for Social Security and unemployment insurance. For employers, such firms fill an important niche by providing qualified workers on short notice to fill in for permanent employees who are ill or on vacation or maternity leave. "Temps" also may augment the company's regular workforce during a period of increased staffing needs (a seasonal surge in orders, for instance) or bring specialized skills that the company needs only occasionally. For some employers, going through temporary help firms is a way to "audition" prospective employees.

For workers, temping meets a need for short-term, flexible employment for mothers, older workers, and others who do not want a long-term job. Some workers prefer the variety of temporary assignments to the predictability of a regular job. Temping also gives workers opportunities to obtain experience and training, explore the local job scene, and test a variety of job settings before making a permanent commitment. To be sure, not all workers are motivated strictly by personal preference. Workers may temp to fill in the gap between "regular" jobs. When permanent jobs are scarce, temping may be one of the few employment options available.

Characteristics

The 1.2 million workers paid by temporary help agencies were more likely than workers in traditional arrangements to be young, female, and black. (To the extent that permanent staff of temporary help agencies— a fairly small group—indicate that they are paid by their agencies, the estimate of the number of workers whose employment was mediated by temporary help agencies is somewhat overstated.) One-fourth of the temps were under the age of twenty-five, making this the most youthful of the alternative arrangements (Table 2.9). Most young people who temped were not enrolled in school. Temps were somewhat less educated than other workers; just 20 percent were college graduates, compared with 29 percent of traditional workers.

The survey data confirmed that many women combined family responsibilities with their temporary work. Over 60 percent had at least one child under the age of eighteen, and nearly half of the mothers had at least one preschooler. Both proportions were somewhat higher than those for women in traditional arrangements.

Surprisingly, perhaps, temps were not, as a rule, part-time. Nearly four-fifths of temps worked full-time, a proportion only slightly lower than that of traditional workers (Table 2.9). There was a notable difference in the reasons given for working part-time, however. About one-half of the part-time temps gave an economic reason for their short hours, compared with only 18 percent of traditional workers.

Congruent with the popular image of the industry, temporary help agency workers were heavily concentrated in clerical and machine operator and laborer positions (Table 2.10). There was a sharp division of labor by sex; half of the men were in the latter category, while half of the women were in the former. Manufacturing and services accounted for 72 percent of the industries to which temps were assigned.

Workers' satisfaction with the arrangement was relatively low; nearly two-thirds of temps reported that they would prefer to work in a traditional job, the highest of the arrangements (Table 2.11). A majority of workers, both male and female, gave an economic reason for working through a temporary help agency, although a sizable minority of the women provided a personal reason. Most temps were relatively new to the arrangement, and few had been in it for more than three years. Most assignments were fairly short-term; 42 percent had been on their current assignment for less than three months. However, 16 percent had been working at their assignment for more than a year, implying that temporary help agencies act as intermediaries for some relatively long-term employment relationships.

Compensation

Temporary help agency workers had the lowest earnings of any of the four alternative arrangements. The median earnings of full-time workers was $290 per week, 60 percent of the traditional worker wage (Table 2.12). Female temps actually had higher earnings than male temps ($297 compared with $277). This reflects, in part, the concentration of the men in low-paying laborer positions and the concentration of the women in somewhat better paying clerical jobs. About one-quarter of temps were eligible for health insurance coverage through their temporary help firms; only 6 percent had signed up for it, though a total of 45 percent had health insurance from any source (Table 2.6). Pension plans offered through temporary help agencies were uncommon—just 3 percent of the workers were included in such a plan, compared with about 50 percent of traditional workers.

Another Source of Data

The temporary help industry is unique among the four employment arrangements under study, in that BLS has produced limited but regular information on the industry for some time. BLS's other major survey of employment, the Current Employment Statistics (CES) survey, obtains from employers information on the number of workers on company payrolls (as well as their average hours and earnings), which is then dis-aggregated into specific industries, including temporary help supply. CES data have clearly established the rapid expansion of this industry, which had grown from four hundred thousand employees in 1982 to more than two million in 1995.[7]

Contract Company Workers

The other form of intermediated employment examined was work arranged through a contract company. Generally speaking, contract companies supply employees to other organizations to provide services that the client companies prefer to be carried out by contract staff rather than "in-house" employees. Examples of services that can be contracted out are computer programming; building security, cleaning, and food service; and construction. To be counted as a contract company worker in this study, individuals had to work for only one customer and usually work at the customer's work site. These requirements were imposed to focus on workers whose employment appeared to be very closely tied to the firm for which they are performing the work, rather than including all workers employed by firms that provide services.

For client companies, contract workers have many of the same advantages as temporary help workers. Contract workers can reduce the size of the client companies' permanent staff, mitigate the cost of recruiting employees, moderate the effect of fluctuations in product demand, and provide access to specialized skills.

7. Temporary help supply is Standard Industrial Classification code 7363. At first glance, there appears to be a large discrepancy between the number of temporary help workers as measured in the CPS (1.2 million) compared with the CES (2 million). On closer inspection, much of this difference can be explained by important differences in the concepts and methods of the two surveys. For a reconciliation of the estimates, see Polivka, 1996a.

Characteristics

Compared with traditional workers, those employed by contract firms (a total of 650,000) were disproportionately male, younger than thirty-five, and college educated (Table 2.9). Most worked full-time. The largest proportion of contract workers was employed in the services industry, and substantial proportions worked in manufacturing and transportation and utilities (Table 2.10). Contract workers were more likely to be in professional specialty or service occupations than were traditional workers. The single largest occupation was security guards, which accounted for 15 percent of the total. Construction workers and computer specialists accounted for 12 percent each. A relatively large share of contract company employees worked in the public sector.

A substantial share—40 percent—had been working for the current client company for more than a year. Nearly half had been working for a contract company for more than a year. (Information on reason and preference for working in the arrangement was not available for contract company workers.)

Compensation

The earnings of contract company workers ($512 per week for full-timers) were higher than earnings of workers in traditional arrangements and nearly matched those of independent contractors (Table 2.12). About 43 percent of contract company workers had health insurance coverage through their employer, less than the proportion for traditional workers (57 percent), but considerably higher than that of the other alternative arrangements (Table 2.6). A relatively large proportion of contract company workers—70 percent—had coverage from any source. About 29 percent were included in their company's pension plan, compared with one-half of traditional workers. As with the other arrangements, the likelihood of receiving benefits increased with education.

Comparison with Temporary Help Workers

While the conceptual distinction between the two types of intermediated arrangements may be somewhat blurred, individuals who worked for a contract company differed markedly from temporary help workers. Compared with temps, contract company workers were more likely to be male, white, at least twenty-five years old, and college graduates (Table 2.9). They were more heavily represented in professional and service occupations and very underrepresented in the clerical and machine operator jobs which dominate the temporary help workforce (Table 2.10). Further, contract company workers had been at their current assignment much longer than temps. Judging from the magnitude of the differences between the two groups, it would appear that the distinction between contract companies and temporary help agencies is meaningful to workers in those arrangements.

Workers in Alternative Arrangements by Contingent Status

As noted earlier, alternative work arrangement status and contingency were independently determined. Table 2.13 presents the proportion of workers in the various arrangements who were contingent. Under the broadest estimate of contingency (estimate 3), two-thirds of employees of temporary help agencies were in contingent jobs, as were about one-third of on-call workers; however, only about 20 percent of contract workers and 4 percent of independent contractors were contingent.

The four alternative work arrangements accounted for only one-third of the nearly 6 million contingent workers. (The remainder includes those hired directly by their employers for a temporary position.) Thus, it appears that most contingent workers are in non-intermediated, regularly scheduled positions, and most workers in alternative arrangements hold permanent (noncontingent) jobs.

Table 2.13 Contingent and noncontingent workers by type of work arrangement, February 1995

| | | *Percent distribution* | | | |
| | | *Contingent workers* | | | *Noncon-* |
Arrangements	*Total (thousands)*	*Estimate 1*	*Estimate 2*	*Estimate 3*	*tingent workers*
In alternative arrangements:					
Independent contractors	8,309	NA	3.8	3.8	96.2
On-call workers	1,968	17.6	18.0	35.2	64.8
Temporary help agency workers	1,181	39.4	48.0	66.5	33.5
Workers provided by contract firms	652	7.7	11.7	19.8	80.2
With traditional arrangements	111,052	1.6	1.8	3.6	96.4

Note: Noncontingent workers are those who do not fall into any estimate of contingent workers. Workers in traditional arrangements are those who do not fall into any of the alternative arrangement categories. Independent contractors, as well as the self-employed, are excluded from estimate 1.

Conclusion

The U.S. labor market has given rise to a profusion of work schedules and employment arrangements. With this have come concerns about the quality of jobs in general and job security in particular. This study, the first to measure directly the overall incidence of contingent work, shows that permanent employment is still the norm for an overwhelming majority of Americans. When asked in February 1995 if their job was temporary (for an economic reason) or could not continue for as long as they wished, only 4.9 percent of workers responded affirmatively. Moreover, one-third of contingent workers preferred their temporary job to a permanent one. Workers in the largest alternative arrangement studied, independent contracting, described themselves as very content with their work. Still, the survey found that several million workers considered their job situation to be at least somewhat unstable, and this has important implications for the workers, their families, their communities, and the economy as a whole. As a result, BLS plans to continue to collect and analyze data that help us to understand the evolving nature of employment relationships.

CHAPTER THREE

Gauging the Consequences for Gender Relations, Pay Equity, and the Public Purse

Roberta Spalter-Roth
Heidi Hartmann

S ince the mid 1980s, labor market researchers have become increasingly convinced that the United States is witnessing a restructuring of the labor market. An important aspect of this restructuring is reflected in the growth of "contingent" work, jobs that are temporary, part-time, or on a contract or on-call basis, and that offer little security, lower pay, or fewer benefits (Barker, 1993; Belous, 1989; Callaghan & Hartmann, 1992; Christensen, 1988a; duRivage, 1992a; Harrison & Bluestone, 1988; Heckman, Roselius, & Smith, 1994; Howell, 1993; Martella, 1990; Polivka & Nardone,1989; Rose, 1995; Spalter-Roth, Hartmann, & Shaw, 1993; Tilly, 1991a, 1992b, 1996). According to many of these researchers, the growth of contingent work is based on the desire of employers—more than employees—for flexibility and cost savings.

Much of the evidence for claims regarding the growth, characteristics, or sources of growth of contingent work is indirect or anecdotal, based on small-scale studies or on inferences from large but inadequate data sets. Defining, identifying, and establishing trends in the extent of contingent work and determining its characteristics have been difficult because of the lack of data. Until recently, no nationally representative data on the extent of contingent work has existed, and now there is disagreement about its results.[1] As a result, contingent work has been measured by proxy variables such as involuntary part-time work, self-employment, seasonal work, employment in the temporary help services industry, moonlighting, or length of job tenure.

Despite the lack of precise evidence, there is a growing consensus that contingent work reflects deteriorating work relations between employers and employees as employers strive to gain greater control over the pro-

---

1. A special supplement of the Current Population Survey attempting to measure the extent and characteristics of contingent work went into the field in February 1995. The initial results of this survey are presented in this volume. This supplement, thus far, contains data for only a single year.

duction process and reduce labor costs. In the face of deteriorating work relations, many workers feel an increased sense of economic insecurity.

In this chapter, we join the effort to investigate the distribution and consequences of contingent work. As part of this effort we examine two less studied aspects of these changing work arrangements: their relation to the gendered division of labor and the costs they impose on taxpayers through public subsidies to employers who hire contingent workers. We stress the relation between contingent work and the gendered division of labor because women still hold a disproportionate share of these jobs despite their increased presence in the labor market. Declining employer commitment to workers can be masked because the majority of contingent workers are women, whose need for economic security is often discounted. We stress the issue of public transfers because the wages provided by contingent work are not enough to support families. Women receiving these wages must seek additional income sources. Means-tested welfare benefits have been a source of wage subsidy for those women without access to the higher earnings of a male breadwinner.

Currently, women make up more than two-thirds of the temporary workforce (unpublished data from the March 1994 Current Population Survey) and about two-thirds of the part-time workforce (U.S. Bureau of Labor Statistics, 1995a). It is likely that the availability of women workers, who have traditionally earned less than men and worked in jobs with fewer advancement opportunities, has facilitated the growth of contingent work. According to Barbara Reskin and Patricia Roos (1990), the gender composition of a firm's workforce reflects how the employer thinks about staffing and human resource decisions, in terms of willingness to provide stable employment, to develop workers' skills, and to provide livable wages and benefits. If employers think of women as "secondary" workers rather than as breadwinners, as workers who are more committed to their families than to their careers, then employers are likely to pay women less and to provide fewer opportunities for training and advancement. Women will tend to work in jobs with lower pay and fewer benefits because these are the jobs that are open to them. Over time, the available jobs seem to have become increasingly contingent in nature, and women have been considered the ideal persons to fill them. (Wherever men have fewer alternatives, they, too, have been induced to take similarly contingent jobs).

In an idealized gendered division of labor in which it is assumed that women specialize more in family care, it is also generally assumed that mothers can depend for much of their financial support on the earnings of husbands who specialize in market work. Many economists assume that families maximize their well-being through this gendered division of labor (see, for example, Becker, 1991; Fuchs, 1988). The result of this tradeoff (whether voluntary or imposed by employment opportunities) is the economic dependency of women or their reduced ability to be self-supporting.

Many women do seek alternative, more flexible employment to accommodate their family care responsibilities and to provide the supply that meets employers' demands for a more flexible workforce. According to a 1994 survey by the National Association of Temporary Services (National Association of Temporary Services, 1994a), 66 percent of those who responded said that temporary work did provide flexibility (down 14 percent from a 1989 NATS survey), 44 percent said they engaged in temporary work to spend more time with their families, but a surprising 78 percent also looked to temporary work to provide a foot in the door for full-time employment. Although some of those who work in contingent jobs are likely to have access to other family resources, many do not. And many married women find it increasingly necessary or desirable to contribute substantially to family income themselves.

Women's financial responsibility for themselves and their families has increased significantly as dual-earner families and single-mother families have replaced male breadwinner families. Male breadwinner families fell from 44 percent of all families with children in 1975 (Hayghe, 1990) to 20 percent in 1994 (unpublished data from the March 1994 Current Population Survey). Yet the majority of women still receive low wages in their jobs, especially those in alternative work arrangements or those in other than full-time/full-year jobs with a single employer (duRivage, 1994; Spalter-Roth, Hartmann, & Shaw, 1993; Tilly, 1991a, 1992b).

As long as employers create contingent work and women hold a disproportionate share of contingent jobs, women's dependence on men or on other income sources is reinforced (Negrey, 1993). If additional earnings from male breadwinners are not available to women engaged in contingent work, then they are likely to require income supplements from taxpayers through state-provided means-tested welfare benefits. Unlike dependence on men, dependence on the state as a source of income support is negatively sanctioned, even stigmatized (Hartmann & Spalter-Roth, 1994; Spalter-Roth & Hartmann, 1994). As welfare benefits are cut back in the current round of "reforms," contingent workers without additional family income sources are put at even greater risk of poverty (Spalter-Roth, 1996; Hartmann, Spalter-Roth, & Chu, 1996).

This chapter first defines permanent and contingent work relations based on information available from the U.S. Bureau of the Census's Survey of Income and Program Participation. Most of the chapter is devoted to presenting findings. The first set of findings describes the share of the workforce employed at permanent, contingent, or questionable jobs, and how these shares changed between 1987 and 1990. Next, we describe the gendered patterns of permanent and contingent work. Third, we examine the financial consequences of current work relations for women compared to men. Then we test the idea that contingent work reflects a gendered trade-off in which women specialize in family care in exchange for support by a male breadwinner. Finding that this trade-off does not appear to be possible for many women employed at contingent jobs, we go on to examine the role of welfare benefits as a substitute income subsidy. Finally we suggest a series of policies to improve the economic well-being of contingent workers that go beyond the breadwinner and housewife model.

Method

Defining Contingent Work

In the absence of an agreed-upon definition of contingent work, most researchers have relied on a series of proxy measures to capture its dominant characteristics. As Kathleen Christensen has stated, "Contingent work is an umbrella term used to describe changes in employer-employee relations. It typically covers a variety of forms including part-time, temporary, self-employed independent contracting and occasionally home based work" (1988a:82).

Three dominant characteristics of this work are usually emphasized. The first, and relatively easily measured, characteristic is a work schedule dimension—usually emphasizing temporariness or unpredictability in terms of hours and weeks of work. Contingent work is often defined as an "other" (and less desirable) category; according to some analysts contingent workers include all those who do not work full-time and full-year for a single employer (Polivka & Nardone, 1989). For example, Cynthia Negrey (1993) defines contingent work to include all part-time workers who are employed for fewer than forty hours per week (in contrast to the standard U.S. Department of Labor definition of part-time work as fewer than thirty-five hours per week). Kathleen Barker and Kathleen Christensen (this volume) label it as less than full-time or permanent work. Jobs that last less than a full year might themselves be considered temporary, unless they simply reflect entry into or voluntary exit from the labor market or a transition between jobs. Although the hours worked per week or weeks worked per year are relatively easily measured with existing data sets, measuring the unpredictability of work schedules is more difficult because specific questions about such a feature of work are rarely included in large-scale surveys.

A second (and also relatively easy to measure) characteristic of contingent work has to do with wage and benefit adequacy. Contingent work is characterized as providing low pay and few or no fringe benefits (duRivage, 1992a; Tilly, 1991a, 1992b). Many surveys routinely ask workers about their earnings and benefits, though benefit data are less common and thorough than wage data.

A third characteristic (more difficult to measure using most current data sets) is an impermanent or conditional relation between employers and employees, usually connoting a lack of attachment (Polivka & Nardone, 1989). Barker and Christensen (this volume) describe contingent work as consisting of "tenuous" arrangements between employers and employees. William Lewis and Nancy Molloy (1991:2) refer to the contingent work relationship as a "no strings attached" relation. Jon Pierce (1989) refers to contingent workers as "leased" or "as-needed" workers. Few surveys ask workers about the contractual arrangements of their employment or their expectations of its duration.

Most researchers attempt to include more than one of these three dominant characteristics in any measure of contingent work. In this chapter, we measure contingent work using information about workers' schedules during a twelve-month period and about the number of different employment relations they have. We then examine the wages and health benefits of the workers we identify as contingent and compare them to those workers we identify as permanent.

Data Set and Definition of Contingent Work

The definitions used throughout this chapter rely on information available from the U.S. Bureau of the Census's Survey of Income and Program Participation (SIPP). The SIPP is a panel survey that tracks a nationally representative sample of respondents for approximately thirty-two months, revealing changes in their work behavior, jobs, earnings, family structure, and participation in government assistance programs. As a representative survey, findings based on the survey sample can be extrapolated to the total population. The SIPP is a useful data set for measuring contingent work because it provides longitudinal information on the characteristics of up to two wage or salary jobs and two self-employment "jobs" that workers hold in any given month. Thus, researchers can determine the number of jobs and employers at any one time or across the year. Because of the longitudinal design of the SIPP, researchers are also able to determine the workers' schedules across the year. In addition, the wages and benefits attached to each job can be observed. Unlike many studies of contingent work that use cross-sectional (or point-in-time) data, we can distinguish between full-time/full-year workers with only one job and full-time/full-year workers packaging several jobs. We can also distinguish between full-time or part-time workers who work full-year and those who work part-year.

Because the SIPP includes self-employment as well as wage or salary jobs, we can distinguish between those who rely primarily on wage or salary work and those who package it with self-employment. And we can distinguish between those self-employed workers who work full-time/full-year in one business and those who combine two or more self-employment jobs over the year. The wealth of information on job statuses, job packages, and work schedules enables us to develop a typology of permanent and contingent work that is more reflective of its complexity than are definitions based on part-time status or employment in the "temp" industry alone. The SIPP was not specially designed to measure contingent work, however. It does not distinguish between voluntary and involuntary part-time workers, nor does it ask respondents if jobs are permanent or contingent.

We use three major distinctions to construct a typology of work relations. The first distinction is whether or not the worker holds a single job with a single employer or multiple jobs with multiple employers. The second distinction is whether or not the worker is employed full-time or part-time (with fewer than thirty-five hours per week defined as part-time). The third distinction is whether or not the worker is employed full-year or part-year. Full-year is defined as fifty weeks or more; part-year is defined as forty-nine weeks or fewer.

As Figure 3.1 shows, workers with multiple employers who work less than full-time/full-year are considered to be *contingent workers*. We consider the number of different jobs held during the year as a proxy for "tenuousness" or "contingency," while the less than full-time/full-year work schedule is itself considered a dominant characteristic of contingent work and is also included. We reason that a worker with more than one employer who still does not work full-time /full-year is likely to be a worker who is trying but unable to achieve a more permanent full-time schedule. In addition, all those who work part-time/part-year are defined as contingent workers regardless of the number of employers. The result is a broad definition of contingent work. *Permanent workers* are defined as those who *do* work a full-time/full-year schedule, even if for more than one employer (such as moonlighters and job changers) *and* those who work part-time throughout the year but only for one employer (these part-time workers are likely have stable employment relations and are more likely to be working part-time voluntarily than those who are patching together several part-time jobs and are still not obtaining work throughout the year).

Workers whom we cannot categorize as either permanent or contingent are identified as *questionable*. They include workers who work full-time/part-year who held only one job or changed jobs, and job changers who worked part-time but all year. These workers are of questionable status because they may have just begun a stint of permanent employment or may be experiencing temporary hires. Self-employment is treated in the same manner as wage and salary jobs. Full-time/full-year self-employed workers are considered permanent workers rather than contingent workers, regardless of the number of businesses they operate. Those working at one business all year long, even if part-time, are considered permanent workers. In contrast, those who package two or more self-employment jobs or package self-employment with wage or salary work and still do not have a full-time/full-year schedule are

Figure 3.1 Classification grid of permanent and contingent workers

| | Full-year | | Part-year | |
	Full-time	Part-time	Full-time	Part-time
Single job holder	Permanent	Permanent part-time	Questionable	Contingent
Job changers	Other Permanent	Questionable	Questionable	Contingent
Multiple job holder	Other Permanent	Contingent	Contingent	Contingent

Source: Institute for Women's Policy Research.

defined as contingent workers. The Appendix shows all the subgroups of workers included as permanent, contingent, or questionable workers.

To conduct the analysis, we created special 1987 and 1990 files of workers who worked at least two hundred hours during the year and were neither over the age of sixty-five nor teenagers living with parents. Each file contains a calendar year (twelve months) of data. We chose the two-hundred-hour rule because we wanted to focus on prime-age men and women who seek an attachment to the labor force rather than on the most marginal workers. As a result of these exclusions, we probably underestimate the number and proportion of contingent workers in the labor force.

Findings

Distribution of Workers

This section first considers the distribution of workers among the three employment categories.

Permanent Workers

In spite of the concern with the growth of contingent work relations, Figure 3.2 shows that more than seven out of ten workers held permanent jobs in 1990. The largest subcategory were those workers, either wage or salary earners or self-employed, with one full-time/full-year job with a continuous relationship with a single employer or business. Still, only half (51 percent) of all U.S. workers with two hundred or more hours of employment during a calendar year held this type of traditional breadwinner job.

About 11 percent of all workers were labeled as "other" permanent workers. The largest subgroup in this category comprised those who worked full-time/full-year schedules but worked at more than one job; many of these likely worked full-time/full-year at one job and moonlighted at a second or even a third job. The second largest subgroup of other permanent workers included job changers who were employed full-time/full-year despite the job change. In this case, the job change might well have been voluntary, with the worker moving to a better job. Other small groups of workers (including those full-time/full-year workers who mixed wage or salary work with a secondary self-employment job) were also included in this category since many of these are permanent wage or salary workers who have a minor business, such as consulting, on the side.

Figure 3.2 All workers grouped by work relation, 1990 (millions of workers)

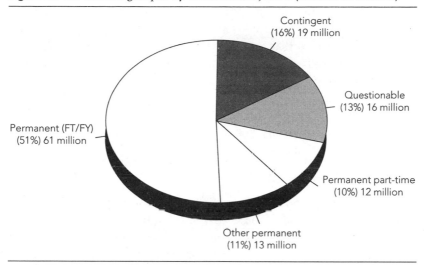

Source: IWPR calculations based on the U.S. Census Bureau Survey of Income and Program Participation, 1990.

Note: "Permanent" represents those workers who are the most likely to have stable employment relationships, i.e., those working full-time/full-year at one wage or salary job, or are self-employed workers at only one business during the year. "Other Permanent" workers include those who are employed full-time/full-year, but who hold multiple jobs or mix wage and salary work with self-employment. "Permanent part-time" workers are single job holders who work part-time/full-year for only one employer or at one business throughout the year. "Contingent" workers are those who work part-time/part-year, regardless of the number of employers; those who work full-time/part-year for more than one employer; and those who work part-time/full-year while mixing self-employment with wage or salary work. "Questionable" workers are those who could not be classified as contingent of permanent, including full-time/part-year single job holders and job changers who work either full-time/part-year or part-time/full-year.

The final subcategory of permanent workers, labeled "permanent part-time," consisted of those individuals who worked fewer than thirty-five hours per week but worked for a single employer or operated only one business over the course of the calendar year. Figure 3.2 shows that 10 percent of workers fell into this subcategory. Although all part-time workers are often lumped with contingent workers, we follow Chris Tilly's (1991a, 1992b, 1996) distinction between permanent and marginal part-time workers. Those with a single employer who work year-round have a degree of job stability and are categorized as permanent.

Contingent Workers

Figure 3.2 shows that about 16 percent of the workforce could be labeled as contingent workers in 1990. About three out of ten of these workers had more than one employer and packaged a variety of jobs but worked less than full-time/full-year. The second largest subcategory of contingent workers were employed by a single employer, but only part-time/part-year. More than one-quarter of contingent workers fell into this category in 1990. We assumed that the majority were seasonal or as-needed workers. Smaller categories included job changers who worked part-time/part-year (21 percent of all contingent workers in 1990) and various groups of workers who packaged more than one self-employment job or wage or salary and self-employment jobs but still worked less than full-time/full-year.

Questionable Workers

After categorizing workers as permanent or contingent, 13 percent remained. More than half of these were single job holders who work full-time but only part-year. These wage or salary workers may have just started a permanent job or may have been hired only on a seasonal or temporary basis.

Changes in Work Relations

Table 3.1 indicates whether contingent work appears to be a growing work relation. Between 1987 and 1990 the structure of work relations remained relatively stable despite the growth of about five million workers, a 4 percent increase.[2] In both years, the majority of workers—seven out of ten—held permanent jobs, 1.6 out of ten held contingent jobs, and slightly more than one out of ten held jobs that were questionable—it is unclear whether they are permanent or contingent. No category of work relations increased or decreased by more than one percentage point; the share of permanent workers fell by one percentage point, that of questionable workers increased by one percentage point, while the share of contingent workers in the labor force remained stable between 1987 and 1990.

Despite this seeming stability in structure, however, there were some notable rates of increase and decrease during this four-year period in several subcategories.

Permanent Workers

Overall, the total number of permanent workers increased by less than 4 percent between 1987 and 1990, slightly less than the growth in the

---

2. Defined as those with at least two hundred hours of employment in a calendar year.

workforce as a whole. Among permanent workers, the category of full-time/full-year wage or salary workers with a single employer—the kind of job that is most likely to allow a breadwinner to provide a stable source of income for a family—grew by 7 percent, from 53 to 57 million workers. Although this category continued to grow, belying fears that all jobs are becoming contingent, it is important to note that fewer than half of *all* workers held full-time/full-year wage or salary jobs with a single employer.

The second largest category of permanent wage or salary workers consists of those who package multiple jobs (either holding these jobs simultaneously or sequentially). Of this group, simultaneous job holders (moonlighters) increased by 6 percent. This increase suggests that workers with breadwinner type jobs were seeking additional sources of income and jobs in order to increase earnings or reduce feelings of economic insecurity.

The number of permanent part-time workers (including the self-employed) increased by 5 percent between 1987 and 1990. As of 1990, this category of part-time workers represented only about one-third of all workers with part-time schedules (fewer than thirty-five hours per week).

In 1987 more than two-thirds of self-employed workers were labeled as permanent workers but only 61 percent were so labeled in 1990—a decline of about 11 percent in the number of permanent self-employed workers. This finding suggests an increase in "as-needed" self-employment.

Contingent Workers

Between 1987 and 1990, almost one million contingent workers were added to the workforce for an increase of about 5 percent. This was a slightly larger increase than for the workforce as a whole. As defined here, the contingent work category is composed of a jumble of work relations (including wage, salary, or self-employment), none of which amount to full-time/full-year work. As can be calculated from Table 3.1, job holders who work part-time/part-year for a single employer, probably on an on-call or as-needed basis, constituted the largest group of contingent workers in both years (28 percent in 1987 and 26 percent in 1990). Despite the growth in the contingent workforce, this subcategory of workers declined by two percent.

Greater than average growth occurred in the percentage of workers who packaged multiple jobs but did not work full-time/full-year. This subcategory grew by 7 percent between 1987 and 1990. These differential growth rates suggest the development of more tenuous arrangements

Table 3.1 Number and percent distribution of permanent and contingent workers, by gender, 1987-1990 (number in thousands)

	Total				Women				Men			
	1987		1990		1987		1990		1987		1990	
	Number	%	Number	%	Number	%	Number	%	Number	%	Number	%
All workers[a]	116,233	100	121,186	100	53,234	100	55,690	100	62,999	100	65,525	100
Permanent workers	83,468	72	86,437	71	35,326	66	37,361	67	48,142	76	49,106	75
Full-time/full-year/single job holder	57,942	50	61,441	51	22,128	42	24,184	43	35,814	57	37,257	57
Wage or salary	53,192	46	56,948	47	21,213	40	23,243	42	31,979	51	33,705	51
Self-employed	4,750	4	4,493	4	915	2	941	2	3,835	6	3,552	5
Other full-time/full-year	13,857	12	12,786	11	4,896	9	4,741	9	8,961	14	8,076	12
Wage or salary	11,977	10	11,423	9	4,544	9	4,435	8	7,433	12	6,989	11
Self-employed	1,880	2	1,363	1	352	1	306	1	1,528	2	1,087	2
Permanent part-time[b]	11,669	10	12,210	10	8,302	16	8,436	15	3,367	5	3,773	6
Wage or salary	9,872	8	10,524	9	7,373	14	7,676	14	2,499	4	2,847	4
Self-employed	1,797	2	1,686	1	929	2	760	1	868	1	926	1
Contingent workers	18,268	16	19,110	16	11,125	21	11,434	21	7,143	11	7,675	12
Wage or salary	15,737	14	16,344	13	9,801	18	10,073	18	5,936	9	6,269	10
Self-employed	2,531	2	2,766	2	1,324	2	1,361	2	1,207	2	1,406	2

Questionable workers	14,497	12	15,639	13	6,783	13	6,895	12	7,714	12	8,744	13
Wage or salary	13,153	11	13,552	11	6,336	12	6,319	11	6,817	11	7,233	11
Self-employed (single business/FT/PY)	1,344	1	2,087	2	447	1	576	1	897	1	1,511	2
Proportion of women to men in each work category											
All workers	100		100		46		46		54		54	
Permanent workers	100		100		42		43		58		57	
Full-time/full-year/single job holder	100		100		38		39		62		61	
Other full-time/full-year	100		100		35		37		65		63	
Permanent part-time[a]	100		100		71		69		29		31	
Contingent workers	100		100		61		60		39		40	
Questionable workers	100		100		47		44		53		56	

Source: IWPR calculations based on the U.S. Census Bureau Survey of Income and Program Participation, 1987 and 1990 Panels.

[a] All workers in this study are those who worked 200 hours or more in a twelve-month period and were neither older than age 65 nor teenagers living with parents.

[b] Permanent part-time consists of single job holders who work part-time/full-year, either as a wage or salaried worker who worked for only one employer throughout the year, or as a self-employed worker who had only one business throughout the year.

between employers and employees and more patching together of jobs on the part of contingent workers. Another growing subcategory of contingent workers were those who combine wage or salary work with self-employment as a secondary source of earnings but work less than full-time/full-year. These findings further suggest that self-employment may be a growing source of income for workers attempting to supplement a less than full-time wage or salary job.

Questionable Workers

This remaining category of workers, whose status we deem questionable, increased by 8 percent between 1987 and 1990 (from 14.5 to 15.6 million workers), about twice the rate of increase of the workforce as a whole, and substantially more than the increase among permanent or contingent workers. This large growth in the questionable category may suggest a growing instability in work relations and work patterns, but further research over a longer time period would be needed to confirm this trend.

Gender Patterns:
Structure and Change

The structure of work relations remained relatively stable between 1987 and 1990. Likewise, the differential structure of work relations among women and men remained relatively stable. Men remained substantially more likely than women to be permanent workers; in both 1987 and 1990 about three-quarters of male workers could be described as permanent compared to about two-thirds of women workers (see Table 3.1). Figure 3.3 shows that in 1990 women still held only four out of ten permanent full-time/full-year jobs with a single employer or own business, but held six out of ten contingent jobs.

Some evidence of shifts in these gendered patterns did occur during this period. As Table 3.1 shows, the number of women working in permanent jobs grew by 6 percent while the number of men grew by only 2 percent. In contrast, the number of women working in contingent jobs grew more slowly than the number of men in such jobs (less than 3 percent for women versus more than 7 percent for men). Thus women's share of permanent jobs grew slightly, while their share of contingent jobs fell slightly. In contrast, men became somewhat less likely to hold breadwinner jobs and somewhat more likely to work at secondary jobs between 1987 and 1990.

Figure 3.3 Percent of women and men in each permanent and contingent work relation, 1990

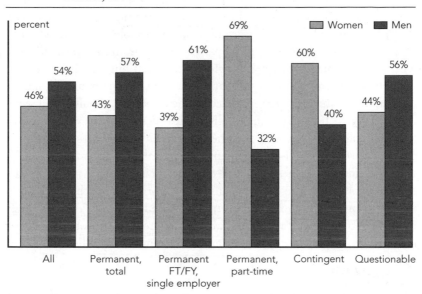

Source: IWPR calculations based on the U.S. Census Bureau, Survey of Income and Program Participation, 1990 Panel.

Permanent Workers

For both women and men the largest subcategory of permanent workers consisted of wage or salary workers employed full-time/full-year by a single employer. By 1990, twenty-three million women and thirty-four million men had this type of employment (a 10 percent increase from 1987 for women versus a 5 percent increase for men).

Despite women's increased participation as permanent full-time/full-year workers, they were still substantially more likely than men (16 percent versus 6 percent) to hold permanent part-time jobs. This was the second largest category of permanent jobs for women. Despite a small decline (of two percentage points in their share), women were 69 percent of permanent part-time workers in 1990 (see Figure 3.3).

In contrast, men were more likely to package jobs to attain full-time/full-year employment. Moonlighting or simultaneous job holding has been more common among men than women in the past (see Stinson, 1990). Yet the percentage of women who were moonlighting increased slightly while the percentage of moonlighting among men decreased slightly between 1987 and 1990 (data not shown). This finding suggests that women's need for full-time earnings has increased and that packaging jobs is an important strategy for obtaining these earnings.[3] Job change, another type of packaging to attain full-time/full-year work, has remained relatively stable among men but has decreased by 28 percent among women—perhaps reflecting a greater unwillingness to change jobs during a period of economic insecurity. Finally, men were more likely to be permanently self-employed than were women. The data in Table 3.1 show that men held about three-quarters (or 74 percent) of permanent self-employment jobs in both years.

These findings suggest that full-time permanent employment is still disproportionately the province of male workers, but that women's efforts to attain the level of earnings provided by these jobs (through multiple job holding, if necessary) are on the increase as women become increasingly responsible for their families' economic well-being.

Contingent Workers

Although women increased their share of permanent workers, they still represented six out of every ten contingent workers in 1990 (see Figure 3.3). Women still were substantially more likely than men to experience tenuous rather than permanent relations with employers. Among contingent workers, women's packaging of multiple jobs increased between 1987 and 1990.

Still, the largest category of women contingent workers were those employed part-time/part-year for a single employer. In 1987 this category made up one-third of all women engaged in contingent work. By 1990 this employment relation had dropped slightly (to 31 percent). For men, only one-fifth (21 percent) worked part-time/part-year for a single employer in 1987, with a slight decline to 20 percent in 1990. Men who were employed less than full-time/full-year were more likely than women to package jobs with two or more employers. Between 1987 and 1990, however, the number of women holding two or more jobs (but working less than full-time/full-year) increased. In contrast, the number of men working at a single contingent job increased slightly. The number of contingent workers for whom self-employment was the major type of work in their employment package increased for both genders.

3. The data also show, however, that women who combine multiple jobs to equal full-time work are, more often than men, combining two or more part-time jobs rather than one full-time and one part-time job.

These findings suggest that women appeared to be moving toward more attachment to the labor market even when they were employed in tenuous work arrangements. And they suggest that although the gendered patterns of contingent work still reflect the notion of women as secondary workers, contingent employment is no longer just a women's issue.

Questionable Workers

Men held more than half of the jobs whose employment relations we deemed questionable in both years (53 percent in 1987 and 56 percent in 1990—see Table 3.1 and Figure 3.3), and the rate of increase in these questionable work relations was greater than women's (13 percent compared to only 2 percent for women). The faster growth rate for men in this category may reflect the slow ungendering of contingent work, but this conclusion is tentative and deserves additional research.

Economic Well-Being: By Work Relations and Gender

Given the ideology that contingent workers are supported by primary breadwinners, it is not surprising that the hourly wages of contingent workers are substantially lower than those of permanent workers. Because women held a disproportionate share of these jobs, they bore a disproportionate share of the negative financial consequences of this work relation (although men in this category also experienced low pay).

Table 3.2 shows the median hourly wages in 1990 for all workers and for female and male workers. It also shows the female-to-male wage ratio in hourly earnings, for several categories and subcategories of work relations. The median hourly wage for all workers in our sample (regardless of work relation or gender) was $8.74 per hour in 1990; the highest paid were two small subcategories of workers—a group of self-employed questionable workers ($12.40) and a group of wage or salary workers who combined this employment with self-employment, probably as consultants ($11.18). The next highest paid workers were full-time/full-year workers with a single employer—"strings-attached" workers—who earned an average of $10.85 per hour. Self-employed workers with a single full-time/full-year business earned $9.44 per hour. In contrast, permanent part-time workers earned $6.51 per hour if wage or salaried, and $7.10 per hour if self-employed. Contingent workers earned $5.15 per hour and questionable workers earned $6.88 per hour. Clearly, contingent work was the least financially rewarding work relation.

On average, women earned about 70 cents for every dollar earned by men in terms of median hourly wages. This differential reflects women's

Table 3.2 Median hourly wages of permanent and contingent workers, by gender, 1990 (number in thousands)

	All		Women		Men		
	Number	Median wage ($)	Number	Median wage ($)	Number	Median wage ($)	Hourly wage ratio[a]
All workers[b]	121,186	8.74	55,690	7.30	65,525	10.45	0.70
Permanent workers	86,473	9.97	37,361	8.42	49,106	11.54	0.73
Full-time/full-year/single job holder	61,441	10.75	24,184	9.02	37,257	12.21	0.74
Wage or salary	56,948	10.85	23,243	9.16	33,705	12.35	0.74
Self-employed	4,493	9.44	941	5.68	3,552	10.90	0.52
Other full-time/full-year	12,786	9.24	4,741	7.93	8,076	10.19	0.78
Wage or salary	11,423	9.32	4,435	8.00	6,989	10.14	0.79
Mixed wage or salary/SE (SE secondary)	2,384	11.18	582	9.40	1,802	11.95	0.79
Self-employed	1,363	8.59	306	6.88	1,087	10.50	0.66
Permanent part-time[c]	12,210	6.59	8,436	6.32	3,773	7.25	0.87
Wage or salary	10,524	6.51	7,676	6.39	2,847	6.77	0.94
Self-employed	1,686	7.10	760	5.66	926	8.74	0.65
Contingent workers	19,110	5.15	11,434	4.89	7,675	5.61	0.87
Wage or salary	16,344	5.05	10,073	4.89	6,269	5.39	0.91
Self-employed	2,766	6.90	1,361	4.98	1,406	8.44	0.59
Questionable workers	15,639	6.88	6,895	6.01	8,744	7.89	0.76
Wage or salary	13,552	6.59	6,319	6.01	7,233	7.30	0.82
Self-employed (single business/FT/PY)	2,087	12.40	576	6.13	1,511	16.64	0.37

Source: IWPR calculations based on the U.S. Census Bureau Survey of Income and Program Participation, 1990 Panel.

[a] Ratio of women's to men's median hourly wages.

[b] All workers in this study are those who worked 200 hours or more in a twelve-month period and were neither older than age 65 nor teenagers living with parents.

[c] Permanent part-time consists of single job holders who work part-time/full-year, either as a wage or salaried worker who worked for only one employer throughout the year, or as a self-employed worker who had only one business throughout the year.

greater likelihood of employment in less financially rewarding permanent jobs (for example, permanent part-time jobs) and the greater likelihood of employment in contingent work. Even when employed in similar work situations, however, women earn less than men in every category and subcategory shown in Table 3.2. Among major employment categories, equality in wages is greatest at the bottom of the wage scale, among permanent part-time workers and among contingent and questionable workers. The least equality is found among self-employed workers, whether they are permanent or contingent.

Permanent Workers

Men benefited financially from holding a larger share of permanent jobs, especially the traditional male breadwinner category of full-time/full-year jobs with a single employer—jobs that are most likely to result in raises, promotions, and benefits. Table 3.2 shows that men who held these jobs earned $12.35 per hour (the highest paid male workers except for a tiny category of "questionable" self-employed single job holders who reported earnings of $16.64 per hour). When women were employed at theseries, equality in wages is greatest at the bottom of the wage scalmanent workers earned an average of $8.42, and those with the most "attached" work situations—full-time/full-year workers with a single employer—earned $9.16 per hour. Those women who combined wage or salary work with secondary self-employment (probably as consultants) earned the highest median hourly wages, $9.40 per hour.

Among all permanent workers, women earned about 73 cents per hour for each dollar earned by men; they earned 74 cents per hour for every dollar men earned among full-time/full-year workers with a single employer. The wage gap was greatest among the self-employed, especially among the questionable groups who may or may not be contingent workers, the contingent self-employed, and the self-employed who work full-time/full-year at one business. In fact, the wage ratio between women and men in this last group was 0.52, the lowest wage ratio (and largest gap) of any group of permanent workers.

Equality at the Bottom: Contingent and Part-Time Work

Table 3.2 shows that women's hourly wages were lowest in contingent, questionable, and permanent part-time work relations. Because women were overrepresented in these jobs, they bore a disproportionate share of the costs of working in these less desirable arrangements. Women employed as contingent workers earned an average of $4.89 per hour in

1990. Those employed as permanent part-time workers earned $6.39. Men were less likely to experience this type of work and therefore were less likely to hold jobs that paid low wages or could not support a family. When they were employed as permanent part-time or contingent workers, they still earned more than women ($6.77 per hour for permanent part-time work, and $5.61 per hour for contingent work). Yet the wage gap between men and women is smaller at this low end of the wage scale, a situation we refer to as "equality at the bottom." Women employed as permanent part-time wage or salary workers earned 94 cents per hour for every dollar earned by men (the highest ratio and smallest gap in the wage structure). Women employed as wage or salary contingent workers earned 91 cents for each dollar earned by men. The exception to the equality at the bottom generalization was among the self-employed. Here women contingent workers earned only 59 cents per hour for every dollar earned by men, and permanent part-time women business owners earned only 65 cents per hour for every dollar earned by men. This is because men's earnings in the self-employment categories were higher than men's earnings as wage or salary workers.

Average Months of Health Insurance

Studies have shown that part-time workers are substantially less likely than full-time workers to have employer-provided health care benefits through their own employment (Employee Benefit Research Institute, 1990; Yoon et al., 1994). Only 13 percent of women and 20 percent of men employed for fewer than twenty-five hours per week (and about one-quarter of both men and women employed from 25 to 34 hours per week) received direct employer-based coverage. This low rate of coverage contrasts with 62 percent of women and 66 percent of men who were employed for more than thirty-five hours per week and received employer-provided benefits (Yoon et al., 1994). Other researchers have suggested that the growth of self-employment, multiple employment, and other contingent work arrangements is an important cause of the decline in health care benefits (see for example, duRivage, 1992a).

Table 3.3 shows the average months per year of employer-provided health insurance for each of the categories of workers and the differences by gender.[4] Not surprisingly, those workers with more permanent

4. Included in each category are those workers with zero months of direct employer-provided health insurance. Those categories of workers who are more likely to have health insurance through their employers include a smaller proportion of workers with zero months.

employment arrangements were more likely to be covered directly by their employers, and women were less likely to be covered directly than men. Wage or salary employees who worked full-time/full-year jobs for a single employer were most likely to have this coverage; men in this category had insurance for an average of ten out of twelve months and women for an average of nine out of twelve months. Among permanent workers, part-time/full-year wage or salary workers were substantially less likely than full-time/full-year workers to have direct coverage from their employers (women had insurance for only four out of twelve months, and men for only five). Self-employed workers, whether full-time or part-time, were the least likely to have insurance among permanent workers.

As a group, contingent workers are the least likely to have health insurance, and women contingent workers had this type of coverage for fewer than two out of twelve months. Men who were contingent workers had direct employer coverage for fewer than three out of twelve months. Some of these contingent workers may have been covered by the health policies of spouses or other family members, but many probably did not have such access because they were not married to a worker with a full-time job.

Reproduction of the Gender-Based Division of Labor

As we have suggested, women's higher rate of participation in part-time and contingent work is often taken as evidence of conflicts between the demands of work and family, in which women bear the primary responsibility for housework and child care. An alternative explanation, that employers make decisions not to invest in women workers and to structure jobs for an idealized gender-based division of labor, is seldom suggested. Women's participation in this lower-paid work is also assumed to reflect their access to additional income sources, primarily the earnings of male breadwinners.

In this next section we see that women employed as contingent workers are the workers who are most likely to have young children. This finding can be used to suggest that these women have made a trade-off in which they specialize in housework and child care in exchange for the support of a male breadwinner. But, contrary to expectation, women with contingent jobs were less likely than other groups of women to live with spouses who themselves had full-time/full-year jobs. As a result, this group of women workers was more likely to meet their family's income needs through the receipt of means-tested welfare benefits. Women in

Table 3.3 Average months of direct employer provided health insurance for permanent and contingent workers, by gender, 1990 (number in thousands)

	All		Women		Men		Health/gender ratio[a]
	Number	Average no. of months	Number	Average no. of months	Number	Average no. of months	
All workers[b]	121,186	6.8	55,690	5.9	65,525	7.6	78%
Permanent workers	86,473	8.3	37,361	7.6	49,106	8.9	85%
Full-time/full-year/single job holder	61,441	9.3	24,184	8.9	37,257	9.6	93%
Wage or salary	56,948	9.8	23,243	9.2	33,705	10.2	90%
Self-employed	4,493	3.1	941	1.9	3,552	3.4	56%
Other full-time/full-year	12,786	8.2	4,741	8.0	8,076	7.9	101%
Wage or salary	11,423	8.6	4,435	8.4	6,989	8.6	98%
Self-employed	1,363	4.5	306	2.3	1,087	3.4	68%
Permanent part-time[c]	12,210	3.9	8,436	3.7	3,773	4.5	82%
Wage or salary	10,524	4.3	7,676	3.9	2,847	5.4	72%
Self-employed	1,686	1.5	760	1.2	926	1.7	71%
Contingent workers	19,110	2.2	11,434	1.9	7,675	2.7	70%
Wage or salary	16,344	2.2	10,073	2.0	6,269	2.7	74%
Self-employed	2,766	1.9	1,361	1.1	1,406	2.7	41%
Questionable workers	15,639	3.9	6,895	3.4	8,744	4.2	81%
Wage or salary	13,552	4.0	6,319	3.6	7,233	4.4	82%
Self-employed (single business/FT/PY)	2,087	2.8	576	1.2	1,511	3.4	35%

Source: IWPR calculations based on the U.S. Census Bureau Survey of Income and Program Participation, 1990 Panel.

[a]The Health/gender ratio is the average number of covered months for women over the average number of covered months for men.

[b]All workers in this study are those who worked 200 hours or more in a twelve-month period and were neither older than age 65 nor teenagers living with parents.

[c]Permanent part-time consists of single job-holders who work part-time/full-year, either as a wage or salaried worker who worked for only one employer throughout the year, or as a self-employed worker who had only one business throughout the year.

the subgroup of permanent workers who were employed part-time for a single employer appeared to have successfully made this trade-off; they were among the most likely to have children under six and the most likely, by far, to be married to men who work full-time/full-year. (Men in the lower-earning work arrangements were much less likely to have children than men in the full-time/full-year permanent arrangements).

Percent with Children under Age Six

We use the variable "percent of workers with children under age six" as a proxy for the time that needs to be spent by working people to meet the demands of young children. Figure 3.4 shows that women with contingent work patterns were the most likely to have young children. One-quarter of women contingent workers had children under age six compared to 17 percent of all female permanent workers and only 16 percent of those female permanent workers who were employed full-time/full-year by a single employer.

Women employed as permanent part-time workers and those whose status is questionable came closest to contingent workers in terms of

Figure 3.4 Percent of permanent and contingent workers, by gender, with children under age six, 1990

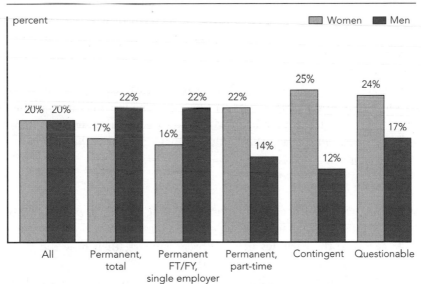

Source: IWPR calculations based on the U.S. Census Bureau, Survey of Income and Program Participation, 1990 Panel.

having responsibility for young children (with 22 percent and 24 percent having children under six). In contrast, men who were employed full-time/full-year for a single employer were the most likely to have children under age six (22 percent), while male contingent workers were the least likely (12 percent) to have young children. These data appear to suggest that contingent (and permanent part-time) work for women does represent a trade-off in which lower wages were accepted in order to have the time to care for young children. Male part-time and contingent workers did not appear to have made this trade-off. In order for this trade-off to work, employees in low-paid part-time and contingent work arrangements needed additional income sources to support their children.

Percent with Full-Time/Full-Year Working Spouses

Were women with young children found in low-wage contingent and permanent part-time jobs more likely than full-time permanent employees to have access to the earnings of a male breadwinner? The answer appears to be no for contingent workers and yes for permanent part-time workers.

A breadwinner was defined as a worker with a full-time/full-year permanent job. Figure 3.5 shows that only 35 percent of women workers with contingent jobs had access to the income of a male breadwinner with a permanent job. In contrast, 43 percent of women with full-time/full-year jobs with a single employer (who earned more than most categories of women workers) had access to income from male breadwinners. Those women with permanent part-time jobs did appear to have made a trade-off in which their lower earnings were supplemented by those of a primary breadwinner; they were the most likely to obtain income support from male breadwinners (53 percent). But for contingent workers, almost two-thirds did *not* have access to this source of income support.

Reliance on the State

If women with contingent employment are the group of workers who were the most likely to have young children but were also least likely to have access to the earnings of male breadwinners, then how did they support themselves and their children?

Figure 3.6 shows that about one out of seven women employed as contingent workers relied on income from means-tested welfare benefits (including Aid to Families with Dependent Children, Food Stamps, and

Figure 3.5 Percent of permanent and contingent workers, by gender, with a spouse employed full-time/full-year, 1990

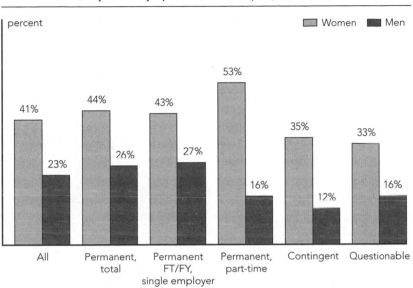

Source: IWPR calculations based on the U.S. Census Bureau, Survey of Income and Program Participation, 1990 Panel.

WIC) as a supplement to their earnings, and presumably as a source of income between jobs. Fourteen percent of women with contingent work patterns, and 15 percent of women in the questionable category, relied on means-tested benefits as an income supplement, compared to 3 percent of all women with permanent work and 6 percent of permanent part-time women workers. Contingent workers who held more than one job were particularly likely to rely on these benefits as part of an income package (data not shown). These women may have been less likely to have had access to additional earnings from a breadwinner and were more likely to have been solely responsible for the support of children year-round than were women employed at a single contingent job during the year. Male workers were less likely to receive means-tested benefits than their female counterparts. Even in contingent work categories, men generally earned more than women. Men in these categories were also far less likely to have children or to be single parents with full-time financial and care-giving responsibilities for children. For these reasons they were less likely to qualify for means-tested welfare benefits. Because women earned less than men and because they are more likely to be

Figure 3.6 Percent of permanent and contingent workers, by gender, with means-tested benefits, 1990

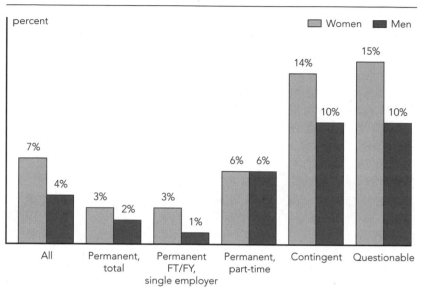

Source: IWPR calculations based on the U.S. Census Bureau, Survey of Income and Program Participation, 1990 Panel.

responsible for the care of children, if single, they were more likely to be dependent on means-tested benefits as a wage supplement.

These findings indicate that state welfare programs (funded by taxpayers) serve as a source of support for the low wages and tenuous work relations of contingent workers, especially for those with children.

Summary and Policy Recommendations

In 1990 about half of all workers held a single full-time/full-year job— what has traditionally been viewed as a breadwinner job, but more than one out of six workers were classified as contingent. Another 13 percent could possibly fall into this latter category. Between 1987 and 1990, the number of contingent and questionable workers grew slightly more than did the labor force as a whole, while the number of permanent workers grew somewhat less. Overall, the structure remained relatively stable

Although women's share of permanent jobs is increasing while that of men is decreasing, women remained substantially more likely to hold contingent jobs. Women held 60 percent of all contingent jobs while men held 61 percent of all permanent jobs. Within the category of permanent jobs, women were substantially more likely to have held permanent part-time jobs than were men. Although men and women's work patterns are gradually becoming more alike, the gendered division of labor, in which women hold the secondary or non-breadwinner jobs, has not disappeared.

Since women are more likely to hold contingent and permanent part-time jobs, women also bear a disproportionate share of the costs of these secondary work relations. This cost can be seen in the gap between women's and men's overall wages (a ratio of 70 cents to the dollar for all workers, or a wage gap of 30 cents). The wage gap was the smallest among the lowest-paid permanent part-time and contingent workers (for both, a ratio of 87 cents to the dollar or a gap of 13 cents)—the situation referred to as equality at the bottom.

Women with contingent work patterns were the most likely group of women workers to have children under age six. In order to support their children financially, the low wages that they received required supplementation. In contrast to permanent workers, however, they were less likely to have had access to the earnings of a male breadwinner. For many contingent workers, the model of trade-offs between men's specialization in market work and women's specialization in family care did not appear to apply. In practice, they supplemented their earnings with income from means-tested government transfer programs.

These findings indicate that state welfare programs (funded by taxpayers) serve as a direct source of support for many contingent workers and an indirect source of support to their employers. Employers who offer jobs that fail to provide a "living wage" and who assume that contingent workers are supported by other breadwinners are imposing costs on society and taxpayers in the form of welfare benefits and income tax credits (the Earned Income Tax Credit).

Policy Recommendations

Public policy makers may opt to do nothing to increase the economic well-being of contingent workers but rather to call for the return of the traditional male breadwinner family. Given that contingent work relations are growing at a time when threats to welfare benefits are increasing, the likely outcome of these two tendencies is that more women, especially single mothers, will be at risk of falling into poverty.

Instead, solutions are necessary that assume that all adult workers have financial responsibilities. Solutions must be directed at low and unreliable earnings and the lack of benefits offered by employers. The purpose of the policies proposed here is to improve work relations rather than to allow them to continue to deteriorate. These proposed solutions permit employers to continue to benefit from the flexibility of contingent relations when necessary, without reinforcing an outdated gender-based division of labor where the greatest equality between men and women is at the bottom of the wage scale. These suggested solutions include creating pay equity between the sexes at all levels of the wage scale, creating parity between permanent and contingent workers, and regulating employers' ability to create contingent relations. These policies specifically include:

- Developing and implementing pay equity and fair wage policies;
- Developing and implementing labor standards that create wage and benefit parity between permanent and contingent workers;
- Easing eligibility requirements for programs that provide job and income security for workers who have lost jobs or must leave them due to illness or family emergencies (for example, unemployment insurance, temporary disability insurance, and family leave);
- Strengthening enforcement of regulations preventing employers from misclassifying workers (as independent contractors, for example) to avoid paying social security taxes and providing other benefits and to avoid complying with federal and state equal opportunity laws and other workplace standards;
- Decreasing the barriers that unions face in representing these workers and that these workers face in gaining union representation;
- Monitoring firms' use of contingent workers and their pay, benefits, and working conditions;
- Regulating the number of contingent workers that firms can hire.

Policies such as these can improve the pay and benefits of contingent workers, enhance their relative bargaining power, and make flexible work less costly to the workers who do it. By creating a floor beneath which employees will not fall and by increasing their ability to bargain, most of these solutions will also increase equality between women and men at all levels of the wage scale, not just at the bottom. These policies could also benefit employers if flexibility itself (rather than simply lower per-unit labor costs) is important to them. If employers wish to continue to create contingent work relations for the advantages they can provide in terms of scheduling production as needed, then it should be possible to raise the costs of contingent work to a par with permanent workers (by requiring wage and benefit parity, for example) without eliminating the benefits of flexibility.

Unfortunately for the workers involved, employers' desire for cost savings seem to be as much a part of the growth of contingent work relations as their need for greater flexibility. Also unfortunately, all of these policy prescriptions are likely to be rejected by organizations of businesses and employers as unwarranted or unpaid federal mandates, or as interventions that will raise the cost of doing business and interfere with free markets. None of these solutions is likely to gain much support during a period when the politics of the untrammeled market and the ideology of the two-parent family are in the ascendancy. It is clear that these new work arrangements place costs on society and taxpayers. There is some evidence that layoffs of full-time workers and their replacement by contingent workers may not even increase the corporate bottom line (Brown, Reich, & Stern, 1992; Cascio, 1993; Reichheld, 1996). And there is one possibly positive note, if contingent work is increasingly experienced by male workers and can no longer be masked as a choice made by married mothers, then the necessary labor-market reforms may be easier to legislate into practice.

The currently popular views, which are so damaging to the rights of workers and women and which will, if enacted in future legislation and programs, reduce living standards and working conditions further, need to be challenged. Researchers who understand their probable effects, can point to policy solutions that can make a difference. They can also work to persuade opinion leaders and the public that policy solutions based on gendered models of primary and secondary workers do not make sense in the long run.

Further Research Needs

While the general attributes of contingent work have been known for some time—lower pay, fewer benefits, and reduced opportunity for advancement and income security—many specifics remain unknown. The welcome arrival of the special supplement on contingent work of the Current Population Survey provides much-needed data. This new survey should be repeated periodically. The information it contains about the distribution of contingent work across industries and occupations as well as by gender could also enable researchers to create a better sample frame with which to develop a case-study strategy.

Extensive as it is, even the new Current Population Survey data set will provide only a partial view of contingent work. It surveys households and workers, not employers, and workers do not always know the contractual arrangements under which they work or the likely duration of their jobs. Employers know such facts more precisely and should also be surveyed to determine their use of various types of contingent work. Direct-hire temporaries (those hired directly by the firms in which they work rather than through temporary help services firms) have been especially difficult to identify, as have independent contractors who are self-employed but really have only one client—their de facto employer.

Comparisons of data from the special supplement with data from longitudinal surveys will allow researchers to compare workers' views of the temporariness of their work with the actual longevity of workers' jobs. Case studies, in-depth qualitative studies of appropriate occupations and industries, could also contribute to our knowledge of employers' decision making and may uncover the best uses of contingent work (as well as the worst). We also need further information about how workers and their families cope with the unpredictability of the work schedules and earnings that characterize contingent work. If the growth of contingent work is a demand-side phenomenon that assumes the presence of an additional full-time breadwinner, then what survival strategies are employed by those without additional breadwinners? Further research that demonstrates how much of an income cushion current government welfare programs provide is critical, especially given recently enacted cutbacks in welfare and food stamps. These family studies need to be continued over time so that they can reflect changing coping strategies, especially if contingent work continues to grow and government means-tested benefits continue to decline.

Appendix
Definitions of Work Relations Used in this Study

All workers in this study are between the ages of eighteen and sixty-five and worked at least two hundred hours during the calendar year.

Permanent Workers

Single Job Holders FT/FY: Workers who work for one employer only or are self-employed with only one business throughout the year.

Other Permanent: Workers who hold multiple jobs but package together full-time/full-year schedules, at wage or salary jobs or at self-employment, or both.

> *Wage or Salary Simultaneous Job Holders*: Workers who hold two regular jobs in any month but work full-time/full-year schedules. They also have no self-employment (often referred to as "moonlighters").

> *Wage or Salary Sequential Job Holders*: Workers who are employed by one employer for at least two separate periods in the year. During the break in employment, they hold at least one other job and have no self-employment. They work full-time/full-year schedules.

> *Wage or Salary Job Changers*: Workers who change from one job to another during the year and have no self-employment, but work full-time/full-year.

> *Mixed Salary and Self-Employment (Self-Employment Secondary)*: Workers whose primary job is wage or salary, but supplement this work with self-employment.

> *Mixed Salary and Self-Employment (Self-Employment Primary)*: Workers whose primary job is self-employment, but supplement their earnings with wage or salary jobs.

> *Two or More Self-Employed Jobs*: Workers who work full-time/full-year by packaging together two or more self-employed jobs.

> *Permanent Part-Time*: Single job holders who work part-time/full-year, either as a wage or salary worker for only one employer throughout the year or as a self-employed worker who had only one business throughout the year.

Contingent Workers

Wage or Salary Single Job Holders PT/PY: Workers who work only part-time/part-year for one employer only or are self-employed part-year with only one business.

Wage or Salary Simultaneous Job Holders FT/PY, PT/FY, PT/PY: Workers who hold two jobs in any month but do not work full-time/full-year schedules. They also have no self-employment.

Wage or Salary Sequential Job Holders FT/PY, PT/FY, PT/PY: Workers who are employed by one employer for at least two separate periods in the year. During the break in employment, they hold at least one other job and have no self-employment, but do not work full-time/full-year schedules.

Wage or Salary Job Changers PT/PY: Workers who change from one job to another during the year and have no self-employment and work part-time/part-year.

Mixed Salary and Self-Employment (Self-Employment Secondary) PT/PY, PT/FY, PT/PY: Workers whose primary job is wage or salary but supplement this work with self-employment.

Self-Employed Single Job Holders PT/PY: Includes those who are self-employed, part-time/part-year, with only one business throughout the year.

Mixed Salary and Self-Employment (Self-Employment Primary) FT/PY, PT/FY, PT/PY: Workers whose primary job is self-employment but supplement their earnings with wage or salary jobs.

Two or More Self-Employed Jobs: Workers who package together two or more self-employed jobs but do not work full-time/full-year.

Questionable Workers

Single Job Holders FT/PY: Workers who work for a single employer full-time, or are self-employed with only one business, for part of the year.

Wage or Salary Job Changers, FT/PY, PT/FY: Workers who change from one job to another during the year, have no self-employment, and do not work full-time/full-year.

Part II

The Workplace: Tension and Trends

CHAPTER FOUR

Countervailing Human Resource Trends in Family-Sensitive Firms

Kathleen Christensen

According to recent surveys, the largest U.S. firms have bifurcated their internal workforces into two groups: core employment and nonstandard work arrangements, including contingent work (Nollen & Axel, this volume; Christensen, 1989; Kalleberg, Hudson, & Reskin, 1997). This bifurcation has stemmed from, and further reinforces, dual and competing sets of staffing philosophies. Core employees are seen as, and typically treated as, valuable human capital into which the firm makes investments and from which it expects returns. Contingent workers, on the other hand, are seen as highly fungible commodities that can be expended as needed for business purposes. Core employees constitute what is typically referred to as the regular or "permanent" workforce, while contingent workers constitute a just-in-time workforce. What is not recognized, however, is that different departments often assume the responsibility for handling compensation, training, and grievances for these two sets of workers. Human resource (HR) departments are responsible for core employees, while in those large firms that have negotiated sole-source contracts with temporary firms, the purchasing departments are often responsible for agency temporaries. Two workforces, two staffing philosophies, and often two distinct/different responsible departments—how does this play out in the treatment of workers?

In an attempt to determine this, I conducted a set of case studies of some of the most progressive U.S. firms regarding work-family benefits and policies. The assumption was that these firms would have some of the most highly articulated beliefs and policies about employees as valuable human capital. The purpose of these case studies was to determine how these large firms used contingent staffing; how and if these contingent workers were eligible for the family-oriented benefits and policies available to core employees; what constraints, legal and otherwise, could hamper these firms—which clearly saw value in investing in workers—

from extending "family-friendly" policies to contingent workers; and who, if not the employers, will help to take care of the family needs of contingent workers.

Family-Friendly Benefits and Policies: What Are They?

The majority of women with children under the age of six are now gainfully employed. With this increased participation of mothers in the workforce, the traditional division of labor in the home, with the male as breadwinner and female as homemaker, has changed. As a result, American businesses which had long operated from the notion of the at-home spouse, began to recognize, beginning in the early 1980s that their core employees, men and women, needed supports to enable them to balance their work and family responsibilities. Over the course of the last fifteen years, these supports have taken a number of forms: information and referral services for dependent care, including care for children and elders; on-site child care; alternative work schedules, such as flextime, job sharing, compressed workweeks; alternative work sites, such as home and satellite offices; and leaves for the birth or adoption of children or for family-related medical purposes. Not all companies offer all benefits. But increasingly many firms offer some supports, and a core group of progressive firms offer a generous array of options. These are the firms which are most likely to show up on the annual survey by *Working Mother* magazine of the 100 Best Firms for Working Mothers.

How do contingent workers fare when they work in firms that are recognized for their emphasis on a human capital view of employees? Does the human capital philosophy spill over to the contingent workers or not? In effect, are they eligible for any of the family-friendly services, benefits, or policies offered by the firms to their core employees? Do we have evidence that they need them?

Work-Family Challenges Faced by Contingent Workers

Although large numbers of American families experience financial stresses and job worries, those with relatively secure wages or salaried jobs have a degree of stability and predictability to their financial futures that many families with contingent workers lack. Contingent work often appears in nonsystematic ways, with a highly intense work period followed by a fallow. The work rarely comes with any kind of health or pension benefits or paid time-off options such as vacations, sick leave, or family leave. In addition, and perhaps most significant, are the financial penalties associated with contingent work. According to a 1997 report by the Economic Policy Institute, contingent workers, regardless of occupation or industry, suffer an earnings penalty compared to their counterparts in full-time regular jobs (Kalleberg et al., 1997).

The extent to which these earnings penalties pose serious problems for a family is a direct function of two conditions: the degree to which the household depends on the income of the contingent worker, and the degree to which the skills of the contingent worker are in demand in the marketplace. Some contingents workers, such as married women living with employed spouses, have a financial buffer to offset these penalties. And contingent workers whose skills are in demand can potentially experience the greatest degree of choice in the marketplace, regardless of the degree to which their households depend on their incomes for support. These workers can set rates that can offset the loss of benefits and cushion the unpredictability of the job market. They may even have the freedom to pick and choose assignments to suit their lifestyles.

Contingent workers who provide the sole income for their families and whose skills are not in demand are in the most vulnerable of conditions. In a recent analysis of the family characteristics of contingent workers, single mothers were found to make up a disproportionate share of employees of temporary agencies and to be the most economically vulnerable of contingent workers (Spalter-Roth et al., 1997). They are the ones whom Jean McAllister profiles in her chapter in this volume. They experience severe financial stresses and view contingent work arrangements as the most unpredictable, unstable, and unforgiving of worlds. They are also the ones who have the fewest resources available for responding to their work-family needs.

In the course of my research over the last ten years (Christensen, 1988b, 1993), it has become clear to me that the unpredictable nature of contingent work can lead to a variety of work-family problems, including financial worries and a limited ability to plan or pay for the amount, kind, or timing of child care needed. The fact that contingent work generally provides no health insurance can put a family in financial jeopardy. And the lack of options for paid time off limits parents' abilities to take care of themselves and their sick children or relatives. Worries that preoccupy the contingent worker's thoughts may translate into very specific fears for children: Will anything happen to my house? Will mommy and daddy be able to take care of us?

Although financial worries can be very real for many contingent working families, more subtle and at times intangible psychological issues may be at play for others. Some, albeit not all, contingent workers often report feeling like second-class corporate citizens within an organization. As temporary workers or contractors, they typically have an ambiguous status within the organization, with no job title or sense of being part of that community. Perhaps what is most troubling to many of these workers is not having a defined career path (Barker, 1997; Christensen, 1988a, 1988b; McAllister, this volume). These issues are quite real for those contingent professionals and managers who have lost their status as core employees and involuntarily work as temps or contract workers.

Some corporations have intentionally or unintentionally translated this policy of a two-class culture into tangible symbols. One major corporation in the food industry requires all on-site workers to wear color-coded ID badges. The IDs of core employees are one color, while the IDs of the temporaries and contract workers are coded the color of visitor IDs. At a glance, any worker knows who is in the core and who is on the periphery. In the corporate cafeteria, different colors result in different food prices, with core employees receiving a discount and "visitors" (including contingent workers) not. Prior to the two-colored ID system, contingent workers were allowed into work-family brown-bag lunch workshops sponsored by human resources. A company executive I spoke with speculated that contingent workers may now be denied access to these gatherings once it becomes clear that they are not core employees.

The subtle and not so subtle financial and psychological consequences for contingent workers can generate serious consequences for their families. Yet the current corporate thinking about contingent workers has not yet directly addressed either the work-family issues experienced by contingent workers or the consequences for the firm for failing to do so. The reasons are multiple, but at root is one axiom: contingent workers fall outside the human capital framework that many large firms adopt toward their core salaried employees.

Before we can address how firms treat the work-family needs of the contingent workers, we need to determine exactly how these firms integrate contingent workers into their organizations.

Organizational Models of Contingent Work Arrangements

Within an organization, there are at least three different organizational models that govern how a firm uses contingent workers (Christensen, 1995). Each model is based on a different strategic use of contingent workers, so it is not uncommon for some firms to have up to three strategic models of contingent workers operating simultaneously. Although these models have been established by most organizations in a staged order, the developmental nature of these models varies from firm to firm.

Stage 1: Traditional Personnel Model

Firms have always had a set of secondary workers they can call on to cover basic personnel needs. Temporary workers, hired either through a temporary help service or directly by a firm, have historically been brought in to cover for personnel out due to sickness, vacation, and leaves or to smooth out peak or cyclical workloads. Consultants, hired as self-employed independent contractors, have regularly been brought in to provide training to employees or to offer very specialized skills for a special finite project.

Within this tradition, departments are allocated a certain dollar amount annually to cover the costs of their fill-in personnel. Other than these dollar allocations, firms at this stage rarely have any centralized data as to who their contingent workers are and what exactly they are used for. Even when firms have expanded their use of temps and contractors in ways characteristic of Stage 2 and Stage 3, there typically remains a certain amount of work that requires the use of these traditional "fill-in/special case" type of contingent workers.

Stage 2: Crisis-Driven Model

The economic turbulence that began to rock many large U.S. firms in the mid-1980s created crises on many fronts. In response, many companies focused on identifying ways to cut head counts and to improve productivity. Widespread workforce reductions precipitated significant alterations in the corporate landscape and prompted a more crisis-driven use of contingent workers (Doeringer et al., 1991). What these companies quickly realized was that *although their manpower decreased as a result of layoffs and early retirements, the amount of work that needed to be done did not diminish.* The same, or in some cases, greater amounts of work needed to be accomplished by a fewer number of workers.

During the late eighties and the early nineties, we began to see evidence of questionable contingent hiring practices: employees being laid off one day as employees and hired back the next as self-employed contractors. Firms began hiring more and more secondary workers in ad hoc ways in order to get their work done. Work associated with key business operations was increasingly being done by consultants, not by employees, or being outsourced to entirely separate businesses—some of which hired ex-employees from the original firms to service the needs of that firm. Temps, hired through other agencies, were being employed in larger numbers and for longer periods of time. In other words, work that was integral to the organization began being done increasingly by workers who were not.

For firms which adopt the crisis-driven model, contingent workers offer the company the means to get the work done without the workers showing up as "heads" on the balance sheet. As a result, the use of contingent workers gives the illusion of improving productivity.

Stage 3: Strategic Staffing Model

The adoption of a Stage 3 orientation represents a significant shift in a firm's thinking about contingent work arrangements. Not all firms are there yet, but anecdotal and journalistic evidence indicates that increasing numbers are moving in this direction (Struve, 1991; Messmer, 1992). Rather than hiring contingent workers in an ad hoc manner to react to immediate circumstances, these "new age" firms are becoming more strategic in their planning and use of contingent workers. These firms are engaged in what has popularly become known as strategic staffing. According to the CEO of Robert Half, a temporary help company, "The concept [of strategic staffing] involves analyzing a department's staffing needs based on the long-term objective and those of the overall company—and finding a combination of permanent and temporary employees with the best skills to meet these needs" (Messmer, 1992). The key to successful use of contingent workers lies in their strategic integration into an overall corporate plan. Some companies have target ratios for how many workers are to be hired as core employees and how many as contingent workers.

The use of the payroll transfer plan has become an important staffing strategy for many firms. Under the plan, the client company selects the individuals and sets the wages—for as many employees as they need at that time. The workers may even be former employees the client would like to recall on a consultant basis. These people are then hired by a temporary personnel company that takes charge of their payroll and insurance, thus eliminating some of the overhead costs incurred with permanent employees (Maniscalco, 1992:66–67). The use of the payroll transfer plan can be advantageous for several reasons:

> It allows firms to circumvent some recent enforcement efforts by the Internal Revenue Service that are making it increasingly difficult for firms to hire independent contractors.

It distances the firm from directly hiring a contingent workforce by transferring their contingent work decisions to an outside organization. Some companies, such as Hewlett-Packard, have recognized that the emergence of a two-tiered workforce system (for example, core employees and contingent workers) can affect the morale of the entire organization. For these firms, the payroll transfer plan can minimize some of the unintended consequences of a two-tiered workforce (Pierson, 1994).

It gives firms the flexibility they need to fix the number of workers who can and should be brought in on a contingent basis.

Many companies have implemented actions to streamline and consolidate their use of contingent workers and to reduce cost. As a result, some of the largest corporations which used to deal with up to one to two dozen different temporary help companies are now negotiating sole-source contracts with one large firm, in which a coordinator from the temp firm works on site as a full-time coordinator. In some cases, the coordinator sits in the human resource department and in others, in the purchasing department.

Tensions Surrounding Contingent Workers within Firms

Contingent work can and does create friction at a variety of organizational levels within a firm. At the plant or floor level, resentment can flare up between core employees and contingent workers over issues as diverse as rates of pay, productivity levels, and commitment to the job.

Core employees, sometimes unaware that contingents receive no benefits, see contingents as making more on an hourly basis for doing the same work. Core employees at the clerical and administrative support levels often end up supervising the temporary and, in doing so, may seek to ensure that the temp does not exceed normative production levels. Core employees working on teams often find contingent workers less than satisfying members of the team; contingents are seen as having substantially less allegiance to the firm and to the project.

Contingent workers, on the other hand, may resent that no matter how hard they work, they remain on the outside, with little hope of a more secure, permanent position. Contingent work reminds everyone on the floor of the reduced level of commitment of the firm to its workforce.

At an organizational level, it also remains unclear as to whether or not contingent workers are cost effective. Recent research, in fact, indicates that the higher rates of attrition, and therefore of recruiting and training, actually make contingent workers *more* costly than intended

(Nollen & Axel, this volume; Nollen, 1993). In previous research, I have done, human resource staff indicate higher levels of satisfaction with the job performance of contingent workers than with their ease of supervision or their cost (Christensen, 1989).

The increased placement of the contingent workforce within the purchasing department also severs a group of workers almost entirely from the traditional functions of the human resource department. And within HR departments, the different models of contingent workers get played out differently and with different levels of friction. The traditional personnel model of contingent work fits in well with the traditional core human resource philosophy of investing in employees. However, with the emergence of the more crisis-driven and strategic- staffing models, human resource staffs have begun to see the underpinnings of their human investment paradigm eroded to the extent that the contingent workers are placed entirely outside HR and in purchasing departments. HR departments are out of the loop for increasing numbers of workers in the organization.

At the psychological level, human resource staff are faced with having to adopt two entirely different and contradictory approaches to their workforces: one sees workers as costs to be cut while another views them as human capital in which to invest. It is not surprising that within such a contradictory climate, many people might find it easier to ignore the contingent workers on the grounds that they fall outside their organizational or legal purview than to face the contradiction of having one part of the workforce treated so differently than the other.

Contingent Workers in Family-Sensitive Firms

To date, there has been little attention paid to how firms treat the work-family needs of their contingent workers. Not only are these workers seen as outside the core of permanent employees, they are often simply not seen in any systematic way. The primary reason for this lack of systematic attention is that most firms do not make centralized decisions about contingent staffing; that is, they are not Stage III organizations as described above. Most decisions are made incrementally by unit or department heads. Institutionally, no one person is assigned to monitor contingent staffing decisions. As a result, few firms possess overall knowledge of the range of contingent workers hired in the firm or access to any centralized data on these workers, since data tend to be disaggregated over departments or not collected at all (Christensen,

1989). As a result, contingent workers remain organizationally invisible. The fact that few, if any, people within an organization think about the work-family needs of the contingent workers should not be surprising; these workers tend to be viewed as the appendix rather than the heart of the organization.

If we are to understand whether and under what conditions contingent workers are eligible for a firm's family-friendly benefits, we must first establish a baseline description of contingent work arrangements within specific firms.

With that aim in mind, I conducted a study of twenty-one large U.S. corporations, in collaboration with the Center on Work and Family at Boston College, that would achieve three purposes: (1) establish firm-specific baseline data on contingent work arrangements; (2) collect firm-specific information on the availability of work-family services, benefits, and policies; and (3) determine the contingent workers' eligibility for these work-family options.

Description of Study

The twenty-one firms which agreed to participate in the study were all members of Boston College's Work-Family Roundtable, a national membership group of thirty-three major U.S. corporations, each of which has demonstrated leadership and commitment to work-family issues. These firms were queried, through a written survey and selected follow-up interviews, as to their use of contingent staffing and as to the eligibility of their contingent workers for the firms' work-family benefits. The lead work-family person in human resources agreed to collect whatever information was available within the firm.

Fifteen of the twenty-one firms studied were clustered in three major U.S. industries, including manufacturing, pharmaceuticals, and telecommunications. Over half (55 percent) of the employees in these firms were male and half were younger than forty-five. Although not by any means a statistically representative sample, it remains a fairly mainstream selection of firms.

Eleven of the twenty-one firms which participated in this study reported that their answers reflected policies and practices for their *entire* companies, which had an average workforce size of 43,797 employees. Seven of the firms reported only on practices at their corporate headquarters, which employed, on the average, 5,030 employees. The remaining three firms answered for specific business units, which averaged 3,125 employees each.

Three types of contingent staffing arrangements were studied:

- *Direct-hire temporaries*: employees hired directly by the firm for a finite project or period of time
- *Agency temporaries*: employees of an external temporary help service firm who are assigned to work on site for the client firm, but who legally remain employees of the temp firm
- *Independent contractors*: self-employed consultants who are hired for a specific project or for a specific period of time

Baseline Data on Contingent Work Arrangements in Twenty-one Firms

Although extensive data were collected in the survey and in follow-up interviews for this study, only that data directly relevant to how contingent work arrangements are used and evaluated within the firms will be reported here (for a complete report see Christensen, 1995).

Numbers

Contingent work arrangements, including direct-hire temps, agency temps, and independent contractors, were in place, during the year prior to the survey, at virtually all of the twenty-one firms. During that year,

- 20 firms hired, on the average, 96 direct-hire temps;
- 21 firms used, on the average, 2,231 agency temporaries;
- 20 firms hired independent contractors, but none of these companies had any record of the number of contractors hired, or the tasks or projects on which they worked.

As is obvious by these figures, although firms hired both direct-hire temps and agency temps, they were likely to use a substantially larger number of agency temps than to hire them directly through their own HR departments.

Assignments

The temporary workers were typically assigned to clerical or administrative support jobs, although it is interesting to note that slightly over a quarter of the direct-hire temps were assigned to do professional or skilled technical work (Table 4.1). Just as the firms had no data on the number of independent contractors hired, they also had no record of the assignments on which they worked.

Table 4.1 Jobs assignments and temporary workers

	Direct-hire temporaries (%)	Agency temporaries (%)
Clerical/administrative support	70	85
Sales	2	2
Production/labor	23	13
Professional/technical	27	11
Managers	3	2
Other	9	5

Perceived Benefits and Problems of Contingent Work Arrangements

It is not surprising that given the pervasive use of contingent staffing, companies hope staffing arrangements will meet human resource objectives. To that end, the companies reported specific benefits associated with each of the three forms of contingent work arrangements.

The most frequently cited benefit of using temporary workers (90 percent for direct-hire temps and 76 percent for agency temps) is that these arrangements allow firms to provide coverage for absent core employees. This is in keeping with the traditional personnel model governing the use of contingent workers.

The most frequently cited benefit achieved by using independent contractors is that it allows the firms to access workers with specialized skills.

Frequently cited benefits for all three contingent staffing arrangements include the ability to maintain adequate staffing during peak business periods, to access personnel for specific cyclical or seasonal needs, and to cut direct labor costs. These benefits are what firms hope to achieve in Stages II and III regarding their organizational use of contingent workers.

As is clear from the responses in Table 4.2, firms identify a number of benefits from using contingent staffing. Some of these benefits, such as covering for absent core employees or acquiring special skills, fit into the goals outlined for Stage I firms. Other benefits, such as cutting labor costs and staffing for peak periods, allow a firm to achieve the goals specified in Stages II and III. Firms can acquire staff without incurring the costs of full-time permanent employees, or they can buffer their core employees from a potential layoff.

Respondents were also asked to identify problems associated with the use of contingent work arrangements. The problem most frequently

Table 4.2 Perceptions of benefits associated with contingent work arrangements

	Direct-hire temporaries (%)	Agency temporaries (%)	Independent contractors/ consultants (%)
Arrange coverage for absences of permanent employees	90	76	19
Avoid head count limits	81	62	38
Access workers with specialized skills	76	67	67
Maintain adequate staffing during peak business periods	76	67	38
Access personnel for specific cyclical or seasonal needs	76	67	38
Cut direct labor costs	52	48	43
Audition job candidates	52	29	14
Reduce health care costs	38	19	29
Avoid additional lay-offs	33	14	14
Provide transition for workers layed-off	29	19	19
Just-in-time staffing philosophy	24	14	14

associated with temporary workers (both those hired directly by the company and those hired through an external agency) was training. They did not have the training adequate for the job. The most frequently cited problem associated with independent contractors was that they were seen as being "too costly and not cost efficient."

It also interesting to note that although the greatest growth in contingent staffing has been and is anticipated to be among agency temporaries, the problem frequently associated with agency temporaries was that they had lower productivity compared to permanent employees and, not surprisingly given their temp status, had high turnover and reduced loyalty.

Table 4.3 compares the responses for the three categories of contingent work arrangements.

Overall Satisfaction with Contingent Work Arrangements

The survey asked the respondents to provide an overall assessment of their satisfaction with the three types of contingent work arrangements on three dimensions: job performance, cost, and ease of supervision.

When considering temporaries (both direct hires and agency temporaries), the highest percentage of companies reported satisfaction with job performance.

Table 4.3 Problems associated with contingent work arrangements
(percent reporting problem specified)

	Direct-hire temporaries	Agency temporaries	Independent contractors/ consultants
Difficulties with training	43	48	19
Workers outside of head count system	43	19	33
Poor morale among temporary workers	33	14	5
Creation of a two-tiered work force	33	24	14
Not cost efficient/too costly	5	29	52
Resentment from permanent employees	24	19	29
Difficulties with supervision	24	29	24
Reduced productivity compared to permanent employees	19	43	0
High turnover	24	38	5
Reduced loyalty	19	33	19

Although three-fourths of respondents indicated satisfaction with the job performance and ease of supervision associated with contractors/ consultants, only 37 percent stated that they were either "somewhat satisfied" (25 percent) or "very satisfied" (12 percent) with the cost. Table 4.4 profiles the respondents' satisfaction ratings.

Past Trends

When queried about their hiring practices over the past three years, the survey respondents reported that their firms had experienced the greatest increase in their use of agency temporary workers. The hiring of agency temps had increased "somewhat" or "significantly" for sixteen of the twenty-one firms. The hiring of independent contractors, on the other hand, had decreased "somewhat" or "significantly" for seven firms. And the numbers of direct-hire temps had stayed about the same or increased slightly.

Table 4.4 Satisfaction with contingent work arrangements
(percent "somewhat satisfied" or "very satisfied")

	Satisfaction with ease of supervision	Satisfaction with cost	Satisfaction with job performance
Direct-hire temporaries	72	83	89
Agency temporaries	67	55	83
Independent contractors/consultants	74	37	74

Projected Trends

When asked to anticipate how their companies' use of contingent work arrangements might change over the next three years, most of the survey respondents felt their use would either stay the same or increase. Nearly a quarter of the respondents predicted that their use of independent contractors would increase "significantly." Given the fact that no firm has available numbers on their current use of contractors, it is not clear how reliable an estimate that may turn out to be. The usage of both types of temp workers is expected to increase, with more reported increases for agency temps than direct-hire temps. Table 4.5 presents the anticipated use of contingent work arrangements in the near future in these twenty-one firms.

Summary of Corporate Patterns

The results of this study of twenty-one firms are admittedly limited to a select, nonrepresentative sample of firms, but they raise some interesting patterns that must be noted.

Contingent work arrangements are almost universally present at these twenty-one firms. Based on available figures, agency temps are much more prevalent within firms than are direct-hire temps.

Despite their existence in twenty of the twenty-one firms, we know virtually nothing about independent contractors. No firm collects centralized data on them, so it is impossible to know exactly how many, on the average, work at these firms, much less what kinds of assignments they work on or for what periods of time. Recent data released by BLS (see Cohany et al., this volume) indicate that they would be more likely to do professional or technical work than temps would be.

Not only do companies indicate that there has been an increase in the overall numbers of these work arrangements, they anticipate that their

Table 4.5 Anticipated changes in use of contingent work arrangements over the next three years (percent)

	Will decrease significantly	*Will decrease somewhat*	*No change expected*	*Will increase somewhat*	*Will increase significantly*
Direct-hire temporaries	19	5	24	38	14
Agency temporaries	14	0	9	57	19
Independent contractors/consultants	23	12	18	23	23

use will increase in the near future. The most likely increases will be in agency temps.

Eligibility of Contingent Workers for Work-Family Benefits

Given the commitment of the Roundtable members to work-family issues, it was expected that all of the respondents would offer a range of work-family programs and policies to their permanent employees. In fact, all of the twenty-one respondent companies offered most of the fifteen options identified in Table 4.6.

When asked about the availability of these options to contingent workers, only a minority of the respondents reported that a fraction of their work-family programs and policies were available to contingent workers. Direct-hire temporaries were most likely to have access to some of the benefits and policies available to permanent employees. These included access to flextime, work-family seminars, child care location and referral information, parent support groups, and information and assistance for dependent care (Table 4.7). This is not surprising since the category of direct-hire temporaries is the only contingent work

Table 4.6 Availability of work-family policies and benefits in 21 firms studied

Programs/policy	*No. of respondent companies*
Flextime	21
Flexplace or work-at-home options	21
Job sharing	21
Relocation assistance	21
Counseling	21
Seminars on work-family issues	21
Child care information assistance	20
Child care location and referral assistance	20
Part-time positions	20
Unpaid childbirth leave for women beyond provisions through disability insurance	20
Pre-tax spending accounts for child care and elder/adult dependent care (DCAP)	18
Parent support groups	18
Dependent care information assistance	17
Dependent care referral assistance	16
On-site fitness center or subsidized memberships in external fitness programs	17

arrangement addressed by our survey that maintains a traditional employer-employee relationship.

In contrast to these direct-hire temps, the agency temps are technically employees of the temporary firms and, as such, the firms in this study would not have a legal obligation to offer the same benefits to them as they do to their permanent employees. Not surprisingly, therefore, agency temps were eligible for very little in the way of family support, other than flextime and informational services. The self-employed contractors/consultants have no employer and hence, like agency temps, are eligible for very few benefits. The work-family supports offered to contingent employees by the highest percentage of corporate survey participants are highlighted in Table 4.7.

Constraints on Firms Offering Work-Family Benefits to Contingent Workers

Of the three types of contingent work arrangements, the direct-hire temps are the only ones who have a legal employer-employee relationship with the firm. In principal, contractors (being "self-employed") have no employer. By law, the agency temporaries' employers are the agencies, not the firm that purchases these services.

This legal quagmire surrounding contingent workers may actually make firms reluctant to offer work-family benefits to their non-employee contingent workers, the independent contractors and agency temporaries. If a firm were to offer work-family benefits to these non-employees, they could then be making themselves potentially liable under law if one of these contingent workers would want to sue the firm under any number

Table 4.7 Benefits available to permanent and contingent workers (number of companies reporting benefit specified)

	Available to permanent employees	Available to direct-hire temporaries	Available to agency temporaries	Available to contractors/ consultants
Flextime	21	11	4	6
Seminars on work family issues	21	10	5	4
Child care location and referral	20	8	1	1
Parent support groups	18	8	3	3
Child care information assistance	20	7	1	1
Elder care/adult dependent care information assistance	17	7	0	0

of the conditions, such as alleged discrimination, harassment, or health and safety violations. So long as the firm does not in any way treat non-employees as employees they limit their liability. But the net effect of this decision is that the contingent worker has, as is evident in this study, few if any work-family benefits.

Yet, there is no reason to suspect that families with contingent workers do not confront the same work-family issues and conflicts experienced by families with permanent employees. The question, therefore, remains: *Who might respond to the family concerns of contingent workers?*

The answers are not straightforward. The traditional firm-based employer-employee relationship has been severed for contract workers and agency temps, and it may hold up more in principal than in practice for direct-hire temps. Contingent workers cannot look to their "employer" in the same way as core employees can for help with their work-family needs. But can they look to the federal law for protection on issues that are also central to their concerns as family heads of households? Are they accorded any protection for periods of unemployment, for time off for birth or adoption, for personal illness or that of a family member, or for costs incurred as a result of an injury on a job? If we consider family needs to include basic protections for health and welfare, is the federal government providing any protection for contingent workers?

Limits of Employment Law to Meet Needs of Contingent Workers

It is apparent from the foregoing discussion that corporations have a limited sense of responsibility for meeting the work-family needs of their contingent workers. But they are by no means alone. Federal law for the most part excludes some contingent workers entirely from their protective labor laws while limiting their protections for others.

One of the most striking aspects of the public discussion of contingent work is that insufficient attention is directed to the fact that, under the law, the different types of contingent workers are defined quite differently and as a result are accorded different protections and privileges. For example, independent contractors are legally defined as self-employed and are outside virtually all protective federal and state labor protection. On the other hand, temporary and part-time workers are employees and are eligible under the law for different protections such as unemployment compensation or employer contributions to social security. Whether or not they can take advantage of such is often a function of how many hours they work. Temporary workers who are placed through a temporary help service agency are technically employees of that agency, whereas temporary workers hired directly by a firm and part-time workers are employees of that firm. These differences in the legal definition of employee status and the identity of the actual employer all lead to a range of issues that must be examined in light of current employment law.

To understand the laws governing contingent workers we must return again to the point that, under the law, temporary workers are employees and eligible under certain conditions for certain protections, while contract workers are not employees and effectively excluded from the protection under many, if not most of, the federal labor laws (see also Carnevale, Jennings, & Eisenmann, this volume).

Federal Employment Law and Contingent Workers

Federal employment law historically was written to protect the needs of full-time, permanent employees. These laws include, but need not be limited to, the following:

- Fair Labor Standards Act (FLSA)
- Equal Pay Act of 1963
- Title VII of the Civil Rights Act of 1964
- Age Discrimination in Employment Act (ADEA)
- Occupational Safety and Health Act (OSHA)

Many contingent workers are excluded from the protections afforded by much of the existing labor legislation because they either (1) are not considered to be "employees" (because they are independent contractors/consultants) or (2) are employees but work fewer than the minimum number of hours set for eligibility.

Agency temporaries also have a complicated situation because, according to law, their employer is the temporary agency, while in practice their day-to-day supervising employer is the client company to whom they have been assigned. As a consequence, there is some ambiguity to whom an agency temp would report concerns regarding issues such as harassment, wage discrimination, and health or safety violations. Their "co-employer" situation has prompted confusion about interpretations of existing laws.

Minimum Wage and Wage Equity Protection

The FLSA sets minimum wage and overtime laws, while the Equal Pay Act of 1963 expanded coverage of the FLSA to ensure equal pay for equal work regardless of gender. Eligibility for these laws is limited to employees. According to the prevailing economic reality test, the status of an employee is determined by five points:

Degree of control over work and materials used for work
Opportunities for profit or loss
Investment in facilities
Permanency of relationship
Skill required

The more dependent a worker is on an employer, the more likely that worker is to be judged an employee.

The FLSA extends minimum wage to employees, including temporary employees, but not to contractors. The Equal Pay Act of 1963 gave employees (*not* contractors) the right to expect equal pay for equal work regardless of gender. Contractors fall outside of any rights under these laws for filing pay discrimination cases.

What is particularly troublesome about the rise of the contingent workforce is that employers have been known to arbitrarily change the status of a worker from employee to self-employed contractor. This has not been uncommon during the recent wave of downsizings and the emergence of the crisis use of contingent workers, in which employees were laid off one day and hired back, virtually the next, as contract workers. According to a recent study by the General Accounting Office many workers are misclassified as independent contractors rather than employees and consequently unprotected in terms of minimum wage, overtime, and equal pay laws (General Accounting Office, 1989).

Civil Rights and Equal Opportunity

Title VII and the ADEA have as their primary goal to prohibit discrimination in employment. Yet if one is to seek protection under these laws, he or she must once again prove to be an employee. No one test is uniformly used to determine employee status for these laws (Carnevale, 1994). In general, temporary workers do have recourse to sue under Title VII. Contract workers, however, have no rights regarding these affirmative action laws.

Another way firms can circumvent these laws is by how they count their number of employees on the payroll. Title VII has a minimum of fifteen employees, while ADEA has a threshold of twenty. Depending on the counting method used, a firm could operate with part-time employees and not meet the threshold level, and consequently even employees working in the firm would not have recourse to sue on antidiscriminatory grounds (Carnevale, 1994).

Health and Safety Protections

In 1970 Congress passed the Occupational Safety and Health Act (OSHA). Its goal was to provide "so far as possible every working man and woman in the Nation safe and healthful working conditions." Yet in effect, OSHA only protects the health and safety of employees.

Self-employed contract workers fall outside the protective net of OSHA. Egregious exploitation of contract workers can be found perhaps nowhere as dramatically as in the petrochemical industry (see Rebitzer, this volume). Following a massive explosion and fire at the Phillips 66 Chemical Plant in Pasadena, Texas, in 1989, which took twenty-three lives and injured another 232, the Occupational Health and Safety Administration mandated a study on the safety and health issues in the use of contract workers in the petrochemical industry in the United States. The study concluded that the contract workers incurred a higher probability of injuries than did employees (Kochan, Wells, & Smith, 1992). The authors found that these contract workers experienced a higher accident rate than did employees for several reasons: (1) "[they] are more likely to be engage in high risk maintenance and renovation work; (2) [they] are less experienced at the workplace; (3) [they] receive less safety training; and (4) the training they receive is less effective in reducing injuries than the training received by direct hire workers" (Kochan, Wells, & Smith, 1992:84). Ironically they received less training by their "employer" for fear that if they received more they would be considered employees and the firm would then be liable for their injuries. In fact, lawyers for the firms often advised employers to avoid supervising contract workers too closely in order to avoid being judged in court as a co-employer. In the petroleum industry, which is likely not atypical, neither the plants nor OSHA keep accurate or adequate data or safety records on the contract workers.

Family and Medical Leave

Once again a worker must have "employee" status to be eligible for family and medical leave under the Family and Medical Leave Act of 1993 (FMLA), yet employee status is not sufficient to guarantee eligibility. *Hours of service* or *time on the job* are the crucial variables in determining eligibility. According to this act, an employee must have worked for an employer for one year and for at least 1,250 hours to obtain the unpaid job-protected leave. In addition, only firms of a certain size must offer this unpaid job-protected leave; firms of fifty or more employees are required to do so.

So although a temporary worker hired either directly by a firm or by a temporary agency could be eligible for a leave under the act, the firm must be of a certain size and they must have worked a certain period of time or number of hours to be fully eligible. Contract workers are excluded entirely from benefits of the Family Medical Leave Act.

Unemployment Insurance

As is the case with the protections provided by federal labor laws discussed above, only employees are eligible to receive unemployment insurance (UI). The federal Internal Revenue Service (IRS) and the states are responsible for determining an employee's status and hence eligibility for the state UI programs.

Toward the Future

Contingent workers include both employees, in the case of temporary workers, and non-employees, in the case of self-employed contract workers. Virtually all protective employment law is written to protect the rights of employees. Virtually none thus far has been extended to protect non-employees. In effect, minimal effort has been expended at the federal level to protect the rights of contingent workers to fair wages, to an equal and safe workplace, and to access to the Family Medical Leave Act provisions. In effect, firms are not alone in failing to meet the individual and family needs of contingent workers. The federal government, through its employment law, has colluded.

The basic conclusions of this chapter are threefold:

First, contingent work continues to grow in importance at large firms. In the twenty-one case studies that form the basis of this chapter, all of the firms offer at least two of the contingent work arrangements. Agency temps appear to be the most numerous within the firms, although that cannot be said definitively since none of these firms collected any information about their independent contractors.

Second, despite their active support for helping core employees meet their work-family needs, even the most family-sensitive firms have limited commitment to the family needs of contingent workers.

Third, the federal government continues to operate with a set of regulations and laws that effectively exclude large numbers of workers from basic rights under law either because they are not defined as employees or because they do not meet certain conditions such as hours worked.

What is to be done? The most obvious answers are twofold. First, the federal government should rewrite current employment law to take into account this excluded group of workers. Second, the private sector should consider the direct and indirect impacts that the work-family needs experienced by contingent workers may have on their business operations.

In the short run, neither of these scenarios are likely to happen, and for very real and complex reasons. Yet given that these contingent work trends are likely to continue, other alternatives must be pursued. These may include the following:

Advocate that temporary agencies should provide work-family benefits to their temporary employees. Under law, temporary agencies are the legal employers of a large percentage of the contingent workforce and as such could and should be more cognizant of the work-family needs of these employees. One avenue for pressuring these agencies would be through demands made by corporate clients. Clients, particularly those interested in negotiating large sole-source contracts with temporary firms, could require that the temp firms show evidence of a work-family commitment to their employees. Since many of the most family-sensitive corporations are large and likely to be considering the use of sole arrangements with a temporary firm, they could take the lead in changing the work-family climate within the temporary help services industry.

Form an organization to represent contingent workers. Within many labor unions there is the possibility for affiliate memberships, which could provide an initial forum in which contingent workers might be able to find a voice. Outside the labor movement, contingent workers of different trades or professions might consider the formation of guilds that could be used to serve several functions: sharing information about pricing or markets; obtaining reduced rates for health benefits or pensions coverage; lobbying for changes in laws; or serving as umbrella organizations for basic work-family benefits such as dependent care information or referral. To work effectively, these guilds would need to be organized by trade or profession, with one possible model being the Writer's Guild. The notion of a guild would probably be particularly relevant to independent contractors, as they would have no employer to which to turn.

Prepare intensive case studies of firms' uses of contingent workers to determine the benefits and costs of these arrangements to the firm. Initial research has shown there can be hidden costs due to turnover and training (Axel, 1993; Nollen, 1993; Nollen & Axel, 1996, this volume), but much more extensive work across firms needs to be conducted.

In conclusion, the results of this study indicate clearly that contingent workers are largely ineligible for both employer-provided work-family benefits and protections under federal employment law. As the United States moves toward an increasing reliance on this contingent work-force, greater numbers of contingent workers will fall outside safety nets. This is an increasingly vulnerable and unprotected set of workers. These contingent workers, faced with unstable sources of income, equipped with few if any health or welfare benefits, and afforded limited opportunities for training or skill upgrading, quickly are becoming a second class of workers within many large U.S. firms, even those committed to providing work-family benefits to their core of permanent employees.

CHAPTER FIVE

Benefits and Costs to Employers

Stanley D. Nollen
Helen Axel

*T*he growing interest of employers in contingent labor over the last decade comes in part from managers' beliefs that staffing on a contingency basis provides workforce flexibility and reduces labor costs. This is the message that is delivered in the popular business press. However, the benefits and costs of contingent labor to organizations are more likely to rely on the employers' assumptions than on hard statistical evidence. A recent Conference Board report, based on a survey and interviews with corporate managers, reveals a widespread absence of data collection and record keeping by corporations on workers who hold temporary, hourly part-time, or contract jobs (Axel, 1995). More specifically, relatively few employers are able to provide accurate and comprehensive information about how many contingent workers they are using at any given time, how many hours these individuals work, how long they remain on the job, how well they perform, and whether or not they are a cost-effective resource to the organization.

Information gaps within companies and other organizations about the dimensions of contingent staffing can be attributed largely to the absence of strategic planning and evaluative studies concerning this practice. Lacking mandates to plan or assess their workforce strategy, organizations that use contingent workers—and most do—frequently do not maintain centralized statistics about them or even monitor their use in areas of the company where they are most prevalent. In the 1995 Conference Board study, for example, almost half of the U.S. corporations surveyed indicated that using contingent workers was not part of any strategic plan; between 40 and 60 percent (depending on the type of contingent work arrangement) had no policies or guidelines for using these workers; and close to 40 percent admitted that no cost controls were imposed upon their use (Axel, 1995). The desire for quick action, guided perhaps by previous patterns of use in the organization, it appears, often substitutes as justification for hiring on a contingency basis. As a result, contingent staffing is more likely to evolve as a series of ad hoc arrangements than as thoughtful decisions made within the framework of a company's principal business objectives.

Despite the ad hoc nature of many contingent work arrangements and current deficiencies in data collection and measurement, employers believe there are advantages in using contingent labor that can produce both monetary and nonmonetary benefits for the organization. At the same time, however, they are also increasingly aware of the costs associated with these staffing arrangements. With this growing awareness, a few organizations are beginning to compare both the costs and benefits of contingent labor and to look for ways to influence the cost-benefit ratio in their favor (Nollen and Axel, 1996).

This chapter examines the benefits and costs of contingent staffing to companies that make use of this practice. The first objective is to identify its benefits—quantifiable ones such as wages and productivity, intangible ones such as management tasks, and potential ones such as buffering the core workforce from layoffs. The second objective is to explain how the real costs of contingent labor and its cost-effectiveness to employers are determined; how benefits less easily measured, such as workforce flexibility, offer value to an organization; and why legal issues, particularly with regard to joint employer relationships and the use of independent contractors, can affect the cost savings anticipated from a contingent workforce. The third objective is to recommend actions that managers can take to maximize the benefits and minimize the costs of contingent staffing. The audience is twofold: human resource managers who are responsible for formulating policies about contingent workers, and operating managers who implement policies and supervise the daily activities of contingent workers. In sum, the benefits and costs reviewed in this chapter reflect the perspective of the employer rather than the worker.

Most of the information presented in the following pages is derived from the authors' research in connection with a recent book on managing contingent workers (Nollen and Axel, 1996). Research for the book is based primarily on in-depth case studies of contingent worker use in five corporations and involves analyses of company data as well as discussions with managers and supervisory personnel in each firm. For several of the case studies, more than one company location was visited. Additional recent findings about corporate experiences with contingent labor come from a Conference Board survey of ninety-three companies

and fourteen follow-up telephone interviews with officials in these organizations (Axel, 1995). It should be noted that while the research is based
on experiences within the business community, its findings on managing
contingent workers are relevant to other employers as well. Hence,
"company," "employer," and "organization" as used in this chapter are
largely interchangeable terms.

The Benefits to Employers—Assumed and Real

The reasons companies and other organizations choose contingent
staffing are likely to depend on assumptions they make about the advantages of temporary, part-time, and contract work. But conditions in the
workplace, including management practices, ultimately determine how
or whether employers will benefit from having contingents in their workforce. When questioned, companies today are likely to identify contingent labor with workforce flexibility and cost control—in addition to its
more traditional uses as purchased expertise and temporary fill-ins. In
fact, four out of five companies in the Conference Board survey consider
workforce flexibility to meet fluctuations in demand a major reason for
using contingent workers (Axel, 1995). The flexibility and cost control
objectives can be realized only if contingent workers are properly man-
aged, however. To do so, employers must maintain adequate controls on
their numbers and length of time on the job, and they must provide work
assignments that are appropriate for the workers' skills and their expected tenure.

Cost Cutting and Cost Control

Employers who hire contingent workers generally see that decision as a
way to control or cut labor costs. Cost cutting occurs in a most obvious
way: contingent workers, unlike regular employees, perform services
and are paid only when they are needed—during seasons of the year,
days of the week, or hours of the day when the workload is heaviest. In
periods of slack demand, the workers can be dismissed or put on hold
in an on-call status. A just-in-time workforce can also help employers
avoid costs associated with recruiting, overtime, and layoffs.

In addition, by reducing the core workforce and refraining from hiring permanent staff to meet increases in demand, companies are able to
exchange typically higher employee wage and benefit compensation for
lower wages and few or no benefits paid to contingent workers. And
they can shed responsibility for income tax withholding, social security

and unemployment tax payments, and related employment costs. The absence of a traditional employer-employee relationship, as in temporary and leasing arrangements (where workers supplied by a staffing company are employees of the provider, not the client company) and in independent contractor relationships (where the workers are self-employed), allows for a distancing between company and contingent worker. But even with direct-hire temporaries and hourly part-timers, who are company employees, separate treatment in terms of compensation is possible, particularly if they are placed on a payroll separate from regular employees. While some business managers are uncomfortable with paying contingent workers smaller wages and benefits, it is possible to do so, and it is a widespread practice (for details and sources see the later section on managing for cost-effectiveness). Despite these more distant relationships, however, employers are not absolved from all legal obligations toward their contingent workers (see section on legal considerations later in this chapter).

Assumptions about cost control rely in part on a labor market that has a plentiful supply of contingent workers so that a sufficient number of qualified workers are available and the prevailing wage rates including providers' fees can remain below employment costs for comparable employees. A favorable wage differential may be difficult to attain in a job market that has relatively few adequately skilled workers seeking contingent employment. Freelancers, consultants and other professionals working as independent contractors are the exception. Organizations are often willing to pay high fees for special expertise not available in-house. The justification here is usually based on need, not cost, although the finite period of a contract limits the company's financial obligation toward these workers.

As employers have learned, however, expectations about cost savings can be derailed in an organization, particularly during a period of downsizing. If jobs of displaced employees are refilled by contingent workers (who, in many cases, may be the very employees who were let go), many of the costs remain although they no longer appear as payroll expenses. If head-count restrictions freeze hiring but not other costs, understaffed managers are likely to circumvent company mandates by replacing downsized employees with temporary and contract workers, thus undermining the intended cost benefits. In one instance, a midwestern retailer found that the combined outlays for overtime, temporary, and contract work accrued by managers in its downsized operations more than offset the savings gained from the cutbacks in payroll (Axel, 1993).

Many organizations use contingent employment to achieve the benefits of workforce flexibility, to buffer regular core employees from job loss during business downturns, or to lighten the personnel administration tasks of managers. All of these intended benefits are plausible, and cases can be cited for which they apparently are realized, although measuring these benefits is quite difficult (some are described in the following paragraphs). None of these motives for using contingent staffing is based primarily or directly on costs. However, there are almost always cost implications, such as unstated expectations for cost containment, if not actual cost savings. Or there are cost implications in terms of organizational effectiveness, broadly conceived.

Workforce flexibility is a major reason organizations use contingent workers because adjustments in labor hours can be made quickly as demand fluctuates. Cost factors such as wages and benefits or agency fees may then be only a secondary issue. For example, Avon Products, Inc., a direct-sales consumer products company, faces heavy demand for its products in the holiday-rich fourth quarter of the year and slack demand in the first quarter. It is not possible to produce for inventory and thus smooth out fluctuations in labor demand because each order received from field sales representatives is unique. Avon must match current labor input to current product demand.

To do so, Avon employs "reserves" who are on-call part-year employees on the payroll. They are called in to work full days when needed. They are paid the same wage rate as core employees when they do the same job, and they get prorated benefits after they have met a certain threshold length of service.

Avon gains little or no cost advantage from its use of contingent workers in the sense of saving wages and benefits. Instead, the "reserves" permit the company to achieve the flexibility it needs to operate its plant and serve its customers. Moreover, the favorable wages and benefits provided to these on-call employees make it easy for Avon to attract qualified workers who, once trained, return year after year. Many of them eventually are hired into the core workforce, giving the company a source of proven workers.

In some cases, supplemental workers are viewed as a means for protecting the jobs of core employees, making it possible for the company to avoid hiring and firing cycles by keeping a "ring" of external workers readily available to work when needed. Such arrangements succeed in some situations, but in others not. An example of the core-ring approach is provided by Hewlett-Packard Company, which set up a "FlexForce" in 1988 and has never had a mass layoff. The FlexForce, which helped prevent downsizing through layoffs, consisted of on-call part-timers who worked as needed but less than full-time year-round, plus on-contract direct-hire temporaries who worked under short-term contracts renewable up to two years maximum. Both groups were on HP payroll and were paid slightly premium wages but no benefits. Movement from ring to core was officially not allowed in order to keep the two workforces separate. However, in 1994 the FlexForce was abandoned and was replaced by a new system of external contingent staffing from selected preferred providers.

Hewlett-Packard's core-ring approach failed because separation of core and contingent employees violated the company's "people philosophy" and its culture of shared values and inclusiveness. Flexibility was achieved, but the existence of two categories of workers, one more privileged than the other, could not be maintained. By contrast, in the Avon example, perceived inequities between contingent and core workers are diminished because ring-to-core mobility is expected and benefits are provided to contingent workers.

The core-ring structure in a third firm was created following a series of major layoffs in the early 1980s, a painful experience the company did not want to repeat. However, the decision to use contingent workers as a buffer to the core was founded on an expectation of cost savings, without consideration to the impact of turnover on quality and teamwork. Managers in that company are now rethinking their strategy.

Another assumed benefit in using contingent labor is that employers will be able to avoid many of the administrative tasks associated with managing their regular workforce. By using temporaries from a staffing company or retaining independent contractors, companies are not only freed from the paperwork required for legal and regulatory compliance, they are also able to relinquish many human resource management responsibilities. Independent contractors, of course, are expected to maintain their own businesses and generally work off-site. With temporary or leased employees, the client company can require that a representative from the staffing firm be on the company's premises to coordinate and oversee the management of its workers. When this occurs, the client is able to shift some of the human resource management and supervisory tasks to the staffing company. This does not come free, of course, and is another example of how assumed indirect cost advantages do not always materialize. Staffing companies that provide extra services to their clients account for them in higher fees negotiated in their contracts.

Treating core and contingent workers differently, especially when they do the same jobs, can create other problems for companies. Hewlett-Packard, for example, found a two-tiered workforce incompatible with its organizational culture, and managers were uncomfortable with the workforce distinctions implicit in a core-ring structure. Different treatment may also cause friction between the two groups of workers, which in turn may interfere with their productivity. According to interviews with corporate managers, contingent workers may resent the imbalances in pay and benefits that favor core employees. Resentment from the core staff, on the other hand, may stem from perceived differences in expectations and workload that seem to put the onus on regular employees, from misunderstandings about pay rates to contingents that show the company's willingness to pay third-party fees rather than higher wages to employees, and from the lack of commitment and acculturation of contingent workers (Axel, 1995).

Finally, since contingent workers by nature are expected to remain with an organization for only short periods of time, no extensive training is (or should be) required. As the analysis later in this chapter shows, the amount of training needed for satisfactory work performance is likely to be a pivotal factor in determining the cost-effectiveness of contingent workers in any given situation. All of these potential benefits to companies and other organizations have a common underlying cost component—management time—which translates into administration, supervision, and training. Where these can be reduced, the organization is likely to gain an advantage.

Assessing the Costs of Contingent Labor

As noted in the previous discussion, most company managers assume that contingent workers are cheaper than regular employees. The assumption is easy to make because of the natural tendency to reckon labor cost according to wages and benefits—contingent workers usually do get lower wages and benefits than regular employees. But other factors must be considered in assessing the true costs involved in using contingent labor. First and probably the most important of these is the question of *cost-effectiveness,* which takes into account other situation-specific variables beyond the wages and benefits paid to contingent workers. Other potential cost considerations for employers include training, productivity issues, legal liability, workplace safety, and managerial problems arising from friction between core and contingent workers.

Managing for Cost-Effectiveness

The key variables in determining cost-effectiveness are wages and benefits, productivity, fixed employment costs such as training, and length of service. Although managers seldom check them out, these variables need to be included in calculations comparing contingent workers to regular employees in order to arrive at an accurate assessment of the cost-effectiveness of contingent labor.

Wages and Benefits

In most cases, companies are able to pay lower wages to contingent workers than to regular employees. The labor market permits it because the supply of contingent workers appears to be ample. One indicator for this is the unemployment rate, which is higher for part-timers, a major component of the contingent workforce, than it is for full-timers, putting downward pressure on part-time wage rates. Also, many of the people who are contingent workers bring little bargaining power to the labor market because they have fewer resources than regular employees and fewer options.

Statistics on wages show that hourly paid part-timers averaged across all occupations earn one-fourth less than regular employees—none of these data include independent contractors who are contingent workers. (These statistics as well as those in the following paragraphs are reported in Nollen and Axel, 1996, from original sources in the U.S. Bureau of Labor Statistics, 1993, and Nardone, 1994). Some of the wage gaps may be explained by differences in the jobs that these groups of workers do. For example, agency temporaries who are in top-end professional specialty jobs actually earn more than full-time employees, while temporaries who are operators or laborers at the bottom end of the occupational distribution make scarcely half as much as their regular full-time counterparts. The fact that contingent workers are younger and less experienced than core employees also helps to explain their lower wages. However, from our case study research in companies, we see that contingent workers are sometimes paid less than core employees in the same work units who do the same jobs. In other cases, they are paid more to partially make up for lack of benefits.

The cost of benefits for contingent workers is almost always less than for regular employees because few contingent workers get any benefits. This is one of the reasons why companies use contingent workers. At the very best, 25 percent of part-time employees get paid vacation, and many of these part-timers are core rather than contingent workers (Nardone, 1994). At the worst, perhaps 1 percent of agency temporaries actually receives health insurance benefits.

For contingent workers who are not employees—i.e., independent contractors or temporaries supplied by a staffing company—the company has no obligation to pay employment taxes or provide company benefits. Some exceptions apply here, however, when a joint employer relationship with the staffing company has been determined or when employees have been misclassified as independent contractors. These issues are discussed in a later section on legal considerations. Even when contingent workers are employees, as part-timers are likely to be, the company may place these workers on a separate payroll to differentiate their status within the organization.

Although benefits are made nominally available to temporaries by many staffing companies that employ them, few temps are actually eligible for these benefits because most have short tenure with their employers. The statistics are revealing: paid vacation is nominally available to three-fourths of all agency temporaries, but actually received by just one-tenth of them; health insurance is nominally available to half, but received by only one in one hundred.

Productivity

Labor cost also depends on productivity. The key variable is unit labor cost, which is wages and benefits divided by productivity. (Unit labor cost $= W \times L/Q$, where W = wage and benefit rate per hour, L = hours worked, and Q = quantity of output produced. Labor productivity is Q/L.) For example, when wages and benefits are low, but productivity is also low, the unit labor cost may be high.

Managers who have experience with contingent workers doing the same work as regular employees usually say that the contingent workers' productivity is "about the same" as for regular employees. But if productivity were actually measured, it might turn out to be less. In two cases of backroom operations of commercial banks where physical productivity data were available, the output rate for contingent workers fell short of that for regular employees by 7 or 8 percent (Nollen and Axel, 1996). If no objective physical productivity measure can be made (for example, the worker's output cannot be easily quantified), appraisals by supervisors can then serve as a substitute measure of performance.

Managers should not be surprised if contingent workers do not perform quite as well as regular employees. Productivity depends partly on the skill of the worker, and contingent workers generally have a little less education and presumably less training and experience on the job than regular employees. Many contingent workers are also likely to be less motivated to put forth maximum effort—they are less involved in the workplace, have less security, and may sense that their rewards are inferior.

Even if the productivity of individual contingent workers is good, teamwork may be what really matters in the work unit. When output is produced by teams and team members have to work cooperatively together, the presence of contingent workers may hamper the performance of the team as a whole simply because the group process is disrupted when one contingent worker leaves and another comes in. The necessarily high turnover rate of contingent workers suggests they will not be good performers in teamwork settings.

Training and Length of Service

If the unit labor cost is lower for contingent workers than for regular employees—because their lower wages and benefits more than make up for any shortfall in their productivity—they still may not be cheaper. Other costs of employment, such as recruiting, selecting, and training, need to be considered. Although temporaries from staffing companies incur no costs in recruitment and selection, the company must pay a fee to the provider above and beyond the wages actually received by the workers. Moreover, almost all new workers need some initial orientation and job training.

The training cost, which is incurred up front before the new contingent worker produces output, is a fixed cost that is incurred per person, not per hour worked or per unit produced. Training and other fixed employment costs pose a special problem for contingent workers. Employers ordinarily view training as an investment in the future productivity of workers. It may begin with classroom instruction, or it may be only on-the-job training with a supervisor followed by a period of learning-by-doing. The costs of training may include direct costs, such as a trainer's salary and the rental value of equipment and space used, but it almost always includes the opportunity cost of lost output from supervisors and trainees while they are paid a salary but engaged in training.

After training is completed, the employer's investment will be recovered as long as the trained workers' output exceeds their wages and benefits (G. S. Becker, 1975; Mincer, 1962). But it takes time to recover the investment, and contingent workers do not have long tenure on the job (excluding the unintended instances of "permanent" temps). When a company does not recover its training investment, it becomes another cost of employment.

Measuring Cost-Effectiveness

To determine the cost-effectiveness of contingent workers, their extra cost of employment represented by any unrecovered training investment must be netted against their unit labor cost saving, if any, for the length of time they spend on the job (see Table 5.1 for a summary of the methodology).

The cost-effectiveness equation is a situation-specific outcome. In three company case studies (reported in Nollen and Axel, 1996), contingent workers had lower wage and benefit costs than regular employees doing the same work. They also had lower measured productivity in

Table 5.1 How to determine the cost effectiveness of contingent labor

Row	Variable	$ Value
1	Wage and benefit rate or fee to staffing company	
2	Productivity (output rate or performance appraisal	
3	Unit labor cost or pay/performance appraisal)	
4	Training cost	
	Initial classroom training (direct + opportunity cost)	
	On-the-job training (direct + opportunity cost)	
	Learning-by-doing (opportunity cost)	
	Continuing training (direct + opportunity cost)	
5	Unrecovered training cost (total training cost from Row 4 less recovered training cost, which is training cost recovery rate × time on job after training)	
6	Cost effectiveness for contingent labor (unit labor cost saving after training less unrecovered training cost from Row 5)	

Source: S. D. Nollen and H. Axel (1996), *Managing Contingent Workers: How to Reap the Benefits and Reduce the Risks.* (New York: AMACOM).

Notes: Comparisons can be made to regular employees for wage and benefit rate, productivity, and unit labor cost.

Not all types of training will take place in every work unit.

Training cost recovery rate is the value of output produced by the trained worker less the wages and benefits paid.

two cases (no measurements were taken in the third case), but their unit labor cost was still about 5 to 6 percent lower. Training costs ranged from less than $300 to more than $2,000 per worker in the three cases, and time spent on the job varied from an average of 7 to 14 months. Training costs were not recovered in two of the three cases, and contingent workers were not cost-effective in one or perhaps both of these cases (see Table 5.2 for details).

To conclude that contingent labor is not cost-effective is not to conclude that it should not be used. Even when contingent workers cost more than regular employees, the company may have a flexibility need that contingent workers meet. The extra cost of contingent labor in this case is the price of achieving flexibility, which may still be a better alternative than layoffs and overtime—or better than turning down business, missing deadlines at peak times, or paying for idle regular workers during slack times.

Table 5.2 Cost effectiveness of contingent labor in three work units

Variable	*Company A*	*Company B*	*Company C*
Type of contingent worker	Part-time employees on payroll	Temporaries from staffing company	Temporaries from staffing company
Type of work	Data entry in backroom	Data entry in backroom	Electronics assembly
Wages and benefits or agency fees compared to regular employees	14% less	12% less	16% less
Productivity compared to regular employees	8% less	7% less	no measure; team-based production
Unit labor cost compared to regular employees	6% less	5% less	16% less if productivity equal
Training cost per new contingent workers	> $ 900	< $ 300	> $ 2,000
Training payback period	20 months	5 months	12 months
Average time on the job	14 months	7 months	8 months
Is training cost recovered?	no	yes	no
Is contingent labor cost-effective?	no	yes	maybe

Source: S. D. Nollen and H. Axel (1996), *Managing Contingent Workers: How to Reap the Benefits and Reduce the Risks.* (New York: AMACOM).

Improving Cost-Effectiveness

To improve the cost-effectiveness of contingent workers, managers can try to increase their productivity, cut back on training, or lengthen their tenure with the company. But these options often have the drawback of added cost.

Raising productivity is hard to do and costs money. Managers can try to recruit people with better skills if they are available in the labor market, or they can turn to staffing companies that may be able to supply more productive workers. Both of these options are likely to raise compensation rates.

Policies on pay and benefits can also be used to improve performance. A pay-for-performance or incentive pay scheme could replace straight wage payments that are equal for all. Or, using opposite causal reasoning, a policy of paying higher (above-market) wages and benefits in some situations could be used to attract better workers with higher productivity.

Raising workers' effort is another way to raise productivity. Effort can be attributed to many sources, among them commitment and equitable rewards. Contingent workers are unlikely to show high commitment since it is not reciprocated by the company. If the contingent workforce is the entry port into regular employment, however, some of these workers may put high effort into their jobs in order to improve their chances for moving into the regular workforce. In some cases, commitment is not an issue. Specialized high-level professionals who are independent contractors are likely to work hard because they are committed to their profession; commitment to the company is unimportant. And for some jobs, for example, jobs that are highly structured and machine paced, commitment is not very critical to performance.

Providing equitable rewards is another way to improve effort and productivity. Equity does not require equality. For example, employers can provide a wage premium to contingent workers instead of offering benefits, which may be complicated to administer. For young contingent workers, current earnings are likely to be more important than benefits, such as pensions, to be received in the future.

Training costs can be reduced by hiring already-trained workers or by shifting this responsibility to staffing companies, which in turn can supply clients with workers who meet their exact qualifications. Both options have the tradeoff of increasing compensation costs. Jobs can also be simplified so that less training is needed, leaving machines to do the training-intensive parts of the work. (But "dumbing down" jobs has its own limits from a human relations perspective.) Finally, a lower training wage can be paid to new contingent workers and raised when training is completed and full productivity is achieved.

To recover more training costs requires companies to induce trained workers to stay in that job or in the organization long enough to become a profitable investment. But long service and contingent work are a fundamental contradiction. Contingent workers are by definition short-term—by their own intent as well as the employer's. These workers have other interests or obligations—school, child care, spouse's situation, second careers—that cause them to leave of their own volition. For their part, organizations cannot afford to have permanent temps. Still, premature quits can be stemmed by designing benefits to appeal to some contingent workers (for example, partial tuition reimbursement); linking pay to time on the job; providing definite short-term contracts; and hiring contingent workers into regular jobs.

Using Fewer Contingent Workers

Using fewer contingent workers can also improve the company's cost-benefit position if these workers are not cost effective. Overuse of contingent workers tends to occur in downsizing companies, as noted earlier. Once brought in to replace lost talent, their numbers are likely to creep up over time without regard to any flexibility purpose they may have been expected to serve.

To use fewer contingent workers, given no overuse at the start, requires companies to reduce their need for workforce flexibility or to achieve it in other ways. Alternative forms of flexibility may be the easier route to follow. Organizations can consider work schedule options for regular employees. These can include work sharing for all employees during temporary slack periods to reduce labor input; variable work hours for regular part- or full-time workers within defined limits that are agreed to by manager and worker and respond to company needs to add and subtract labor hours; and work-year contracts that allow an uneven distribution of work hours over the year.

Companies need to recognize, however, that only some regular employees will want or be able to vary their work hours to meet their employer's needs because they are constrained by the time schedule of other aspects of their lives, such as carpools and day care. And only some regular employees are likely to tolerate the uncertainty of earnings that might vary with significant swings in their work schedule. But even a small margin of additional flexibility from the core workforce can go a long way toward taking the pressure off the need for a contingent workforce. For example, suppose contingent workers make up 15 percent of a company's total labor input and core employment accounts for 85 percent. Then if labor input needs to be reduced temporarily by, say, 15 percent, that target can be reached by eliminating all contingent workers. Alternatively, the company could adopt work sharing and reduce the hours of full-time core employees by just four (from 40 to 36 hours per week), which results in a 10 percent reduction in labor hours. Such a move would take care of two-thirds of the required cutback.

A different approach to getting flexibility from the core workforce is to use functional flexibility as a partial substitute for numerical flexibility. Functional flexibility refers to the ability of employees to perform a variety of tasks and do several types of jobs. In a large company with multiple products and production processes, it is possible for periods of temporarily weak demand for labor in one work unit to be partially offset by strong demand for labor elsewhere in the organization. Instead of bringing contingent workers in to match workload fluctuations and then discharging them when demand weakens, companies can move workers internally. Such an approach requires workers to be cross-trained so that they are able to handle different assignments.

Accounting for Other Potential Costs

A cost consideration that many companies are aware of, but do not always factor into their decision making about contingent labor, lies in the area of their legal responsibilities toward contingent workers. Their obligations and potential liability vary according to different relationships they have with these workers in the eyes of the law. For example, companies are almost always under obligation to contingent workers as the job-site employer; they often share responsibilities as a joint employer with the staffing company; and, in some instances, they are in fact the employer of record for individuals they do not consider their employees.

As the job-site employer, companies have responsibility under OSHA (Occupational Health and Safety Administration) and Title VII to maintain working conditions that are safe and nondiscriminatory. As a result, even though a third party is used to supply contingent workers and is their employer of record, the client company has responsibility for the work environment not only for its employees but for external workers as well. The Americans with Disabilities Act, for example, which does not explicitly delineate the job-site employer's responsibilities, has implications for the client company to provide reasonable accommodation for disabled contingent workers since it is in the best position to modify the physical environment or the tasks to be performed by these workers.

On a related issue, a study of safety issues in the petrochemical industry (Kochan, Smith, Wells, & Rebitzer, 1994) revealed that inadequate training and lack of supervision of contract workers in high-risk jobs can lead to increased accidents and dangerous working conditions at the job site. In this instance, the study suggested that managers who were eager to avoid joint employer liability did not provide the necessary oversight and training of contract workers that might have prevented accidents.

Joint employer relationships with a staffing company are determined by the amount of control an organization retains over its contingent workers. Practically speaking, almost all companies maintain some control over these workers since they typically provide the day-to-day supervision and determine the work to be done. Beyond this, however, a company may demonstrate additional control, for example, by determining hiring criteria or participating in the recruitment process, by setting pay rates or controlling compensation payments, or by retaining the right to discipline or discharge the worker. As a rule, the more a company chooses to control its contingent workers, the more likely it will be judged a joint employer with the staffing company and the more likely it will be considered liable when a violation of the law occurs. Companies may also be liable for illegal acts of a staffing company when it has been determined that it knew or should have known of these acts but did nothing to stop them.

Another major area of concern for employers revolves around independent contractors or, more specifically, employees who are misclassified by companies as independent contractors in order to avoid employment tax payments and withholding requirements. The Internal Revenue Service has stepped up scrutiny of this category of contingent workers, giving particular attention to certain industries (such as high-tech businesses and "temp-intensive" industries) where significant numbers of independent contractors are concentrated. Government interest in this issue stems from concern about tax revenues lost when a company misclassifies workers as independent contractors and does not withhold income tax payments. In 1996, for example, misclassification is projected to cost the federal government in excess of $2 billion in terms of uncollected tax revenues (Coopers & Lybrand, 1994). If these workers are reclassified as employees, the company faces stiff penalties in the form of back taxes and accumulated interest. Companies found to have intentionally disregarded withholding and 1099 form filing face additional penalties.

While legal challenges involving contingent workers do not necessarily result in major losses for the organization, they are certainly a cost consideration—at the very least in time spent responding to the complaint. In addition, since few employers are eager to go to court because of the adverse publicity, the possible setting of precedents in case law, and the threat of big awards to the plaintiff from a potentially unfriendly jury, many of these complaints are settled out of court. Thus, from the company's perspective, the best way to avoid problems—and costs—is to be as well informed as possible about the legal ramifications of contingent employment arrangements. In the end, employers may find that contingent staffing relationships present more complications, and thus less of an advantage to the organization, than they anticipated.

Maximizing the Benefits, Minimizing the Costs

Contingent employment is likely to remain a significant component of the workforce, and companies are likely to continue and, in some cases, expand their use of these workers. But contingent work is a flawed strategy. Sometimes its benefits to organizations are less than imagined, and its costs more than expected. To take advantage of the benefits of contingent labor and avoid significant costs, employers need to consider the following:

- Have sound goals for using contingent workers. Be clear about what the organization wishes to accomplish. Is it workforce flexibility? protecting core workers? screening candidates for regular employment? acquiring special skills? How important are the costs associated with contingent work arrangements?
- Develop policy guidelines for managers regarding use of temporary, part-time, and contract workers. Clarify whether or not these workers are to be separated from core employees in terms of the types of jobs they do, their conditions of work, and their access to core employment. Make sure managers understand the appropriate uses of these workers and their responsibilities in hiring and managing them.
- Establish a system for monitoring or controlling the numbers and costs of contingent workers, as well as the length of time on the

job, in work units where they are likely to be most heavily used. Conduct cost-effectiveness tests in these units. Maintain centralized records in business units or at the corporate level.
- Know the potential legal liabilities the company faces with different types of contingent work and communicate these issues to managers.

Contingent work is at the center of the radically changing relationship between organizations and workers. It is an integral part of business strategy. It accomplishes its main purpose of providing workforce flexibility. Whether it does so cost-effectively for the employer, or whether flexibility or another objective is of significantly greater importance to the organization, depends on managerial decisions.

CHAPTER SIX

New Systems of Work and New Workers

Robert Drago

T he U.S. economy appears to be headed in a variety of contradictory directions. While managers of major corporations create family-responsive policies on the one hand, those same managers expand the domain of "family-unfriendly" contingent work arrangements with the other (Christensen, this volume). Very differently, some of America's largest corporations (for example, IBM, General Motors, and Hewlett-Packard) espouse the values of employee commitment and loyalty while simultaneously downsizing a substantial portion of their employees.

Given these circumstances, even the most casual observer must wonder if there is any systematic direction to these initiatives or if, instead, the economy is in a period of experimentation. Following Eileen Appelbaum and Rosemary Batt (1994) and David Levine and Laura Tyson (1990), it is perhaps most reasonable to take the intermediate view that coherent patterns of employment relations and work practices are emerging, but within a context of experimentation.

The specific relationships of interest here concern high-performance workplaces and contingent work, and the issue is whether there are patterns to these relationships or instead a hodgepodge of unrelated practices. The central question I address is whether practices associated with high-performance workplaces exist in tandem with contingent work arrangements. Given evidence that both phenomena are expanding at present (see Osterman, 1994; Spalter-Roth & Hartmann, this volume), the answer to this question can potentially shed much light on the future of work and the economy. For example, it may be that high-performance work practices dictate that firms avoid contingent work arrangements. If high-performance workplaces require a committed and loyal workforce

The author thanks Iain Campbell, John S. Heywood, Jane Slaughter, Mark Wooden, and the editors for valuable advice, and the Australian Department of Industrial Relations for providing the data.

and contingent work undercuts commitment, then the practices will not coexist in the same workplace. Alternatively, high-performance workplaces might be consistent with contingent work arrangements. Core workers may view the presence of secondary, contingent workers as ensuring job security for the core. Given the intense interest these two trends have attracted, it is surprising that little effort has been made so far to connect them. What follows represents an initial effort to fill this gap.

As highlighted earlier in this book, there is substantial debate over the definition and extent of contingent work (Cohany et al., this volume; Spalter-Roth & Hartmann, this volume). These same difficulties afflict the literature on high-performance workplaces (Appelbaum & Batt, 1994; Levine & Tyson, 1990; Lawler, Mohrman, & Ledford, 1992; Osterman, 1994). To cut through these issues, we define and operationalize the terms in a multiplicity of ways. The minimal definition of contingent work used here concerns employment relations with little or no job security that was provided by economists at the Bureau of Labor Statistics (BLS) (Cohany et al., this volume). An expanded definition includes part-time employment, temporary agency workers, subcontractors, and home workers, all categories where workers are likely to be viewed by the corporation as "costs" instead of valued employees (Barker & Christensen, Chapter 1, this volume). High-performance workplaces are also difficult to define, so again multiple definitions are employed. As an initial indicator, we consider employee involvement (EI) practices emphasizing teamwork since these are included in virtually all research as an important element of high-performance workplaces. We also consider job security, as this is also considered a critical ingredient for high-performance workplaces by many researchers. The question of job security, however, is central to understanding both contingent work and high-performance workplaces, so is treated with some caution. Finally, as Appelbaum and Batt (1994) argue, there are at least two paths to high performance; we consider both "workplace transformation" and the "disposable workplace" (described below) as such paths, and we examine the linkages between these paths and contingent work.

The policy stakes involved in the present exercise are significant. If high-performance workplaces are consistent with contingent work, then there is every reason to believe that both phenomena will enjoy continuing growth and success. Efforts to promote practices supportive of high-performance workplaces would simultaneously support further expansion of contingent work, and efforts to reduce the economy's reliance on contingent work may reduce the potential for high-performance workplaces and, by implication, the competitiveness of the economy. On the other hand, if high-performance workplaces are inconsistent with contingent work, then efforts to promote high-performance work practices will undermine the extent of contingent work and, by the same logic, restrictions on contingent work will promote high-performance workplaces.

The analysis below helps to shed light on these issues by examining the empirical relationship between high-performance workplaces and contingent work using the Australian Workplace Industrial Relations Survey, or AWIRS. While the Australian and U.S. settings are far from identical, no currently existing U.S. data set aside from Osterman's is adequate for this task. Furthermore, so long as differences in underlying conditions are acknowledged and accounted for, it will still be possible to draw out conclusions relevant to the United States.

The first section below introduces various possible causal arguments by considering the experience of one high-performance workplace—the Saturn automobile factory—and the role of contingent work there. Building on this discussion, the second section outlines methods for creating high-performance workplaces and connects these to contingent work. The third section shifts our focus to Australia's unique system of industrial relations, to the AWIRS, and to the extent of contingent work found in the AWIRS data. The fourth section outlines various indicators for high-performance workplaces and tests the empirical relationship between these indicators and contingent work. The fifth section provides a brief summary of the results, policy conclusions, and relevant qualifications.

The Saturn Experience

We begin with a look at one high-performance workplace: General Motors' highly touted Saturn automobile factory. Saturn is virtually dripping with employee involvement, or EI, one signal of a high-performance workplace. Since the project was conceptualized in 1982, the United Automobile Workers (UAW) union local has been intimately involved in decisions regarding virtually every aspect of Saturn, from the design of the car and the factory to personnel, marketing, training, and industrial relations. On the shop floor, work teams elect supervisors, determine who will be hired on to the team, change work processes as needed, and participate in firing and other disciplinary decisions as well. At higher levels, UAW representatives are closely involved in decisions concerning prospective Saturn dealerships, the choice of suppliers to Saturn, design changes in the automobile, and training programs (Bluestone & Bluestone, 1992; Rubenstein, Bennett, & Kochan, 1993).

EI is generally considered a hallmark of high-performance workplaces (Appelbaum & Batt, 1994; Levine & Tyson, 1990), so if we use EI as a measuring stick for high-performance workplaces, Saturn clearly falls into the category.[1]

Levine and Tyson (1990) consider job security another necessary ingredient for high-performance workplaces. How does Saturn fare on job security? The original Saturn agreement of 1985 set up a two-class system, with most workers enjoying complete job security except due to unforeseen or catastrophic events or severe economic conditions, while a second—contingent—group would have no job security. This arrangement echoes that of many Japanese firms which use the flexibility of a constellation of subcontracting firms to ensure the job security of the core workforce (Brown et al., 1993). When market conditions deteriorate, the contingent workforce can be let go and their jobs taken over by core workers while, conversely, during a temporary expansion, contingent workers will be added. As Kathleen Barker and Kathleen Christensen (Chapter 1, this volume) describe the logic, core workers, who are valued, work alongside contingent workers who are viewed as a cost. This logic suggests that *contingent workers support core-worker job security and are for that reason associated with high-performance workplaces.*

Two additional opportunities for contingent work are related to Saturn proper. First, most components are subcontracted out, and subcontracting firms might rely heavily on contingent workers. Second, workers engaged in cafeteria, janitorial, and delivery services at Saturn are subcontract workers not subject to the job security provisions of the Saturn agreement. While it is difficult to imagine cafeteria, janitorial, and delivery services being taken over by the core workforce to protect job security during a downturn, such subcontracting may nonetheless be associated with low wages and hence protect high core-worker wages by reducing the overall Saturn wage bill.

As things have worked out, the classlike distinctions envisioned in the original Saturn agreement have been largely if not entirely ameliorated. While 20 percent of core Saturn workers are not covered by the job

---

1. Note that I define EI as increasing worker participation in managerial, supervisory, and technical decisions relative to either the past or comparable settings elsewhere in the economy.

security clause, many if not all workers are not even aware of whether they fall within this 20 percent,[2] so neither management nor the UAW local are stressing the logic of job security for the core through contingent work at the periphery of Saturn. The treatment of some workers as a "cost," as Christensen and Barker describe it, is avoided at Saturn. Indeed, the UAW local has organized and now represents subcontract workers at Saturn, and the union leadership has used its involvement in management to ensure that most parts coming into Saturn are produced at UAW-organized plants (Rubenstein, Bennett, & Kochan, 1993). The latter strategy, in particular, suggests Saturn is not explicitly attempting to rely on contingent workers. That is, *high-performance practices may dictate the avoidance of contingent work arrangements* as management strives to create perceptions of job security, trust, and commitment on the part of all involved parties.[3]

Finally, Mike Parker and Jane Slaughter (1994) suggest that Saturn—like General Motors' other well-known example of a high-performance workplace, the NUMMI plant in California jointly run with Toyota—actually runs on job insecurity. Like Saturn, NUMMI has job security provisions in its contract but, as a NUMMI employee puts it, "The main thing we are concerned with is keeping our jobs"(55). Concerning Saturn proper, Parker and Slaughter claim that Saturn workers discount the job security provisions and that "the atmosphere is one of great fear for their jobs"(104). These arguments suggest that Saturn workers have been molded into a large team for high performance, but team members are motivated to cooperate with each other through threats of collective job insecurity. From the shop floor to top-level management, the entire Saturn "crew" may believe that they all sink or swim together. By implication, *high-performance workplaces may be consistent with employees being treated as collectively contingent.*

Within the story of Saturn we can therefore identify three possible linkages between high-performance workplaces and contingent work: (1) contingent workers may function as a cheap and flexible periphery, supporting core-worker job security and wages, and hence promoting high-performance workplaces; (2) contingent workers may be anathema to high-performance workplaces, undercutting the trust and long-term

2. Jane Slaughter provided this information in a telephone conversation with the author, September 1994.

3. Similarly, Susan Helper and Levine (1994) argue that automobile companies have moved toward long-term relationships with supplier so that worker participation within the companies meshes with the same phenomenon within supplier firms.

relationships required for success; or (3) high-performance workplaces may be associated with collective threats to employee job security, thereby making all workers appear contingent.

Recent research suggests it is no accident that we were able to draw diverse and contradictory linkages out of the Saturn experience, since there is now a loose consensus that there are multiple pathways to the high-performance workplace (Appelbaum & Batt, 1994; Osterman, 1994). I outline two of these paths below—workplace transformation and the disposable workplace—and then discuss their connections with contingent work. This discussion will put later empirical work on a firmer theoretical footing.

Two Models of High-Performance Workplaces

Before linking high-performance workplaces and contingent work, it is worth considering two specific models of high performance, "workplace transformation" and the "disposable workplace." Workplace transformation is reasonably well known (Appelbaum & Batt, 1994; Levine & Tyson, 1990; Osterman, 1994). The disposable workplace as a route to high performance is an idea I have developed in a series of theoretical, empirical, and historical papers (see Drago, Garvey, & Turnbull, 1996; Drago, 1996, 1997, respectively). The disposable workplace bears more than a passing resemblance to what Appelbaum and Batt (1994) label "American lean production." What follows draws heavily on the empirical analysis in Drago (1996).

The basic ideas informing the detailed descriptions immediately below are as follows: there are two roads to high performance, and both involve high levels of employee effort and involvement (EI) in the production process. One road, workplace transformation, motivates through job security and the creation of perceptions of trust, fairness, and commitment to both the enterprise and the individuals in the enterprise. The other road, the disposable workplace, motivates through collective insecurity, by creating a sense that employees and workplace managers are all part of a team pitted against the rest of the world.

Workplace Transformation

I have argued (Drago, 1996) that the workplace-transformation road to high performance will be marked by job security, profit sharing, egalitarian wage structures, guaranteed individual rights, union voice, high levels of worker training, internal promotions, large firm size, and flat hierarchies. Together these elements of workplace transformation should support EI and high levels of workplace performance.

The first four "ingredients" for workplace transformation listed above are drawn from Levine and Tyson (1990). *Job security* is required both to promote trust and to convince employees they will not work their way out of a job through high levels of performance and innovations in the production process. *Profit sharing* fosters high performance because workers receive a monetary return on their contributions. Profit sharing also causes wages to fluctuate with product market conditions and so facilitates job security. *Egalitarian wages* are required because they reduce conflict and foster teamwork. *Individual rights* such as grievance procedures are required to ensure that speaking the truth will not result in managerial retribution.

Appelbaum and Batt (1994) note that workplace transformation, as described by Levine and Tyson's four ingredients, is empirically associated with unions. Adrienne Eaton and Paula Voos (1992) attribute this phenomenon to *"union voice"* (Freeman & Medoff, 1984). A strong union voice supports workplace transformation by improving communications, trust, and perceptions of fairness. Furthermore, because the union provides a voice for workers, union involvement in the development of EI programs typically improves outcomes (Cooke, 1992; Drago, 1988). Voice is also linked to workplace transformation because unions typically promote Levine and Tyson's four ingredients.

An implication of job security is that it will foster long-term employment and hence motivate managers to provide, and workers to seek, *high levels of training* (Levine & Tyson, 1990:210–211). Long-term relations ensure that such investments are more likely to be recouped. Training in turn facilitates productivity and quality improvements.

Workplace transformation should also be related to *internal labor markets* with relatively *flat management structures,* such that promotions are mainly internal but occur infrequently. Such characteristics will enhance communication, trust, perceptions of fairness, and hence quality and productivity.

Firm size should be positively related to workplace transformation for two reasons. There may be economies of scale in the creation of workplace transformation, and in particular large firms may be able to better afford job security. Of course, transformed workplaces *per se* could then be large or small, but the relevant firm should be large.

Product market structure is ambiguously related to workplace transformation. Competition in output markets can provide the initial impetus for workplace transformation, but if conditions remain highly competitive then job security might be undermined (Appelbaum & Batt, 1994; Levine & Tyson, 1990).

As described by Barry Bluestone and Irving Bluestone (1992), Saturn fits nicely into this description of workplace transformation and has achieved high levels of performance as a result.

The Disposable Workplace

Empirical studies find that a key ingredient in workplace transformation—job security—is not usually associated with another key facet of high-performance workplaces, namely, EI programs (Drago, 1988; Eaton, 1994; Osterman, 1994). As of 1987, only 17 percent of U.S. managers with EI programs viewed job security as facilitating the program, a figure which fell to 9 percent by 1990 (Lawler, Mohrman, & Ledford, 1992:48). This is where the disposable workplace comes in.

The notion of the disposable workplace flows from the literature on rank-order tournaments (Lazear & Rosen, 1981). In this literature, the firm motivates worker effort through a tournament or contest which offers a fixed number of guaranteed promotions distributed to the best performers regardless of whether average performance is good or bad. While tournaments can generally motivate worker effort, they also encourage sabotage and discourage helping efforts (Drago & Turnbull, 1991), so they may not produce high levels of workplace performance.

It is possible to overcome these problems if the tournament is collective, pitting one workplace against another and forging workers and managers within each workplace into a cohesive team (Drago, Garvey, & Turnbull, 1996). That is, a collective tournament can align the interests of workers, supervisors, and managers, promoting high levels of effort and generally fostering intraplant cooperation.

To strengthen the incentives provided to each workplace "team," managers will push wages up for winners and down for losers, with the bottom limit on wages for losers set by job loss. Particularly when unemployment is high, the threat of losing one's job can keep employees performing at high levels.

The "disposable workplace" exists when a firm uses a collective tournament among workplaces with job loss for the losers. The strategy may be explicit (as is common in the automobile industry), but may frequently be implicit, with the firm pitting domestic against foreign plants or workplaces in one industry versus those in another.

Next, consider how the characteristics of disposable workplaces match up against those outlined earlier for workplace transformation. The disposable workplace relies upon job insecurity. Profit sharing should be absent since disposability depends on severing the interests of the firm and of the workplace. There is no obvious reason why wages would be equally or unequally distributed in the disposable workplace, or why individual rights would or would not appear. Both issues seem less relevant in the disposable workplace. By way of contrast, recall that workplace transformation dictates job security, profit sharing, wage equality, and individual worker rights.

Union voice should be negatively related to the disposable workplace. Managers and supervisors will listen to worker ideas in the disposable workplace regardless of union voice because the cost of not listening is job loss. Furthermore, to the extent that unions successfully provide Levine and Tyson's four ingredients for workplace transformation, the disposable workplace cannot emerge. In nonunion disposable workplaces, employees will find unions unattractive because union wage increases raise the probability of shutdown. Similarly, Parker and Slaughter (1994:105–106) argue that the UAW local at Saturn is relatively weak because its relations with other UAW locals are limited (largely by the unique nature of the Saturn contract) while the plant itself remains in competition with other GM plants.

Investments by the firm in the form of worker training should be more substantial under workplace transformation relative to the disposable workplace. Why train someone you plan to abandon? Nonetheless, managers in the disposable workplace maintain some interest in training because it enhances workers' ability to reduce costs and improve quality both directly and through EI programs. Therefore, the disposable workplace should exhibit above-average levels of training but less than that found in transformed workplaces.

Since the disposable workplace strategy reduces required levels of supervision and bureaucracy, it should yield flat managerial hierarchies. This does not, however, imply the existence of internal labor markets. Workers will not value promotions highly when they are temporary.

To strengthen the credibility of the shutdown threat, the workplace should be small and the firm large. To the extent a workplace represents a modest proportion of the corporation's investments, shutdown is less costly to the firm and opportunities for interplant competition are enhanced. Furthermore, a very large firm may only need a few shutdowns to produce a credible threat.

Product market competition will also support the disposable workplace, since competition reinforces corporate threats of collective job insecurity.

The disposable workplace—with high levels of employee involve-ment, a weak or nonexistent union, and collective job insecurity—is represented by Parker and Slaughter's (1994) description of Saturn. Both disposable workplaces and transformed workplaces should exhibit high levels of EI, be associated with large firms, and exhibit above-average levels of training, but they will diverge in other ways and particularly regarding job security.

Contingent Work and the High-Performance Workplace

We are now poised to pull together the relevant arguments concerning contingent work and high-performance workplaces. Recall that contin-gent work can be conceived most narrowly as concerning workers with little or no job security, while an expanded definition concerns workers likely to be treated as a cost factor rather than as valued employees. High-performance workplaces are defined minimally by EI, by job secu-rity at least for core workers, or by the characteristics of workplace trans-formation or the disposable workplace. How are these practices likely to fit together?

First consider contingent work as job insecurity and EI as a signal of high-performance workplaces. On the one hand, as Levine and Tyson (1990) argue, job security may be required for EI so that workers trust management and believe that improving productivity will not lead to job loss. On the other hand, as Clair Brown and her colleagues (1993) suggest from the experience of large Japanese corporations, it may be that a constellation of subcontracting firms with flexible employment supports job security for core workers, and hence their commitment to improving productivity and quality, often through EI programs. If we broaden the definition of contingent work to include all workers viewed as costs to the firm, similar arguments apply: if core workers believe that management sees them through the lens of the dollar, then they will not be committed to their work or the firm, whereas if they view the pres-ence of contingent workers as making it easier for the firm to support core worker jobs and wages, then contingent work might support EI and high performance among core workers. Note that with *any* of these arguments, job security for core workers, at least, is viewed as a require-ment for EI and the high-performance workplace.

Next consider job security as a hallmark of the high-performance work-place. The discussion immediately above suggests that high-performance workplaces might provide job security for core workers either by avoiding contingent workers or instead by hiring them. However, research on EI and job security suggests that job security for core workers might not be a necessary condition for high-performance workplaces (Lawler, Mohrman, & Ledford, 1992). Instead, the firm might motivate high levels of performance by creating disposable workplaces with job insecurity for core workers. In this case, the logic presented above gets turned on its head: high-performance firms which avoid contingent workers may do so to signal job insecurity for core workers, while those who employ contingent workers may be telling core employees that "your job is next."

Given these conflicting and contradictory possibilities, an empirical analysis could help us understand the relationship between high-performance workplaces and contingent work by addressing three questions. First, is there a net positive or negative relationship between a key element of high-performance workplaces—employee involvement—and contingent work? Second, is there a net positive or negative relationship between job security for core workers and contingent work arrangements? Third, if traditional, disposable, and transformed workplaces can be isolated, does one type or another rely more heavily on contingent workers? We now turn to relevant evidence.

The Pattern of Contingent Work in Australia

A glimpse of Australian industrial relations is provided here, then a look at the legal and practical meaning of contingent work in Australia (which is quite different from the United States). We conclude the section by looking at contingent work as described by the AWIRS data.

Australian industrial relations are unique but only a few relevant issues are discussed here.[4] Australia has historically been characterized by high levels of union density, centralized determination of wages and working conditions, and informal relations on the shop floor (Strauss, 1988). Government appointed tribunals hand down or ratify awards (the rough equivalent of collective bargaining agreements) and often assign jobs and workplaces to particular awards (and implicitly particular unions) through "conveniently belong to" and "roping-in" provisions in awards. Figures from the late 1980s find awards covering 85 percent of all employees, but only 40.5 percent of employees are union members (Drago, Wooden, & Sloan, 1992). Australia, like the United

4. For broader treatments, see Strauss, 1988; Callus et al., 1991; or Drago, Wooden, & Sloan, 1992.

States, has experienced increasing international competition (partly facilitated by tariff reductions) and declining union membership.[5]

The Status of Contingent Workers

For the most part, contingent workers do not provide a low-wage alternative to full-time permanent employment in Australia. In part, Australian government policies on pension and health care arrangements heavily limit such strategies. Pensions are portable since the government maintains an individual's account and health care is provided through a tax-funded single-payer system. Therefore, employers need not consider health care costs when hiring employees, nor is there a pension cost advantage to dismissing high-seniority employees and replacing them with contingent workers.

Australian unions have developed a unique and explicit distinction between "permanent" and "casual" employees through the awards system. Casual employees look very much like those which the BLS describes as contingent—they are employed "at will" (Cohany et al., this volume). Permanent employees receive award wage rates, nine or ten paid holidays per year, four weeks of paid vacation, paid sick leave, and due process rights in case of dismissal. Casual employees, who form the bulk of Australia's contingent workforce, typically receive none of these benefits. Instead, they usually receive 20 percent higher hourly wages relative to permanent employees in an equivalent position. The 20 percent wage loading is intended to equalize the hourly costs of hiring casual and permanent employees. Casual employees are often hired for a matter of days, weeks, or months. Though a small proportion will hold a position for even a decade, their casual status means that at-will dismissal is always a possibility. This distinction between casual and permanent employees provides a clear and powerful way to distinguish contingent employees in Australia using the definition of the BLS.

If we expand the definition of contingent work to include any workers who are likely to be treated as a cost, then part-time employees can be added. Part-time employees in Australia can be hired either on a permanent or casual basis, but they are typically casual. Part-time permanent employees are usually covered by awards and receive the same hourly pay and benefits (the latter prorated) as their full-time counterparts. As is the case for casual employees, employers who depend upon part-time employees receive at most a minimal cost advantage.

5. Note that the industrial relations system has changed dramatically since the data used here was collected.

Table 6.1 The extent of contingent work in Australia (commercial establishments with at least 20 workers)

Type of contingent work	Proportion of workers with characteristic	Proportion of female workers in category
Part-time, permanent employees	.052	.860
Part-time, casual employees	.154	.705
Full-time, casual employees	.036	.521
Subcontractors	.034	.160
Temporary agency workers	.008	.693
Home workers	.003	.756
Total contingent workers	.287	.601

Source: Australian Workplace Industrial Relations Survey (AWIRS), 1081 weighted observations at the workplace level.

Expanding the definition of contingent work further, it can take three additional forms in Australia: temporary help agency employees, subcontractors, and home workers. Employees associated with temporary help agencies are covered by awards, so they receive either the full entitlements of permanent employees or the wage loading for casual workers. As in the case of the United States (Gonos, this volume), the circumstances of subcontractors are less clear-cut because firms can reach agreements with self-employed contractors independently of the awards system.[6] Nonetheless, *employees* of subcontracting firms are covered by awards. Similarly, home workers might either function as independent contractors, and hence fall outside of the award system, or appear on the payroll of the firm and be covered by awards.

Six types of contingent workers can be identified in the AWIRS—part-time permanents, part-time casuals, full-time casuals, subcontractors, temporary agency workers and home workers—but later analysis is greatly simplified by focusing on only four groups. These include the sum of all contingent workers from the six categories, casual employees, part-time employees, and temporary help agency workers. The casual category (part-time plus full-time) captures workers directly hired into jobs which are explicitly insecure. Part-time employees capture the non-standard working time arrangements often associated with contingent work. Temporary help agency employees are indirect hires who lack job

6. This is a bit of an oversimplification, since legislation at the state or federal level can be used to supplement award conditions and can affect independent contractors as well. For example, Victorian legislation dictates that the system of workers compensation for injury cover independent contractors as well as employees under awards.

security at their current place of employment but might experience work continuity through their employing agency.

If we had to pick a single group out of these to view as more contingent than the others, my suspicion is that casual employees are the best candidate. These workers explicitly lack any job security and, unlike either temporary help agency or permanent part-time workers, firms may maintain only limited records on casuals, thus facilitating abuses such as underpayment of awards to this group.[7]

The AWIRS Data

This study draws on the Australian Workplace Industrial Relations Survey, which was modeled on the two Workplace Industrial Relations Surveys undertaken earlier in the United Kingdom.[8] The data was constructed from a sample of Australian workplaces with a least twenty employees administered between October 1989 and May 1990. A workplace was defined as a business establishment with a single geographical location, so a single firm might have many workplaces in the survey. The response rate was roughly 90 percent, yielding a sample of 2004 workplaces (see Callus et al., 1991, for more information).

Because the theoretical views outlined earlier apply to market economies, the sample is restricted to commercial workplaces, defined as "workplaces which undertake activity for the purposes of making a profit," thus reducing the usable sample to 1,453 workplaces. Of these commercial workplaces, 11.5 percent are owned by various levels of the Australian government. Such workplaces account for a substantial component of economic activity in Australia (for example, Australian Airlines, Qantas Airlines, and the Commonwealth Bank) and should be included in the sample.[9] Purging workplaces which did not respond to all pertinent questions resulted in a working sample of 1,081 workplaces.[10]

---

7. I thank Iain Campbell for suggesting this possibility in an e-mail to the author, March 3, 1995.

8. For a general description of the survey and results, see Callus et al., 1991.

9. Note that these are commercial operations in the usual sense of the word, since the government uses them to generate revenues and employees are covered by awards shared with the private sector. For example, Australian Airlines and the privately held Ansett Airlines have very similar awards.

10. The major culprits were questions on female employment, union density, occupational data, workplace employment, and the union voice variable (see discussion below). The "scqwt" weighting variables in the AWIRS is applied. Note that three further observations are missing on two variables (see Table 6.3). These observations are kept for other purposes so the cluster analysis from Drago (1996) can be used. Note that the sample was stratified, so the data employed here are weighted.

Contingent Work in the AWIRS Data

The 1,081 workplaces in our sample report total employment of 233,865. That total includes 6,406 part-time permanent employees, 20,275 part-time casuals, 5,695 full-time casuals, 7,089 subcontract employees, 1,480 agency workers, and 202 home workers. Weighting these figures permits economy-wide projections as shown in Table 6.1.[11] Around 29 percent of Australian employees are engaged in contingent work, with over half of these (above 15 percent of total employment) composed of part-time casuals. The second largest group, part-time permanents, represents slightly over 5 percent of employees, while full-time casuals and subcontractors each account for less than 4 percent. The temporary help industry and home work together account for around 1 percent of employees.

The real surprise in these numbers is the projected percentage of the Australian workforce classified as casual. Where the most liberal estimate of contingent work provided by the BLS for the U.S. is 4.9 percent (Cohany et al., this volume), in Australia we find a full 19 percent of employees classified as contingent according to the BLS definition. Given the relatively weaker incentives for firms to employ contingent workers in Australia and the cleaner legal definition of casuals in that country, it is at least plausible to suggest that the higher figures of Roberta Spalter-Roth and Heidi Hartmann (this volume) more accurately reflect the U.S. situation.

Less surprisingly, women are overrepresented among Australia's contingent workers. Women represent only 33.2 percent of full-time permanent employees, but as Table 6.1 indicates almost two-thirds of contingent workers are women. For the two largest categories of contingent work—part-time casuals and part-time permanents—women hold over two-thirds of the jobs, and only in subcontracting are women underrepresented.

Contingent Work and High-Performance Workplaces

Three gauges of high-performance work systems are analyzed below: employee involvement, job security, and the categories of transformed, disposable, and traditional workplaces. In each case we check for a positive, negative, or insignificant correlation with the four categories of

---

11. The projections are not random since the sample excludes employees in workplaces with less than twenty employees and those in the noncommercial public sector as well.

contingent work: the proportions of all contingent workers, casual employees, part-time employees, and temporary help agency workers.[12]

Employee Involvement

Employee relations managers are asked whether any of ten employee involvement practices exist at the workplace. The average percentage of contingent workers in workplaces where EI exists is listed in Table 6.2 (the proportion of contingent workers in workplaces without EI is given in parentheses). Where contingent work and EI go together statistically, the degree of significance is noted for the nonparenthesized figure. Where contingent work and EI tend to be found in different workplaces, the significance is noted for the parenthesized figure.

Considering the connection between EI and the sum of contingent workers, every significant relationship shows a lower incidence of contingent work arrangements where EI practices exist, implying that *firms with employee involvement tend to avoid the hiring of contingent workers*. For example, contingent workers are around 30 percent of the workforce where there are no quality circles programs or joint labor-management committees. Contingent workers make up only around 16 percent of the workforce where quality circles programs or joint labor-management committees exist.

As suggested earlier, casual workers arguably provide the best single gauge of contingent work in Australia. Here the connection (or lack thereof) with EI is more complex, as shown in the second column of Table 6/2. Figures for casual workers echo those for all contingent workers with respect to quality circles and joint committees, but casual workers are positively and significantly related to suggestion schemes, a daily walk around by a senior manager, and informal meetings with senior managers and employees. The pattern for part-time employees is broadly similar to that for casuals. Temporary help agency employees, however, break with the patterns just identified. Here we find strong positive and significant relationships with newsletters, meetings with senior managers or supervisors and employees, task forces, joint committees, and employee representatives on the board of directors.

---

12. The key theoretical arguments in this paper center on the question of whether contingent work and high performance are *consistent*. Correlation coefficients are appropriate given the theoretical approach. Nonparametric (Spearman) correlation coefficients (Seigel, 1956) are applied.

Table 6.2 Proportion of contingent workers where employee involvement practice exists (does not exist)

Employee involvement practice	All contingent workers	Casual workers	Part-time workers	Temporary help agency employees
Workplace newsletter	.263 (.305)[b]	.172 (.204)	.184 (.224)[a]	.009[b] (.006)
Meetings with senior managers and employees	.294 (.267)	.190[a] (.185)	.219[b] (.178)	.009[b] (.005)
Meetings with supervisors and employees	.246 (.334)[a]	.156 (.231)	.170 (.250)	.008[b] (.007)
Task forces	.175 (.307)[b]	.096 (.207)[b]	.108 (.225)[b]	.012[b] (.007)
Daily walk around by senior manager	.282 (.297)	.194[b] (.155)	.205 (.205)	.007 (.012)[b]
Joint consultative labor-management committee	.149 (.298)[b]	.087 (.199)[b]	.080 (.217)[b]	.008[b] (.008)
Quality circles/productivity groups	.169 (.303)[b]	.095 (.203)[a]	.104 (.221)[b]	.005 (.008)
Suggestion scheme	.317 (.271)	.218[a] (.176)	.249[b] (.187)	.007 (.008)
Employee reps on board of directors	.299 (.284)	.123 (.191)	.224 (.204)	.012[a] (.008)
Regular social functions	.244 (.322)[a]	.145 (.227)[a]	.175 (.232)	.010[b] (.005)

Source: AWIRS, 1081 weighted observations.
Note: Two-tailed test for significance of Spearman correlation coefficients, significance attached to figure which is significantly above the other.
[a]significant at 5% level.
[b]significant at 1% level.

If we view EI as an indicator of high-performance workplaces, there are at least three reasonable interpretations of these results. First, as suggested by the results for all contingent workers, it may be that high-performance workplaces are inconsistent with contingent work. Second, using a stricter definition of contingent work—casual employment—it could be argued that contingent work is associated with more faddish and less substantive moves toward the high-performance workplace (for example, meetings between managers and employees, a daily walk around by a manager, and suggestion schemes), but that more substantive forms of EI are again inconsistent with contingent work. Third, while temporary help agencies are projected to account for less than

3 percent of contingent workers, their positive association with EI might signal a trend toward high-performance workplaces that rely on temporary workers. Stated baldly, our analysis of EI and contingent work does little to resolve the question of the connection between high-performance workplaces and contingent work.

Job Security

I concluded earlier that to the extent that high-performance workplaces require job security, this security is clearly intended for core workers. Where present, contingent workers would be treated separately since they are generally viewed by management as holding insecure jobs. Regarding core workers, the AWIRS includes four questions relevant to job security. First, were there layoffs of permanent employees during the previous year? Second, are there many competitors in the market for the workplace's major product or service? Third, was market demand down during the previous year? And, fourth, is demand for the work-place's major product or service largely unpredictable? In all cases, positive responses indicate job insecurity for core workers.

Parallel to Table 6.2, Table 6.3 shows the average percentage of contingent workers where respondents answer job insecurity questions in the affirmative (percentages for respondents answering negatively are shown in parentheses). Layoffs are inversely related to contingent work. For example, workplaces with no layoffs averaged a 31 percent contingent employee base, while workplaces that experienced layoffs maintained a 22 percent contingent base. This finding suggests that contingent workers are associated with workplaces where jobs for core workers are secure, as suggested by Brown's analysis of Japanese workplaces (Brown et al., 1993). That is, contingent workers may serve as a protective buffer for core workers.[13]

Results for the competition variable suggest, to the contrary, that contingent workers are typically employed in highly competitive industries (with the exception of temporary agency workers). Even though this result looks quite different from the finding with regard to layoffs, it is possible to provide the same interpretation as above: jobs are insecure in such industries and workplaces, and contingent workers serve as a buffer for core workers.

---

13. It is possible that workplaces experiencing layoffs had large numbers of contingent workers prior to the layoffs, but the magnitude of the differential—a 10 percent difference in workplace employment of contingent workers—is so large that this seems implausible.

Table 6.3 Proportion of contingent workers where jobs are insecure (secure)

Job security characteristic	All contingent workers	Casual workers	Part-time workers	Temporary help agency employees
Layoffs during previous year	.218 (.310)[b]	.136 (.209)[a]	.124 (.236)[b]	.013 (.006)
Many competitors in output market	.334[b] (.228)	.236[b] (.134)	.245[b] (.159)	.007 (.008)[b]
Market demand down during previous year	.232 (.295)[a]	.154 (.195)	.170 (.212)[a]	.006 (.008)
Market demand unpredictable	.252 (.297)	.146 (.202)[a]	.164 (.219)[a]	.012 (.007)

Source: AWIRS, 1081 weighted observations for layoff and competitors, 1078 for demand down and unpredictable variables.

Note: Two-tailed test for significance of Spearman correlation coefficients, significance attached to figure which is significantly above the other.

[a]significant at 5% level.

[b]significant at 1% level.

Figures concerning demand reductions in the previous year and unpredictable product markets seem to contradict the other job security findings. Here we find significant relationships linking contingent workers to workplaces where markets are stable or improving, and not to situations where jobs are insecure due to poor market conditions. These findings suggest that contingent workers do *not* serve as a buffer for core worker job security. Instead, such employment arrangements are used as a stopgap to meet growing product demand, or perhaps they are part of more sophisticated employment systems which are used by firms and workplaces with substantial resources. Again, I am led to conclude that job security for core workers, as an indicator of high-performance workplaces, sheds little light on the question of how these workplaces are linked to contingent work.

Transformed and Disposable Workplaces

Two explanations for the inconsistent pattern of results from our attempts to link contingent work to either EI or core-worker job security are suggested by the discussion at the beginning of this chapter. Either we are witnessing a period of experimentation, such that coherent patterns have yet to emerge, or there are multiple paths to high performance, and these are conflated in the analyses of EI and of job security. We now turn to the latter possibility.

The theoretical characteristics of transformed, disposable and traditional workplaces, outlined earlier, are summarized in parentheses in Table 6.4. Workplace transformation should rank high (+) on job security (no layoffs during previous year), worker rights (grievance procedures), profit sharing, union membership, union voice, formal training, on-the-job training, internal labor markets (percentage of managers promoted from within workplace), firm size (proxied by the workplace being owned by a multinational firm). Workplace transformation should rank low (–) on hierarchy (proportion of managers), while the number of workplace employees and the degree of competition in the output market is not predicted (0 or intermediate rank).

Quite differently, the disposable workplace should rank low (–) on job security (no layoffs), profit sharing, union membership, union voice, hierarchy (managerial proportion), and employee numbers at the workplace. The disposable workplace should rank high (+) on firm size (multinational) and competition in the output market, and rank at an intermediate level on the training variables.

These theoretical predictions allow us to assign workplaces to either the transformed, disposable, or traditional workplace categories. The specific variables used to do so are described in an appendix to this chapter. The method used for classification is confirmatory cluster analysis. Cluster analysis is a statistical procedure originally designed to classify flowers using a series of characteristics such as color, smell, height and size. With confirmatory cluster analysis, we tell the computer what characteristics we expect to see running together (parentheses in Table 6.4) and the process attempts to locate workplaces that have all of the relevant characteristics (see Cutcher-Gershenfeld, 1991, for further explanation).

A cluster analysis from Drago 1996 is reported in Table 6.4, where numeric figures give the average characteristics of workplaces within each category.[14] Note from the weighted number of observations at the bottom of the table that the cluster analysis assigned over one-half of workplaces to the "traditional" category, leaving under 30 percent as

14. Note that the traditional category might better be labeled a "residual" category since it will pick up any workplace types that are neither transformed or disposable. Note also that, as the Saturn experience suggests, cluster analysis is consistent with the notion that most firms fall along a multidimensional continuum between traditional, transformed, and disposable workplaces. Although not reported here, the vast majority of differences between the categories are statistically significant at conventional levels (see Drago, 1996).

Table 6.4 Average workplace characteristics, categories from cluster analysis
(predicted size in parentheses)

Variables	Workplace transformation category	Disposable workplace category	Traditional workplace category
No layoffs during previous year	.730 (+)	.394 (−)	.830 (0)
Profit sharing	.131 (+)	.054 (−)	.070 (0)
Grievance procedure	.773 (+)	.242 (0)	.330 (0)
Union membership proportion	.773 (+)	.194 (−)	.428 (0)
Union voice	2.37 (+)	.188 (−)	.495 (0)
Formal training	.774 (+)	.551 (0)	.339 (−)
On-the-job training	.611 (+)	.411 (0)	.160 (−)
Proportion of managers	.057 (−)	.084 (−)	.090 (+)
Promotion opportunities	.749 (+)	.320 (0)	.473 (0)
Multinational	.194 (+)	.456 (+)	.020 (−)
Employees at workplace	180.8 (0)	68.7 (−)	65.2 (0)
Market competition	.468 (0)	.650 (+)	.516 (0)
Number of observations in category (weighted #)	435 (5339)	171 (3440)	475 (10171)

Source: AWIRS, 1081 weighted observations.

"transformed" and under 20 percent as "disposable."[15] As expected,
while 73 percent of transformed workplaces avoided layoffs during the
previous year, only 39 percent of disposable workplaces did so. Similarly, while 13 percent of transformed workplaces exhibit profit sharing,

15. This result is a little surprising, since Paul Osterman (1994) finds over 36 percent
of U.S. workplaces can be classified as transformed. However, given the different method-
ologies employed here and in Osterman's study, it is possible that some of the workplaces
he classifies as transformed in fact belong in the disposable category.

only 5 percent of disposable workplaces do so. Also consistent with predictions, grievance procedures, union membership, union voice, levels of formal and on-the-job training, and internal promotions of managers are substantially higher in transformed workplaces, while disposable workplaces rank lowest on grievance procedures, union membership, union voice, and internal promotions. An intermediate level of training provision in disposable workplaces is also found, and disposable workplaces are themselves very small (particularly relative to transformed workplaces) and are likely to be owned by a large, multinational firm.

The resulting workplace categories are linked to the incidence of contingent work in Table 6.5. The sign and significance of correlation coefficients are provided in parentheses while numeric figures show the proportion of contingent workers in the category. For example, according to the broadest definition of contingent work, 22.4 percent of employees in transformed workplaces are contingent, 31.8 percent of employees in disposable workplaces are contingent, and 30.9 percent of employees in traditional workplaces can be labeled as contingent.

The figures in Table 6.5 are generally consistent with the possibilities that (1) contingent workers are related to job insecurity for all employees, (2) transformed workplaces avoid contingent workers to maintain job security, and (3) disposable workplaces are associated with job insecurity and hence contingent workers.

In terms of precise figures, transformed workplaces employ significantly fewer contingent workers in total, over four percentage points less than the overall average of 28.5 percent (see Table 6.1). Disposable workplaces employ significantly more contingent workers and are over

Table 6.5 The proportion of contingent workers in transformed, disposable and traditional workplaces

Form of contingent work	Transformed workplaces	Disposable workplaces	Traditional workplaces
All contingent workers	.224(–)[b]	.318(+)[a]	.309
Casual workers	.134(–)[b]	.234(+)[a]	.204
Part-time workers	.151(–)[b]	.224(+)[a]	.229
Temporary help agency employees	.004	.015	.008

Source: AWIRS, 1081 weighted observations.
Note: Two-tailed test for significance of Spearman correlation coefficients for transformed as opposed to average and disposable as opposed to average workplaces.
[a]significant at 5% level
[b]significant at 1% level

three percentage points above the average. Figures for part-time workers reflect this same pattern and are significant as well. Results for casual employees are perhaps most striking, since casuals fit the most narrow definition of contingent work. The casual component of the workforce in disposable workplaces is a full ten percentage points higher than in transformed workplaces. Results for temporary help agency workers exhibit the same ordering as the others, but are not significant.

If both transformed and disposable workplaces offer viable routes to high performance, and if the latter is consistent with contingent work, it should also be the case that contingent work and employee involvement coexist within disposable workplaces. That is, the job insecurity represented by contingent work should serve as one more signal to employees in disposable workplaces that productivity and quality improvements (largely through EI) are the tickets to avoiding job loss. Results provided in Drago 1996 support this assertion. There it is found that both transformed and disposable workplaces are significantly more likely to exhibit a variety of EI practices relative to traditional workplaces. Compared to traditional workplaces, transformed and disposable workplaces are around ten percentage points more likely to have informal meetings with senior management and employees, informal supervisor-employee meetings, and suggestion systems; and they are over five percentage points more likely to exhibit quality circles. Similarly, a direct test for whether EI practices and contingent work are connected within disposable workplaces reveals that none of the significant negative correlations reported in Table 6.2 remain except that contingent workers broadly defined are negatively connected with employee representation on the board of directors (no surprise here). Indeed, three of the significant positive correlations found for temporary agency workers and EI remain (those for informal employee meetings with senior managers, meetings with supervisors, and task forces). These results confirm my supposition that employee involvement and contingent work are both at home in the disposable workplace.

Discussion

This chapter examined the connection between contingent work and high-performance workplaces using the Australian Workplace Industrial Relations Survey. A major advantage of the data is the Australian distinction between "casual" workers, who have no job security and extremely limited rights on the job, and "permanent" employees, who cannot be terminated at will by managers. Casual workers are clearly contingent as the term is used by the BLS (Cohany et al., this volume). Contingent work was then broken into four categories: all contingent workers as broadly defined, casual employees, an overlapping group holding part-time positions, and temporary help agency workers or indirect temporary hires. Over 28 percent of workers in the sample are contingent in the broadest sense, and 19 percent are casual employees. Given the much weaker incentives to employ contingent workers in Australia relative to the United States, these figures provide indirect support for the higher figures for U.S. contingent work provided by Spalter-Roth and Hartmann (this volume) as compared to the BLS.

We considered employee involvement and, alternatively, job security for core workers as central to high-performance work systems; we tested for any association with contingent work, but no strong patterns emerged.

We then entertained the possibility that the apparent absence of patterns was due to the conflation of two distinct paths to the high-performance workplace—workplace transformation and the disposable workplace. Workplace transformation is based on job security, worker rights, a sharing of the monetary fruits of the workplace, and a strong union voice, and should further be associated with high levels of training, flat managerial hierarchies, internal labor markets, and EI. The disposable workplace depends upon motivating workers to cooperate through threats to close the entire workplace if high performance levels are not achieved. Using results from Drago 1996, the sample was split into three groups—transformed, disposable, and traditional workplaces. Both transformed and disposable workplaces are significantly more likely to exhibit employee involvement practices relative to traditional workplaces, and results reported in Drago 1996 suggest that both paths offer a route to high performance.

The major result of the study is the finding that transformed workplaces avoid contingent work arrangements while disposable workplaces rely heavily on them. Using the most narrow definition of contingent work as casual employment, we find just over 20 percent of employees in traditional workplaces are casuals, just over 13 percent of employees in transformed workplaces exhibit the characteristic, but over 23 percent of employees in disposable workplaces are casuals. Moreover, this patterns holds for each definition of contingent work used in this study.

At least in Australia, these results are consistent with the conclusion that contingent workers signal job insecurity for all employees, and do not generally serve as a buffer for core employee job security. By implication, contingent work arrangements are inconsistent with the workplace transformation road to high performance but fit easily into organizations using the disposable workplace strategy to achieve high performance.

Of course, caveats are required here. First, it is not clear that the results carry over to the United States (more on this below). Second, further research should be undertaken to confirm or invalidate these results. Third, there is no causal analysis here so we do not know, for example, whether contingent work arrangements invite attempts to make the workplace disposable or vice versa. Therefore, the results and conclusions here should be treated with some caution.

If the results reported here do stand up to further scrutiny, the relevant policy conclusions are straightforward. First, policies that restrict contingent work arrangements may help to promote workplace transformation, as suggested by Appelbaum (1993). Similarly, policies supporting worker job security or a strong union voice in the workplace might simultaneously undercut the expansion of contingent work and advance workplace transformation. These conclusions are not surprising. More novel is the implication that government efforts to facilitate employee involvement initiatives (e.g., Levine & Helper, 1993) could induce employers to take the low road of the disposable workplace and expand contingent work arrangements. More precisely, the analysis here suggests that an increasing incidence of employee involvement programs could either undercut or support contingent work arrangements.

The major unanswered question here concerns the applicability of these Australian findings to the United States. Most concretely, it would be difficult to replicate this analysis using U.S. data because the casual-permanent distinction found in Australia is missing here. Brushing this (admittedly substantial) empirical issue aside, I suspect the main results found in the present analysis would hold in U.S. data but that the disposable workplace strategy would appear as far more prevalent than workplace transformation. U.S. union membership is far lower than in Australia, and job insecurity—due to the at-will employment doctrine—is more widespread in the United States. Both conditions tend to favor the disposable workplace strategy. If these conjectures are correct, then the United States may witness the simultaneous expansion of high-performance workplaces and contingent work arrangements through the disposable workplace strategy. That is, Parker and Slaughter's (1994) pessimistic assessment of Saturn may tell us more about where the United States is heading than Bluestone and Bluestone's (1992) more optimistic view.

APPENDIX
Description of variables for cluster analysis

Proxies for the relevant characteristics are as follows, where most are dummy variables (yes = 1, no = 0). The variable means and standard deviations are listed after each proxy. Job security is represented by a dummy for No Layoffs during Previous Year (.723, .448). Profit Sharing (.084, .278) is positive where a program exists. Because workplace data is used, an adequate proxy for wage equality is not available, so this characteristic is ignored. Employee rights are indicated by whether a formal Grievance Procedure exists in the workplace (.439, .496). To proxy union voice, Union Membership is the proportion of union members in each workplace (.482, .377). A more precise indicator is constructed from a set of questions which ask union delegates whether "management 'always' consult[s] with your union on" issues of employment levels, wage increases, physical working conditions, occupational health and safety, introduction of new technology, dismissals and disciplinary action, changes to work practices, or a major change in product or service. Setting "yes" answers equal to one and adding up the responses yields the Union Voice index (.967, 1.916).[16] Two variables proxy worker training. Formal Training (.500, .500) is a dummy for implementation of a formal training scheme during the previous five years. Less formal mechanisms for acquiring skills might take the form of on-the-job training, so an On-the-job Training (.333, .471) variable is added for workplaces where a new worker in the main occupational group would require at least three months to achieve expected work standards. The degree of hierarchy in the firm is proxied by Proportion of Managers (.079, .057). managers as a fraction of all employees.[17] Internal labor markets are proxied by Promotion Opportunities (.530, .499), which measures the proportion of managers promoted to their current position from within the organization. The size of the corporation is indicated by a dummy variable for Multinational (.148, .355) or foreign ownership of the establishment. Given the presence of Exxon, Ford, GM, IBM, ICI, and Mitsubishi facilities in Australia, and given the scarcity of comparably sized Australian corporations, this seems a reasonable proxy. Workplace size is measured by Employees at Workplace (98.41, 203.41). Market Competition (.526, .499) exists where many competitors are reported being in the market for the workplace's main product or service.

---

16. To recover missing observations due to nonresponses by union delegates, we set Union Voice to zero for nonunion workplaces (using the Density variable), and set any remaining missing observations equal to zero if managers claimed not to have bargained with union delegates at the workplace over any issue during the previous year.

17. The AWIRS defines one-digit occupations such that professional and technical workers are excluded from the managerial occupation indicator.

CHAPTER SEVEN

The Interaction between Market Incentives and Government Actions

George Gonos

To date, much of the literature on contingent work in the United States has displayed an *economistic* bias. That is, it has suggested that the greatly expanded use of these forms of employment over the past twenty years has been merely the result of changing human resource strategies on the part of business managers in response to new "global" market imperatives, as if no environmental factors such as government regulatory policy or established legal precedent had existed as potential barriers to their plans. Thus the literature has typically neglected the specific actions that have been required of government in allowing and supporting these developments.

This chapter explores the interaction between business and government that was involved in bringing about the institutionalization and growth of one form of contingent employment, "temporary work," as this has been promoted by the temporary help industry (THI). It will provide a brief overview of the rather obscure history of the battle that the THI has persistently fought since its appearance after World War II to bring about specific changes in law and public policy that were necessary in ratifying its version of the temporary employment relationship as legal and legitimate. The evidence will show that without the supportive framework ultimately provided by government, temporary work as we know it could not have become the staple part in the scheme of employment relations that it is in the United States today.

Not all analysts, of course, have overlooked the importance of political processes in relation to the growth of the various forms of contingent work. Thomas Kochan, Harry Katz, and Robert McKersie (1986:xii) took the position that these "experiments" aimed at labor market flexibility were carried out by business "acting largely without an active government

For helpful comments on an earlier draft I want to thank D. Randall Smith, Judith Gerson, Charles Nanry, Jeffrey Keefe, and the editors of this volume.

role" but noted the important part played by public policy makers in "diffusing and institutionalizing" the innovations afterwards. Bennett Harrison and Barry Bluestone (1988:5–7) postulated that the moves to alter employment practices were "taken first by the leaders of American business in the early 1970's and then ratified by policies of government, beginning in the latter half of that decade." In their analysis, "these radical 'innovations' . . . in the management of workers could not take place in the absence of a supportive public policy" (1988:76). Yet, neither of these works dealt specifically with the actual mechanics of the political processes that allowed for and supported the growth of contingent work. This is the gap that this chapter hopes to fill with respect to temporary work.

It is important to note that for their expanded use to be made possible, not all forms of contingent work necessitated government involvement to the same degree. This is because each discrete form of what has been called contingent work represents a distinctive social arrangement, the continued viability of which depends on the *presence* of a favorable regulatory environment and supporting legal doctrine—or the *absence* of specific institutional barriers to its legitimacy.[1] For example, though part-time work is defined for the sake of gathering statistics as work of less than thirty-five hours per week, no law prohibits an employer from working a "part-timer" more than this, or from denying "part-time" employees who do work more the same benefits that accrue to those who are full-time workers on the books (see Kilborn, 1991). Moreover, most part-time employment rests on a direct employer-employee relationship—that is, it is not mediated by other social agents who historically have been regulated (cf. Abraham, 1990). Thus, though supportive public policy has no doubt played a part in the growth of part-time work, employers have been able to greatly expand their use of "part-timers" largely without facing legal or regulatory obstacles.

However, this was not true in the case of temporary work, for which this kind of barrier-free environment did not exist. The expanded use of this form, as we will see, *required* changes in prevailing legal interpretation and existing government regulation.[2] Because each form of employment

1. Arthur Stinchcombe (1983) provides a framework for understanding the political supports underlying economic arrangements. Karl Klare (1981) focuses specifically on legal doctrine as ideological support for employment practices.

2. Similarly, as Martin Greller and David Nee (1989:69) point out, the expansion in the ranks of the "self-employed" in recent years could only happen under the condition that this development was "politically blessed." This is because, as Kathleen Christensen (1988) has shown, much use of the category was actually fraudulent in that it did not conform in practice to prevailing legal definitions.

has a distinctive structure and function and its own social history, the study of contingent work has in some instances not been served well by the tendency to conflate many kinds under a single umbrella. Any study of the interaction between business and government in the expansion of contingent work requires that generalization be eschewed and attention be paid to details. Though space allows only a fairly brief summary, this chapter—based on the author's extensive fieldwork, interviews with key informants in government and industry, and analysis of legal, government, and industry documents (see Gonos, 1994)—attempts to do so in the case of temporary work.

The chapter begins with an examination of the temporary employment relationship and the precarious socio-legal foundation on which it rests. It then provides some details of the post–World War II history of business-government interaction in the growth and institutionalization of this employment arrangement in the United States, focusing on the protracted, and ultimately effective, lobbying effort carried out by the THI for recognition as sole legal employer of the workers it sends out to client firms. The chapter concludes with a look at recent developments and prospects for the future. Overall, it will show that the existence of temporary work, as currently practiced by the commercial THI, is itself "contingent" on government policy as it has developed over this period.

The Temporary Employment Relationship

Despite the growing literature on temporary work in recent years, the characteristics of the temporary employment relationship have not been clearly explicated. As it is commonly applied to work arranged through commercial temporary help firms (THFs), which first appeared in the late 1940s, the term "temporary work" is actually a misnomer. This is because the limited duration of work assignments has never been its defining characteristic. Rather, the principal feature of this form of employment is its arrangement in what, following Efren Cordova (1986) and Robert Moberly (1987), we call a triangular employment relationship. This means that THFs, while "assigning" workers to their clients (or user firms), simultaneously place these workers for legal purposes on their own payroll, billing client firms in an amount covering wages, overhead, and profit. THFs thus claim the status of sole "employer" of these workers and assume, ostensibly at least, the formal responsibility for compliance with the legal requirements connected with this role— even as a third party, the client firm, utilizes the labor power provided.

In itself, use of the triangular employment relationship long predates the birth of the THI, having been prevalent in the United States since late in the nineteenth century when labor market intermediaries made their widespread appearance. Such intermediaries, which most states made extensive efforts to regulate as "employment agents" early in this century, procured workers for employers, often provided commissary and other services, and sometimes served as paymasters—after deducting their fees—much as THFs do now (see Gonos, 1994, chap. 4). What *is* new in the THI's use of this triangular arrangement is its claim to be the actual "employer" of the workers it "sends out," which, as we will see, is the key point of contention surrounding the industry. In using this arrangement, THFs established a different form of practice than that of the "permanent" employment agency which collects a one-time fee as compensation for the *placement* of a worker as a regular employee with another firm. In that scenario, a standard employer-employee relationship is established between the worker and the firm with which she is placed, and the agency steps out of the picture. The THF, on the other hand, maintains a formal tie to this worker, as her "employer," whether her stint of employment with a particular client firm lasts a few hours, a week, or several months or years, thereby profiting from the arrangement every hour that work is being performed.

The central purpose served by maintaining this ongoing arrangement—which we call the *temporary help formula*—is that it effectively severs the employer-employee relationship between workers and those user firms on whose premises they work and for whom they provide needed labor inputs.[3] That is, this arrangement allows the THF's client to utilize labor without taking on the specific social, legal, and contractual obligations that have increasingly been attached to employer status since the New Deal (see, e.g., U.S. Department of Labor, 1994:24–25; Weiler, 1990). As Sergio Ricca (1982:147) says, relieving client firms of these legal obligations toward workers, especially those connected with hiring and dismissal, is the *raison d'être* of the "temporary work" arrangement. The user firm's ability to choose to utilize workers on a short-term, or temporary, basis is its *byproduct*. The growing number of long-term assignments made by the THI in recent years, that is, the phenomenon of the "permanent temp" (see, for example, Lewis and Molloy, 1991:116–117), brings out this point clearly.

---

3. As Garth Mangum, Donald Mayall, and Kristin Nelson (1985:603) state, the THF "offers an assured supply of at least minimally qualified workers *without the responsibilities of the standard employer-employee relationship*" (emphasis mine).

In allowing core firms throughout the economy to rid themselves of legal and social obligations with respect to a portion of their workforce, the "temporary help formula" became one of the key mechanisms for the dramatic restructuring of employment relations that began in the 1970s, that is, for the breakup of what Kochan, Katz, and McKersie (1986) call the New Deal model of industrial relations. The use of temporaries provided large employers with a means of responding to what many saw as the "rigidity" of the labor market by offering the possibility of enhanced workforce "flexibility" (see Harrison and Bluestone, 1987; Rosenberg, 1989). By increasing user firms' control over the duration of a worker's stay and over what tasks workers could be directed to do while on the job (practically unencumbered by laws or contracts governing dismissals or work rules), the "temporary solution" held the potential for significantly increasing both the numerical and functional flexibility of the firm's workforce. Similarly, by taking wages out from under existing contracts and putting them "back into competition," the arrangement also provided wage flexibility (Rosenberg, 1989:11–13; see also Christensen, 1989). As a number of researchers have shown (for example, Belous, 1989; Mangum, Mayall, & Nelson, 1985), the great majority of large firms made use of these possibilities.

In effect, the use of temporary help constituted an effective means of relocating work out of primary (or "core") labor markets and into secondary (or "competitive") ones, that is, into a situation where workers typically experience lower wages, fewer benefits, less ability to use established "employee rights," and less protection from certain social programs of the so-called safety net (see Callaghan and Hartmann, 1992; Harrison and Bluestone, 1987; U.S. Government Accounting Office, 1991).[4] Moreover, as the U.S. Department of Labor (1994:66) has noted, temporary work and other contingent arrangements have "effectively excluded" many workers from union representation (despite the fact that they are nominally covered under national labor law), since such arrangements posed serious difficulties for traditional modes of trade union organizing inherited from the New Deal period.[5] It is for these reasons that the growth of temporary work has played an impor-

---

4. It should be noted, further, that this effect applies across a wide range of skilled, unskilled, and professional occupations, and in various economic sectors. For more detailed analysis of the growth of contingent work in relation to theories of labor market segmentation, see Gonos, 1994, chap. 3.

5. For current efforts within organized labor to combat this problem, see Service Employees International Union, 1993; Carré, duRivage, & Tilly, 1995.

tant role in the drift toward lower wages and greater employment insecurity for a significant portion of the U.S. workforce.

But for this role to be possible at all, the THI and its clients had to
insure the existence of a legal and regulatory framework supportive of
their definition of the situation, that is, the "temporary help formula."
The most essential ingredient in this formula, as we have seen, is the
recognition of THFs in practice as the legal "employers" of the workers
they assign to client firms. On this point the entire enterprise rests, for
if it were not for that recognition, THFs could not perform the function
of relieving core firms of their responsibilities as employers. Thus, it is
on this point that the THI strove to gain the support of government
institutions.

The THF as "Employer"

Despite the fact that both popular and academic accounts of temporary
work, even those critical of the industry as exploitative (e.g., Parker,
1994), unanimously accept as given the legitimacy of the THF as employer, this status has been anything but a foregone conclusion. It is a
determination for which the THI and its corporate backers have battled
for four decades, and one which is still in doubt. This is because the THF's
claim of employer status rests on a fragile legal foundation, as the rulings
of U.S. and European courts from the 1950s through the 1970s—mostly
adverse to the industry's position—attest (see, e.g., Veldcamp and Raetsen, 1973). In short, substantial grounds exist in American and international legal tradition, and in social history, for the nation's policy makers
to have disallowed the THI's version of "temporary help."

Based on the standard tests by which employer status is determined,
the THF's claim can be seen as questionable on several points (see, e.g.,
International Labour Organization, 1966; Moore, 1965a, 1975; Valticos,
1973). Considering the typical THF's operations and pattern of practice,
these points are as follows:

1. It is not the THF but its "customer" or client firm that exercises
   direct control over the work, which is normally carried out on the
   client's premises and with the client's supervisory personnel in
   charge.
2. The worker is not technically "employed" until she begins work on
   the premises of the THF's client, and she is paid only so long as
   she is on assignment with this outside party. Although, in the THI's

interpretation, the "customer can end a temporary employee's assignment but cannot 'fire' the employee" (Lenz, 1991:40), the THF's official "firing" of this worker may be seen as a mere formality.

3. The THF normally does not supply its own materials or utilize its own tools, nor does it guarantee or take responsibility for a final product or service, in the usual manner of an independent contractor. Furthermore, THFs do not typically specialize in the delivery of a specific or distinct service or product; instead they provide workers for a wide range of labor inputs and hence may be seen as "labor only contractors" (Epstein and Monat, 1973).

4. The work performed by temporary workers is part of the regular business of, and therefore directly benefits, the customer or client firm, not the THF.

These considerations all lend themselves to forming an opinion that THFs are not employers but labor market intermediaries or, in common terms, employment agencies. In this view, the fact that THFs collect withholding taxes, comply with minimum wage law, carry worker's compensation insurance, and perform the role of paymaster, etc. is seen as compliance with mere formalities only; it is not in itself determinative of employer status, which normally means control over the manner and means of work performance (Alito, 1992:3–4).

Yet, despite the serious questions raised by the THF's claim of employer status, the meanings of the terms "employer" and "employee" are elastic enough in practice to allow a legal determination of this issue in various ways. As with most cases in the area of employment law, this one would be decided as much on the basis of social and political context as on strict jurisprudence.[6] For the THI, then, winning its claim as the legal employer of "temporary workers" involved much more than a simple application of established legal doctrine. Settling the issue in its favor would take a protracted campaign with legal, political, and public relations aspects, and this is how the industry approached the matter.

It must be stressed just how much depended on the outcome of this issue. For instance, would "temporary workers" supplied to core firms by THFs be covered under collective bargaining agreements along with regular employees, or would they be excluded? Likewise, would they be eligible for health insurance and other benefits along with the user firm's

6. "The word [employment] is not of the technical language of the law . . . and must be construed according to the context and the approved usage of the language" (*30 Corpus Juris Secundum,* Employment 682).

own employees? Would "equal pay" law apply? Would "temps" be able to utilize their rights as employees vis-à-vis the core firms for which work was being performed? Unlike certain issues, this one would not be decided by a single case in the high court. Rather, a tentative answer emerged over a considerable period of time and only after an extended contest between the THI and various governmental bodies, as the next sections will show.

The Battle over the THF as Employer

It was just a few years into the post–World War II period that the battle ensued over whether THFs are legal employers or employment agencies subject to the state laws that have historically regulated that business. National labor legislation of the New Deal period had not addressed the question of employment agencies; their regulation remained therefore at the state level, where it had been since the appearance of the business in the 1890s. In the half century since that time, the employment agency business had been vexed by the vigorous efforts of the states, with the backing of various reformist constituencies, for strict regulation, if not abolition, of private fee-charging agencies. As the post–World War II period began, broad regulation of employment agencies existed in all but a few states. Regulation of fees had been fought fiercely by the industry but allowed by a Supreme Court decision in 1941. All signs seemed to indicate that the anti-agency mood in government would continue, as the U.S. Department of Labor advocated strict, comprehensive regulation. Moreover, from the industry's point of view, the strengthening of the nation's public employment system during World War II was seen as another serious threat. Though the private placement industry continued to grow, as it had in fits and starts since its beginning (despite the outwardly harsh regulatory climate), these conditions could easily be seen as threatening the very existence of the business as a whole (Gonos, 1994, chaps. 4–5). It was in this context that the THI was born in the late 1940s (Finney & Dasch, 1991:33–43; Moore, 1965b).

Although its identity was far from clear even to its own proponents at first, within a few years the strategy of the THI began to take shape, and continued to undergo refinement over the years. The position of the industry was that THFs were not employment agencies but a "new" kind of business or service, and the actual employers of the workers that they assigned to client firms. In effect, the industry waged a two-pronged fight: avoiding the designation of employment agency would satisfy the THI's own desire to be free from unwanted state regulation, while being declared the actual employer of workers would satisfy its clients' desire to have access to labor without obligation. While the former goal was important, the latter was absolutely essential, for unless THFs were accepted in practice as legal employers their raison d'être would quite literally disappear (Gonos, 1994, chap. 6).

The industry's position was not by any means immediately perceived as valid. Evidence from the early years of the THI's existence shows that state and federal regulators, in a simple application of long-standing assumptions, intuitively regarded THFs as employment agencies, subject to state laws regulating their operation. Or as the official history of the THI published by the industry trade group puts it, "Since most state governments didn't really understand what temporary help companies were, they generally lumped them in with employment agencies" (Finney & Dasch, 1991:64–65). Fighting this "confusion" would become the main mission of the industry's leaders, most notably Manpower, Inc., and its national organization, the National Association of Temporary Services (NATS), when it was formed in the mid-1960s.[7]

During a brief phase in the mid-1950s, the question of whether THFs were employers or employment agencies was heard in the state courts. The cases yielded mixed results. Court decisions adverse to the industry's position in Nebraska and New Jersey held that Manpower and other THFs were not employers but employment agencies subject to state licensing laws and other regulation. Only in Florida (1956) was an opinion favorable to the industry rendered, in which the court decided that Manpower was not an employment agency but an independent contractor, as the company claimed.[8] The court found, in its words, that "Manpower hires its own employees and sends them to the customer to perform the service required" and that this customer thus contracts with Manpower not for labor *per se* but "for the particular service to be performed." In the view of the Florida court, THFs were a "new type of service" comparable to a painting contractor, a detective agency or an accounting service (*Florida Industrial Commission v. Manpower*, 1956:197–199).

Based on statutory definitions of employment agency that were virtually the same as that in Florida, courts in Nebraska (1955) and New Jersey (1957) reached the opposite conclusion: Manpower was an em-

---

7. The organization has since been renamed the National Association of Temporary and Staffing Services (NATSS).

8. A lower court in Pennsylvania also found in favor of Manpower, but the state's courts did not have an opportunity to consider the matter further, since an appeal by the state was dismissed on a technicality (U.S. Congress, 1971:192).

ployment agency subject to the state laws regulating their activity and not the actual employer of workers it assigned to client firms. Based on a detailed description of Manpower's standard practices, the Nebraska court decided that the company "obviously" fit its statutory definition of a fee-charging employment agency, that is, that it functioned as an intermediary in the labor market, procuring work for job applicants and supplying "help" for employers (*Nebraska v. Manpower,* 1955). The opinion rendered in New Jersey is probably the sharpest critique of the THI's position on record in the U.S. context. It directly criticized the "very narrow interpretation" made by the Florida court a year earlier. In essence, the New Jersey court found that Manpower "undertakes only to furnish a certain type of temporary help and not . . . to do a particular job," and that such activity clearly falls within the meaning of employment agency, the sole purpose of which consists of *procuring help* for its corporate customers. The court noted that "it is the customer who directs and controls the worker, assigns the work to her, directs the manner of doing it, fixes the hours of work, recess and the like," and, therefore, that the temporary worker is "like any other employee of the customer and subject to the same direction and control" (*Manpower, Inc. of New Jersey,* 1957).

Though the results of this litigation were on the whole negative for the THI, the actual meaning of these adverse decisions in practice was not as problematic for the industry as might be supposed. The decisions in Nebraska and New Jersey simply meant that THFs were subject to the states' licensing requirements and other regulations applying to employment agencies. Yet, historically, such regulations had been merely nuisances for the industry, not roadblocks to success. The THI would continue to survive and grow because, even in the face of such decisions, THFs could continue in practice to act as employers. The reason for this is that another government agency, the Internal Revenue Service (IRS), accepted their payroll taxes, and this was much more significant in the overall scheme of things than the nuisance represented by state employment agency regulations. As early as 1951, the IRS had ruled (in a case involving Employers Overload, an early THF) that for the purpose of federal withholding taxes, the THF was the "employer of the employees furnished" to its customers (Parker, 1994:25).

A look at the situation existing in New Jersey at that time shows how the inconsistent policy operating within government worked in the THI's favor. Even as the judge in the New Jersey case cited above reached the conclusion that THFs were employment agencies, not employers, he faced the contradictory fact that the state accepted unemployment insurance taxes from Manpower as an "employer." Yet, in ruling the company an employment agency rather than a legal employer, the judge did not direct that the state's tax collection practice be changed. Rather he decided that his ruling placing THFs under employment agency law could exist concurrently with a different interpretation operational under the state's tax system (*Manpower, Inc. of New Jersey,* 1957:12). Conflicting interpretations made by different government agencies in relation to THFs continue to exist today (see, e.g., Lewis & Molloy, 1991:153–157). In effect, they allow the THI to thrive on the use of the temporary help formula despite apparently sound rulings in the judicial arena rejecting its legal claims of employer status. Clearly, it is the tax question that has often been preeminent, exercising ultimate control over the outcome of the THF issue.[9] But although the IRS decision to collect payroll taxes from THFs was in practice much more crucial than any state court's determination to regulate THFs as employment agencies, this decision was never challenged. Hence, the THI continued to operate as the "employer" of workers it sent out and to build its business in an ongoing state of legal ambiguity, which surrounds it to this day.[10]

Still, the battle had only just begun. The industry was determined to get THFs out from under state regulation. And, on the other side, many government regulators and policy makers continued, at least for the time being, to put up a great deal of resistance to the THI's claims. There are numerous examples of this. In the early 1960s, the tendency of state and federal bodies to identify THFs as employment agencies continued to be widespread (Moore, 1965a). As we have seen, the U.S. Department of Labor (1960, 1962) held the view that "temporary placements" should be covered by the same regulations as traditional employment agencies. Similarly, Senator Wayne Morse's 1962 bill to strengthen regulation of employment agencies in the District of Columbia included language specifically designed to insure the inclusion of THFs under its regulatory provisions (S. 3259, 1962). And in at least

9. Because THFs collect withholding taxes as "employers," they are from the standpoint of the IRS a desirable alternative to large numbers of "self-employed" individuals, since THFs facilitate greater efficiency and volume of collection. Thus, Greller and Nee (1989: 68–69) suggest that IRS efforts in recent years aimed at "pushing people" out of 1099 (self-employed) status and into W-2 (employee) status represent a potential "bonanza" for THFs, especially those specializing in technical services. The THI plays up its favorable position with respect to this powerful government agency for all it is worth, selling its services to potential corporate clients as a way for them to avoid the "dangers" of making excessive use of the "self-employed" designation for its workers (see Lenz, 1990:50).

10. On the function of ambiguity within the law, see Bourdieu, 1987; for ambiguity in employment law in particular, see Selznick, 1969; Klare, 1981:469.

five states (including Wisconsin, Manpower's home state), bills intended to bring THFs under regulation as private employment agencies were introduced (Moore 1965a:623–626; U.S. Congress, 1971:228). Yet the strength of the THI and its corporate backers, who made tenacious efforts to oppose all such legislation, was demonstrated by the fact that none of these new regulatory efforts made it past the committee stage.

Well into the 1960s many observers in the United States assumed that temporary workers would ultimately be regarded as employees of the firms that directly utilized their labor, not THFs. One example involved the use of "temps" in unionized defense plants during the Vietnam war. *Business Week*, reporting on the "storm brewing" over their employment status, predicted that the prospects were "fairly good" that the temporaries would be ruled employees of the manufacturers that were utilizing their labor and, as such, would be covered under existing collective bargaining agreements. "The decisions in these cases," the magazine stated, "are based on the so-called 'right-of-control test,' which holds that the company that controls an employee's hours, duties, and working conditions is the actual employer no matter who hands him his paycheck." A labor law expert quoted in the story agreed, stating, "That's how most past cases have gone" (Labor-for-rent war, 1966: 160–162). But at this point in time "past cases" were no longer a good gauge of future policy, because the THI was in the midst of making a breakthrough in its efforts to establish itself as the sole legal employer of temporary workers, and the prevailing legal interpretation was about to take a turn in a different direction. From this point on, the question of who was the legal employer of the "temporary worker" would indeed be judged on the basis of "who hands him his paycheck." The next section recounts these new developments.

The Deregulation of the THI

Inconsistent results in the courts in the 1950s and the continuing widespread tendency to define THFs as employment agencies in the 1960s led the THI to pursue a strategy of statutory change through legislative lobbying and to seek influence over state administrative agencies. THI lawyers crafted legal definitions of such key terms as "employer," "employee," "agency," and "fee" which were designed to back up the claim of employer status for THFs (see, e.g., Lenz, 1985a, 1991). State legislatures across the country were systematically approached in a campaign to alter employment agency law in every state. Bills were drafted and redrafted, and willing sponsors found. Year after year, if necessary, bills written specifically to exempt THFs from coverage under employment agency law, and to define THFs as "employers," were introduced into state legislatures. Strong national and state industry associations were built in the process, and the persistence and good organization paid off.

The earliest successes took place in New York (1958–60) and California (1961–63), the two largest markets, as well as in Oregon (1961), which all passed legislation to exempt THFs from coverage under employment agency law. The amendment to employment agency law enacted in New York excluded from regulation "the business of furnishing services to employers through the employment of temporary employees." As the state Department of Labor later explained, "The temporary help supply firm is considered to be the 'employer' and is therefore not an employment agency within the meaning of the N.Y. Employment Agency Law" (U.S. Congress, 1971:52, 103). During the same period attorneys general in three other states and the District of Columbia were moved to render opinions in favor of exempting THFs from regulation within their jurisdictions (U.S. Congress, 1971:192).

The THI's campaign soon achieved rapid success in the rest of the country, as deregulation bills swept through state political processes. From 1965 to 1971 all but two of the remaining states made accommodations of one kind or another with the position of the THI. (Only New Jersey and Missouri continued to regulate THFs). Over this six-year period twelve states passed legislation specifically exempting THFs from regulation, and numerous others achieved the same result through administrative interpretation (U.S. Congress, 1971:6, 191–193). The typical legislation consisted of a brief, specific amendment to the existing statute, obviously written to serve the interests of the THI. For example, Maryland amended its "Fee Charging Employment Agency Law" with the following: "'Employment Agency' shall not include any person conducting a business which consists of employing individuals directly for the purpose of furnishing part-time or temporary help to others" (quoted in U.S. Congress, 1971:205). In most cases, state legislatures gave no rationale for exempting THFs from regulation or for defining them as employers, and many observers saw the actions as only a matter of "semantics" or "mere technicality" (U.S. Congress, 1971:53). There was little or no public debate on the issue.

We are left with a clear picture of the dominance of the THI and its backers over the state legislatures and administrative agencies. A U.S. Department of Labor memo on the subject attributed the sweeping success of deregulatory legislation in the states to "the very active campaign for exclusion [i.e., exemption], with Manpower, Inc., carrying the ball" (U.S. Congress, 1971:199). In Congressional hearings on proposed federal regulation,[11] its sponsor, Congressman Mikva of Illinois, spoke of the THI's "clout in the [state] legislative halls."

> It should not be surprising then that when on occasion court cases run against the interest of the industry the immediately next [*sic*] following session of the legislature corrects whatever harm has befallen the industry in that recent court decision. . . . I say this with no disparagement intended of the State legislative process, but simply in recognition that in any given State arena the industry can pack a considerable wallop. (U.S. Congress, 1971:11–12)

The THI's collective strength, as a distinct branch of the personnel placement industry as a whole, had been mobilized on a national level in 1966 with the formation of the Institute for Temporary Services, later to be renamed the National Association of Temporary Services (Finney & Dasch, 1991:66–70). Its leadership always saw NATS's political function as most critical, and the organization kept an especially sharp eye on the details of lawmaking and the legislative process, as quotations from its official publication indicate.[12] For example: "One of the most important reasons for NATS' existence is to keep the industry free of regulation. . . . NATS constantly monitors all [government] actions—national, state and local" (Legislative monitoring, 1982:15). "Freedom from regulation has resulted from significant legislative efforts undertaken by members of the temporary help industry" (Co-mingling, 1982:20).

NATS's method called not simply for avoidance of adverse legislation but for stringent efforts to initiate and shape the precise language of legislation and to work with government regulators on the drafting of administrative codes. As one industry representative put it, "Action, rather than reaction, is . . . NATS' goal by introducing helpful legislation where possible" (Legislative monitoring, 1982:15). Ultimately, the THI

11. From 1971 to 1977, bills were introduced in Congress that would have reregulated the THI under the U.S. Department of Labor. The bills accepted the status of THFs as employers and were aimed solely at the industrial sector of the industry. Although hearings were held (U.S. Congress, 1971), the bills met strong THI opposition and never made it out of committee to a floor vote. In many ways, the episode strengthened the THI's position and actually helped clear the way for its further institutionalization (see Gonos, 1994, chap. 7).

12. *Contemporary Times*, NATS's official journal, or reprints of articles cited in this chapter, are available from National Association of Temporary and Staffing Services, 119 S. Saint Asaph St., Alexandria, Va. 22314-3119.

demonstrated how the intricate fashioning of seemingly minor provisions within state statutes or administrative codes could yield big payoffs for business. NATS utilized a two-tiered organizational structure, with strategic planning taking place on the national level and state-level chapters doing the legwork. In this way the THI epitomized and was an early example of the "politicization" of business that would occur throughout the business world in the 1970s (see Edsall, 1984, chap. 3) and the so-called grassroots methods it utilized (see Lenz, 1985b).

The typical character of state legislatures during the 1960s and early 1970s no doubt facilitated the THI's efforts toward the passage of self-serving deregulatory legislation during that period. The often "part-time" working schedules of legislators, their high rate of turnover, and the declining influence of strong local party organizations at that time meant an increased reliance on the growing number of lobbyists, most of whom represented business organizations (see, e.g., Burch, 1975). Of the rapidly increasing number of bills sponsored to appease interest groups, the successful ones were those drafted and backed by powerful groups that lobbied vigorously. On issues like employment agencies, representatives and legislative committees typically lacked sufficient expertise to provide a critical function. Moreover, the state legislators were often small businesspeople likely to be favorably predisposed to the message of "new entrepreneurialism" the THI represented. Overall, the functioning of state legislative bodies can be summed up, in the words of an analyst of New Jersey's legislature during this period, as "weak" and "permissive" (Rosenthal, 1975:148–152). Combined with the growing organizational strength of the THI, this description of the workings of the state legislatures is clearly relevant to understanding the events whereby THI deregulation took place.

Thus, without benefit of public debate, the THI had, through deliberate and concerted action, won its deregulation, about a decade before the well-known industry-specific cases (trucking, airlines, banking) of the late 1970s. Perhaps because it took place in a decentralized manner on the state level, and because of the obscurity or seeming triviality—the purely "legal" or "technical" nature—of what was done, THI deregulation has never been recognized as such in the recent literature on business deregulation (e.g., Galambos and Pratt, 1988:241–245). Yet it may be argued that it has had far greater ramifications than any of the better-known examples, since THI deregulation affected the norms surrounding the utilization of labor throughout the economy. In effect, it constituted a step in the deregulation of the employment relationship itself.

With its deregulation throughout most of the country by 1971, the THI entered its take-off period. Although in popular perception, and in some of the academic literature, the 1980s is seen as the decade of the "temporary revolution" (e.g., Lewis and Schumann, 1988:1), this is actually misleading. In fact, despite downturns during recessionary periods, the industry has experienced an extremely rapid rate of growth over each of the past four decades. From small beginnings, the THI established itself quickly in the 1950s as a major business (Finney & Dasch, 1991:46–48, 55), and it continued to grow at a phenomenal pace during the 1960s, when Manpower, Inc. reported increases of 513 percent in corporate revenues and 345 percent in the number of its "employees" (U.S. Congress, 1971:190).[13] And although, as Polly Callaghan and Heidi Hartmann (1992:28) point out, the THI was more affected by the business cycle in the 1970s, by some measures its growth was more rapid in that decade than in the 1980s. During the 1970s, its total payroll grew at a faster rate (Parker, 1994:26–27), and its gain in total employment exceeded 20 percent in more years (see Table 7.1). In both these areas, that is, payroll size and total employment, NATS reported higher compounded annual growth rates for the 1970s than the 1980s (see Table 7.2). Although, for numerous reasons, such statistics on temporary work lack reliability,[14] it is clear that the explosive growth of temporary employment should not be singularly associated with the 1980s.

In the long view it appears that the THI's greatest spurt forward began in 1973, as the greater "uncertainty" of the market—commencing at that time, and continuing since—proved to be the perfect condition for its growth by providing corporations wary of new commitments with an alternative to adding "permanent" employees to their payrolls. Significantly, the early 1970s also saw the end of federal efforts to improve the effectiveness of the nation's public employment service and the beginning of a serious decline for that potential THI competitor (Janoski, 1990:99–103). The deregulation of the THI by the early 1970s

13. Mangum, Mayall, and Nelson (1985:601–602) report that, between 1963 and 1977, the THI grew by 469 percent in total payroll, 550 percent in total employment, and 280 percent in the number of temporary firms.

14. Statistics reported by different sources vary substantially. The government's manner of classifying temporary workers has changed over time. Moreover, it collects and classifies employment data by industry, not by the type of employment relationship involved. As a result, government statistics have excluded large numbers of temps in technical and professional fields and other temps working out of specialized THFs, who are all reported in different categories. For these reasons, an undercount is likely. For a more complete treatment of such counting problems, see Gonos, 1994, chap. 2.

Table 7.1 Growth of temporary help industry: employment (average daily employees) and total payroll, 1970–1989

Year	Average daily employees (thousands)	Percent change	Total payroll (millions of dollars)	Percent change	Year	Average daily employees (thousands)	Percent change	Total payroll (millions of dollars)	Percent change
1970	184.4	13.7	547.4	n/a	1980	416.1	-4.7	3,117.2	11.1
1971	150.6	-18.3	431.6	-21.2	1981	401.4	-3.5	3,483.8	11.8
1972	164.6	9.3	506.3	17.3	1982	406.7	1.3	3,427.5	-1.6
1973	203.7	23.8	661.4	30.6	1983	471.8	16.0	4,008.7	17.0
1974	250.6	23.0	955.4	44.5	1984	622.4	31.9	5,399.0	34.7
1975	186.6	-25.5	853.0	-10.7	1985	708.2	13.8	6,375.6	18.1
1976	233.3	25.0	1,081.4	26.8	1986	807.6	14.0	7,147.6	12.1
1977	293.7	25.9	1,470.5	36.0	1987	948.4	17.4	9,823.0	37.4
1978	348.2	18.6	1,970.5	34.0	1988	1,042.6	9.9	11,898.0	21.1
1979	436.4	25.3	2,805.4	42.4	1989	1,031.5	-1.1	13,218.0	11.1

Sources: National Association of Temporary and Staffing Services (Steinberg, 1995); Parker, 1994, 26–29; and Callaghan and Hartmann, 1991, 40.

Table 7.2 Temporary help industry compounded annual growth rates

	1970–1979	*1980–1990*
Total payroll	19.9%	12.5%
Employment	10.0%	9.3%

Source: National Association of Temporary Services (Whalen and Dennis, 1991).

securely positioned the industry to play a key role in the tremendous growth of contingent work and in the restructuring of employment relations that has taken place since. It has now become widespread and accepted practice for corporations to use the industry's "services" to relocate work from their core to what would become known as the "outer rings." Not coincidentally, it was 1973, the year the great spurt in THI growth began, that marked the beginning of the "Great U-Turn" in the incomes of American workers (Harrison and Bluestone, 1988; see also Newman, 1994) .

Further Institutionalization of the Temporary Help Formula

The 1980s saw the further institutionalization and growth of "temporary work" in the United States, as the federal government and the courts provided further support for the version of the temporary employment relationship promoted by the THI and its corporate clients. Here we can only touch very briefly on certain of these later developments.

During the 1980s the federal government greatly expanded its own use of part-time and "temporary" workers. At first this involved only "direct hires" who, according to new federal regulations promulgated in 1985, could be hired for up to four years without benefits (Kornbluh, 1988:18). Long-standing civil service regulations seemed to prohibit the use of "temps" supplied by outside agencies or contractors. But after some consideration, the Office of Personnel Management (OPM) decided in 1988, per the THI's definitions, that using temporary workers would not obligate the government as an employer. In its words, OPM felt assured that by this time "the role of the temporary help service firm is well established and clear cut, and the temporaries are legally its employees" (Office of Personnel Management, 1989). The United States thus approved, with some restrictions (see Office of Personnel Management, 1991), utilization of "temps" by its own agencies, and beginning in January 1989 the practice spread rapidly through virtually every federal department. In dealing with THFs, the government said, it was not hiring workers but purchasing services, and thus the practice would be treated according to guidelines covering purchases, not employment. Thus the new federal policy further helped institutionalize the idea of THFs as legal employers of employees, to whom users of labor had no obligation. As one might expect, NATS takes credit for having provided this "correct interpretation" of the employer-employee relationship to OPM and for helping to shape the new regulations (Mackail, 1988:47).[15]

The federal government took another step toward acceptance of the THI's formula when in the mid-1980s it strongly encouraged the U.S. Employment Service to begin to refer job seekers at its free public offices to private employment agencies, including temporary help firms. The referral of workers to commercial fee-charging agencies had until that time been prohibited by law and long-standing policy, but a new interpretation that excluded THFs from that category was put into effect with the passage of the Job Training Partnership Act in 1982. The new policy was initially opposed by the Department of Labor but was finally implemented under pressure from the General Accounting Office and other government sources (U.S. Government Accounting Office, 1986). With this move, the federal government was again helping to legitimate the idea that THFs themselves provide real "employment," and put itself more squarely behind the drift toward contingency.

The federal courts also provided support for the idea of THFs as legal employers in the 1980s. In the 1960s the courts had established clear grounds for the determination of "joint employer" status in cases where a firm utilizing labor exercises what is seen as a sufficient degree of control over the terms and conditions of work. But research by Jonathan Axelrod (1987) shows that during the 1980s the courts failed to issue "joint employer" judgments against user firms, even in cases where the facts could easily have warranted such judgment.[16] His analysis of the *Clinton's Ditch* case,[17] for example, revealed substantial evidence that the firm utilizing "leased" employees trained and supervised

15. The OPM is currently considering loosening the original restrictions placed on the use of temporaries by federal agencies (personal communication with OPM specialist).

16. Although Axelrod focuses his study on users of "employee leasing" firms, the same conclusions can be applied with respect to THFs, which are, despite their protests (see Lenz, 1991), a close relative of the former. (The Bureau of Labor Statistics has classified them under the same code.) Like THFs, employee leasing firms are, as Axelrod (1987: 862) says, "designed to be an extra layer of supervision to shield the customer from employer status."

17. *Clinton's Ditch Coop. Co.*, 778 F.2d 132 (1985), *cert. denied*, 93 L.Ed.2d 25 (1986).

workers in their day-to-day activities and exercised a significant degree of control over the terms and conditions of work. Yet the court found a "single employer relationship" to exist between the workers and the firm leasing them, and refused to recognize the user firm as a "joint employer." Viewing user firms as joint employers would constitute a first step toward insuring equal treatment for temps (for example, by imposing a legal obligation on user firms to include long-term temps in bargaining units along with regular employees).

As for the states, the 1980s saw their legislatures further liberalize the restrictions they had historically placed on the activity of the private personnel placement industry. (Even New Jersey, the last holdout, finally fell into line with THF deregulation in 1981.) With corporate "downsizing" now releasing large numbers of workers, including professionals and skilled technicians, into circulation in the labor market, there was a proliferation of private placement firms, especially those types working within the more lucrative or "upscale" segments of the workforce. Though many of these firms used the temporary help formula more or less exactly as it had been developed by the THI, they avoided the appellation "temporary help firm," a term they associated with firms working in the industrial or clerical sectors, that is, the "lower end" of the industry. Though they went by other names ("personnel consulting," "executive search," etc.), they wished to be exempted from state regulation as THFs had been. Thus the states were approached again, and began to extend the exemptions they had granted to THFs to other kinds of firms engaged in personnel placement (Gonos, 1994, chap. 8). By now, practically the entire personnel placement industry has in effect been deregulated, returning millions of workers in the United States to the conditions that prevailed early in the century.

This chapter has provided a brief overview of the little-known history of the battle over the legal status of the THF and the temporary employment relationship it has promoted. In effect, it constitutes a case study of the complex interaction between market forces and government in the growth of one form of contingent work in the United States. Although the story clearly points to the dominant role of business in shaping the public policy on this issue, it also demonstrates the important role played by both state and federal government—in their legislative, judicial, and administrative functions—in ratifying the "temporary help" formula as legal and legitimate within the current system of employment relations in the United States.

It is well to remember that legality and social legitimacy are two very different things. Legitimacy refers to a condition in which a given social practice finds widespread acceptance in a society because it lies within the general framework of accepted social norms and widely held beliefs. With respect to this, it must be said that "temporary work," as it is currently practiced in our society, still violates the sense of what is acceptable or "right" to many workers and students of work, this despite the massive public relations campaign carried on by the THI consciously aimed at promoting its legitimacy. In short, as the constant flow of materials critical of the industry suggests, temporary work cannot be said to have achieved legitimacy in any final sense. Legality, of course, is also anything but a fixed state of affairs. Hence, the THI's victory, as described above, is at best a tentative one.

Another issue has to do with the time frame in which the growth of contingent work and the restructuring of employment relations has occurred. It is often mistakenly stated that the "fundamental transformation of work commenced in the 1980s" (Wood, 1989:1). As this chapter has shown, it was during the 1950s and 1960s—literally at the height of the reign of the New Deal model of industrial relations—that the THI and its backers were working behind the scenes to implement an employment relationship very different from the "standard" one. The events related above, which resulted in THI deregulation and the acceptance in practice of the THF as employer, paved the way for the acceleration of trends in the 1970s and 1980s when the use of temporary workers, and contingent workers in general, was greatly increased.

With those early events, the nation's policy makers had in effect made what Kochan, Katz, and McKersie (1986) call a "strategic choice" in relation to the kind of industrial relations system we now have. Simply put, their actions pointed us in the direction of a low-wage/high-turnover workforce. The notion of "choice" is important to keep in mind, since so much recent analysis of contingent work, both popular and academic, holds the view that overwhelming and uncontrollable "market" forces (such as "globalization") have made the trend toward contingency as we know it inevitable. Certainly the THI's effort to shroud the history of these events in obscurity has served both the industry and the notion of inevitability. The conclusion of this chapter, however, is that a choice was indeed made: different actions and ideas could have taken our industrial relations system in a very different direction. Given the fragile legal foundation on which "temporary work" rests and the existence of viable alternatives within American legal tradition and labor history, the nation's policy makers could have rejected the THI's claims and made a very different "strategic choice."

It is important to stress, then, that the battle is an ongoing one. As part of its fact-finding report, the Dunlop Commission (U.S. Department of Labor & U.S. Department of Commerce, 1994a:94) has recently posed the question of whether the definition of "employer" should be "retailored to include the enterprise that owns the structure or finances the project on which work is being done, but utilizes a contractor to hire and manage the people who perform this work." Thus, the question of the THF's status has been put on the public agenda. Perhaps now, real public debate on the issue, a debate that includes a broad spectrum of interests and concerns, can take place, and previous answers will be reconsidered. It is hoped that a new answer will emerge, one based on the realization that alternative forms of workforce flexibility, which do not necessarily increase employment insecurity or widen the gap between rich and poor, are feasible.

Part III

The Human Face of Contingent Workers

Toiling for Piece-Rates and Accumulating Deficits: Contingent Work in Higher Education

Kathleen Barker

When looking back over life, many individuals consider their years of experience to be as important as almost any other aspect of their employment. Many adult workers take care, if not pride, in their occupational growth, especially the development of job-relevant knowledge and skills. The centrality of accumulating resources in an individual's career is a theoretical foundation in labor and workplace scholarship. Insofar as the workplace represents a level playing field, peers have equivalent potential for the accumulation of resources associated with job tenure. Workers invest in their education and expect to receive, and many times do receive, job training and development, equitable compensation, job security, promotions, and adequate feedback and responsibilities.

A general assumption is that time or tenure with an employer signifies to others that a particular worker has been of value to the employer. Does this assumption hold for all workers, however? For those working in many fields, especially the professions, a social contract of reciprocal rights and responsibilities has governed employment relations. For contingent workers, however, a different set of workplace assumptions, a different social contract, may influence their employment relations. For example, does job tenure signify that a worker is of value when "time" with an employer is short term or tenuous? Given that contingent work experience is new to evaluators, will the accumulation of job experience be advantageous, benign, or disadvantageous? As highly skilled workers find themselves working temporarily, or in "piece-rate" situations, how will that experience be evaluated, especially when it does not fit the normative expectations of peer evaluators?

One example of a highly educated and skilled worker is the college teacher working as an adjunct instructor. Like other professionals, these

The author thanks Gary Holden, Barbara Reskin, and an anonymous reviewer for comments on an earlier draft.

individuals look forward to working within jobs that will prepare them for positions with increasing amounts of responsibility and status. As many adjunct instructors vie to teach undergraduate classes, however, a cruel hoax may accompany their work experience.

Job tenure (Krecker, 1994; Rosenfeld, 1992) and work experience (Fusilier & Hitt, 1983, Hitt & Barr, 1989; Olian, Schwab, & Haberfeld, 1988; Stone & Sawatzki, 1980; see Singer & Bruhns, 1991, for a review) are viewed as playing a key role in, respectively, the accumulation of individual resources or skills and the desirability of candidates in the selection process. Yet contingent workers have tenuous attachments to employers and insecure futures within organizations. These workers, as well as their employers and coworkers, may not perceive themselves as belonging to the full-time and permanent community of workers. After years of working from semester to semester in tenuous arrangements, adjunct instructors expect to accumulate increasing levels of knowledge, skills, and abilities that signify their development and achievement in the workplace. These contingent workers, however, may also be acquiring more than just experience. Due to the institutional and organizational constructions of contingent work that mediate worker identity and value (Barker, 1995), contingent workers *accumulate deficits*. To the degree that workers are negatively valued or stigmatized due to their contingent status, a deficit model of work experience is created. One implication is that employers will not evaluate contingent work experience fairly or positively when a worker competes for subsequent employment. Moreover, if contingent work is segregated by race and gender, discrimination may be amplified (see Chapters 2 and 3, this volume).

The purpose of this chapter is to organize findings and develop a social psychological framework of contingent employment. Two studies weave a narrative regarding the construction of difference, tensions between different groups in the workplace, and the social costs of exclusion such as the denigration of work experience. Exclusion from organizational, interpersonal, and skill-related activities is central to the social construction of difference in the workplace (Barker, 1993). While some exclusions may be benign, others are stigmatizing and present potential long-term difficulties in a workplace that historically has assigned less value to individuals working on the margins in peripheral employment (Chapter 1, this volume). In the first part of this chapter, a study of contingent workers in one profession, adjunct instructors in higher education, explores these issues. The perspectives of these instructors provide the data for the study, which is organized thematically. Contingent relationships were found to mediate not only adjuncts' experience in the workplace but their identity as well. One hypothesis that adjunct instructors generated concerns the association of contingent employment with the accumulation of deficits. This hypothesis is tested in a survey, and the results regarding the evaluations of academic employers toward such workers are presented in the second part of the chapter. This chapter starts, then, by sorting through the response of contingent workers to their workplace and concludes by examining employers' perceptions of contingent work experience.

Study I. Workplace Communities and Moral Exclusion: The Contingent Workers of Academe

Over the past fifteen years, the restructuring of the American workplace has been achieved through reorganization, downsizing, and the expansion of contingent employment. In many instances, contingent workers and permanent workers labor side by side at the same jobs but under different conditions. Yet just as conditions for full-time, permanent employees vary, so are there differences among nonpermanent, less-than-full-time workers based on their occupation and industry setting. In this section, we examine contingent workers in one occupation and setting, instructors in higher education.

Academe has not been exempt from the restructuring observed in the private sector. References to the "ivory tower" appear grossly inaccurate to many professionals working within higher education. Uncertainty in higher education originated in the recessions and budget slashing of the 1970s and 1980s (Benjamin, 1995). The financial crisis of the 1970s in higher education converged with experimentation in flexible faculty staffing to achieve curriculum goals. Uncertainty was also magnified by the decline of public support for higher education. Higher education in the 1990s suffered financially from the reneging of the federal government on financial aid for qualified students, an increase in the number of middle-management administrators, and the falling rate of traditional-age students (Zemsky & Massey, 1990). The result was an increase in uncertain or contingent arrangements: jobs held by individuals referred to as adjunct or part-time faculty. These faculty are rarely referred to as temporary, although many are working on a semester-to-semester basis. Cost containment in academic human resources is now entrenched and committed to providing a "just-in-time" professoriate.

From the early 1970s, there has been a steady increase in the number of adjunct instructors (Gappa & Leslie, 1993). In a survey of 974 public and private nonproprietary higher education institutions in 1992–93, there was a final weighted total of 1,035,055 faculty and instructional staff, of which 510,141 were full-time permanent; 29,070 were full-time temporary workers; 400,981 were part-time, a figure that includes both those working permanently and temporarily (U.S. Department of Education, 1996). Of the 400,981 faculty working part-time, approximately half are temporary part-timers (Linda J. Zimbler, personal communication, March 28, 1997). Temporary replacements and graduate teaching assistants were not included in the survey. Therefore, to some degree, these figures underrepresent non-core faculty and instructional staff. Even so, full-time temporary, part-time temporary, and part-time permanent instructional faculty comprise 42 percent of instructional faculty. According to the survey, male faculty comprise 66.8 percent of full-time faculty and 55.4 percent of part-time faculty. Although some part-time and temporary faculty are topic experts who prefer flexibility in the form of temporary arrangements and some are supplementing retirement benefits or nonacademic full-time earnings (Gappa & Leslie, 1993), many are involuntarily employed on an as-needed, "piece-rate" basis and are multiple job holders (dubbed "subway dons" or "freeway fliers"), traveling from campus to campus to make a living wage (Abel, 1984).[1] Recent analyses indicate that as many as 62 percent of part-time faculty work on a semester-to-semester basis (Gappa & Leslie, 1997).

The increasing presence of contingent workers in higher education—temporary and part-time adjunct instructors—is emblematic of contemporary workplace transformation. Adjunct instructors are a permanent feature of college life. Yet, academe prides itself on the ideal of a unified "collegium" (Warme & Lundy, 1988). The contradiction of workplace transformation in higher education is that it institutionalizes privilege for one set of citizens (tenured and tenure-track faculty) at a cost to oth-

---

1. There are a number of arrangements in academe with varying pay structures. For example, a visiting professor working full-time on a one-year renewable or nonrenewable contract can earn close to what a regular faculty member would earn in that position. Individuals who are packaging jobs, such as two courses at University A and two courses at University B, are not paid as well. These individuals are "adjuncting." For example, a major university in New York offered the author of this chapter $2,000 to teach a graduate course in social psychology. In New York City, the colleges and universities pay as low as $1,500 to a high of $3,000 for a course taught by an adjunct. Many adjuncts earn a "living" wage by packaging course contracts over the fall, spring, and summer semesters. To earn $20,000, the adjunct must teach ten courses at the major university mentioned above. This does not include benefits, pension, etc.

ers (Warme & Lundy, 1988). The failure of inclusion within academe, or the success of exclusive membership, is revealed when a system of layered citizenship is constructed, made coherent, and legitimated.[2]

The construction of difference at the institutional level, whether in ideology or practice (cf. Wells, Kochan, & Smith, 1991), may create a personal disadvantage for the worker that is unjust at two levels. The first injustice concerns an inversion regarding organizational stances. That is, organizational actions that distance a worker are reinterpreted as a function of workers' attributes or discretion. The second injustice is the loss of value that adheres to a worker's identity and which then appears *normal*. In writing about psychological processes involved in the construction of difference, Erika Apfelbaum (1979:197–198) commented that "marking, excluding, and grouping make up the first sequence of processes necessary to establish domination. . . . The segregated, subordinated group, its autonomy removed, now exists only by reference to the norms, rules and regulations set by the dominant group; that is, it exists within an imposed dependency relation that benefits the latter."

When tensions between groups in the workplace arise, the cause of the tensions can be diverted by referring to an asymmetry of qualifications, capabilities, and/or demographic traits that yield the naturally occurring distribution of rights, privileges, and deficits.

From a social psychological perspective, the concept of moral exclusion is implicated in the construction of privileges, entitlements, and penalties associated with the emergence of contingent work in higher education. The literature on the scope of moral community and moral exclusion is found in the writings of Morton Deutsch (1985), Susan Opotow (1990), and Ervin Staub (1987). Moral exclusion is said to occur "when individuals or groups are perceived as *outside the boundary in which moral values, rules, and considerations of fairness apply* . . . they

---

2. The discussion of adjunct instructors in this chapter does not use the "adjunct as expert" model. Individuals who work full- or part-time at another job or are self-employed and who *choose* to work as adjuncts are not the concern of this chapter. Due to the multiple jobs these workers hold, they choose to work in a voluntary, peripheral position (the adjunct position) which may even expand their primary job in ways either intellectual or financial. Work conditions that are described in this chapter probably hold true for individuals who are working as adjuncts but are also multiple job holders, that is, they work as an adjunct but are also employed in a full-time job. These individuals elect to teach one or two courses to reap the psychological and financial rewards of teaching. But "professional" adjuncts who supplement a primary job can be considered "moonlighters" and should not be confused with those working on an involuntary basis in a job or jobs which represent their primary source of earnings.

are perceived as nonentities, expendable" (Opotow, 1990:1). Opotow notes that instances of "moral exclusion occur when we fail to recognize and deal with undeserved suffering and deprivation. . . . in this case harm doing results from unconcern or unawareness of others' needs or entitlements to basic resources, such as housing, health services, respect, and fair treatment" (2).

From the literature on harm doing, Opotow extracted a series of over two dozen symptoms that operationally define moral exclusion for empirical research. The symptoms were divided into two groups: exclusion-specific processes and "ordinary" processes. Examples of exclusion-specific processes included, for example, derogation, dehumanization, blaming the victim, and self-righteous comparisons. Processes that Opotow labeled as ordinary included groupthink, transcendent ideologies, deindividuation, psychological distance, condescension, double standards, euphemisms, and normalizing of violence, to name a few.

The concept of moral exclusion provides an organizing framework within which contingent work can be explored and theorized. When considering contingent work from the perspective of moral exclusion, otherwise invisible aspects of such work become apparent.[3] In *Webster's Unabridged Dictionary*, invisibility is defined as that which cannot be seen or is out of sight and not apparent, as well as that which is imperceptible, indistinct, and kept hidden. In fact, there is little empirical research or systematic inquiry which focuses on the workplace experiences of adjunct instructors. Most of the articles on adjunct instructors are of an anecdotal nature (Gappa & Leslie, 1993).

Case study material within a particular context—academe—provides glimpses into the contingent work experience of highly educated workers, who are rarely studied and for the most part invisible in workplace scholarship. One limitation of the data is that new instructors were voluntarily employed in apprenticeship arrangements, whereas those who had completed or nearly completed doctoral requirements were seeking full-time academic work and were involuntarily working in contingent employment arrangements. Another limitation concerns the generalizability of findings from exploratory studies. Although the interview data provide interesting glimpses into the nature and terms of exclusion for

3. The notion of invisibility or embeddedness of workers is readily apparent in the work of Katherine Newman (1988:91), who uses the anthropological notion of "liminality" rather than moral exclusion. Liminality refers to the idea that an individual is hanging between states and, for workers in particular, that an unemployed individual is in seclusion or shunned.

contingent workers in academe, generalizability to the larger population remains to be empirically established.

Research Questions and Method

Due to the absence of systematic research on adjuncts, a number of open-ended questions were developed with an eye toward subsequent systematic study: Do adjuncts feel different from full-time faculty, and if so how is this expressed in the workplace? What is the nature of the professional community? What is the quality of the mentoring, if any, they receive on the job? Do adjuncts express entitlement to a full-time job? What do adjuncts think about their future prospects, and does this include union activities? How central is professional identity in their lives? What is the importance of teaching compared to scholarship. If they resort to cutting corners, which corners do they cut?

Individual interviews and two group interviews were conducted with adjunct instructors. The first group included those who had averaged three years of teaching experience in higher education and were working as graduate or teaching assistants (this low-experience group I refer to as GA/TAs). The second group, which included those who either had received their Ph.D.'s or had completed all the degree requirements except for the dissertation (ABDs), possessed a range of teaching experience averaging nine years (this high-experience group I refer to as adjuncts). Ten one-hour semistructured interviews were conducted with GA/TAs and adjunct instructors. Some of these instructors also participated in focus groups. Fourteen instructors participated in two separate two-hour focused discussions, one for the low-experience group and the other the high-experience group. The GA/TAs in the low-experience group were actively apprenticing, and all the participants were in early stages of their careers. Individuals in the high-experience group were not working in formal graduate assistantship programs but were tenuously attached to an employer, renegotiating their contacts on a semester-by-semester basis. The high-experience group was working contingently. Most of my discussion will focus on the highly experienced adjuncts, but throughout I will draw upon data concerning the GA/TAs for comparison.

Results and Discussion

Although the GA/TAs discussed their work in the terms commonly associated with apprenticeship, the contingently employed adjuncts did not. The findings of this study point to a number of organizational and individual actions that support the notion of moral exclusion as described by Opotow: organizational and interpersonal exclusionary devices and stigmatizing processes. Findings from this research extend the literature on moral exclusion to include processes and outcomes such as declining beliefs in meritocracy, muzzled protest, resistance strategies, and accumulating deficits.

Organizational and Interpersonal Exclusionary Devices

Generally, the highly experienced adjuncts reported more discouragement and disappointment than the less experienced GA/TAs. Many adjuncts reported being made to feel like second-class citizens compared with tenured or tenure-track faculty. Exclusionary devices were the typical lack of office space, mailboxes, and support staff. Only two GA/TAs reported being assigned a mentor. Individuals working as adjuncts scoffed at the question as naive. When asked what support was provided, adjuncts unanimously agreed it was "nonexistent." At points during the discussion, adjuncts brought up instances in which their invisibility receded, but many of these instances were apparently painful. One instructor reported attending festive departmental parties (always invited by posted notices, not by personal invitation) but gave up trying to engage tenured and tenure-track faculty. Another recalled: "At the last party, I was standing with the chair of the department, who looked distracted. I was conscious of not trying to ask about next semester's opportunities. Professor M——, the one who never says hello to me, waved to us across the room. She came up to us, planted herself between the chairperson and me—with her back to me. That was one of my worst moments" (Arièl, English).

Contingent workers of higher education were not consistently "invisible," but visibility was a problem for certain adjuncts. An ABD in social psychology at an urban public university made this point:

> When they want something from you, it changes. All of a sudden, for just a couple moments, they [the department chair] are actually talking to you like a colleague. "Will you teach the drug course?" "Can you make it more of a health psych course than a biopsych course?" . . . At my school they don't tell you when they are going to evaluate your class. So, this department chair, who I helped out [by teaching the course], sent the most hostile evaluator in the department, who of course [also] happened to be a physiological psychologist . . . and this woman hated the syllabus. After that class, I sat outside the chair's office until he would see me. . . . Then I made this decision [to retrain]. (Sharon, now retraining in clinical psychology)

Resentfulness and bitterness did not dominate all of their comments about jobs and working conditions. Many instructors reported frustration, others appeared resigned, and a few were deeply disappointed. Yet, almost every adjunct expressed enjoyment about their teaching, as well as some frustration about their teaching assignments.

> How much satisfaction do you get from your job? . . . I feel very frustrated at [A] College. . . . Less is expected of the students and I consistently wind up teaching down, and I find that exasperating. . . . And then I realized after a while, wait a minute, there's got to be more to life than teaching high school to college-age students. . . . By contrast, I find [B] College very satisfying . . . there's a good percentage of the students that do their homework, are prepared, and are attentive, and I find that immensely satisfying, even for the remedial classes. (Matthew, math)
>
> I have been teaching so many intros in so many places that I start wondering, "Am I any good?" And so I ask my students, "Am I?" And they consistently tell me that even on a bad day I'm more interesting than almost any other class they have! (Penelope, sociology)

Finally, adjuncts, many who were still students themselves, reported the importance of suppressing concerns about their future livelihood. Older ABDs and Ph.D.'s talked about denial as an everyday form of coping with the lack of jobs in their fields, and this denial about the lack of academic openings was clearly something that they had in common with their own teachers and supervisors: "The first class I ever took in graduate school, I remember [that] the first professor in my first class said, 'We're not here to think about jobs or money . . . we are here to [discuss] literature'" (Arièl).

Identity and Stigma

An adjunct with eleven years of experience made one of the more riveting statements during this research. What the adjunct, who is white, observed was that adjuncts acquire a stigma, a racelike quality in a racist society, that permanently changes the identity of the worker to others: "Working as an adjunct is like becoming a Black. You cannot become White again" (Arièl). This adjunct's comment illuminates the privileges associated with the political, social, and cultural constructions of whiteness (Fine et al., 1997; Frankenburg, 1993). The adjunct's error is believing that whiteness is equivalent with goodness. Michelle Fine (1997: 58) has commented on how institutions are particularly prone to constructing hierarchies of privilege: "Whiteness, like all 'colors,' is being manufactured, in part, through institutional arrangements. This is particularly the case in institutions designed 'as if' hierarchy, stratification, and scarcity were inevitable."

The same institutions that erect conditional or contingent relationships with workers also provide a filter through which identity is valued or stigmatized. Schools may not provide a formal employment contract until after the first or second week of school so that if there are not enough attendees, the course can be "bumped," and the contingent worker is left without a class, work, and earnings. The notation "TBA" for course instructors in a semester's catalog was vigorously derided by almost all adjuncts. One instructor commented that "TBA" was used to describe her as the instructor of a course even though she had been teaching this course every fall for three years.

Finally, one adjunct commented that some adjuncts internalize the messages they receive about their work and status: "There is this very subtle, insidious and pernicious attitude that many adjuncts adopt about being second-class teachers . . . that a person teaching adjunct has less experience and less expertise. They come to believe it and . . . it is erroneous" (Arièl). Other adjuncts develop defenses in reaction to such messages. "At [C] College, many of the teachers in the English department think they're at Cambridge. There is this incredible arrogance, insensitivity. Some adjuncts adopt the arrogance, the arrogance and snootiness of the full-time people. . . . They're in denial . . . it's like they adopt the mannerisms with nothing behind it, not realizing that they are totally insecure, they have no *real* job" (Arièl).

Declining Beliefs in Meritocracy

Graduate teaching assistants and the experienced adjunct instructors expressed very different views regarding their belief in meritocracy. Meritocracy, a term introduced by Michael Young (1958) in the book *The Rise of Meritocracy,* signifies a system of thought meant to advance merit (intelligence plus effort) in education as a basis of individual achievement. More recently, the term has assumed greater meaning in the sense that all job holders attain their jobs on the basis of merit alone, rather than gender, race, or other social indicators. There are few beliefs as strongly supportive of the American Dream as the belief in meritocracy.

Although the GA/TAs, who are second- and third-year graduate assistants, were not uninformed about the limited job prospects in academia, none challenged department actions and goals in supplying individuals with doctorates to a job market that was nearly nonexistent. These less experienced students were not naive, but they were more upbeat about their future than the ABDs or Ph.D.'s who felt stuck or insecure in their contingent jobs. The more experienced instructors believed that they had *not* made many errors in their career lives. They believed that colleagues who did obtain full-time work were *not* more capable, only more fortunate. The legitimacy of their graduate school training and the mission of faculty were greatly undermined, as the adjuncts focused on whether scholars of their generation were getting a fair deal.

> You are force-fed the idea that if you work hard you get good grades and then you go on and get more good grades, then you go to a good college and you get more good grades, then you go to graduate school. And of course, you work hard, you get good grades, therefore there should be this reward! *(group laughter)* And then you suddenly realize that this is fine in the ivory tower, but it has nothing to do with the world out there that will someday pay your salary. (Fiona, music)
>   Like a Ponzi scheme. (Matthew)

Those with the most experience reported a sense of dwindling legitimacy of their role in the academy, accompanied by a negative interpretation of their role in maintaining the status and well-being of full-time faculty members. These views are distinct from those reported by Emily Abel (1984), in which many interviewees blamed themselves for their plight. This change may have to do with the greater awareness regarding the restructuring of the workplace and, specifically, the role of adjuncts in cost savings for institutions in higher education. The ability to locate causes outside the self may be realistic and healthy; however, it underlines the inability of these professionals to view themselves, rightly or wrongly, as directing their career or occupational fates. Thus, contingent work contributes to a decline in the belief in meritocracy. If meritocracy is the glue of institutional life, then contingent work may be the solvent that dissolves a belief in the fairness of institutional systems.

Muzzled Protest

Most participants in the research believed they could not engage openly in a politics of resistance. Many instructors found novel ways, however, to resist exclusion, and these strategies are discussed below. Like temporary workers in clerical industries (Tucker, 1993), instructors mostly reported discouragement and disappointment in their workplace, and when they did try to engage the system, it was at the level of nonconfrontational tactics such as gossip or exit. Unlike temporary workers in clerical jobs, however, Ph.D.'s and doctoral candidates have been professionally socialized.

One aspect of professional socialization is learning to mute or muzzle protest concerning injustice in order to gain a footing in the profession. This may appear to resemble loyalty, but for many of these workers, they are experiencing "entrapment" (Withey & Cooper, 1989). When voicing discontent is too costly, the *appearance* of loyalty through silence or cooperation protects the worker from the costs associated with voice. Workers may learn these costs from observing others or, less fortunately, personally experience these costs.

All instructors commented on their uneasiness with the power relations of their department. One GA/TA felt it was impossible to counter unfairness at the interpersonal or organizational level but that organizing a union or coalition was "a waste of time." The same person later commented on the politics of course scheduling. In his department, some adjuncts were given coveted classes and time slots, and he was one of this "loyal" group. "Troublemakers" were given the worst meeting times on a "take it or leave it" basis. Almost all of the respondents approved of union organization but complained that their union, which also represented full-time faculty, did not actively recruit adjuncts. A few adjuncts suggested that the union was less interested in adjunct issues and therefore was not a vehicle through which adjuncts could freely articulate their concerns. Researchers have noted that dual tracks in the academy may ultimately disempower tenured and tenure-track academics who have benefited from the use of contingent workers to preserve their positions (Warme & Lundy, 1988).

Resistance

Using the distinction between oppositional behaviors and resistance as a guide (Giroux, 1983), resistance is defined as behaviors that counteract individual or group oppression by challenging either the explicit or implicit rules that govern employment relationships between adjuncts and colleges or universities. Oppositional behaviors are those that oppose the system but hurt the individual in the long run. Oppositional behaviors, such as lessened attention to teaching in the areas of grading, lecture preparation, and to a lesser extent advising, were not reported in interviews. One instructor did, however, talk about the need to *manage* unpredictable course loads and very large classes.

> I'm in a different position [from full-time faculty] walking into these [large classes], especially when I teach three or four Intro to Social Science [classes]. I have graduate degrees in three fields. [I think I can] do this off the top of [my] head. . . . But the other piece of it is that my standards

often slip in the larger class [because they do] less work per student. . . . You give me forty-five people, multiple-choice tests, give me a Scantron, and to me, it doesn't matter what I get paid for the course, there is only so much time that I'm going to budget for a course. . . . I keep reminding myself that I am only human, that I am not cheating them in relation to full-time faculty, if anything, because I am doing dissertation work . . . that they are getting new stuff that a lot of the full-timers . . . who are teaching four and five every term can't give them. . . . Those full-timers [have] a flat EKG! (Penelope)

Penelope developed a set of comparison standards that departed from norms regarding full-time faculty status. She observed problems with those teaching full-time, one of which was burnout. She responded with a calculus that she considered just and fair given her adjunct status, a time budget for her courses. She was realistic about the job and pointed to conditions of the job itself as justifying various reactions and behaviors. Penelope resisted efforts to define her job as similar to those working full-time and therefore was more insightful in appraising her situation than those coworkers of Arièl's who adopted the mannerisms and even the work attitudes of full-time faculty.

Adjuncts were acutely aware of the job market and their precariousness within it, and they reported two coping strategies. The first strategy entailed *not* reporting all teaching experience on the CV when applying for full-time positions. The second coping strategy they reported has been commonly misinterpreted by chroniclers of academe. It is generally acknowledged that social science research funding has declined and Ph.D.'s have been overproduced (Bérubé & Nelson, 1995). Observers often point out that this has had an undesirable effect on doctoral students because it has prolonged their time in the academy as they seek alternative sources of financial support. This is undoubtedly correct. Adjuncts, however, also report deliberately postponing the "minting" of their doctorate for as long as they could until they acquired what one adjunct called "that mythical, full-time job" (Fiona).

Accumulating Deficits

Older adjuncts reported receiving two messages: teaching general courses is good, but anything taught by adjuncts is less than adequate.

It's a course taught by an adjunct. How good can an adjunct be? . . . Or they ask you, "What can you teach that's basic?" . . . I'd kill to teach something slightly more specific than everything! . . . Gee, what happens if I find that mythical full-time job and they suddenly ask me to teach something specific, and I'm going, "Can I do that?" Can I remember anything beyond that Beethoven was a composer in this century? . . . Can I be more specific than to say, "Yes, he wrote nine symphonies"? . . . There's this real fear that someone's gonna ask me a real tough question, faculty to faculty, job interview or something, and I'm just gonna go, "I have to go home and look it up." There's this feeling that, yeah, I've been doing this for ten years . . . I've paid my dues with my Ph.D., when do I get to use it? (Fiona)

Working as an adjunct may give the individual needed teaching experience among other benefits. Research needs to specify, however, the costs of working contingently over time. For example, as workers are enveloped within a system of contingent relationships, are they valued for their skills and their readiness to apply them on short notice, or are they devalued because their merit has a planned obsolescence? In addition, does the transience or campus-to-campus migration of these workers— the subway dons and freeway fliers—foster a process of devaluation?

Fiona's comments are suggestive regarding the long-term consequences of contingent work. For example, consider the beliefs and expectations of permanent medical personnel in a hospital. Technological advances require periodic training on new medical equipment. If, for example, a contingent nurse is consistently passed over when training on new equipment is conducted, over time that individual could be considered to be *accumulating deficits* of contingency.

Various sources of evidence suggest differential treatment is associated with part-time, temporary, and contractor status (Barker, 1993; Carré, 1992; duRivage, 1992a; Shockey & Mueller, 1994; Wells, Kochan, & Smith, 1991). "Difference" may also subsequently create a deficit model when employers use such jobs as a way to evade worker protections such as unemployment compensation and occupational safety and health protections (see Chapters 9, 10, 11, and 12, this volume). Deficits also accumulate to the individual from structural conditions of work, such as when promotion opportunities, autonomy, challenge, the opportunity to learn new skills, and other conditions are unavailable or denied (Barker, 1993).

In concluding this section, some issues merit consideration. Amid the restructuring of higher education, faculty continue to pride themselves on a number of ideals. These ideals persist even in the face of an emerging two-tier faculty system. One of these ideals concerns the notion of community. Discussing the psychological sense of community, Katherine Klein and Thomas D'Aunno (1986) note that the individuals with whom one works are more a part of one's daily life than any other group of individuals except for one's family. Community, in the academic sense, refers to progressive notions regarding mutual citizenship and commonality linked through the missions of teaching and research. Yet, a number of assumptions are embedded in this notion of community, and these deserve further examination and articulation. The continued expansion of positions with a flexible status, as distinct from the prized status of tenure or a tenure-track job, is proof of a divided community in a two-tier system. Such a system diminishes, or contributes to diminishing, the status of scholar-teachers in the bottom tier. There is no doubt that institutions are flexible because of the adjunct workforce (although they may also lose some stability because they rely increasingly on adjuncts). *As institutions gain in flexibility and other advantages from adjunct instructors, however, those instructors are absorbing some of the costs that institutions shed.* Instructors could be viewed as *accumulating deficits* associated with their contingent status. But just how does the accumulation of deficits emerge? One way to study whether contingent workers are accumulating deficits associated with their status is to examine what impact contingent work has on the credentials of workers. For example, when workers attempt to leave contingent work arrangements for more traditional arrangements—such as a permanent job—how are their credentials evaluated?

Study II. Does Experience Count or Cost the Individual? Contingent Work Experience and Accumulating Deficits

Adjunct instructors believe they accumulate deficits associated with their contingent work status even though their work experience is highly relevant to future jobs in higher education. They fear that their job-relevant experience actually hampers their future chances. They report that they are unable to teach advanced courses and that this results in a "numbing" of their skills and knowledge base. Although they know they fill an increasingly important role within colleges and universities, they worry that the more experience they report, the more the prejudice they will face. Finally, they fear that a permanent and negative change in their perceived identity will result from working as an adjunct. The purpose of this section is to test selected findings from the qualitative study reported above.

The notion that job-relevant experience might harm rather than help a worker is not intuitively appealing. Acknowledging that other factors are relevant as well (references, education, perceived quality of dissertation and doctoral program, advisor, a suitable number of publications appropriate to the stage of an individual's career, etc.), job-relevant work experience, such as classroom teaching, would still appear to be important in the decision to hire an academic. In fact, experience accounts for a substantial portion of variance in explaining income. Job knowledge and capability to perform a job have been reasoned to be positively affected by work experience (Schmidt, Hunter, & Outerbridge, 1986). Abel (1984), however, has noted adjuncts' fear of reporting all of their experience to potential employers. In her survey of California educators, adjuncts worried that too many publications would result in damaging their prospects of getting a job by pricing themselves out of the market. Adjunct instructors felt that working as an adjunct was a high-risk job in still other ways: "We have seen that adjuncts rarely are promoted to the ranks of the full-time faculty. In addition, many displaced academics were convinced that the longer they remained part-timers, the more elusive any regular position became. No matter how glowing their past records, they incurred some of the stigma of part-time employment" (Abel, 1984:115).

Before testing the hypothesis of accumulating deficits reported by adjuncts, we need to examine what is known about work experience in the selection process. How does work experience psychologically impact on a recruiter and determine whether a candidate is perceived as fit or unfit for a job?

Work Experience

While there is ample literature urging recruiters to focus on work experience, there is little on what types of information influence perceptions of job candidates. According to Ming Singer and Chris Bruhns (1991: 551) in their review of the literature, "Work experience as an independent variable and its effect on selection-interview decisions have been examined in only a few studies." In his study of impression formation, Stephen Knouse (1994) used resumes to predict interviewer response. He found that when resumes contained job-relevant education and job-relevant experience, perceptions of the applicant were more enhanced than when the resume also contained job-irrelevant qualifications. Other researchers, however, report that job-irrelevant sources of information are weighted in the selection process (Kinicki & Lockwood, 1985; Hitt & Barr, 1989). In examining academic qualifications and work experience of hypothetical managers in their own study, Singer and Bruhns found that work experience accounted for a greater proportion of variance in deciding that candidates were suitable, that they had a good chance of success on the job, and that they also were suitable for hiring. Singer and Bruhns manipulated quantity and quality of work experience—low (five years of experience in an unrelated position) and high (up to ten years of service in two related previous positions)—and found that candidates who were more than qualified (possessing M.B.A.'s) for employment as a sales-representative supervisor were more likely to be hired when they also possessed a high level of relevant work experience. This result supported prior findings (Stone & Sawatzki, 1980) that evaluation and likelihood of hire were positively affected by relevancy of work experience. In terms of *length* of work experience, researchers have found that work experience (none vs. five years) was more important to evaluators than age, race, and sex (Fusilier & Hitt, 1983; cf. Macan, Detjen, & Dickey, 1994), and fifteen years of experience was found to have greater positive impact on evaluations than ten years (Hitt & Barr, 1989).

These studies suggest that increasing quantities of job-relevant experience should result in more positive evaluations when job-irrelevant facts are equivalent across conditions. Yet due to the limited number of studies that have explored the issue of work experience, very few positions (e.g., sales, marketing, management) and industries have been studied. The variable of job experience is typically manipulated as dichotomous— it is either relevant or irrelevant, long or short. No study has considered increments of experience within occupations that have multiple tiers such as contingent and noncontingent. If such tiers present a potential for stigmatization, due to the devaluation of a contingent tier of an occupation, we need to learn how this affects job candidates in a selection process. That is, we need to learn whether length of work experience can indeed have a negative impact when a candidate is working in what is perceived to be a nonnormative capacity, that is, contingently.

The reaction of evaluators to work experience can also be measured by exploring their reaction to a series of closed-ended questions ("How likely is it that this person would be recommended for an interview?"). Reactions can be explored less directly as well. In the latter instance, researchers are interested in the type of questions that interviewers or evaluators generate themselves. For example, in the context of a job interview, confirmation behaviors are behaviors that corroborate a priori notions regarding an individual. Such behaviors are enacted by recruiters who seek to confirm that their first impressions or what might be termed "initial suspicions" are valid. Mark Snyder and William

Swann (1978) explored the confirmatory bias in inquiry strategies used by interviewers. This research revealed that interviewers will select questions in the search for information that will confirm, rather than disconfirm, hypotheses they hold about the individual interviewee. Robert Dipboye (1982:579) proposed a model using self-fulfilling prophecies to explain why "interviewers may notice, recall, and interpret events that occur in the interview in a manner that is consistent with their initial impressions." Most studies, however, have not utilized open-ended questions to elicit participants' evaluative responses to candidates. The combination of closed-ended questions and the study of fairly homogenous occupations could lead to an incomplete understanding regarding the meaning of work experience in the selection process of particular worker categories. Some researchers, however, failed to find that interviewers conform to Snyder and Swann's predictions (e.g., McDonald & Hakel, 1985; Sackett, 1982). John Binning and colleagues (1988) found much stronger support for the confirmatory bias when participants were permitted to freely produce their questions rather than select from a list of predefined questions, as participants did in Paul Sackett's (1982) study. Others found some support that poorly qualified candidates were asked fewer positive questions and more difficult questions (Macan & Dipboye, 1988).

Research Questions and Method

The first research prediction is that the more job-relevant contingent work experience a candidate reports, the more negatively evaluated the candidate will be. That is, due to the stigma attached to the adjunct work status, the more experience the candidate reports, the lower the likelihood that a candidate will be recommended for a campus visit or recommended for hire.

A common belief in academe concerns the notion that the "minted" year of a Ph.D. is critical in the evaluation process and may interact with other variables, such as with work experience. Academic qualifications will also be manipulated such that the candidate's degree is "minted" one year earlier or six years earlier than respondents' receipt of the questionnaire. Therefore, the next set of research predictions concern year of degree. Will the candidate with the older degree have less of a chance of being recommended for a campus visit and hire than the candidate with the more recent degree? The combination of greater adjunct work experience *and* older degrees, it is predicted, will result in more negative evaluations than fewer years of adjunct work experience and recent degrees.

Confirmatory question generation will also be examined. Given the sparse and highly competitive job market that many ABDs or Ph.D.'s face when searching for full-time and permanent positions, the advantages or disadvantages of having held a particular job are critical. In the eyes of the beholder, different types of experience may influence a number of subsequent interviewer impressions concerning a candidate. Given the high investment that is associated with obtaining the doctorate in the United States, job-relevant work experience should be evaluated positively. This evaluation should lead to positive or at least neutral attributions in open-ended questions generated by interviewers. Yet, given the reports of individuals in Study II above and comments by Abel (1984), it is expected that a job candidate with more adjunct experience will be asked more negative questions by evaluators than job candidates with less adjunct experience.

The research questions led to the development of a survey that tested four conditions for length of work experience and two conditions for year of degree. Each respondent received *one* survey representing one of *eight* possible combinations of study. In February 1994, a survey and follow-up requests for survey completion were mailed to a random sample of 450 department chairpersons and deans in universities and four-year colleges in the United States. Seven surveys were returned as undeliverable. After two follow-up reminder mailings, the final survey sample was 113 for a response rate of 26 percent. The final sample of survey instruments was evenly distributed across all eight conditions of the study ($\chi^2 = (3) .10, p\ ns$).

The survey instrument consisted of a set of questions regarding a hypothetical candidate and a separate section of questions regarding the respondent and her or his institution. The hypothetical candidate for the position was presented in a brief vignette that represented a variation on the conditions (length of work experience and year of degree). Respondents were instructed to "react to the vignette regarding a candidate 'RM' for a position within your department." The following vignette was varied for each condition:

> RM has provided a CV in application for a tenure-track teaching position in your department. RM was awarded the doctorate in 1988 (1993) and is 33 years of age. You are familiar with the dissertation advisor that RM specified in a cover letter. In terms of qualifications, RM has an appropriate

number of publications in journals, considering the date of the doctorate. RM has 3 (5, 7, 9) years experience working as an instructor in adjunct positions. RM has complied with your institution's request for all supporting documentation, excepting one letter of reference which took longer to arrive than other letters.

Testing four levels of experience allowed an analysis of low to moderate to high amounts of experience. Since the median number of years to complete a doctorate was 10.9 in 1988 and 11.2 among those graduating in 1993 (U.S. Department of Education, 1995), nine years of experience was selected as the maximum number of years for the Work Experience variable. The statement regarding respondents' knowledge of the advisor, as well as the candidate having an appropriate publication record, was included to discourage standard questions about these areas. One ambiguous and irrelevant job cue (a late letter of reference) was also included to help disguise the variables under study. Items regarding the likelihood of the respondent recommending a campus visit and the suitability of the candidate for hiring purposes were the main items of interest in answering the first research question. Respondents were asked to rate the candidate on a ten-point, Likert-type scale, indicating from 1 (very unlikely) to 10 (very likely) their responses to the questions "How likely is it that you would recommend RM for a campus *visit*?" and "Should RM be brought to campus, how likely is it that RM would be *hired*?" To test the second research question regarding confirmatory bias, respondents were asked to generate at least three questions in response to the vignette. Respondents were also asked to list any other questions they might have. These open-ended responses comprised the data for analysis of confirmatory bias. The resultant question type and within-question subcategories are presented in Table 8.1. The questions coded as Job-Related or Personality Trait were subcategorized as either positive or negative. Finally, each open-ended response was coded as invasive-noninvasive and this dimension will also be tested.

Results and Discussion

The first two research predictions concerned whether adjunct work experience and year of doctorate would have a negative impact on the likelihood of being recommended for a campus visit and being hired. In a 2 × 4 analysis of variance tests for the effects of degree and years of adjunct experience, respondents did not differ in their evaluation that RM be recommended for a campus visit. Respondents did, however, react differently in their responses to RM's chance of being hired. In ana-

Table 8.1 Questions generated by deans and chairpersons in academic survey: category codes and sub-category codes

---

1 Job-related: knowledge, skill or ability

Quality of research, service, publications
Teaching issues: quality of teaching evaluations, teaching commitment
Letters of recommendation: contents and whether they address teaching, research, etc.
Candidate-institution fit
Time-frame questions regarding degree and job fit
Professional goals
General strengths
Why leaving adjunct job?
Unusual requirement issues (e.g., must have all experience in one adjunct job)
Candidate experience or publication: "something wrong" with experience or publications

2 Personality trait, personal situation

What is race/ethnicity?
What is gender?
Letters of recommendation: what are contents regarding personality
Cognitive abilities
Interpersonal abilities
What is age or age related questions
Why interest in position/institution?
Family or uncontrollable forces as problem
Focus on late reference letter
Something wrong with candidate traits

3 Status

Qualities of graduate institution
Quality of journals in which published
Renown of dissertation advisor

4 Other category

Years to earn Ph.D.
Comparison with other candidates
Nonacademic experience
Institutional financial
Limits/salary
  Geographic limitations for bringing candidate
  Interviewee impression formation
  Interviewers' discretion/communication process
  Focus on stimulus letter as late
  More information needed

lyzing responses to the question regarding the likelihood of RM's being hired, an analysis of variance test for the effects of year of degree and years of adjunct experience revealed that only work experience was significant ($F(3, 82) = 3.524, p < .02$). The more adjunct experience, the lower the chance the candidate had of being recommended for hiring. A two-way interaction between work experience and year of Ph.D. was only marginally significant ($F(3, 82) = 2.6, p < .06$). Figure 8.1 presents mean scores and depicts the relationship between the two independent variables on the likelihood of the hire variable. The likelihood of hire drops to lower levels for candidates with 1988 and 1993 degrees with more than five years of experience (although for candidates with 1993 degrees and only three years of experience, the likelihood is lower still).

The next set of research questions concern whether respondents would engage in confirmatory question generation such that the longer the adjunct experience of the hypothetical candidate, the more negative and fewer positive questions would be generated. The first four analyses probed for differences in respondents' strategies in asking Job-related positive/neutral questions, Job-related negative questions, Personality trait positive/neutral questions, and Personality trait negative/potentially negative questions. Of these four, the two Job-related categories of ques-

Figure 8.1 Mean scores on likelihood of hire by years of adjunct experience and year of degree

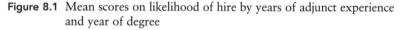

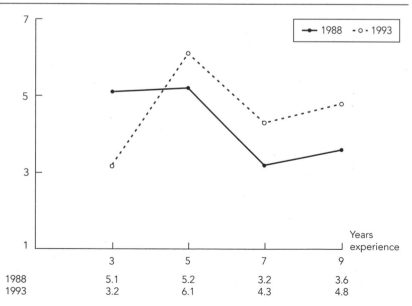

	3	5	7	9
1988	5.1	5.2	3.2	3.6
1993	3.2	6.1	4.3	4.8

tions were significantly different. In 2 × 4 analysis of variance testing for the effects of year of degree and years of adjunct experience, the greater the number of years a candidate worked as an adjunct, the more they were asked Job-related negative questions ($F(3, 105) = 5.31, p < .02$) and the less they were asked Job-related positive questions ($F(3, 105) = 4.33, p < .03$). No interactions were significant. Possessing a recent or older degree did not result in different strategies about Job-related questions.

Next, Status questions were examined. Status questions pertain to discretionary information, questions typically phrased as concerns with "candidate quality" (see Table 8.1). When the hypothetical candidate possessed an older degree (1988), respondents were more curious about the quality of their graduate institution, journals of publication, and renown of dissertation advisor ($F(1, 105) = 3.8, p < .05$). Adjunct work experience was not significant ($F(3, 105) = .34, p < ns$). None of the questions that were coded as "Other" (Table 8.1), including the irrelevant cue of a late reference letter, were significantly different by year of degree or teaching experience. Finally, questions were coded as to their invasiveness. Respondents tended to use more invasive questions when the hypothetical candidate possessed an older degree ($F(1,105) = 8.51, p < .002$).

Although the results do not indicate that department evaluators are using work experience as a *single* criterion for determining the adequacy of candidates, there is evidence that cumulative contingent work experience was negatively related to perceived likelihood of hire and impacted negatively on respondents' use of confirmatory questions regarding applicant information. While respondents did not differ regarding the likelihood of a candidate being invited to campus, they were much more likely to rate the candidate as unlikely to succeed in the hiring phase. As Figure 8.1 shows, contingent work experience is less valued by evaluators when considering a recent Ph.D.; it is similarly valued at five years of experience for both a recent and older degree; but after five years, contingent work experience is appraised negatively. There was a non-significant tendency for the individual with the older degree and more than five years of contingent work experience to be appraised more negatively than a similar individual with a more recent doctorate.

By generating more negative and fewer positive approaches to gathering information regarding job relevant characteristics, respondents appeared to be confirming their own initial suspicions that a significant amount of contingent work experience was a negative factor in the evaluation process. This negative evaluation occurred in reaction to some of the most important data in screening candidates' employment background. Adjunct work experience was not related to discretionary questions regarding the "quality" of the candidate's credentials or the invasiveness of the question, but year of degree was related. The more recent Ph.D. was questioned less about status—and questioned in a more appropriate or less invasive manner—than the individual with the older doctorate. The older degree may have served to organize a perceptual set that granted the evaluator an immunity. Such immunity enabled the evaluator to ask more invasive or inappropriate questions. Personality trait questions—positive, neutral, and negative—were unrelated to either year of degree or teaching experience. Respondents were probably aware of the illegalities or irrelevancy of some of these questions, and most may have hesitated to report them.

The two variables, experience and year of degree, did not interact to form a cumulative model of disadvantage. Contingent work experience, however, appears to affect a number of key areas for academic evaluators. Unlike other studies that show that length of work experience positively affected candidate evaluations (Fusilier & Hitt, 1983; Hitt & Barr, 1989), length of work experience exerted a downward trend on some variables in this study. These findings support Singer and Bruhns's (1991) contention that studies of workplace experience should control for both quantity and "quality" of that experience. In addition, the present study yielded a rich array of questioning strategies used by academic evaluators. In terms of job-relevant questions concerning knowledge, skills, and abilities, candidates with an older degree may face a more challenging interview situation. Older degrees led to closer questioning regarding the "quality" of the candidates' background.

A rival explanation for the above findings is that many (seven to nine) years of contingent work experience is not normative. Such experience could be viewed as inconsistent with other information provided about the candidate. Candidates with many years of experience are simply not prototypical and therefore elicit more negative responses from evaluators. This explanation, however, begs the question. First, there was not much information about the candidate in this study, and so it would be more difficult for evaluators to determine which features were inconsistent with others. Second, given that the *median* time to achieve a doctorate among graduates in 1993 ranged from a low of 7.8 in the natural sciences to a high of 19.7 in education, seven to nine years of adjunct instruction would be high but hardly excessive. In fact, it is supportive of the general findings of this study that evaluators were *underestimating* what could be the normative employment experience for recent doctorates.

A secondary issue concerns the evaluator in higher education. Are evaluators knowledgeable regarding academic job markets and contemporary experiences of recent doctoral graduates? For example, in 1970, 80.3 percent of new doctoral recipients in the social and behavioral sciences had definite employment plans in higher education (U.S. Department of Education, 1993). By 1993 this percentage was reduced to slightly more than *half* of all new recipients, 53.4 percent. Even so, a number of evaluators in this study wanted to know why the individual in the vignette wanted to *leave* their adjunct position for a permanent position! Some academic evaluators appear to underestimate the competitiveness of the job market or other factors, such as geographic limitations or family responsibilities, that may influence a candidate's job history. It is as if there must be *something wrong* with the candidate—in the candidate's background or job-related skills—if he or she has not acquired a permanent job. Evaluators were counting years of experience in temporary positions, but they were also doing more than that. After a cutoff period of approximately five years of experience, evaluators counted years of experience but subtracted a value from the individual as a candidate. Counting years of experience and devaluing that experience resulted in injustice, because individuals are typically led to believe that experience *counts*—that it does not cost the individual. The result is, in effect, blaming the victim (Ryan, 1971) for structural features that may be beyond the control of the individual candidate.

Future research on the evaluation of experience should be attentive to the development of different attachment schemes in the workplace, academic or corporate. We need to understand what heuristics an evaluator uses and their relationship to contingent vs. noncontingent work experience. To the degree that evaluators retain outdated or incorrect expectations regarding employment conditions in the academy, thereby making assumptions concerning the merits of applicants' experience, they will penalize individual applicants for structural disadvantages. Blaming the victim for participating in "stigmatized" workplace activities results in an accrual of disadvantages, both economic and social. That a two-tier academy emerges and stabilizes during a period of an intense "ratcheting up" (Burgan, 1997:5) of tenure standards for junior faculty is especially disquieting.

One strength of the current study is that rather than relying on proxy respondents, such as students, the participants are actual decision makers in academe. A limitation of the study, however, is the moderate response rate. This response rate means that the findings of this study require replication for further theorizing about contingent workers in the academy.

Finally, additional study is needed. Given some of the unusual features of occupational life in higher education, we need to study other occupations, professional and nonprofessional, to learn more about the generalizability of these findings.

A central feature of discrimination was recognized by G. W. Allport (1954:50) when he wrote that discrimination functions to reinforce "the inferiority of out-group standards to our own." Certainly the contingent workers of each industry face particular challenges, benefits, and disadvantages that are historically and socially rooted within particular occupations and histories. Not all contingent workers will be viewed as members of out-groups and excluded on a systematic basis. For some contingent workers, such as technical "knowledge" workers, such exclusion is not a penalty but a reward and freedom to move between and across organizational, institutional, and occupational membranes. For these "piece-rate" laborers, entrepreneurial conditions dominate their workplace experiences (Kanter, 1995). For contingent workers toiling in the knowledge factory, however, conditions are less favorable. Many of these workers do not start out thinking that their temporary experiences are a weak element in the scaffolding of work experience, and yet others simply do not have a choice but to try to stay within higher education. For these piece-rate workers, contingent relations may be especially cruel.

Research is needed that not only expands and improves on some of the ideas discussed above but that also addresses the possibilities of an activist research program. Research is needed concerning the emergence of a permanent two-tier faculty in higher education, with privileges reserved for some at the cost to others. Privileges enjoyed by tenured and tenure-track faculty are not neutral, for they function to silence and blame those restricted to the borders of permanent employment possibilities. Considering the unease that some might feel in approaching these issues, it becomes particularly important for both groups to participate in the design, execution, and analysis of research. Adjunct instructors need to be full partners in the research enterprise, whether it concerns conditions of employment or the heuristics utilized in the evaluation process. Most promising of all would be for all researchers to look inward and illuminate areas of inequity within the academy itself.

Contingent work is a social issue *and* a social process . Research that probes the human face of contingent work will unveil opportunities for transforming contingent work and contribute to a reordered and more humane workplace.

CHAPTER NINE

Sisyphus at Work in the Warehouse: Temporary Employment in Greenville, South Carolina

Jean McAllister

A current debate in popular, academic, and policy media centers on the question of whether the proliferation of temporary employment arrangements is good news or bad for American workers. This essay enters this debate by exploring the day-to-day experiences of one subgroup within the temporary workforce who find temporary employment to be an inadequate substitute for the permanent jobs they seek, exposing them to difficulties not faced by the nontemporary workers doing equivalent work for the same employers. Like Sisyphus, condemned to push a stone from the bottom to the top of a hill for all eternity, each of these workers struggles up from the bottom rung of the ladder of employment each day only to wake up at the bottom again. Their daily efforts are erased overnight so that each day's labor has been, and will likely continue to be, no more rewarding or secure than the day before.

The Arguments in Brief

The temporary services industry has claimed for many years that temporary employment arrangements liberate workers from unwanted commitments and so are in demand by workers with priorities (and sources of support) outside of paid employment, such as new workers who want to shop around, struggling artists, women with school-age children (and working spouses), seniors (with pensions or social security), or students (with parents or grants). The industry also maintains

This essay is based on a research study conducted by the Carolina Alliance for Fair Employment with assistance from the Poverty & Race Research Action Council and the Tennessee Industrial Renewal Network. Earlier drafts of this essay were greatly improved by the criticisms offered by Kathleen Barker, Tom Brooks, Kathleen Christensen, Florence Gardner, Louisa Meacham, Joan McAllister, Keith McAllister, Deborah Merrill Sands, and Kristin Nelson. The people whose stories are retold below have my heartfelt gratitude for the efforts they made to help me understand, as well as my apologies for the inevitable simplifications and distortions that any writing entails.

that by working for (or through) a temporary services agency, workers can retain all the material and occupational benefits of working for a traditional employer.[1]

On the other hand, researchers working with broad economic and demographic data have asserted that temporary employment is an employer-driven phenomenon and that—while some workers prefer temporary employment—most workers are temporary involuntarily; that temporary workers do not receive occupational and material benefits (both cash and noncash) at the same rates as other workers, whether they work through temporary agencies or not; and that a correlation exists between "flexible" employment arrangements like temporary work and relative economic distress.[2] Advocates and researchers have asserted that temporary employees are outside of the protective web of labor legislation that regulates the relationship between employers and workers and provides a material safety net for workers in trouble.[3] Descriptive case studies of particular workers and their experiences of temporary employment have demonstrated that working as a temporary employee can also entail social, emotional, and psychological costs invisible to formal data collection techniques.[4] These explorations into the complex, mundane experience of working as a temporary employee have also suggested that the structure and dynamics of particular temporary employment relationships constrain workers in ways that are predictable and that begin to explain the negative material and occupational consequences of temporary work suggested by the statistical record.

It was with the desire to explore the details of the particular local temporary employment arrangements and the significance of these arrangements to workers in Greenville, South Carolina, that the study reported below was undertaken. Members of the Carolina Alliance for Fair Employment (CAFE), a community organization that promotes research, education, and community action on issues of importance to working families, have been increasingly concerned by the proliferation

1. For example, Canter, 1988; National Association of Temporary Services, 1994a, 1994b.

2. For example, Golden & Appelbaum, 1992; Belous, 1989; Callaghan & Hartmann, 1992; duRivage, 1992a, 1992b; Hartmann & Lapidus, 1989; Segal & Sullivan, 1995; Spalter-Roth, Hartmann, & Shaw, 1993.

3. For example, Asian Law Caucus et al., 1994; Christensen, 1988; New Ways to Work, 1992; 9 to 5 (National Organization of Working Women), 1994; Southeast Regional Economic Justice Network, 1994; U.S. Government Accounting Office, 1991; U.S. Senate Committee on Labor and Human Resources, 1993.

4. See Barker, 1995; Barrett, 1993; Henson, 1993; Martella, 1992; Parker, 1994; and Rogers, 1995.

of temporary employment in Greenville and the concurrent increase in complaints to the CAFE office by temporary workers. In the fall of 1994, CAFE asked workers who depend on intermittent, low-wage assignments from temporary service agencies in Greenville to describe their relationships with agencies, employers, supervisors, and coworkers as they go about trying to get, perform, and keep jobs. They answered that the arrangements of their employment are such that they are marginal to the organizations for which they work, the relationships within those organizations, and the work process itself. They live under conditions of extreme uncertainty relative to their work schedules, tasks, and incomes. Moreover, they are vulnerable to many types of subtle and blatant exploitation, and are almost entirely powerless to change their status.

Background of the CAFE Study

The city of Greenville, its surrounding county, and indeed the Upstate region of which it and Spartanburg are the center, are all considered exceptionally healthy in economic terms. The strip surrounding Interstate 85 running through Greenville-Spartanburg has been referred to as "the boom belt," a "preferred megacorridor for business," and "the U.S.'s top region for commercial growth" (Foust & Mallory, 1993:98; Levin, 1994:46). Manufacturers, employing about 30 percent of the county's nonagricultural workforce, are the biggest employers in the area. Unemployment figures for the county are consistently lower than those for the state and the country, and the per capita personal income is significantly higher. The temporary employment industry in Greenville is also healthy. Figures on the size and growth of the local temporary labor market in terms of workers or revenue are not available, but the number of agencies grew by 500 percent in ten years. By the fall of 1994, jobs listed in the classified advertisements in the local daily newspaper were almost exclusively available through temporary service agencies.

In November 1994, I joined CAFE in holding a five-day "Temp School" for nineteen experienced temp workers, with staff assistance from the Tennessee Industrial Renewal Network (TIRN) and financial assistance from the Poverty & Race Research Action Council (PRAAC). Participants were recruited through advertisements for "experienced temps" in the local daily paper, and applicants were screened only for the amount of their experience with temporary work and temporary employment agencies. Participating workers, who were paid an hourly wage for their time, spent the week sharing with one another and the workshop organizers their experiences of, and adaptations to, temporary employment.[5] In the weeks following the workshop, I interviewed participants individually about issues raised at the workshop.

Study participants shared two characteristics in particular: The vast majority of the temporary jobs assigned by the agencies to this group were manual and unskilled, such as inspecting parts, cleaning, or packing and moving boxes;[6] and each of the participants was a sole, primary, or significant breadwinner for a household. In other ways, the participants formed a varied group. Ages ranged in the study group from early twenties to fifties, education level varied from sixth grade to college degrees, and work histories varied from manual to management. Before they began temping, about half the group were in the labor force and the other half in school or childrearing. The group was roughly half white and half African-American, and three-quarters women to one-quarter men. For the purposes of this study, however, I will not highlight the significance of demographic variation.[7] I will look, instead, at the common conditions these workers reported experiencing as low wage earning temporary employees.

Some Experiences of Temporary Employment

In an extensive study of work schedules, Kathleen Barker found that workers with part-time hours experienced, relative to workers with full-

5. See Carolina Alliance for Fair Employment, 1995.

6. Industrial work grew from 9 to 23 percent of temporary jobs between 1983 and 1993 (while the percent of total employment in industry fell), according to economists working with data from the Current Population Survey (Segal & Sullivan, 1995), since actual numbers of blue-collar temps grew 468 percent compared to 67 percent and 41 percent for pink- and white-collar temps respectively. A random sample of members of the National Association of Temporary and Staffing Services reported that in 1994 clerical workers and industrial workers brought in about 40 and 34 percent of payroll dollars respectively (despite their low wages relative to workers in the "technical" and "professional" categories) and the percentage of payroll dollars attributed to industrial temps has grown larger since 1991, while that of clerical, technical, and medical temps has grown smaller (Bruce Steinberg, personal communication, June 1995).

7. The study group was more female and more African-American than the total workforce, which according to the Greenville Chamber of Commerce was roughly 53 percent male and 83 percent white in 1991. Data on the other demographic characteristics of the local workforce were unavailable. Data on the characteristics of the local temporary workforce were also unavailable. Fortunately, because the study's goal was to begin exploration into local experiences with temporary employment and agencies, it did not require a representative sample. We were, however, careful to include everyone who responded to our advertisement for "experienced temps," and respondents were screened out only for the amount of experience they had with temporary employment and temporary service agencies.

time schedules, "low participation in organizational activities, high uncertainty, marginality in social relations, and occupational disadvantage vis-à-vis skill development," circumstances she terms "peripherality" (1993: 53). Measured by these dimensions, temp workers in the Greenville study are peripheral in the extreme. Despite the theoretical potential of temporary employment arrangements to provide workers with "Freedom, Flexibility, Choice, and Control" (to quote the industry's trade association brochure), they have created in the lives of these workers only increased marginality, uncertainty, vulnerability, and weakness.

Living on the Margins:
Kimmey Massey Skirts the Edges of the Working World.

Kimmey Massey and her infant son, Darius, share a two-bedroom apartment with a friend and her daughter.[8] The apartment is almost entirely empty, the floors uncovered but for a pristine white carpet and a pot holding a flowering orchid plant. In the bedroom that Kimmey and Darius share, a quilt covers a brass bed, stuffed animals fill the baby's crib, and framed photographs of family stand in a colorful crowd on a small table. Kimmey, now twenty-three years old, was one year short of a college degree when she left school to earn money to send to her parents' troubled household. Three years later, she is delaying her return to school until she has some money saved. Darius's father pays for his son's expenses but cannot provide health insurance. Kimmey has stopped sending money to her parents but must still support herself while paying the balance on her college loan. She desperately wants to get a full-time, year-round job with benefits before Darius's father loses his income and before either she or the baby gets sick. Most recently, Kimmey was making boxes and packing them with very expensive, designer label underwear. "It was a pretty good job, it was just that I thought it was going to be long-term and turn to permanent. I'm going after benefits *wherever* I go!" Kimmey wants most of all the security that comes from being a valued member of an employer's organization, but she can only find work through temporary service agencies, and her relationships with these agencies and their clients do not include benefits, nor any of the other elements of the traditional social contract between employers and employees.

8. This essay includes both pseudonyms and real names, according to the wishes of those interviewed.

Kimmey's face-to-face contact with the personnel at each agency has been limited to the initial sign-up visit, when she was tested and interviewed. Exchanges of time cards and paychecks are usually done impersonally through a drop box and the mail. The dispatcher calls Kimmey's house with assignments, usually at the last minute. If she is home when the agency's call comes, can quickly arrange for someone to watch her son, and has transportation, she accepts the job. None of the agencies have offered her job skills training or useful feedback on any of her myriad completed interviews or assignments. None of the agencies that employ Kimmey have given her a paid sick day, assistance with health insurance, or any other noncash benefit. None of the agencies have even offered her the minimum number of work hours that would meet their eligibility standard for benefits. Kimmey says that the agencies, her legal employers, take money from her real employers for the work she does and give her nothing.[9]

Kimmey's ties to the client employers have been no stronger than her ties to the agencies. They have given her no training beyond simple instructions on each single, narrow task and no information about the shape of, or entry into, internal job ladders. Her temporary supervisors generally end her jobs at a moment's notice, without any explanation. Kimmey told me one of her recent jobs was supposed to be "two weeks to perm."

> I called the woman at the temporary employment service every day, and she said the company was interested in me and that they had another position coming open upstairs, and she said I didn't have anything to worry about because they really liked me. I even talked with the supervisors there and they said, well, all we need to do is to get you to fill out an application and we'll be set. You know they practically told me that they really liked my work and they really liked me being there and that I was guaranteed to get another job through them away from the temp agency. And the next thing you know, it was like, well, do I come back tomorrow, or is the assignment over? And they said, well, we don't have anything else for you today. So that was that.

9. The amount the temporary agencies take above Kimmey's wages is unknown to anyone outside the agencies themselves, but data from the temporary employment services industry indicates that the "average markup is approximately 50 percent" (Segal and Sullivan, 1995:7). In his fascinating analysis of the long-running, high stakes legal negotiations over whether the temporary employment agency is a statutory "employer" or employment agency, George Gonos suggests that "what the worker actually gives up in reduced wages (or if one wishes, fees) is not only for placement per se, but for the privilege of continuing to work" (1994:420).

If Kimmey cannot make it to a job one day because her transportation or child care falls through, then the agency replaces her with another temp, and she is again unemployed.

Kimmey is marginal even to the social interaction among people in the work places. The nontemporary employees usually ignore her, but it is almost as common for them to actively create barriers of silence, space, or regulations to prevent her from interacting with them. Supervisors make no contact with her beyond their initial cursory instructions, talking in low voices to the permanent workers on either side of her, holding meetings from which she is excluded, and posting notices in areas where she, as a temp, is not allowed to go.

Marginal to the organizations of the temporary employment agencies and the employers of Greenville, as well as their internal communities, Kimmey is also marginal to the very process of work. Her assignments are usually the jobs that are most peripheral to the central operation of the factory or the office, such as packing boxes or doing archival filing. Assignments that are more central to the operations of an organization, such as assembly, machine operation, or word processing, are the most intrinsically unpleasant at each work site: the industrial work is grueling, the clerical work is mind-numbingly dull, and all of the work is routine.[10] Kimmey is frustrated that she is not given jobs that challenge her or provide her with experience or skills.

Kimmey's disappointment in her job assignments was shared by all workers in our study. Previous case studies of temporary workers in different cities, recruited by different methods, have also documented an abundance of experience with assignments that are dull, isolating, and dead-end (Barrett, 1993; Henson, 1993; Parker, 1994; Rogers, 1995). Virginia duRivage writes that "the growth of contingent work signals declining employer commitment to career development" (1992:91). Agencies and their clients treat Kimmey and each of the other study participants as one of many interchangeable units, not as a resource to be developed.

Many studies have previously suggested, whether by means of broad, statistical data or case studies, that temporary workers across industries and occupations are far less likely than others to receive either occupational resources or standard noncash benefits (see, for example, Belous,

10. Jackie Krasas Rogers (1995) points out that while increasing narrowness and deskilling of tasks alienates all workers from the product and purpose of their labor, this alienation is greater for those temps who leave each workplace without ever being told the business's goal or product.

1989; duRivage, 1992a; Callaghan & Hartmann, 1992; Hartmann & Lapidus, 1989; U.S. Government Accounting Office, 1991). Some writers have suggested this difference is a result of workers' preference. For example, Lewis Segal and Daniel Sullivan contend that three-quarters of temporary workers do without employer-paid health insurance (compared, for example, to less than one quarter of the full-time workforce) because "many non-permanent workers elect out of this coverage" (1995:7). Kimmey's testimony warns us that being denied access to resources can be mistaken in the statistical record for a lack of interest in them.

Day-to-day, Kimmey finds her social isolation the most irritating aspect of her outsider status, but the least important. However, she may pay for this isolation at many more levels than the emotional. When she has transportation or child care trouble, she cannot protect her job by getting a coworker to cover for her until she can arrange a sitter, or to give her a ride until she can fix the car. Kathleen Christensen has written in her study of home-based workers (1988:164), "not being part of a typical office culture deprives a woman of the practical and professional benefits of having colleagues." Kimmey has no one from whom she can learn about the operations and hierarchies at workplaces, or with whom she can compare notes, theories, and suggestions. Kimmey has been shut out not only from access to tangible benefits but also from the accumulation of intangible personal resources, such as information with which she could adjust her approach, correct for errors, or seize opportunities.

Facing Uncertainty:
Corinna Madison Makes Plans Hour by Hour

Corinna Madison keeps pictures taken on the day after her tenth-grade graduation, when she and her high-school sweetheart, Alan, were married. Other photographs show her singing in the Baptist choir and standing by the house that Alan built. After Corinna had their first child and stopped working outside the house, Alan supported the family at the local mill. When debts piled up, Corinna would work at the mill for a month or two. She was glad for these temporary jobs. Her photo album includes pictures of her grinning kids, who sit with their grandparents on car fenders, or with their father beside them playing the guitar. There is a picture of the cake made by nurses in the hospital where Corinna and Alan celebrated their twentieth wedding anniversary together on the day he died of cancer. Soon after, Corinna was in a near-fatal car accident and spent most of a year in the hospital. So, in her forties, with enormous amounts of work behind her but no history of steady employment, Corinna faced the job market. She studied for and passed her G.E.D., took a computer operating course, and made lists of potential employers. In the last three years, every employer she has approached has sent Corinna to a temporary service agency.

Corinna never knows what she will be doing on any given day to make her income. In the last few years, she has worked in a financial services firm, a fast food restaurant, a mill, a nursing home, a department store, a lawyer's office, and several factories and warehouses. She has operated industrial machines, run a cash register, sorted mail, lifted boxes, cleaned houses, and inserted marketing pamphlets into newspapers. Most of the time, the agencies send her to employers without telling her what the job entails. It is not unusual for her to wait at an employer without being told what to do.

> Like at ——— Publishing you have to just stand maybe thirty minutes, sometimes two hours, waiting on them to even tell you what to do next. And when I say two hours, I'm honest. I'm not joking whatsoever, that's the honest truth. Sometimes it'd be two hours before they'd even come back there and tell us, "Well, we're gonna have to see, well, we're waiting on this,". . . and so we just never knew. . . . I had rather just go, know what my job is. Now mill work was hard, I spooled and I spinned, but I knew what I was going to do.

Uncertainty about tasks was disturbing to most of the temps in this study, as well as temps in other recent studies of temporary workers. Maureen Martella, for example, found that "assignments are frequently miscommunicated" and that "the actual nature of an assignment can greatly differ from the description given to the temp" (1992:88).

Corinna's confusion about her tasks is compounded by her low status in the hierarchy at the workplace: For the temp, everyone is a supervisor. She does not know who to listen to when the personnel manager, the supervisor, and the worker next to her are giving her conflicting instructions. She can be held responsible when she makes one person angry while trying to follow the instructions of another. And with so many supervisors, when disputes have arisen at the places where she has worked, she has had to stumble from one person to another to find out who was in authority.

Corinna does not have the slightest idea what her work schedule will be from one week to the next. She tries to piece together temporary assignments to make a full-time, year-round schedule, but dispatchers ask her to take jobs without guaranteeing that the job will last her a minimum number of days or hours per day. Ultimately, the assignments are too few and far between, too short, and too distant. Between the low pay and travel costs on some jobs, Corinna barely breaks even.

> Oh, the agency called me today, and she said I could go back over to the ———— Company today. Said they had sort of an emergency come in and wanted some people to come in and work. And I said . . . how long is this job going to last? And she said, well, today and tomorrow. That was about twelve-thirty today when she called. And, I thought, I'm going at twelve-thirty, well, one o'clock, and work till four. It wouldn't be enough to pay my gas! I mean, run my car out, run my tires out. And then three or four hours tomorrow—don't know—whatever there was to do. Then they send me home. What's the use going?

Still, she dares not turn down such an assignment, for fear there will be no better one offered that day.

The worst element for Corinna is the uncertainty about what her income will be each week. Given the unpredictable travel costs, hours assigned, and hourly wages, Corinna is unable to even hazard an estimate. With no way of anticipating her income from week to week, she is unable to plan, to get credit, or to invest in any kind of repairs or preventative maintenance either for herself or for her car. She is unable to turn down jobs or to invest her time in anything other than working or waiting by the phone. Corinna enjoys no flexibility as a temporary employee; because she needs as much income as she can get and cannot know in advance how much work she will be offered, she must keep herself constantly available. When I asked Corinna what she hoped the future would be like, she said without hesitation, "I'd like something that I can go to, the same place every day, do the same job everyday, get paid every week, and just come home. I don't really mind doing different jobs. I don't really mind doing anything. I love about any kind of work. But if I had what I wanted to do everyday, I would go do the same job every day, know what I was going to do every day and not have to worry about it."

Uncertainty about schedules and income was a source of tremendous frustration and hardship for all nineteen study participants. The method by which we found these workers would tend to select for underemployed workers, but Segal and Sullivan recently concluded from census data that the percentage of temporary workers who are involuntarily working less than a full week is "significantly higher than in the labor force as a whole," and they suggest that at least 15 percent of temporary workers "work fewer hours than they wish" (1995:12).[11]

Vulnerable on All Sides:
Amanda Ranger Dodges Negligence and Exploitation

Amanda Ranger, twenty-three, shares a small house with a close friend and her friend's enormous collection of stuffed and ceramic figures of animals. She grew up in West Virginia, where her dad supported the family as a coal miner. Amanda has been working since she moved as a teenager to Greenville and trained as an electrician. She worked as a permanent employee for General Electric and "made good money," but GE shut down the facility, and all of the other local employers referred her to the temporary agencies. One of the agencies sends her to do electrical work repeatedly at one company, but not often enough to pay her bills. She has to take the other jobs the agencies offer, which have been a variety of unskilled, industrial jobs.

Working as a temp has made Amanda vulnerable to both irrational and disruptive idiosyncrasies of temporary agency personnel. The manager of one agency recently sent her home from her sign-up appointment to change into jeans out of her large, army-style shorts even though the agency's specialty is manual day labor in warehouses. This second round-trip was a severe penalty for a woman who must carefully ration her gas. The manager at a different agency showed up at her house on his motorcycle asking her to spend the day with him. She declined the offer and has not heard from that agency since.

Exploitative actions on the part of her temporary employers have also presented hazards unknown to her before she began temping. Sometimes employers make her pay money up front for work clothes, safety equipment, and drug tests before they will let her work; sometimes they dock her paycheck for these things after she has begun. Another hazard Amanda faces is unscrupulous employers and agencies who choose not to honor their obligations to her. After one recent temp

11. An accurate picture of the circumstances of the workforce would identify not only the nominally "unemployed" but also these people who are unable to find as much work as they need. Attempts are being made to quantify "labor market hardship" (Parker, 1994), but right now, as Heidi Hartmann and June Lapidus write, "a temporary worker without full assignment for the week would most likely be classified as 'employed part-time involuntarily' *if* interviewed on a day he or she was without work" (1989:31, emphasis added).

assignment, the temporary service agency refused to pay her and a second temp worker for one day's work, on the grounds that the client employer said they had not worked. Amanda argued, but finally walked away without her wages since fighting in court would cost too much in fees and foregone work hours.

Amanda is also facing threats to her personal safety. On a recent temp assignment, she fell from a high scaffold to the ground, breaking her ankle and straining her back. Once she was on the ground, she realized she had been tied off on a line that was longer than the drop from the scaffold to the floor. Amanda had to wonder if this accident was partially a result of her unfamiliarity with the equipment or of the disregard for her safety that the supervisors and other workers had shown her because of her temporary status. Whether or not the accident resulted from her position as a temp, the consequences of the accident were clearly unique to that marginal position. She did not for a minute consider filing a workers' compensation claim, fearing that the employer, for whom she had done temporary jobs in the past, would ask the temp agency to send someone else when they next needed a worker or that the agency itself, dependent on this client, would drop her from their list entirely. She calculated that the doctors bills and the time at home without pay would cost her less than her foregone income should she be blacklisted.

Several other workers in this study had been assigned by employers to do work that was physically dangerous without adequate safety equipment, such as mixing toxic caulking material without gloves or a face mask and clearing out a maze of boxes in an old warehouse with fire doors chained shut. Researchers, particularly those working with contract employees in the chemical industry, have warned that the use of workers who are statutory employees of third-party firms allows companies to downplay and evade responsibility for the accidents and health problems of their facilities and leads to a relaxation of safety standards and precautions.[12] Researchers have long been concerned about the safety of workers doing noncontract temporary work (Hartmann & Lapidus, 1989), but available information on the subject is still anecdotal. Anecdotes are instructive, however. In Amanda's experience, the temporary agency had a nominal policy against sending workers to dangerous jobs, but it was not in control of the employer. Motivated by dependence on that employer, the agency supported Amanda's decision to sit out her injury without reporting it or filing for compensation.

12. For example, Kochan et al., 1994; Kochan, Wells, & Smith, 1992; Rebitzer, 1995.

Little has been written about the kind of petty exploitations of withheld wages and equipment charges suffered by Amanda and the other temps in our study. One person bought expensive work boots that he was told were required for a "two-week to permanent" assignment, but the job lasted no more than two days. Another person paid seventy dollars for prescription safety glasses for a job that ended on the third day. After two days as a telemarketer, another worker cleared seventy-two dollars by her own estimate but was told there was no more work and sent home with a check for twelve dollars. Apparently, a fifty dollar "bond" had been a required prerequisite of the job. These workers are in the position of independent entrepreneurs, purchasing equipment and paying the operating costs of their businesses—except, of course, they are not entrepreneurs but wage laborers, bearing operating costs normally borne by employers.

Other study participants reported that they are also easily, and often, cheated of their wages. In one incident, a temporary service agency quoted one hourly wage to a worker at the start of a job but paid the worker more than a dollar an hour less after a week of work had passed. In another incident, an agency told a worker that she would be paid by the piece on a job, but after two days of work the client employer paid her according to an hourly wage, cutting her expected earnings by over 50 percent. In another incident, a worker found her paycheck did not include wages for nine of the hours she had worked that week. The agency refused to pay her and four other workers for their hours on the client's assertion that he had told the workers to stop earlier.

Starting from a Position of Weakness: Duncan McElroye Builds a Future without the Benefit of Tools

Duncan McElroye, at thirty-six years old, lives in a small apartment in a single-story concrete block of five such apartments, next to a busy downtown highway. Prints and paintings cover three of the living room walls. The fourth wall displays framed documents: Duncan's degree in business administration from Cornell, his training certificates, the copyright he holds for the business he ran as a young man at home in Rochester, New York. In one photograph, Duncan's three-year-old daughter, Indigo, wears a pair of dark sunglasses and mugs for the camera. "That's my baby trying to be cool," Duncan explains with a smile. His baby is in Rochester, where her mother works as a hospital nurse to support herself and the child. Duncan lost his ability to support his family when he was laid off from the corporation where he had worked for twelve years, the last few in management. Discouraged by several months of job hunting in upstate New York, Duncan moved to Greenville on the advice of relatives in the area who saw the economy growing. His family drives to see him twice a year, but will not move to join him unless he has a secure position from which he can support them. After three years of temping, Duncan has begun to wonder if that secure position will ever materialize. Although Duncan is a man of tremendous personal resourcefulness and confidence, he has been unable to imagine or fashion any tools to control, much less escape, a cycle of dead-end, low-wage, temporary assignments.

Getting a nontemporary position is Duncan's top priority, but both the state unemployment office and the local employers direct him to temporary service agencies. In the absence of a secure job, Duncan tries to boost, or at least stabilize, his income from temporary assignments. He is registered at several agencies, and he calls their dispatchers to inquire about work, to keep a picture of himself in the dispatchers' minds, and to find out what employers say of him. He has occasionally called the client employers themselves but is always reprimanded by the dispatchers. He tries to extend each job by doing it well, but he does not think that doing well on a job has, thus far, increased his chance of keeping it. Duncan tries to limit downtime by rejecting distant or short jobs with the hope that longer or closer ones will be offered. But the strategy of turning down bad assignments is risky itself because of uncertainty about the future supply of work.

In addition to more and longer assignments, Duncan seeks "good" assignments, namely those that use his skills and might give him access to a business's internal job ladder. What he gets, however, are marginal, minimum-wage jobs in warehouses and on assembly lines. "I wanted a job," he says, "that would get me back in the same field, at least where I could get closer to management than a forklift. But most of the jobs—I should say every job—that I got through a temp agency, was a bullshit job. . . . It was just something to pay the bills. But I never got what I wanted." Despite his past experience, his careful presentation of himself at interviews, and his requests to the dispatchers, he is never assigned to a job that is remotely related to his training and experience in business administration. Recently, one of the dispatchers suggested that Duncan stop wearing suits to interviews and, instead, dress "like he was ready to work." Duncan told the woman that a suit is what he always had worn to work, but he has begun going to meet employers in sweatshirt and jeans.

Duncan finds himself as powerless to control the conditions of the job at the work site as he is to control the dispatcher's assignments. In one incident, Duncan was put on a team with two permanent employees, who then left. After repeatedly asking the other workers to return, asking the supervisor to speak to them, and trying to do the task alone, he finally began resolutely doing only his own part of the task. This meant sacrificing some of the product, and for this he was let go at the end of the day. When he has complained in the past to employers about conditions—about the nature of his task or the treatment of his coworkers—he has been let go and has had to face additional downtime. When he has appealed to the temp agency, he has been simply removed from the job and again faced more downtime.

It is Duncan's analysis that all power in the temporary employment relationships lies with the agency's dispatchers and their clients, and that he can do nothing to make these people and their organizations serve his needs for additional or more rewarding work. Outside of the range of union organization as a temp, Duncan's one "power" he has is the power to turn down or leave bad assignments.[13] But these gestures of independence, while good for his sense of self, netted him nothing but lost income. The other eighteen people in our study agreed that the choice to turn down work was a pathetic form of "power." "What do they care?" one person said, "There are a thousand people standing behind you to take that job." Economists call this situation a one-sided, small-numbers bargaining problem: where one side has no alternatives, the other will be able to set the terms of the agreement. Each day Duncan and his fellow temps go to the bargaining table alone and without leverage, and have virtually no impact on the terms of the agreement.

Considering workers' demands may not be in the interests of many temporary service agencies. The temporary services industry's trade association asserts that "when a customer order is received, the temporary help firm refers to its files of temporary employees and assigns a worker whose skills and preferences match the customers' needs" (National Association of Temporary Services, 1994b:9). However, many branch managers interviewed by Robert Parker (1994) define their job as providing willing "warm bodies" to clients at a moment's notice and so do not consider workers' preferences, satisfaction, or benefit in making job assignments. Some of the managers "thought that the whole issue of

13. For examples of individual resistance to the alienating conditions of temporary employment, see the zine *Temp Slave! Work! Work!* and Rogers, 1995. Although current law makes it impossible, practically speaking, for temps to join or organize unions (Appelbaum & Gregory, 1988; New Ways to Work, 1992; Service Employees International Union, 1993), projects to organize temp workers have already begun through community organizations such as CAFE, TIRN, and Southerners for Economic Justice.

employees getting improved assignments was irrelevant and ludicrous"
(106), and others "encouraged employers to place the temporary worker
in the boring slot to free up the more challenging positions for permanent employees" (149). As Glenda Barrett points out, to the extent that
"organizations are designing temporary jobs to relieve permanent workers of mundane tasks, they may have little incentive to change these positions" (1993:100). Certainly Duncan and the other workers interviewed
in this study indicated that the agencies in Greenville are delivering them
to employers as last-minute hands to do any boring, low-skill task that
the employers either cannot or will not give to their own employees.
These workers believe that they function as part of a pool from which
they can be indiscriminately pulled by the dispatcher and used at the
employers' discretion. For that purpose, they are uniform objects, whose
interests and needs are irrelevant to the assignment of these jobs.[14]

Besides his powerlessness to influence the terms of his employment
with either the agencies or their clients, Duncan fears he pays a price for
even trying. He suspects that turning down, objecting to, or leaving
assignments that are undesirable—in that they are offered at the last
minute or are low-paid, distant, short, boring, difficult, or humiliating—
will lead the dispatcher to shut him out of future jobs. He takes and
sticks to many jobs out of fear of the dispatchers' displeasure. Christensen found a similar phenomenon in her study of home-based workers: "since these women feel the precariousness of their positions, they
are often afraid to speak up or complain for fear of being let go" (1988:
163). Duncan's fear that agencies would withhold work in the future if
he did not take and perform bad jobs in bad circumstances, shared by
most of the temps in this study, as well as by many interviewed by Kevin
Henson (1993), Martella (1992), and Parker (1994), may be a reasonable fear. Branch managers of temporary service agencies interviewed by
Parker revealed that they believe their key task is to screen out "com-
plainers" for their clients. Our study indicated that their efforts are
largely successful; it was highly unusual for any of these workers to express his or her opinions or needs. This process by which protest is
"muzzled" by the power to withhold work has already been described by
Barker's (1995) research in the university setting, where adjunct profes-

14. In fact, their interests and needs would be an impediment to the assignment of
these jobs, should they have any other options. While the absence of options for these
workers is not the fault of the agencies, this situation may be a prerequisite for their ability to provide employers with workers for unpopular work with almost no advanced
warning.

sors who openly contest employment conditions are punished through the assignment of poor classes and schedules.

The law does not offer a temp like Duncan tools to negotiate with agencies or their clients, but it does—in theory—offer Duncan some last-resort, safety-net protection from inadequate employment or biased treatment. But as Dean Morse indicated twenty-five years ago in his study *The Peripheral Worker*, subgroups of the labor force "subject to inferior conditions of work, inferior wages, and inferior status" are likely to "suffer the added disability of partial or entire exclusion from some of the governmental programs designed to protect and to stabilize the position of the individual worker" (1969:8–9). Governmental programs designed to protect individual workers are, indeed, largely out of Duncan's reach. For example, Duncan wonders if his opportunities as a temp are affected by his being African-American, but he cannot explore the question. Much as activating the protections of workers' compensation legislation is too risky for someone as vulnerable as Amanda, activating the power of equal opportunity legislation is impossible for someone as powerless as Duncan. He does not know the other temps who work at the agencies, much less their qualifications and assignments. He is never at a workplace long enough to identify patterns in the way temps of different races are used. The practical irrelevance of antidiscrimination remedies is particularly disturbing given that, as Hartmann and Lapidus write (1989:27), populations "that are thought to have been historically disadvantaged in the United States and that are protected by civil rights laws are overrepresented in temporary jobs."[15]

The one governmental program that Duncan has been able to seize to "protect and stabilize" his position is unemployment insurance, for which he became qualified after one unusually long assignment. Duncan refers to the income as "a blessing" and is turning down bad short assignments so that he can complete a technical job skills course. Unfortunately, only two of the nineteen participants, in all of their years of underemployment, had been assigned enough work to qualify for unemployment insurance. Research has consistently indicated that it is "either difficult or impossible to collect unemployment benefits" for nontraditional workers, particularly for people doing intermittent, temporary jobs (U.S. Government Accounting Office, 1991:9).[16] Moreover, Duncan and the other workers collecting unemployment insurance may

15. For information about the composition of the contingent workforce, see Belous, 1989; Callaghan & Hartmann, 1992.

16. See also duRivage, 1992b; Callaghan & Hartmann, 1992; New Ways to Work, 1992.

end up paying a price for their "blessing"; Parker found that some managers of temporary agencies think unemployment claims signal trouble and so during the initial screening, "by examining a potential employee's work history, temporary help companies attempt to uncover any periods without work when unemployment insurance might have been collected" (1994:47).

Living on the Periphery

Although our study was confined to work experience, participants raised a number of concerns about the effect of temporary employment on the larger whole of their lives. Every day these workers have to manage the uncertainty and vulnerability inherent in their marginal and powerless position with an eye to simply breaking even at week's end. Every last-minute call from an agency sets in motion a process of weighing the potential rewards from taking the assignment (including pay rate, hours, and the good will of the dispatcher) against the potential costs of taking that job (including travel time and costs, child and elder care costs, opportunity costs in terms of other jobs or family responsibilities, and health care costs). It is a process that repeats in miniature the income optimization planning done by businesses to manage the risks associated with uncertainty in their market. As others have pointed out, temporary employment arrangements essentially represent the shifting of uncertainty and risk—and the costly business of its management—from employers to a small segment of the workforce (duRivage, 1992b; Golden & Appelbaum, 1992; Morse, 1969).

Ironically and sadly, managing these burdens of risk and flexibility requires resource reserves that are difficult for underemployed and poorly remunerated workers to maintain, such as a dependable vehicle, phone service, and a reserved (i.e., prepaid) spot in a day-care center for each child, and cash or credit to finance these assets or living expenses in periods of slack demand (due to market forces, personal injury, etc.). "These jobs don't pay enough to keep your car up!" Amanda pointed out to me. "*That* should be the title of your article."

Workers in this study report that whenever possible they depend heavily on members of their families and, indeed, the form and content of their families conditions their ability to weather the vicissitudes of the temporary job market in Greenville. One person with a broken-down car has been getting rides every day for four weeks from her teenage sister who lives on the other side of town. Her sister and her car are both maintained by the woman's mother, who has a relatively secure job managing a car wash. "Every family needs one killer job," points out one of the study participants who depends on his wife's full-time, permanent job to keep the five members of their family clothed, fed, and sheltered. For another worker, it is her husband's consistent and secure job as a car mechanic that allows her to keep her kids' places in a good day-care facility despite the unpaid downtime during which she waits for a dispatcher to call. For a different woman, it is her proximity to her mother, who provides both her and her best friend the free child care that makes it possible for the two women to take the temp assignments at all. Her mother is supported by an Army pension from her husband's twenty years as an employee of the federal government. For these people, it is that one "killer job," whether it belongs to a living relative or one now gone, that builds the small boat with which they navigate a moving sea.

But the vicissitudes of the temporary employment market influence the formation and dissolution of these families themselves. One worker is considering applying for Aid to Families with Dependent Children even though it means citing her baby's father for desertion, because she cannot earn enough by working. At least two women in the study group are living with men who they want desperately to leave, one because of her husband's criminal activity and the other because her husband beats her. Neither can find work that pays enough to support herself and both fear what destitution might bring. Now we must wonder not only how much temps are obliged to take from their families to get by but also how many additional risks these workers assume in their personal lives to compensate for the poor quality of their employment relationships.

Other Questions:
Looking Around and Looking Forward

It would be a mistake to extrapolate from case study data such as that above to suggest that temporary employment is, in general, bad for workers. However, it would be as great a mistake to dismiss the implications of this information regarding how bad for workers such arrangements can easily be. One of the next questions for CAFE, indeed for everyone concerned with the quality of employment, is how many of the growing number of temporary workers are experiencing the same high level of difficulty as the participants of the Greenville Temp School. Are the temporary employment experiences described at the school anomalous, or are they normal? We also need to explore what variables condition the degree of marginality, uncertainty, vulnerability, and powerlessness experienced by different temporary workers. To what extent is a worker's leverage in day-to-day bargaining with temporary agencies and their client employers affected by personal characteristics, including race, sex, age, degree of specialized skill, local knowledge of employer networks, previously established contacts in the workplace, and so on? To what extent is the worker's ability to get what he or she needs from the temporary agencies affected by characteristics of the agency itself, such as the size of its employee list, the size of its client list, its status as a franchise of a national organization or as an owner operated business, and so on?

We are also concerned to know how these nineteen people—and people around the country working in similar arrangements—will be living ten years in the future. Many researchers have already begun to hypothesize a connection between the deterioration of employment relationships and the growing inequalities of income and wealth at a national level. Segal and Sullivan recently wrote that statistics showing that temps sometimes move into permanent jobs indicate that fears of a temporary underclass are exaggerated. In the same article, however, the authors admit that industrial temp workers are more than three times more likely than "average" industrial workers to be unemployed the following year and more than twice as likely to be out of the labor force altogether (1995:13–14). Comparative longitudinal research is needed to explore how temporary employment arrangements of various kinds affect the incomes and occupations of different workers in the long run. Certainly participants in our study left us fearful not only that they will be unable to get a toehold to lift themselves up and out of this cycle of bad jobs, but that they will suffer a further deterioration in their occupational and material resources over time.

Barker has described how workers' very peripherality in employment can handicap their efforts to achieve a less peripheral employment position and create ever new handicaps, a phenomenon she calls the "accumulating deficits of contingency" (1995:21). In universities, Barker found, moving from job to job is itself disadvantageous, lowering a professor's status and making her less attractive to academic departments. Temp workers often voiced a similar analysis. As Kimmey put it to me, "People don't want to hire you because you haven't been on a job over a year, but if every job lays you off . . . you can't get that experience of working!" Just as Barker found for academic temps, industrial temp workers who are passed over in every job for training opportunities, skill building experience, and office gossip may become increasingly marginal to the workplace and the work process and so become increasingly *less* likely to gain access to these occupational resources in the future.

The difficulty of maintaining crucial resources such as cars and phone service points to another dilemma these workers face, namely, as Robert Chambers has written in reference to rural poverty, a "deprivation trap" (1983:111). Despite their hard work and ingenious solutions, resource-poor farmers struggle against "interlocking disadvantages which trap them in deprivation" (103). The temporary employees in this study report "interlocking disadvantages" that describe an urban counterpart to the rural poverty Chambers studied. In simplest terms, a reliable car is a necessary condition of a steady income for the workers in this study, but a steady income is itself key to keeping a car running reliably. Material deficits that these workers suffer as temps thus decrease their ability to ensure, much less increase, their material security; working fewer hours lowers income, which inhibits car maintenance, which increases the odds of car failure, which decreases the number of work hours. Various methods of finessing tight situations are also out of these temps' reach; a worker in a secure job might overcome a car breakdown by borrowing money or asking a coworker for a ride or two, but these temps cannot get loans from banks or friends and seldom even know the name of a coworker.

The present and likely future struggles of these workers may have serious ramifications for the larger communities where they live, starting, as we have seen, with their families. Personal experience, as well as decades of excellent scholarship, has taught us that the structures of family households are intricately bound up with the structure of the economic relationships in which their members are enmeshed. We need to explore how far the risks that these temporary workers assume travel beyond them into the resources of other people, and how these burdens travel from person to person in a community. In addition, the precipitous position of the workers in this study suggest that risks and uncertainty passed on by businesses to their most vulnerable employees may pass ultimately onto the social welfare system, in whatever form it remains. As Hartmann and Spalter-Roth have previously pointed out, "without reform of the low-wage labor market, the government transfers required to bring all workers out of poverty are needlessly expensive" (1992:1).

It is widely argued that flexible employment arrangements, like temporary jobs, can create important social benefits, especially in the form of job creation by newly competitive businesses. Laying aside the contentious question of whether contingent affiliations between employers and workers are the best way to achieve flexibility in a human resource system even from a narrow goal of profit maximization (see, for example, Belous, 1989), the cost savings to industry from using temps is only part of the temporary employment story. The other part is what happens to the people who assume the costs from industry and the ways those costs are passed on to their families and, ultimately, their communities and neighbors. Hartmann and Lapidus have written that "uncertainty is a constant feature of a market economy; who is going to bear the cost of adjustment to change is often a matter of political strength" (1989:15). We Americans will not avoid risk, but we will certainly decide, whether by our action or inaction, how risk, flexibility, and its costs will ultimately be shared.

CHAPTER TEN

Job Safety and Contract Workers in the Petrochemical Industry

James B. Rebitzer

The use of contract and temporary workers has increased dramatically in the United States in recent years. Payroll survey data indicate that employment in personnel supply services grew at an annual rate of 11.5 percent between 1972 and 1986. Katharine Abraham estimates that in 1986 temporary workers, business service employment, and production subcontracting accounted for about 10 percent of total employment. Moreover, these types of employment relationships all appear to be "growing more rapidly than employment elsewhere in the economy" (1990:114).

Despite their increasing importance, very few studies have examined the implications that contract and temporary employment relationships have for the operation and regulation of labor markets.[1] At the level of the firm, little is known about the manner in which contract employees are trained and supervised. At the economic policy level, little is known about how laws and legal concepts developed for conventional employment relationships work when applied to contract employment relationships.

This chapter examines how human resource practices and legal liability rules affect the job safety of contract workers. The particular object of study is the petrochemical industry. Contract workers are an important and controversial part of the labor force in petrochemicals,

This research project began as part of the John Gray Institute's study of contract labor in the U.S. petrochemical industry under a grant from the Occupational Safety and Health Administration. I wish to thank the project director, John Wells, and my colleague at MIT, Thomas Kochan, for allowing me continued access to the data after the final report was completed. Tom Kochan, David Levine, Lowell Taylor, Kevin Lang, Price Fishback, and participants at seminars at MIT, Carnegie-Mellon, Harvard, and the 1992 NBER Summer Institute also offered helpful comments on earlier drafts. Peter Cebon contributed to this paper through his expert research assistance.

The conclusions and opinions expressed in this paper are my own and do not necessarily reflect the views of OSHA or the John Gray Institute.

1. For exceptions see Abraham, 1990; Appelbaum, 1987; Mangum, Mayall, & Nelson, 1985; and Rebitzer & Taylor, 1991.

accounting for nearly a third of total work hours. Union leaders and industry critics argue that contract employees receive inadequate safety training and supervision and therefore increase the risk of both individual accidents and catastrophic plantwide accidents (Selcraig, 1992). In response, management argues that they take extraordinary precautions to prevent catastrophic accidents. Management further contends that contract workers do not pose a safety risk. Rather, they are an important means by which companies can cope with changes in product demand as well as the periodic maintenance and renovation required in petrochemical facilities.

Both sides can find evidence in support of their positions. Between 1986 and 1990, an increasing proportion of explosions and fires at petrochemical plants have involved contract employees (Wells, Kochan, & Smith, 1991:4) This trend appears to be continuing into 1991. Of the eleven workplace accidents known to involve explosions, fires, and spills in the U.S. petrochemical industry from January to June 1991, nine were reported to involve contract employees. On the other hand, leading employers in the petrochemical industry have a long history of safety-conscious employment practices. Dow, DuPont, and Mobil, for example, are recognized both within the industry and nationally for having developed comprehensive and effective safety management programs for their employees.

The controversy over contract workers was brought to a head when, on October 23 1989, an explosion occurred at a Phillips 66 chemical complex in Pasadena, Texas. Twenty-three workers were killed and 232 others were injured. Contract workers were implicated in the accident. In response to the Phillips disaster, Congress instructed the Occupational Safety and Health Administration (OSHA) to determine whether the use of contract workers in the petrochemical industry posed a safety hazard. OSHA convened a steering committee of all interested parties and selected the John Gray Institute of Lamar University to conduct a comprehensive study of safety issues relating to contract workers. The analysis presented below is based upon the case studies and surveys conducted during the course of the John Gray Institute study.[2]

The chapter proceeds in two parts. The first describes the relevant institutional features of the contract employment relationship in petrochemicals. Particular emphasis is given to the effect that liability rules have on the safety training and supervision of contract employees. The

2. Readers interested in reading the report finally submitted to OSHA should see Wells, Kochan, & Smith, 1991.

second part is an empirical analysis of the roles safety training and supervision play in determining the probability of accidents. The paper concludes with a discussion of the implications the findings have for labor market policy.

Institutional Features of the Contract Employment Relationship

Contract employees are an important part of the workforce in most petrochemical plants. Surveys of plant managers indicate that at the typical petrochemical refinery, contract workers account for nearly a third of the total work hours contributed by hourly personnel.[3] Contract employees are found largely in "maintenance" and "renovation and turnaround jobs," with the former comprising 55 percent of contract employment and the latter comprising 33 percent.

The category "renovation and turnaround" includes jobs in the on-site construction projects that periodically occur at petrochemical plants. Some of these projects involve building or rebuilding parts of plants (renovation) while others involve short-term changes in the configuration of equipment to accommodate changes in product mix (turnaround). Renovation and turnaround projects typically require shutting down expensive pieces of capital equipment and, for this reason, need to be completed quickly. Contract workers are attractive for these projects because they allow firms to bring large numbers of additional employees on site for the duration of the project. Once the project is finished, these contract workers can be sent elsewhere by their contractor.

Contract jobs in the "maintenance" category encompass the variety of tasks involved in maintaining physical plant. In contrast to renovation and turnaround, firms typically do not bring large numbers of maintenance employees on site to work on fixed duration projects. Contract maintenance workers perform many of the routine maintenance tasks also performed by direct-hire employees. For this reason, contractors supplying maintenance workers do not typically act as spot contractors. Rather general maintenance contractors maintain a long-term relationship with the host employer.

3. A national survey of plant managers conducted by the John Gray Institute found that during non-turnaround periods, 32 percent of the average production labor hours in a plant were worked by contract employees. During turnaround periods, contract employees typically account for more than 50 percent of total work hours (Wells, Kochan, & Smith, 1991).

The most striking feature of the contract employment relationship in petrochemicals is the distance that host managers maintain from the contract employees working on site. Case studies of the management of contract workers in petrochemical plants find that host plant management often has little or no involvement with the recruitment, training, or supervision of contract employees. "Contract employees were generally treated as a separate and distinct workforce; it was observed that contract workforces dressed differently, used separate entrances, relied upon medical support in emergencies only, reported and responded first to contract supervisors, and depended principally upon the contractor to prepare them for work in a petrochemical facility" (Wells, Kochan, & Smith, 1991:95–96).

Host plants avoid training and directing contract employees in order to escape potentially expensive legal liabilities associated with being declared the employer of contract employees. In conventional employment relationships, the identity of the employer is clear. For contract workers, however, there are two potential employers: the management of the host plant and the contractor.

In determining who the true employer is, courts generally ask who controls the employee (see Hood, Hardy, & Lewis, 1990:43; Keeton, 1984:501). Control includes the employer's rights to give orders, specify the manner in which work is to be done, and to hire and discharge. In contrast to an employee, an independent contractor is simply given specifications for the final product or result. The means of accomplishing the result is left to the judgment of the independent contractor. This has important implications for job training. Should a host plant require an employee of the contractor to attend a meeting, receive training on how a task is to be performed, or report directly to plant personnel, the appearance is created that the host is interested not only in the final result but also in the means by which the result is accomplished. In this situation, courts are likely to decide that an employment relationship exists between the host plant and contract workers.[4]

4. In the course of the research on this project, we obtained a copy of an unpublished memo by a law firm that advises chemical companies. This memo listed various indicators of employment (or co-employment) status. These included (1) stopping contract employees in the course of their jobs and instructing them how to perform these tasks in compliance with plant safety procedures, and (2) contractual provisions requiring contract employees to report injuries and illness to plant supervisory personnel.

The problem of determining the true employer of contract workers arises most frequently in suits for negligent injuries to third parties.[5] Under the legal principle of vicarious liability (also known as *respondeat superior*) employers are liable for harm to others caused by the actions of their employees in the course of employment. If a contract employee injures a third party during the course of employment, then the contractor is liable for damages.[6] If it can be demonstrated that the contractor was truly an independent contractor, the vicarious liability does not extend to the host (Keeton, 1984). However, plaintiffs can bypass contractors and directly sue the host plant if they can demonstrate that the host plant was the true employer of the contract employee. Given that most petrochemical plants have "deeper pockets" than contractors, this is an attractive strategy for plaintiff attorneys to pursue.

The identity of the employer also determines liability for workers' compensation premiums. Contractors pay the workers' compensation premiums for contract employees and host plants pay premiums for direct-hire employees. Should a contract employee become injured, the contractor's insurance company may sue the host's insurance company, arguing that the host plant was the true employer of the contractor. If the contractor's insurance company prevails, the host plant would become liable for the workers' compensation costs associated with the contract employee's injuries.[7]

As a result of the barriers erected to avoid liability for contract employees, managers at host plants often do not have a good understanding of the human resource practices contractors use to manage their workforce. This is especially true in issues relating to the management of job safety. The following passage from a case study of a midwestern petrochemical plant is revealing on this point.

5. I learned of the importance of third-party liability in shaping the contractor-host relationship through conversations with risk managers and workers' compensation specialists at three major petrochemical firms, with plaintiff's attorneys in Texas, and with staff members at the Workers' Compensation Commission in Texas.

6. The term "third party" here refers to people other than those directly employed by the employer in question. Under the exclusivity provisions of workers' compensation laws, the employer is strictly liable for injuries to employees, and the employee, in turn, forfeits the right to sue an employer for negligence.

7. The legal definition of an employer also plays a role in labor relations. If the union at a unionized petrochemical plant can prove that the host plant has an employment relationship with nonunion contract workers, then the contract workers must be included in the bargaining unit. Once included in the bargaining unit, the contract workers would be entitled to the same wages and benefits as unionized permanent employees.

> The issue of liability and co-employment status looms large. . . . The company is going out to bid for a general maintenance contractor this year and has already notified the current contractor that the company will not be responsible for any training or monitoring of the contract employees nor for the purchase or upkeep of safety equipment and supplies. . . . The contracts between the company and other contractors who provide services such as janitorial services, hydrocleaning and vacuuming, and compressor and turbine repair, are standard and only indicate a few safety and health provisions. They state that the contractor has sole obligation to provide a safe place to work for its employees. (Smith, 1990:III-11)

Clearly the host plant described above seeks to maintain a substantial degree of distance from contractor safety programs. Large-scale surveys of plant managers and contractors conducted by the John Gray Institute reveal that this situation is not exceptional. Fully 76 percent of the three hundred contractors surveyed report having primary responsibility for the safety and health training of contract employees working at a host site. More than a third of the contractors interviewed were not required to submit *any* information on their safety and health programs in order to bid for a job at the host plant where they were currently employed.[8]

The survey of managers of petrochemical plants found that many host employers do not even collect information on the accident rates of contract employees working on site. Of the 243 host plant managers willing to provide accident data for direct hires, 101 could not provide accident rate data for contract employees at their plant (Wells, Kochan, & Smith, 1991:154). Analysis of the data host plants did provide suggest that host record keeping about contractor safety is generally very poor.[9]

While many plants give contractors sole responsibility for the safety of contract employees, it should be pointed out that this practice is not universal. One plant among the nine studied by the John Gray Institute deliberately disregarded distinctions between direct-hire and contract employees in order to ensure a safe and efficient operation (Smith, 1990, case 4). In addition, some companies purchase employer liability and workers' compensation insurance policies *for* their contractors. These owner controlled insurance programs (OCIPs) create strong incentives for host plants to act pro-actively to reduce injury rates among contractors.

8. These figures are from unpublished tabulations of the Harris survey of contractors in the petrochemical industry.

9. Safety practices used to manage contract and direct-hire employees in the firms could not explain any of the variation in contract employee accident rates—even though the variation in direct-hire accident rates was strongly related to these same safety practices (see Wells, Kochan, & Smith, 1991, app. 8A).

In summary, the system of apportioning liability based on the degree of control management exerts over workers has the effect of artificially increasing the cost to petrochemical plants of directly supervising and training contract employees. It follows that petrochemical plants give contractors more control over safety supervision and training than they would under a different set of liability rules. If contract and host management were equally effective in acting to prevent accidents, any distortions created by the legal system would be of little consequence. If, however, host management is in a better position than contractors to prevent accidents, the system of allocating liability may exacerbate safety problems in the industry.[10]

It is likely that contractors in the petrochemical industry do not have the same knowledge or as many incentives to provide effective safety supervision and training as plant management has. Sociologist Charles Perrow (1984) characterizes the production process in petrochemical plants as being "complex" and "tightly coupled." This means that the various components in a petrochemical plant can interact with one another in ways that are both unplanned and difficult to comprehend. Since contractors typically have less experience with the overall facility than plant management, contractors may be less able to predict the safety consequences of the actions taken by employees. Put differently, contractors may lack the facility-specific knowledge that is required for effective safety supervision and training.

Contractors may also not have the economic incentives that host management has to provide high-quality safety training and supervision. In particular, contractors who do not have "deep pockets" may worry less about the costs of accidents than plant management. Consistent with this incentive argument, some reports suggest that the safety training offered by contractors is often perfunctory. In a recent article in *Harper's*, Bruce Selcraig contrasts the safety training received by direct-hire and contract employees at an Amoco plant:

> Upon being hired, permanent Amoco employees . . . go through an intensive "hands-on" two-week training seminar and must apprentice with veteran workers for several months. All employees receive at least eight hours of safety training each year and periodic refresher courses on everything from crane safety to chemical hazards to CPR.

10. The degree to which safety is affected by the system of apportioning liability also depends on host management's perceptions about the likely costs of accidents and the safety benefits of closely supervising contract employees. Unfortunately, no data on managerial perceptions of these costs and benefits are currently available. Collecting information of this sort is an important task for future research.

> For Amoco's contract workers, safety training is sketchy at best. In order to be hired, most are required to do little more than pass a physical, take a drug test, and complete a two-hour course at a contractor's safety school downtown. I took the course and found it so superficial as to be worthless. Some workers even nodded off in their chairs. (Selcraig, 1992:70)

The hypothesis that contractors provide inferior safety training and supervision has potentially important ramifications. Studies of accidents in petrochemical plants and other "complex and tightly coupled" production processes indicate that catastrophic accidents are typically the result of an unexpected concatenation of independent, small, and otherwise innocuous accidents or breakdowns (Perrow, 1984). To the extent that contractor safety training and supervision practices increase the probability of small accidents, they may also increase the probability of catastrophic accidents that effect contractors, direct-hire employees, and surrounding communities.

The Role of Safety Supervision and Training in Determining Accident Rates

The preceding section argued that host employers commonly assign to contractors primary responsibility for supervising and training their contract workforce. This transfer of responsibility will matter for safety if contractors are less effective than host plants in preventing accidents. This section makes use of a unique survey of contract and direct-hire employees in the petrochemical industry to examine the effectiveness of the safety supervision and training employers provide for contract and direct-hire workers.

The survey sample was constructed as follows. A sample of 309 plants was selected from Dun and Bradstreet's list of petrochemical facilities, that is, facilities SIC industries 2821, 2822, 2869, 2911 and 1321 (see Wells, Kochan, & Smith, 1991). Beginning in June of 1990, Louis Harris and Associates sent 120 of these facilities a series of letters requesting lists of direct-hire and contract employees who worked at these facilities during April and May of 1990. Individual employees were then contacted by telephone. The result was a sample of 610 direct-hire employees and 623 contract employees.

Ninety five percent of the direct hires and 93 percent of the contract employees contacted by Louis Harris and Associates responded to the surveys. However, usable lists of direct-hire employees were received from only forty plants while lists of contract employees were received from twenty-nine plants. The low response rate from petrochemical facilities raises the possibility that the facilities included in the survey do not represent a true cross-section of the facilities in the industry. In particular, the sample includes what is likely to be a disproportionately large number of contract employees working at large facilities for unionized contractors (see Wells, Kochan, & Smith, 1991).

There is very little published information about contract workers in the petrochemical industry (or contract workers in any other industry). By way of introduction to this labor force, Table 10.1 presents a comparison of contract and direct-hire personnel. The first two columns refer respectively to direct-hire and contract employees in all work groups.[11] Columns 3 and 4 refer to direct-hire and contract employees engaged in maintenance work. The first row of Table 10.1 presents average values of the variable ACCIDENT, a dummy variable equal to 1 if the respondent experienced an injury at a petrochemical plant over the previous year. Injuries were defined as events requiring either first aid, treatment by a physician, or at least one lost day of work. The mean value of ACCIDENT for direct-hire employees is 19 percent, considerably less than the 26 percent found among contractors. Within maintenance occupations, however, the average values for ACCIDENT are quite similar—27 percent for direct hires and 28 percent for contract employees.[12] Row 2 of Table 10.1 indicates that approximately 36 percent of direct-hire workers are employed in maintenance jobs compared to 56 percent for contract employees. Nearly all of the remaining contract employees worked in renovation jobs, a job category that accounts for only 2 percent of direct-hire employment.

Rows 3 and 4 offer a comparison of the median hours of safety training received by direct-hire and contract personnel over the previous year. Data on hours of safety training was collected in categories. In the median category, a direct-hire employee received twenty-one or more hours of safety training from his employer. The median contract employee received between nine and twenty hours of safety training from

11. Employees in the following job classifications were included in the survey: major renovation and turnaround; maintenance and repair; specialty and operations.

12. The variable ACCIDENT obviously does not record fatal accidents. However, available evidence indicates that fatal accidents are rare in this industry. A recent survey of serious accidents at petrochemical refineries found 51 direct-hire fatalities and 35 contractor fatalities over the period 1985–89. These figures imply that there were 14.3 direct-hire fatalities and 21.7 contract fatalities per 100,000 employees per year (Rusin & Hofmann, 1991:12).

Table 10.1 Comparisons of contract and direct hire employees in the petrochemical industry

	All job categories		Maintenance jobs	
	Direct hire	Contract	Direct hire	Contract
1. FRACTION WITH ACCIDENT[a] IN PREVIOUS YEAR	0.19	0.26	0.27	0.28
2. FRACTION IN MAINTENANCE JOBS	0.36	0.56	1.00	1.00
HOURS OF SAFETY TRAINING IN THE PREVIOUS YEAR (MEDIAN HOURS)				
3. RECEIVED FROM EMPLOYER[b]	21+	9–20	21+	9–20
4. RECEIVED FROM HOST[b]		3		2
5. MEAN YEARS WITH EMPLOYER	12.85	4.20	14.04	4.83
6. FRACTION CONTRACT EMPLOYEES AT HOST 1 OR MORE YEARS	0.41	0.51		
7. FRACTION REPORTING CLOSE SAFETY SUPERVISION BY HOST[c]	0.28	0.29		
8. FRACTION WITH AT LEAST HIGH SCHOOL DIPLOMA	0.93	0.79	0.95	0.78
9. MEAN AGE	42	37	44	37
10. FRACTION BLACK	0.10	0.09	0.07	0.11
11. FRACTION HISPANIC	0.06	0.16	0.07	0.22
12. FRACTION HAVING POOR ENGLISH COMPREHENSION[d]	0.01	0.07	0.01	0.06
13. MEDIAN HOURLY WAGE CATEGORY	$15+	$12–15	$15+	$12–15
14. FRACTION UNION MEMBERS	0.54	0.46	0.64	0.36
NUMBER OF OBSERVATIONS	610	623	218	329

[a]"Accident" is defined as an event at a petrochemical plant over the previous year requiring either first aid, treatment by a physician, or at least one lost day of work.

[b]"Host" refers to the petrochemical plant at which contract employees are currently working. For contract employees, "employer" refers to the *contractor* who currently employs them.

[c]Close supervision by host occurs when contract employees are required to report accidents, injuries, and safety problems to host as well as contractor.

[d]Phone interviewer's assessment of the English language skills of the respondent.

the contractor.[13] In addition, the median contract employee received three hours of safety training from the host (see row 4).

Row 5 compares the job tenure of contract and direct-hire employees. The average direct-hire employee has been working for his current employer for more than twelve years (all the hourly employees in this

13. More than 23 percent of contract employees had 0–4 hours of safety training compared to 7 percent for direct hires. The other training categories were 5–8 hours, 9–20 hours and 21 or more hours. A chi-square test strongly rejects the hypothesis that hours of safety training provided by the employer and contractor status are independently distributed.

survey were men). The average tenure of contract employees with their contractor is much shorter—a little over four years. The data in row 6 indicates that 41 percent of contract employees in all work groups have been at the host site for at least one year. However, more than 50 percent of contract maintenance employees have been at the host plant for at least a year.[14] The large proportion of contract workers employed at their current host site for less than twelve months raises the possibility that the accident figures in row 1 understate the true contract employee accident rates. A contract employee who has spent part of the previous year at a non-petrochemical facility will necessarily have less exposure to potential injury at the petrochemical plant.

Row 7 presents a measure of the intensity with which host employers supervise contract workers. This measure derives from safety reporting procedures governing contract employees. All contract employees interviewed in this survey were required to report accidents, injuries, and safety problems to the contractor supervising them. However, some contract employees were *also* required to report accidents, injuries, and safety problems to host plant management. For this latter group of contract workers, host supervision is said to be close. Consistent with the notion that many host employers keep an arms-length relationship with their contract employees, only 28 percent of contract personnel report close safety supervision.

Row 8 compares the educational attainment of contract and direct-hire personnel. On average, direct hires have spent more time in school than contract employees. More than 90 percent of the direct hires have at least a high-school diploma compared with 78 percent for contract employees. Rows 9 through 11 compare the demographic characteristics of direct-hire and contract employees. On average, contract workers are younger and more likely to be of Hispanic origin than direct hires.

In light of the relatively large proportion of Hispanics' working as contract employees, it is interesting to compare the language skills of the two groups of workers. Row 12 presents average values for a variable measuring the interviewers' assessment of the English-language skills of the respondent. If the interviewer felt that the respondent did not understand the questions very well, English comprehension was specified as poor. Only 1 percent of direct hires had poor English comprehension compared to 6 percent for contract employees.

Finally, the figures presented in rows 13 and 14 indicate that on average direct-hire employees earn higher wages and are more likely to be

14. In contrast, only 2 percent of all direct hires have a year or less of tenure with their employer, and only 2 direct-hire maintenance employees have tenures of one year or less.

union members than contract employees.[15] It should be noted, however, that the unionization rate for contract employees in this sample is higher than other estimates (Wells, Kochan, & Smith, 1991).

Table 10.2 presents analyses of the determinants of accidents in maintenance jobs. Focusing on maintenance jobs is important for two reasons. First, maintenance is the only job category with large numbers of both direct-hire and contract personnel. Second, much of the union-management controversy over the use of contract employees centers on the contracting out of maintenance jobs.

Column 1 of Table 10.2 presents a probit estimate of the determinants of contract and direct-hire accident rates. The positive and statistically significant coefficient on CONTRACT EMPLOYEE indicates that contract maintenance workers with less than a year at the host have accident rates ten percentage points higher than do direct-hire employees in maintenance. The coefficient on CONTRACT EMPLOYEE > 1 YEAR AT HOST is negative but measured imprecisely. As a result, one cannot reject the hypothesis that contract employees having more than a year at the host have the same accident rates as direct-hire employees.[16]

The coefficient on CLOSE SUPERVISION BY HOST in equation one is also negative but it is statistically significant and quite large in absolute value. The magnitude of this coefficient indicates that close safety supervision is associated with a 21 percent reduction in contract employee accident rates. Taken together, one cannot confidently reject the hypothesis that newly arriving contract employees who are closely supervised have the same accident rates as direct hires. Closely supervised contract employees with more than one year at the facility do appear, however, to have *lower* accident rates than direct hires.[17]

The results in column 1 do not distinguish the direct effect of close supervision from other factors that may influence accident rates and be correlated with supervision. Column 2 presents a more fully specified accident equation for contract employees. In this equation accidents are a function of the following: the degree of contractor safety supervision (CLOSE SUPERVISION BY HOST); the length of time the contract employee

15. Hourly wage data in this survey was collected in the following categories: under $6.00, $6.00–$8.99, $9.00–$11.99, $12.00–$15.00, over $15.00.

16. An F-test of the hypothesis that the coefficients on CONTRACT EMPLOYEE and CONTRACT EMPLOYEE AT HOST > 1 YEAR sum to zero yields $F(1, 565) = 0.601$.

17. An F-test of the hypothesis that the coefficients on CONTRACT EMPLOYEE and CLOSE SUPERVISION BY HOST sum to zero yields $F(1, 565) = 3.29$, which is not significant at the 5 percent level.. However an F-test of the hypothesis that the coefficients on these coefficients and CONTRACT EMPLOYEE > 1 YEAR AT HOST sum to zero is $F(1, 656) = 7.96$.

worked at the host plant (CONTRACT EMPLOYEE > 1 YEAR AT HOST); the hours of safety training supplied by the contractor (SAFETY TRAINING); the hours of safety training supplied by the host employer (SAFETY TRAIN-ING BY HOST); and the years of experience with the contractor (YEARS WITH EMPLOYER). Also included in equation 2, as well as all the other equations presented in Table 10.2, are variables that control for the respondent's age, education, non-safety-related job training, English language skills, and union affiliation. The coefficients on these control variables are not presented in Table 10.2, but they are available from the author upon request.

In equation 2 of Table 10.2, the variable indicating close supervision by the host is negative and statistically significant. The effect of close supervision on safety is very large. All else equal, when host management closely supervises contract maintenance employees, accident rates fall by 20 percent. In contrast, none of the variables measuring hours of safety training provided by the contractor or the host plant are statistically significant. Indeed, the hypothesis that all the training variables are jointly zero cannot be rejected at conventional significance levels.[18] Similarly, neither experience with the contractor nor tenure at the host plant have a statistically significant effect on the accident rates of contract employees.

Column 3 presents an accident equation for direct-hire maintenance employees. In this equation the variable SAFETY TRAINING refers to hours of safety training provided by management at the host plant. Similarly YEARS WITH EMPLOYER measures a direct-hire employee's tenure at the host plant. The estimates in column 3 suggest that the determinants of accident rates for direct-hire employees are quite different than the determinants for contract employees. In particular, the hours of safety training provided by the host plant have a large and statistically significant effect on accident rates. Point estimates suggest that, all else equal, moving from 5–8 hours of safety training to more than 21 hours of safety training will reduce the probability of an accident by 6 percent. In contrast to safety training, experience with the employer appears to have little effect on the accident rates of direct-hire maintenance employees.

The host plants supplying lists of contract employees to interview were a subset of the host plants supplying lists of direct-hire employees. It is therefore possible that the different effects of safety training on

18. An F-test of the hypothesis that the coefficients on all the safety training variables are jointly zero yields $F(4, 314) = 1.24$.

Table 10.2 Determinants of accidents for maintenance workers (dependent variable: accident [t-statistic])

Sample:	Contract + direct-hire employees (equation 1)	Contract employees (equation 2)	Direct-hire employees (equation 3)	Direct-hire employees (equation 4)	Contract employees >1 year at host (equation 5)
CONTRACT EMPLOYEE	0.305 (2.098)				
CONTRACT EMPLOYEE 1 YEAR AT HOST	-0.231 (-1.57)	-0.223 (-1.358)			
CLOSE SUPERVISION BY HOST	-0.65 (-3.613)	-0.645 (-3.385)			-0.883 (-2.670)
SAFETY TRAINING 5–8 HOURS		-0.401 (-1.362)	-0.972 (-2.173)	-0.860 (-1.014)	-0.585 (-1.010)
9–20 HOURS		0.211 (0.903)	-1.144 (-3.249)	-1.144 (-2.287)	0.091 (0.268)
21+ HOURS		0.136 (0.675)	-1.159 (-3.391)	-1.211 (-2.510)	0.058 (0.186)
SAFETY TRAINING BY HOST		-0.0027 (-0.876)		-0.001	(-0.240)
YEARS WITH EMPLOYER		-0.014 (-0.907)	-0.019 (-1.225)	-0.01 (-1.250)	-0.009 (-0.451)
IN CONTRACT SAMPLE				-0.091 (-0.153)	
IN CONTRACT SAMPLE × SAFETY TRAINING: 5–8 HOURS				-0.116 (-0.114)	
9–20 HOURS				-0.014 (-0.020)	
21+ HOURS				0.102 (0.155)	
CONSTANT	Yes	Yes	Yes	Yes	Yes
N	569	329	218	218	169
LOG LIKELIHOOD	-325.53	-177.654	-110.128	-110.046	-83.395
Phi	0.328	0.321	0.310	0.310	0.213

Note: All equations estimated as probits. ACCIDENT is a dummy variable equal to one if the respondent reported an accident at a petrochemical plant over the previous year. Accidents are defined as events requiring either first aid, treatment by a physician, or at least one lost day of work. Phi is the standard normal density function evaluated at sample means. Equation 1 evaluates phi at means for direct-hires. Equations 2-5 also include variables measuring education, non-safety-related job training, age, union membership, and the English-language skills of the respondents. IN CONTRACT SAMPLE is a dummy variable equal to 1 if the direct-hire's employer was also a host for a contract employee in the sample used to estimate equations 1 and 2 of this table.

contract and direct-hire accident rates may reflect some unmeasured technological difference between the two sets of plants. This explanation is explored in the equation presented in the next column of Table 10.2. Equation 4 provides another estimate of accident probabilities for direct-hire maintenance employees. It includes all the variables used in equation 3 plus a dummy variable equal to 1 if the respondent's plant was included in the contract employee survey (IN CONTRACT SAMPLE) and a set of interaction terms between this dummy variable and variables measuring hours of safety training. None of these additional variables are statistically significant, and one cannot reject the hypothesis that they are all jointly zero.[19] This suggests that in terms of accident rates, there is little difference between the plants included in the direct-hire survey and the subset included in the contract employee survey.

The safety training variables used in equations 2–4 of Table 10.2 refer to a respondent's experience at petrochemical plants over the previous year. If contract employees worked at a number of different host plants over the previous year and if there exists an important facility-specific component to safety training, this might lead to a downwards bias in the effect of safety training on accidents for contract employees. To examine this issue, the equation in column 5 reestimates the safety equation in column 1 but restricts the sample to contract employees having at least one year of tenure at the host plant. Here again we find that the coefficient on the variable CLOSE SUPERVISION BY HOST is negative and statistically significant while the variables measuring safety training are neither individually nor jointly statistically significant.[20]

The primary result that emerges from the analysis in Table 10.2 is that safety supervision by host employers markedly reduces the accident rates of contract employees. This effect persists even when controls for job type, work experience, levels of education and hours of safety training are included in the equation. The finding that heightened host supervision is associated with reduced contract employee accident rates is important. Requiring contract workers to report safety matters directly to host plant management is precisely the sort of activity that host plants must avoid if they wish to escape vicarious liability for the actions of contract workers.

This interpretation of the results in Table 10.2 presumes that close supervision *causes* lower accident rates. An alternative possibility is that

19. An F-test of the hypothesis that the coefficient on IN CONTRACT SAMPLE and all the interaction terms are jointly zero yields $F(4, 202) = 0.04$.

20. An F-test of the hypothesis that the coefficients on all the safety training variables are jointly zero yields $F(4, 155) = 0.38$.

host plants directly supervise only those jobs that have inherently low accident rates. If this second interpretation is correct and closely supervised contract employees work in safer jobs, then one should observe *lower* levels of safety training for contract employees who experience close safety supervision. Unpublished analysis of the data, however, reveals that closely supervised contract employees receive substantially *more* safety training from the host plant and no less safety training from contractors.[21] An alternative explanation might be that host plants recognize the potential liability problems posed by closely supervised contract workers. In response, plants that closely supervise contractors also try to reduce accidents by both increasing safety training *and* placing contractors in relatively safe maintenance jobs. This conjecture receives some support from the estimates in column 1 indicating that closely supervised contract maintenance employees may have *lower* accident rates than their direct-hire counterparts. This hypothesis would also suggest that the coefficient on CLOSE SUPERVISION BY HOST is picking up both the effects of differential job assignments within maintenance as well as unmeasured aspects of safety training by the host.

The second important result from Table 10.2 is that the safety training offered to contract employees has no effect on accident rates even though safety training dramatically reduces the accident rates of direct-hire employees. These findings may be understood as supporting the hypothesis that contractors are less effective than host plants in preparing their employees to function safely in petrochemical plants. This interpretation of the results would be consistent with journalistic reports of perfunctory training of contract workers (Selcraig, 1992). It would also imply that the practice of giving responsibility for safety training to contractors leads to higher accident rates among contract employees. Other explanations of the training results are plausible, however, and cannot be ruled out with the data currently available.

It may be, for example, that the type of workers who accept contract jobs are inherently more difficult to train than permanent employees. Alternatively, if safety training is a form of investment in firm-specific human capital, the relatively short expected tenure of many contract employees may reduce their incentives to get the most out of the safety

---

21. These supplemental data analyses are available from the author upon request. The association between close supervision and safety training would have to be interpreted quite differently if the marginal benefits of safety training happened to be high (and/or the marginal costs low) in jobs characterized by low accident rates. If this were the case, however, one would expect *both* contractor and host safety training to increase with close supervision.

training offered by contractors and host-employers. If either of these explanations are correct, then the effectiveness of safety training for contract employees would not be improved by simply giving responsibility to host employers. Further investigation of this issue would require more detailed information about safety training and worker characteristics than is possible with the data currently available.

A third result from Table 10.2 is that experience has no significant effect on accident rates. This finding is somewhat surprising in light of the fact that experience typically is found to be an important determinant of accident rates (Kahn, 1987). A plausible explanation for this anomaly is that many of the studies in the occupational safety and health literature do not include measures of safety training as detailed as those used in this study. If safety training is correlated with experience, this would bias upward the coefficient on experience in an accident equation. Alternatively, it may be that the determinants of accidents in petrochemical facilities are simply different than those in other industries.

The legal rules for assigning liability for the costs of accidents penalize host plants that exercise direct control over contract employees. Evidence from case studies, interviews with risk managers, surveys of contractors, and surveys of petrochemical plant managers all indicate that these liability rules lead host plants to give primary responsibility for safety training and supervision to contractors. Analysis of the determinants of accident rates suggests, however, that host plants offer more effective safety training and supervision than contractors.

It follows that accident rates in the industry might be reduced if host plants were given incentives to take more responsibility for safety training and supervision. A natural way to create such incentives would be to assign liability for the actions of contract employees to host plants—irrespective of the degree of control the host exercises over the contract workforce. Given the possibility for catastrophic accidents in this industry, the potential benefits from such a change in legal doctrine might be large.

Part IV

Policy and Research:
Future Directions

CHAPTER ELEVEN

Making Labor Law Work
for Part-Time and Contingent Workers

Virginia L. duRivage
Françoise J. Carré
Chris Tilly

As part-time and contingent employment expand in the U.S. economy, U.S. labor laws have become increasingly out of date. These laws, designed to regulate labor-management relations and to guarantee a worker's right to choose union representation (in order to improve their employment conditions) serve the new "flexible" workforce poorly. In order for part-time and contingent employees to enjoy equal rights to union representation—and thus greater employment protection—labor laws and the institutions that surround them must change dramatically.

Workers in part-time, temporary, and contingent employment account for about one-fourth of today's workforce. We need a few brief comments regarding the definition of this workforce for this chapter. Most analysts use the standard Bureau of Labor Statistics definition of part-time work, which classifies people working fewer than thirty-five hours per week as part-time workers. Defining contingent employment, however, is more contentious. The February 1995 Current Population Survey (U.S. Bureau of Labor Statistics, 1995b) uses a very specific definition of contingent work that is based on the past and expected duration of employment. Under the broadest BLS definition of contingent workers (wage workers and the self-employed who do not expect their job to last), contingent employment accounts for 4.9 percent of total employment. This chapter adopts a broader focus, addressing the hardships (lack of benefits, union coverage, instability) experienced by workers who are considered nonstandard or marginal by their employers and by employment and labor law. We discuss the impediments to union representation experienced, for example, by part-time workers, regardless of the duration of their employment and regardless of their status as "contingent" or not under the narrow BLS definition. Similarly, we discuss the difficulties faced by workers who are in other nonstandard arrangements including temporary workers, contract workers (for example, janitorial services), on-call workers or day laborers, and those who are independent contractors. According to the BLS, part-time employment encompasses 18 percent of those at work in 1995, and the categories of nonstandard employment (regardless of expected job duration) account for 9.9 percent of employment. Of course, there is overlap between measures of "nonstandard" employment (a status) and part-time hours (work schedule). For example, 29.5 percent of nonstandard workers work part-time. Finally, in addition to these definitional ambiguities, the Current Population Survey results on temporary help service workers are also subject to debate. The worker survey yields a size of employment in the temporary help/staffing industry that is about half the size of the industry as reported by other BLS establishment-based data.

Federal laws governing the right of workers to organize into labor unions (labor law) as well as other laws governing wages, social insurance, and other aspects of working life (employment law) have failed to respond to the dramatic growth of the part-time and contingent workforce.[1] Part-time and contingent workers stand outside the traditional permanent, full-time employment relationship upon which the framework of employment and labor law was built in the 1930s and 1940s and thus lack basic protections. Partly as a result, part-time and contingent workers suffer from a series of problems: few or no benefits; low wages; reduced employment security and barriers to advancement; low productivity, due in part to employer and employee's diminished commitment to each other; and the possibility of being trapped in these arrangements involuntarily (Carré, duRivage, & Tilly, 1995). Very low rates of union

---

1. Labor law refers to the legal rights of workers to union representation, as defined in the National Labor Relations Act of 1935 (NLRA), also known as the Wagner Act (which was subsequently amended under the Taft-Hartley Act of 1947). Under this law, American workers are guaranteed the right to form and to join labor organizations, to bargain collectively through representatives of their own choosing, and to engage in other activities related to collective bargaining and mutual aid. When we use the term "labor law" in this chapter, we are referring to the legal framework undergirding the NLRA, as well as the government institutions implementing that law (chiefly the National Labor Relations Board).

Employment law refers to federal laws, regulations, and institutions governing conditions at work, as opposed to union-management relations. Such conditions include minimum wages, hours of work, occupational safety and health, unemployment insurance, pensions, and social security. Federal regulations regarding workplace conditions are codified in laws including the Fair Labor Standards Act, the Social Security Act, the Occupational Safety and Health Act, the Employee Retirement and Income Security Act, and the Family and Medical Leave Act, and are administered by the Department of Labor.

representation leave part-time and contingent workers ill-equipped to address these problems.

Bringing union representation to part-time and temporary workers requires several changes (Carré, duRivage, & Tilly, 1995). First, changes in labor laws are needed to extend coverage to workers who fall through the cracks of current legislation, to facilitate pre-hire agreements through which labor and management can negotiate the use of temporary workers, to institutionalize multiemployer bargaining structures, and in some cases to use government mandates to extend union-negotiated conditions to an entire industry.

Changes in labor law, though critical, will not by themselves be sufficient to guarantee protection for part-time and temporary workers. Unions have also been slow to respond to workplace change. Thus, unions must develop new and creative approaches to organizing and bargaining. Lastly, employment law must also establish direct government regulation of some aspects of nonstandard employment in order to assure a basic level of security for workers and to prevent exploitation.

The remainder of this chapter argues the case for these changes. We begin by outlining the gaps in existing labor law and detail changes that could remedy these flaws. We address how changes in union organizing strategy and in employment law could supplement amended labor laws, and we then close with brief conclusions and suggestions for future research. Throughout the chapter, we repeatedly draw on the examples of the construction and garment industries, where alternative union structures and legal provisions designed for a contingent or marginal workforce have a long history.

Gaps in Current Labor Law

Current labor law falls short by restricting access to union representation to part-time and contingent workers. The National Labor Relations Act (NLRA), the main law establishing rights and procedures for union organizing, was crafted in 1935. Congress designed the NLRA primarily for workers employed permanently full-time by a single employer in a fixed location. As a result, the growing number of workers who depart from this norm experience depressed levels of unionization. In 1990, 7 percent of part-timers were union members, compared with 19 percent of full-time workers (U.S. Bureau of Labor Statistics, 1991). Even after controlling for gender, race, age, and education, over two-thirds of the gap in union membership rates between part-time and full-time workers remains. In the personnel supply service industry (which includes temp agencies), only 7 percent of workers are organized, compared with 17 percent of workers in other industries (Tilly, 1991c).

Indeed, in some cases, employers have expanded flexible forms of employment in order to undercut union organizing drives or exact concessions during contract negotiations (Carré, duRivage, & Tilly, 1995). At Transtech, a nonunion subsidiary of AT&T, fifteen hundred agency temps are performing the same work as bargaining-unit employees at AT&T and have become the company's first defense against union organizing in the Florida firm. In the construction industry, an increasingly common practice is hiring workers as self-employed contractors to avoid hiring through the union. No legislation prohibits the hiring of temporary agency workers as strike breakers. Numerous employers have resorted to this strategy, a practice outlawed in several Western European countries.

There are four primary gaps in labor law coverage that severely limit the protective effects of existing labor law for part-time and contingent workers. First, when the federal government establishes the "bargaining units" that define who will be in a given union, nonstandard workers are often excluded. Second, current laws are ill-equipped to handle joint employment, as when a business hires workers through a temporary agency or subcontractor. Third, subcontracting of public sector jobs creates a gray area between public and private employment where the legal protections associated with either often do not apply. Finally, current labor laws are inadequate for high-turnover workforces.

Exclusion from Workplace Bargaining Units

The National Labor Relations Board, the federal agency charged with enforcing the NLRA, plays the major role in the determination of the "appropriate bargaining unit." In the absence of voluntary employer recognition, when a board election must be held, the NLRB defines the group of workers among whom the board holds a union representation election and who are covered by the collective bargaining agreement once it is in effect. Unfortunately, a narrow and inappropriate bargaining-unit determination by the NLRB often creates an obstacle to representing part-time and contingent workers. In determining an appropriate bargaining unit, the board relies upon a "community of interest" criterion that considers similarity of wages, working conditions, and regularity of employment among workers. Using this criterion, the NLRB has issued inconsistent rulings as to whether part-time and contingent workers hired directly by the firm should be covered by the same contract as regular employees (Bronfenbrenner, 1988). In some cases, the board has found that short-term hires may be part of a bargaining unit if no certain date has been set for their termination. Seasonal employees may be included in the unit if they have a reasonable expectation of reemployment.

Factors that help determine the "community of interest" include performing similar kinds of work, working in the same location, and sharing common supervision and schedules (Service Employees International Union, 1993). Under the original National Labor Relations Act, employees' preexisting patterns of preferences, as evidenced by the "extent of organizing," were often decisive in determining bargaining units. However, since the passage of the Taft-Hartley Act (the Labor Management Relations Act of 1947, which weakened many of the prounion provisions of the NLRA), it is illegal for the "extent of organizing" to be the controlling factor in bargaining-unit determination (Wial, 1993).

Joint Employers

Workers with joint employers can also be excluded from union representation because the NLRB rarely recognizes the role of the client company in controlling employment conditions. Two parties—the client company and intermediary subcontractor or agency—are involved in controlling working conditions and wages. For example, a client company hires a subcontracting firm to clean its office buildings. The client company determines the duration of the contractual relationship with the subcontracting firm and thus controls the employment of workers on its site. It also controls the terms of the contract, which have a direct bearing on wage levels and benefits, while the janitorial contractor exercises direct supervision over the employees.[2]

The NLRB, drawing on outdated notions of a fixed worker-employer relationship, rarely finds a joint employer relationship; that is, it rarely recognizes the employer-like role played by the client firm in controlling the wage levels and duration of employment of the contractor's workforce. Under current labor law, the NLRB uses a narrow "right to control" test to determine joint employer status. This test ignores the underlying economic realities of the client/contractor relationship, focusing instead on whether employers "share or codetermine those matters governing the essential terms and conditions of employment" (Hiatt & Rhinehart, 1993:21). Even in cases where the client is extensively

---

2. L. Engelstein (1996) notes that the bulk of the cost of janitorial services contracts goes to workforce wages.

involved in work assignments and supervision, however, the board has failed to recognize joint employer liability.

As a result, remedies against unfair labor practices by client firms under the NLRA are not available. For example, a building owner or "client" can legally terminate a building service contract in retaliation for union activities without sanction, even though such an action by an "employer" ordinarily violates Section 7 of the NLRA. And no NLRA provision requires a successor contractor to hire the previous employer's workers or to accept the previous employer's collective bargaining contract (Hiatt & Rhinehart, 1993). Furthermore, despite the client company's economic control over contract workers' wages and working conditions, the company is protected from economic retaliation under current labor law. The Taft-Hartley Act regards the client as a "neutral secondary employer," insulated from collective economic actions such as picketing or striking in the event of a labor dispute.

Public Workers versus Private Workers

When public sector work is contracted out to the private sector, not only do workers lose union protection (Dantico, 1987) but their contracted status places them between public and private employers, leaving them outside both the NLRA and state public sector collective bargaining laws. For example, in Michigan fifteen thousand group home workers perform essential services for the state, working under a variety of private employers funded by the State Treasury. When the American Federation of State, County, and Municipal Employees (AFSCME) tried to organize these workers, the NLRB denied representation on the grounds that they were state employees not covered by the NLRA. But when the union approached the State of Michigan Employment Relations Commission, the state successfully argued that the workers were private employees, and the commission denied AFSCME representation on this basis. Such seesawing is common in the public sector. (P. Booth, personal communication, September 20, 1993).

Short Job Tenure

Finally, much of existing labor law is poorly designed for dealing with high-turnover workforces. The NLRA generally assumes that workers have relatively long-term attachments to a single employer, giving them a stake in organizing with coworkers and bargaining with that employer. Contingent workers, such as temporary or leased workers, by definition have short-term employment arrangements. But part-time workers as well tend to turn over much more quickly than do full-timers (Rebitzer & Taylor, 1991). Turnover rates among part-time retail clerks and cashiers run as high as 300 percent annually (Tilly, 1992c). Furthermore, virtually all jobs have become more "contingent," as businesses renege on implicit employment guarantees, raising the possibility of increased job turnover in the labor market.

Current labor laws do include a few historical exceptions to the presumption of long-term employment with a single employer. For example, the NLRA has special provisions for the construction and garment industries, designed to accommodate organizational structures already in place at the time of the NLRA's passage (Wial, 1993). Both sectors have complex employment structures involving subcontracting, short work tenures, and unstable working conditions. However, as these features of business activity and employment relations have spilled over into other industries, labor law has not evolved to respond to them.

Changing Labor Law

We suggest four areas of labor law reform to strengthen representation rights for part-time and contingent workers. First, existing labor law protections should be extended to workers who are currently excluded. Second, permitting pre-hire agreements between employers and unions would allow the latter to bargain for temporary and on-call workers. Third, instituting multiemployer bargaining would greatly facilitate representation in industries where workers move frequently among many small firms. Last, we advocate more extensive use of sectoral bargaining, in which government extends a union-negotiated floor of protections to all workers in an industry, whether unionized or not.

Extending Existing Labor Protections

As the various forms of nonstandard work proliferate, it becomes increasingly important for the National Labor Relations Board to broaden definitions of bargaining units and include part-timers, short-term hires, and others as an integral part of the workforce. Without such broad unit definitions, employers may have an incentive to hire nonstandard workers to avoid complying with union contract provisions.

In addition, employees deliberately misclassified as independent contractors by their employers should be brought under NLRA coverage. Tax reformers as well as unions have begun to tackle this issue; the Internal Revenue Service, which uses a more stringent definition of independent contractors than that included in the NLRA, estimates that 38 percent of employers dodge payroll taxes by misclassifying employees in this way (U.S. Government Accounting Office, 1991). One solution may be to adopt a standardized, stricter definition of an independent contractor across federal employment and labor laws with separate jurisdictions (e.g., NLRA, Internal Revenue Code, and others).

In fact, assuring meaningful representation for both independent contractors as well as other contingent workers requires modernizing and streamlining the concepts of "employer" and "employee." During 1994 the U.S. Labor and Commerce Departments' Dunlop Commission on the Future of Worker-Management Relations (U.S. Department of Labor & U.S. Department of Commerce, 1994a) held special hearings to target the problems of contingent employment. While reluctant to support broad reforms in labor law to address these problems, the commission did recommend administrative and regulatory approaches to interpreting labor law in a manner that more clearly defines the employment relationship. One recommendation calls for Congress to adopt a single, coherent concept of employee and apply it across the board in employment and labor law. The commission also recommended that the NLRA adopt a broader approach to determining who is or is not an independent contractor. This approach would go beyond questions of day-to-day supervision and control and consider the underlying economic realities of the client and contractor relationship in determining whether a worker is an independent contractor or an employee. We would argue that this approach be used in determining the issue of joint employers as well (Engelstein, 1996).

The growth of subcontracting, through privatization, has hit workers particularly hard in the public sector, undermining wages, benefits, and job security. To pull public sector contract workers out of the private sector/ public sector limbo described above, one solution is to extend NLRA coverage to public employees in those states that do not currently have a public sector bargaining law.[3] In addition, the administration of collective bargaining laws, whether public or private, should be coordinated so that no worker falls in between public and private representation.

---

3. The NLRA was initially established to cover the collective bargaining relations between workers and private employers. Thus many states have adopted their own public sector bargaining laws. Currently only twenty-three states have comprehensive, NLRA-like laws regulating public sector collective bargaining, and a number of states—including Virginia, Texas, and Missouri—outlaw public sector unions.

Establish Pre-hire Agreements

In drafting the National Labor Relations Act, Congress recognized the uniqueness of unstable and transient employment patterns in the construction and garment trades. Legislators permitted these two industries to continue their already established practice of pre-hire agreements, in which union and employer agree to hire only union-referred workers. In addition to securing work for their members, unions in these sectors also administer health and pension funds that are funded through employers' payroll contributions, in recognition of the fluidity of employee-employer relationships in these industries and of high turnover among employers.

Today, sixty years after the enactment of the NLRA, the defining characteristics of employee-employer relations of these trades—transience and subcontracting—have expanded to other sectors of the economy. Reforming labor law by permitting pre-hire agreements across all industries would greatly enhance the protective impact of the law for part-time and contingent workers. Pre-hire agreements would empower unions to develop proactive solutions to contingent work by offering training and job referral services to workers tossed out of the "core" workforce who seek a way back in. In high-turnover settings, such agreements allow workers to retain union membership and associated protections as they move from job to job. They prevent an employer from ousting the union by simply hiring a new crop of employees.

Even without changes in the law, some unions are experimenting with labor referral systems which operate as quasi–hiring halls, matching union-preferred temporary workers or contract workers with employers in their industry. In California, the Service Employees International Union has helped to develop a nonprofit consortium of home health care providers, in which workers are involved in setting wages and working conditions. And in Ohio and California, the Communications Workers of America are experimenting with employment centers run by the union that contract with employers to hire union-protected workers on a short-term basis. We discuss these experiments below in a section on supplements to labor law.

Without explicit legal recognition, however, such experiments are in jeopardy. For pre-hire agreements to be effective, unions must be able to exert some control over the employer's hiring decisions. Some unions, who already represent a firm's regular workforce, have been able to control the presence of part-time and contingent employment. This is how the communications workers have won union-run employment centers at some of the regional Bell corporations. To make it possible, however, for broader groups of workers to achieve pre-hire accords, labor law must restore unions' right to pressure employers through secondary boycotts and picketing for union recognition.[4] The Taft-Hartley Act bans both practices outside the garment and construction industries. Historically, construction and garment unions have often secured pre-hire agreements through the use of secondary boycotts. Reinstating the right of secondary boycott, in situations where there is a subcontracting relationship, would enhance the success of organizing efforts among contingent workers, from home-based clerical workers to the growing legions of mobile professional freelancers (Cobble, 1991).

Multiemployer Bargaining

Many of the obstacles to organizing and bargaining for part-time and contingent workers result from a labor law framework that fixes organizing and collective bargaining around an individual employer and a specific work site (Wial, 1993, 1994). This framework is obsolete in an economy in which workers with different employers and employment contracts work side by side in the same work site, while workers in scattered, sometimes even home-based locations are employed by the same firm. Once more, the building and garment trades offer useful precedents. In these industries, unions developed multiemployer bargaining structures that predated the National Labor Relations Act. Workers were organized according to craft or occupational lines, geographic area, or in some cases according to ethnicity or gender. Union locals were grouped into union federations or boards which bargained directly with employer associations, while contract enforcement took place at the level of the business establishment.

Extending labor laws to accommodate occupational and regional unions in industries other than garment and construction would give contingent workers the latitude to construct forms of representation that reflect their patterns of employment. The National Labor Relations Board could be involved in determining the boundaries of the relevant multiemployer labor market (Wial, 1993). Under a reformed labor law, the "community of interest" criterion could be expanded beyond the work site to include multiple work sites or entire geographic areas. Alter-

---

4. A secondary boycott targets a business purchasing from the employer the union is attempting to bargain with—for example, boycotting a retailer that sells apparel manufactured by a nonunion contractor.

natively, a less regulatory approach would allow the parties to negotiate the boundaries of the labor market area relevant to collective bargaining.

Sectoral Bargaining

A potentially more powerful instrument in improving the terms of employment for workers who shift across work sites and employers is sectoral bargaining. Under sectoral bargaining, unions initially bargain a model agreement, either with an industry-wide employer association or with a substantial subset of employers in a given industry and geographic area. The government—local, regional, or national—then extends the terms of the contract to *all* employers in that industry and area. Thus, even if a worker moves from one employer to another, she or he is consistently assured of continued coverage under terms of the union contract. Government support of sectoral bargaining could greatly enhance worker protection in industries where an intermediary employer is involved and workers shift across assignments, such as services to buildings, and could also create the basis for organizing temporary workers *as employees of temporary agencies*, rather than as employees of the client companies.

American labor law currently inhibits sectoral bargaining, with some limited exceptions, such as prevailing wage laws that extend building trades union contract provisions to all construction workers on publicly funded projects. Experiences in France, however, suggest approaches that may be useful in formulating reforms in the U.S. system.

Since 1985, the French government has promoted national collective bargaining agreements in the temporary help industry, improving working conditions for temporary and contingent workers. In France, public opinion and policy concern about the erosion of stable, long-term employment have focused on the temporary help industry as the most visible culprit in this trend. During the 1970s, government action focused on tightening licensing and insurance requirements for temporary help agencies. By 1982, in a move to curb repeated employer abuses and to respond to calls for nationalizing the temp industry, France's parliament passed compromise legislation regulating both user firms and temporary agencies. Regulations included a prohibition on using temporaries as strikebreakers, wage and benefits parity between temporary workers and regular workers of the user firm, requirements to notify workers in advance of the duration of a temporary assignment, and a ban on temporary assignments in some dangerous work sites. The legislation had two important effects: (1) marginal temp help service companies with the worst records of employee abuse were weeded out; and (2) the clerical temporary help service industry, in particular, became more concentrated into businesses that compete on the basis of service quality rather than lower wages.

To further improve employment conditions, and as an alternative to further regulation, the government fostered the development of a sectoral bargaining effort. The first agreement in 1985 and subsequent ones have developed seniority provisions for key benefits which move with a temporary worker from temp agency to agency (not just across assignments for one temp agency), create social welfare benefits such as workers' compensation or supplementary retiree benefits that are comparable to those of regular workers, and maintain worker access to job-related benefits such as sick leave beyond the duration of their assignment with one user firm. Most important, a government decree extended the full range of benefits to all workers in the temporary help supply industry, even those who are not members of a union. National-level sectoral bargaining in the French temporary help industry thus allows all workers in the industry to benefit from the terms of the contract.

Supplements to Labor Law

Revisions to labor law can facilitate union representation of part-time and contingent workers, removing current obstacles to organizing. But to actually achieve representation, two additional changes are needed that go beyond labor law. Most important, unions must take the initiative to create new forms of organizing and collective bargaining that reflect new workplace realities. In addition, employment law, which regulates conditions of employment other than the labor-management relationship itself, needs to set certain ground rules for nonstandard work.

Organizing and Bargaining Innovations

For unions representing a workforce with substantial numbers of part-timers or others with nonstandard work arrangements, regulating the use of these workers has already become a central goal. John Reilly, president of the United University Professions Division of the American Federation of Teachers, states, "The best strategy is to fully integrate part-timers into the union and academic life with prorated benefits and equivalent participation" (Part-time concerns, 1992:3). The first step toward this goal is inclusion of part-time and contingent workers in the bargaining unit, although with a separate status. The next step is to bargain for parity in wages and benefits. For example, the United Food and

Commercial Workers has targeted equal wages and prorated benefits for part-time workers, with some success. In Birmingham, Alabama, UFCW Local 1657, whose membership is 60 percent part-time, has won a package that actually makes compensation for two part-timers more expensive than for a single full-timer, through a package of prorated and in some cases equal benefits.

Though unions have typically opposed the spread of part-time and contingent employment, a growing group of unions has concluded that schedule flexibility can be a benefit for part of their workforce and, accordingly, have bargained to make that flexibility available. The Service Employees International Union Locals 6 (representing private mental health clinics in Seattle), 535, and 715 (representing Santa Clara County workers) have bargained for a full-time employee's right to request job sharing or a permanent part-time arrangement. Part-time workers can also bid to move to full-time jobs, and in many cases parents of young children have moved from full-time to part-time and then back to full-time based on child care needs. Local 6's agreement protects part-timers from overtime demands by requiring that overtime be offset by compensatory time. The contract for Locals 535 and 715 even sets a minimum of part-time positions in the bargaining unit (Nollen, 1982).

Union representation of contingent workers other than part-timers is particularly challenging. Some union contracts mandate upgrading of contingent workers after a fixed duration of employment. Unions have been particularly creative in exploring ways to establish pre-hire agreements, as noted above. For example, at Cincinnati Bell, the Communications Workers of America negotiated the creation of its own temporary agency, the Cincinnati Bell CWA Agency. The agency draws extensively on CWA retirees who seek added work and is run by a manager hired by the union. The union receives a monthly list of who is working for the agency, for how many hours, and for what department and manager. Agency workers receive the full union benefit package, but slightly lower pay. They pay union dues and have access to the grievance procedure. Union officials report that Cincinnati Bell, which was once notorious for using temp agencies, now relies almost entirely on the union-run firm (D. Ditmer, personal communication, January 15, 1995).

A recent settlement between AT&T and CWA Local 1058 offers an interesting twist on the pre-hire agreement model. The union filed a charge with the National Labor Relations Board against AT&T for grossly exceeding the contractually permitted level of agency temporary workers as defined in the labor contract. They documented that 25 percent of

AT&T's total clerical workforce in New Jersey was made up of agency temps doing work usually performed by union members, in direct violation of the collective bargaining agreement. The board found against AT&T and recommended that the company retroactively apply all the terms and conditions of the labor contract to the improperly hired temporary agency personnel, at a cost the union estimated would have come close to $35 million. The two sides agreed instead to settle the dispute by establishing, on a pilot basis, a pool of employees who would serve as a flexible, mobile workforce to fill temporary assignments in positions normally held by bargaining-unit employees. The Administrative Pilot Agreement sets up a new union-protected job classification called "administrative intern." For the first six months of employment, an intern agrees to accept temporary assignments within AT&T offices in New Jersey (Bronfenbrenner & duRivage, 1994).

Even without pre-hire agreements, unions have in some cases succeeded in capturing work that has been shifted out of the bargaining unit. In Wisconsin, correctional nurses in Service Employees International Union District 1199WI successfully regained nursing work that had been subcontracted by the state. When the state awarded the nursing contract to the lowest bidder, they were shocked to find out that the contractor, We Care, Inc., consisted of unionized nurses working at time-and-one-half rates! The nurses, many of whom work part-time on their regular jobs, allocate subcontracted work time among themselves according to need.

Organizing Models

To extend representation of contingent workers beyond these relatively special cases, unions will have to adopt more comprehensive models of organization. The relevant alternative models proposed to date are occupational unionism (Cobble, 1991) and geographical/occupational unionism (Wial, 1993). *Occupational unionism,* a model based on research on waitress unions from the turn of the century to the 1960s, rests on strong occupational (skill-based) identity, union control over the industry's labor supply, definition of rights and benefits as functions of occupational membership rather than work-site affiliation, peer control over occupational performance standards, and emphasis on employment security rather than "job rights." This model could apply to temporary and contract workers who frequently shift among job sites. It depends, however, on homogeneity of skills and union control over labor supply.

Temporary and contracted workforces, while heterogeneous in terms of skill, could instead build a common identity based on their distinctive experiences of the workplace and of the labor market.

H. Wial (1993) proposes a more widely applicable variant of occupational unionism, which entails establishing a uniform wage and benefit structure covering loosely defined occupational groupings across employers within a localized geographical area. Unlike the previous model, this *geographical/occupational unionism* requires neither strong occupational identity nor union enforcement of job performance standards nor union control over labor supply. Without control over labor supply, unions' bargaining power must emanate from their ability to mobilize economic and political pressure, to provide services useful to employers, and to rely on government intervention.

The geographical union model requires portability of benefits to facilitate worker mobility across jobs. Although unions do not control labor supply, they refer workers to jobs within the unions' jurisdictions. Because this is a multiemployer structure, the union can compel employers to invest in training without fear that the costs involved will put unionized businesses at a competitive disadvantage. The prospect of areawide collective bargaining agreements encourages pre-bargaining associations between union and community groups that can turn into union locals.

Can these proposals work? Arts and entertainment unions, which represent workers with short-term, project-based jobs, incorporate many of the elements of both the Cobble and Wial models. These unions provide services to ease job transitions, including referral and placement and transitional loan funds. They bargain for pension portability and for health coverage that can be self-paid during spells of unemployment. The arts and entertainment unions are directly involved in a number of areas traditionally left to management, such as hiring and the administration of compensation. A. Kleingartner and A. Paul (1992:3) note that "unions in arts and entertainment are effective, relevant, and valued by workers in the industry without being powerful in the sense of being able to impose their will on employers through strikes."

Other unions have also begun trying out variants of these models. In the organizing arena, the Service Employees International Union's Justice for Janitors campaign—which inspired Wial's geographical/occupational model—stands out. Justice for Janitors targets employers citywide with a variety of innovative tactics, including lawsuits, theatrical actions directed at the media, and corporate campaigns designed to pressure the customers of building service firms to favor union representation (J. Hiatt, personal communication, November 16, 1993). In another experiment with multiemployer bargaining, SEIU Local 509 is working to extend union protection to about twenty thousand human service workers in Massachusetts who are performing state-funded mental health and mental retardation services but are employed by a couple of hundred private agencies in about two thousand sites. To do this, the union is attempting to gain voluntary employer recognition and create a statewide bargaining unit to represent these workers (Carré & Dougherty, 1995). The success of this experiment could provide a powerful weapon against the public sector's use of contracting-out as a tactic for cutting costs at the expense of worker wages and employment conditions.

Government Regulation of Part-Time and Contingent Employment

A necessary complement to labor law reform and innovative union approaches to organizing and bargaining is employment laws that directly regulate the use of part-time and contingent workers. Here we simply sketch a few elements of these policies.[5]

The most effective short-term policy to boost wages and working conditions for contingent workers is to mandate wage and benefit parity between part-time and contingent employees and the full-time, permanent workforce (in comparable positions) of the firm where they work. This parity provides workers with significant benefits and simultaneously reduces firms' cost incentives to substitute part-time or contingent workers for regular workers.

Part-time and contingent work that brings decent wages, benefits, and security is one side of the coin; a job that allows flexibility in response to changing worker preferences is the other. Measures along these lines include parental leave, flextime, and the right to move between full-time and part-time status. And whether workers choose nonstandard employment or have it imposed on them, key benefits should be socially guaranteed. Universal health coverage is the single most important piece of this package. A logical next step would be a portable pension system with a guaranteed minimum. Part-time and contingent workers would also benefit from revised standards for unemployment insurance because

5. For more extensive discussion of these policies, see Carré, duRivage, & Tilly, 1995; Tilly, 1996.

many of them fall short of eligibility under current work and earnings requirements.

Changes in labor law, innovations in union strategy, and direct regulation of part-time and contingent work are all needed to build basic protections for the nonstandard workforce. In fact, the three approaches complement one another. If and when government regulations mandating wage and benefits parity are adopted, unions will play a critical role in monitoring and enforcing these regulations, just as they do for current wage and hour laws that in principle apply to all (nonexempt) workers. Conversely, union organizing efforts can be greatly assisted by government requirements that build up security and stability for nonstandard workers as well as render transience less costly to workers. And as was the case with the original 1935 National Labor Relations Act, new models of union representation can help shape the labor laws that Congress adopts.

Further research would help to flesh out the types of legal reforms and union strategies that would be most effective in facilitating the representation of nonstandard workers. In this paper, we have referred repeatedly to labor relations in the construction and garment trades as models for labor law reform because policy makers have historically recognized these sectors as entailing transient employer/worker relations and thus made exceptions in labor law for them. But different industrial sectors may require different approaches. A more thorough understanding of the dynamics of labor relations within the construction and garment trades would provide valuable information about what types of contingent work, and what industrial sectors, respond best to pre-hire agreements and multiemployer bargaining. Similarly, more research is needed in examining labor relations in the arts and entertainment industries, which yield other representative models for contingent workers.

Research is also needed on the growing body of union experiments with labor referral systems and alternative organizing and bargaining strategies. Several questions can be asked: What problems do these experiments address? What is gained by having union run referral systems? Under what conditions can jointly run union-management experiments work? A systematic look at proactive union responses to contingent work would provide a clearer understanding of the interplay between social relations in the firm, the market, and the political environment.

We can also learn much from comparative research examining how other countries' governments and labor movements have approached part-time and temporary work. Many countries have moved beyond mere restrictive regulation and toward building social insurance structures which make it possible for workers to experience frequent changes in assignment, site, or employer without dire consequences for their economic well-being.

Today, all too often the "flexibility" in nonstandard forms of employment means flexibility for the employer alone, at the cost of insecurity for the worker. Rectifying this imbalance means updating a labor relations system that dates back more than fifty years and retooling it for the twenty-first century. Through a combination of government action and union organizing, we can start to catch up with the rapid transformation of the American workplace.

CHAPTER TWELVE

Contingent Workers and Employment Law

Anthony P. Carnevale
Lynn A. Jennings
James M. Eisenmann

*T*his chapter will examine the state of the contingent workforce by identifying who is an "employee" in the context of federal employment laws. The discussion will review the Fair Labor Standards Act,[1] Title VII of the Civil Rights Act of 1964,[2] the Age Discrimination in Employment Act,[3] the Family and Medical Leave Act,[4] the Occupational Safety and Health Act,[5] and the Worker's Adjustment and Retraining Notification Act.[6] Even a cursory examination of these statutes reveals that federal protections afforded full-time, permanent employees do not reach contingent workers. Few workplace protections are afforded workers who are unable to prove that they are an "employee" as defined by the statutes. Although the existence of an "employment relationship" is only an initial step in the litigation process, it is a crucial jurisdictional hurdle to meet before a worker qualifies for coverage under these laws. This is a fact that often prevents meritorious cases from being adjudicated. The challenge we now face is how to reconcile the need to furnish contingent workers protections in the workplace similar to those afforded permanent employees while continuing to provide employers with the workforce flexibility they need to be competitive in a global economy and continuing to provide diverse and flexible employment options for individual workers.

The views expressed in this chapter are solely the views of the individual authors and not those of the Secretary of Labor or the Department of Labor.

1. 29 U.S.C. § 201, *et. seq.*
2. 42 U.S.C. § 2000e, *et. seq.*
3. 29 U.S.C. § 621, *et. seq.*
4. 29 U.S.C. § 2601.
5. 29 U.S.C. § 651.
6. 29 U.S.C. § 2101.

The Fair Labor Standards Act and the Equal Pay Act

The Fair Labor Standards Act[7] (FLSA) was enacted in 1938 to "combat the low wages and long working hours then endured by some laborers" and to "free commerce from the interferences arising from production of goods under conditions which were detrimental to the health and well-being of workers."[8] Pursuant to the Act, an "employee" is defined as "any individual employed by an employer."[9] An "employer" includes "any person acting directly or indirectly in the interest of an employer in relation to an employee."[10] The term to "employ" means to "suffer or permit to work."[11] To establish an employment relationship under the FLSA, there must be an "employer" and an "employee," as those terms are defined under the FLSA. Generally, the most difficult task in interpreting the FLSA and other statutes reviewed in this analysis comes not in the determination of who the employer is but in the identification of a worker as either an employee or an independent contractor. It is important to note that only employees, not independent contractors, receive protections under the FLSA.

The test to determine if an employment relationship exists under the FLSA had its genesis in a U.S. Supreme Court case concerning the Social Security Act. In *United States v. Silk*,[12] the Albert Silk Coal Co. sued the Internal Revenue Service for illegally assessing social security taxes against the company. The issue before the Court was whether the railway coal unloaders and the truck drivers who delivered coal for Silk Coal were independent contractors or employees. The Court held that in light of the "economic realities" of the circumstances, the unloaders

---

7. *Supra* note 1. The FLSA, enacted June 25, 1938, is a part of the social legislation of the 1930s of the same general character as the National Labor Relations Act of July 5, 1935, 49 Stat. 449, and the Social Security Act of August 14, 1935, 49 Stat. 620. See *Rutherford Food Corp. v. McComb*, 331 U.S. 722, 723; 67 S.Ct. 1473; 91 L.Ed. 1772 (1947); *Hageman v. Park West Gardens*, 480 N.W.2d 223, 225 (N.D. 1992).

The FLSA was expanded when it was amended by the enactment of the Equal Pay Act (EPA) in 1963. The EPA mandates that workers receive equal pay for equal work regardless of gender. The EPA states that "[n]o employer . . . shall discriminate . . . between employees on the basis of sex by paying wages to employees . . . at a rate less than the rate at which he pays wages to employees of the opposite sex . . . for equal work on jobs the performance of which requires equal skill, effort, and responsibility and which are performed under similar working conditions." 29 U.S.C. § 206(d)(1). Because it is an amendment to the FLSA, the FLSA definitions of employee and employer apply to the Equal Pay Act.

8. *Supra* note 1.

9. 29 U.S.C. § 203(e)(1).

10. 29 U.S.C. § 203(d).

11. 29 U.S.C. § 203(g).

12. 331 U.S. 704, 67 S.Ct. 1463, 91 L.Ed 1757 (1947).

were employees, but that the drivers were independent contractors. In its opinion, the Court reasoned that because the drivers generally owned their own companies and were given a great deal of responsibility for investment and management, they were independent contractors.[13] In reaching its decision, the *Silk* court developed the following five-prong "economic realities" test to determine whether an individual is an employee:

1. degree of control
2. opportunities for profit and loss
3. investment in facilities
4. permanency of the relation
5. skill required[14]

The U.S. Supreme Court recognized this test in the context of the FLSA in *Rutherford Food Corp. v. McComb*[15] and *Goldberg v. Whitaker House Cooperative, Inc.*[16] The *Rutherford* court applied the *Silk* factors to rule that boners in a meat factory were employees under the FLSA rather than independent contractors because their work was part of an integrated process that did not require any special skill.[17] In *Whitaker*, homeworkers who made crafts in their homes were found to be both members and employees of the cooperative pursuant to the "economic realities" test because the members were not self-employed, independent, or selling their products at a price they commanded.[18]

The application of the "economic realities" test has been elucidated further by the federal circuit courts. Generally, it is acknowledged that the *Silk* factors are not exhaustive and that they should not be "mechanically applied to arrive at a final determination of employee status."[19] In *Usery v. Pilgrim Equipment Co., Inc.*,[20] the U.S. Court of Appeals for the Fifth Circuit stated:

13. *Id.* at 716–719, 67 S.Ct. at 1469–1471.
14. *Id.* at 716, 67 S.Ct. at 1469–1470. See also *Bartels v. Birmingham*, 332 U.S. 126, 67 S.Ct. 1547, 91 L.Ed 1947 (1947); and *Rutherford Food Corp. v. McComb, supra* note 7.
15. *Supra* note 7.
16. 366 U.S. 28, 81 S.Ct. 933, 6 L.Ed.2d 100 (1961).
17. *Supra* note 7, at 729–730, 67 S.Ct. at 1476–1477.
18. *Supra* note 16, at 32, 81 S.Ct. at 936.
19. *Brock v. Mr. W. Fireworks, Inc.*, 814 F.2d 1042, 1043 (5th Cir.), *cert. denied*, 484 U.S. 924, 108 S.Ct. 286, 98 L.Ed.2d 346 (1987), *and appeal after remand*, 889 F.2d 543 (5th Cir. 1989), *and cert. denied*, 495 U.S. 826, 110 S.Ct. 2167, 109 L.Ed.2d 497 (1990).
20. *Usery v. Pilgrim Equipment Co., Inc.*, 527 F.2d 1308, 1311 (5th Cir.), *cert. denied*, 429 U.S. 826, 97 S.Ct. 82, 50 L.Ed.2d 89 (1976).

The five [*Silk*] tests are aids—tools to be used to gauge the degree of dependence of alleged employees on the business with which they are connected. It is *dependence* that indicates employee status. Each test must be applied with that ultimate notion in mind. More important, the final and determinative question must be whether the total of the testing establishes the personnel are so dependent upon the business with which they are connected that they come within the protection of the FLSA or are sufficiently independent to lie outside its ambit.[21]

Applying the "economic realities" test with an emphasis on "dependence," the Fifth Circuit in *Pilgrim Equipment* held that operators of laundry pickup stations, working at separate locations, were employees because "all indicia of the economic realities test indicated, singularly and collectively, dependence on Pilgrim."[22] The *Pilgrim* court found that the operators were totally dependent on Pilgrim to provide guidance and control; the operators did not have the opportunity for loss of the capital investment; the investments the operators made in the business were minimal; the operators were tied to Pilgrim because they had nothing to transfer but their own labor; and the skill required to run the laundries was minimal.[23]

In sum, contingent workers are entitled to receive the minimum wage and overtime under the FLSA only if they are not classified as independent contractors. Unfortunately, many workers are unaware of their exact status under the FLSA until they try to pursue a claim. Statistics indicate that contingent workers earn less than their full-time, permanent counterparts. Given the remedial intent of the FLSA, it is both ironic and contrary to the original intent of the law that a contingent worker performing similar tasks with the same skill, effort and responsibility as a permanent employee can receive a lower wage.

Title VII of the Civil Rights Act of 1964 and the Age Discrimination in Employment Act

Title VII of the Civil Rights Act[24] and the Age Discrimination in Employment Act[25] (ADEA) prohibit an employer from discriminating against employees on the basis an individual's race, color, religion, sex, national

21. *Id.* at 1311–1312 (emphasis in the original).
22. *Id.* at 1315.
23. *Id.* at 1312–1314.
24. *Supra* note 2.
25. *Supra* note 3.

origin, or age. These statutes are discussed together because their legislative language and remedial intent often result in similar outcomes. In order to receive the protections of Title VII and the ADEA, an individual must be an employee. Therefore, a worker's status as an employee is crucial for those seeking to redress allegations of discrimination under federal employment laws.[26] Prior to the Supreme Court's decision in *Nationwide Mutual Insurance Co. v. Darden* in 1992, federal courts generally interpreted the provisions of Title VII and ADEA legislation liberally to ensure that the remedial intent of these laws was realized.[27] A great deal of case law has evolved in determining if an employment relationship exists for purposes of Title VII and the ADEA.

Title VII of the Civil Rights Act of 1964

The Civil Rights Act of 1964 was enacted to remedy the inequities of racial minorities in American society. Specifically, Title VII of the Act makes it an unlawful employment practice for an employer

1. to fail or refuse to hire or to discharge any individual, or otherwise to discriminate against any individual with respect to his compensation, terms, conditions, or privileges of employment, because of such individual's race, color, religion, sex, or national origin; or
2. to limit, segregate, or classify his employees or applicants for employment in any way which would deprive or tend to deprive any individual of employment opportunities or otherwise adversely affect his status as an employee because of such individual's race, color, religion, sex, or national origin.[28]

Under Title VII, an "employee" is defined as "an individual employed by an employer."[29] An "employer" is defined as "a person engaged in an industry affecting commerce who has fifteen or more employees for each working day in each of twenty or more calendar weeks in the current or preceding calendar year, and any agent of such person."[30]

26. *Spirides v. Reinhardt*, 613 F.2d 826, 829–830 (D.C.Cir. 1979); *Norman v. Levy*, 767 F.Supp. 1441, 1444 (N.D.Ill. 1991).
27. *Wheeler v. Hurdman*, 825 F.2d 257, 262 (10th Cir.), *cert. denied*, 484 U.S. 986, 108 S.Ct. 503, 98 L.Ed.2d 501 (1987); *Martinez v. Orr*, 738 F.2d 1107 (10th Cir. 1984); *Davis v. Valley Distributing Co.*, 522 F.2d 827 (9th Cir. 1975), *cert. denied*, 429 U.S. 1090, 97 S.Ct. 1099, 51 L.Ed.2d 535 (1977)).
28. 42 U.S.C. § 2000e-2(a).
29. 42 U.S.C. § 2000e(f).
30. 42 U.S.C. § 2000e(b).

The Age Discrimination in Employment Act

The Age Discrimination in Employment Act (ADEA) is a hybrid of the FLSA and Title VII in that its scope of procedures and remedies are modeled after the FLSA and its substantive prohibitions are fashioned by Title VII.[31] In enacting the ADEA, Congress intended to prohibit "arbitrary age discrimination by employers against employees and applicants for employment" and "to promote the employment of older persons based on their ability and not their age."[32] Like Title VII, the ADEA broadly defines the term "employee" as "an individual employed by an employer."[33] As with the FLSA and Title VII, the ADEA provides no protection for independent contractors.[34] Like Title VII, the ADEA, defines an "employer" as "a person engaged in an industry affecting commerce who has twenty or more employees for each working day in each of twenty or more calendar weeks in the current or preceding calendar year."[35]

Prior to the *Darden* decision, the scope of the "liberal" interpretation afforded Title VII and the ADEA varied greatly, but it was generally recognized that the statutes were to be interpreted in a fashion to ensure that the remedial intent of the legislation was to be realized. The courts have generally applied the following three tests to determine when an employment relationship exists: (1) the hybrid economic realities/common law agency test; (2) the pure economic realities test discussed under the FLSA analysis; and (3) the pure common law agency test.

The Hybrid Economic Realities/Common Law Agency Test

As noted above, before the *Darden* decision, most courts applied the hybrid economic realities/common law agency test to determine the existence of an employment relationship for purposes of Title VII and the ADEA. The factors the courts used in making this determination, first enunciated in *Spirides v. Reinhardt*,[36] were

---

31. *Oestman v. National Farmers Union Insurance Co.*, 958 F.2d 303, 305 (10th Cir. 1992) (citing *Lorillard v. Pons*, 434 U.S. 575, 98 S.Ct. 866, 55 L.Ed.2d 40 (1978).

32. 29 U.S.C. § 621(b).

33. 29 U.S.C. § 630(f).

34. *Hyland v. New Haven Radiology Assoc., P.C.*, 794 F.2d 793, 797 (2d Cir. 1986); *E.E.O.C. v. Zippo Manufacturing, Co.*, 713 F.2d 32, 35 (3rd Cir. 1983); *Hickey v. Arkla Industries, Inc.*, 699 F.2d 748 (5th Cir. 1983); *Frishberg v. Esprit De Corp., Inc.*, 778 F.Supp. 793 (S.D.N.Y. 1991); *Carney v. Dexter Shoe Co.*, 701 F.Supp. 1093 (D.N.J. 1988); *Donohue v. Pendleton Woolen Mills, Inc.*, 47 Empl. Pract.Dec. ¶ 38,364, WL 36317 (S.D.N.Y. 1988).

35. 29 U.S.C. § 630(b).

36. *Supra* note 26, at 832. See also *Broussard v. L.H. Bossier, Inc.*, 789 F.2d 1158, 1160 (5th Cir. 1986), and *Wilde v. County of Kandiyohi*, 15 F.3d 103 (8th Cir. 1994).

1. the kind of occupation, with reference to whether the work usually is done under the direction of a supervisor or is done by a specialist without supervision;
2. the skill required in the particular occupation;
3. whether the "employer" or the individual in question furnishes the equipment used and the place of work;
4. the length of time during which the individual has worked;
5. the method of payment, whether by time or by the job;
6. the manner in which the work relationship is terminated, i.e., by one or both parties, with or without notice and explanation;
7. whether annual leave is afforded;
8. whether the work is an integral part of the business of the "employer";
9. whether the worker accumulates retirement benefits;
10. whether the "employer" pays social security taxes; and
11. the intention of the parties. [37]

In applying the *Spirides* factors, the primary emphasis has been placed upon the degree of control exercised over the worker.[38] Courts that have adopted the hybrid test tend to interpret the definition of employee more narrowly under Title VII and the ADEA than under the FLSA,[39] because they contend that the intent of Title VII and the ADEA was not to eliminate discrimination in all business relationships but rather to eliminate discrimination only in employment.[40] In *Spirides*, the issue before the U.S. Court of Appeals for the D.C. Circuit was whether a woman who was a contract foreign language broadcaster for the Voice of America (VOA) was an employee pursuant to Title VII.[41] The *Spirides* court concluded

37. *Id.* Other courts that have applied the hybrid test first enunciated in *Spirides* include: *Broussard, supra* note 36; *Cobb v. Sun Papers, Inc.,* 673 F.2d 337, 340–341 (11th Cir.), *cert. denied,* 459 U.S. 874, 103 S.Ct. 163, 74 L.Ed.2d 135 (1982); *Lutcher v. Musicians Union Local 47,* 633 F.2d 880, 883 (9th Cir. 1980). See also *Oestman, supra* note 31, at 305; *Garrett v. Phillips Mills, Inc.,* 721 F.2d 979, 981–982 (4th Cir. 1983); *Zippo Manufacturing, Co., supra* note 34, at 37–38; *Duke v. Uniroyal, Inc.,* 777 F.Supp. 928 (E.D.N.C. 1991) (each adopting the hybrid test under the Age Discrimination in Employment Act).

38. *Id.* at 831–832.

39. *Knight v. United Farm Bureau Mutual Insurance Company,* 950 F.2d 377, 380 (7th Cir. 1991); *Zippo Manufacturing Co., supra* note 34, at 37–38; *Cobb v. Sun Papers, Inc., supra* note 37, at 340.

40. *Wilde v. County of Kandiyohi,* 811 F.Supp. 446, 451 (D.Minn. 1993).

41. Please note for several years after its enactment, Title VII of the Civil Rights Act of 1964 proscribed only nonfederal employment discrimination. Congress became increasingly concerned, however, about the apparent inability of federal employees to

that Ms. Spirides was *not* an employee. The court held that to determine the employment status of the plaintiff, it would have to consider the economic realities of her situation, but that "the extent of the employer's right to control the 'means and manner' of the worker's performance was the most important factor to review."[42]

The Pure Economic Realities Test

The second test that courts have used to divine whether a worker is an employee is the pure "economic realities" test, which is used to analyze the existence of an employment relationship pursuant to the FLSA. This test had been adopted by only a minority of federal circuit courts for Title VII and ADEA purposes. The focus of the economic realities test is whether an individual is economically dependent for his livelihood on the business to which the person renders service. The test consists of the following elements:

1. The extent of the employer's control and supervision over the worker, including directions on scheduling and performance of work
2. The kind of occupation and nature of skill required, including whether skills are obtained in the workplace
3. Responsibility for the costs of operation, such as equipment, supplies, fees, licenses, workplace, and maintenance operations
4. The method of payment and benefits
5. Length of job commitment and/or expectations[43]

The pure economic realties test is a more expansive standard than the hybrid test and the pure common law agency test because it focuses on an individual's economic dependence rather than the control an employer exerts over an individual.

The leading case which held that the economic realities should be applied to antidiscrimination cases is *Armbruster v. Quinn*.[44] After ex-

---

obtain judicial review of employment discrimination cases. Thus, in 1972, Title VII was amended by the Equal Employment Opportunity Act to forbid discrimination by federal government employers, and to permit federal employees to sue those employers in discrimination cases. *Spirides, supra* note 26, at 828–829.

42. *Id.* at 831; see also *Broussard v. L. H. Bossier, Inc., supra* note 36 and *Zippo Manufacturing Co., supra* note 34.

43. *Hayden v. La-Z-Boy Chair Co.*, 9 F.3d 617 (7th Cir. 1993), *cert. denied*, 511 U.S. 1004, 114 S.Ct. 1371, 128 L.Ed.2d 47 (1994), citing *Rogers v. Sugar Tree Products, Inc.*, 7 F.3d 577, 581 (7th Cir. 1993).

44. 711 F.2d 1332 (6th Cir. 1983). See also *Lilley v. BTM Corporation*, 958 F.2d 746 (6th Cir.), *cert. denied*, 506 U.S. 940, 113 S.Ct. 376, 121 L.Ed.2d 287 (1992) (applying economic realities test in ADEA case).

amining the case law and legislative history of the FLSA, Title VII and the NLRA, the Sixth Circuit in *Armbruster* reasoned that the pure economic realities test should be adopted. The court held that the term "employee," when considered in the context of remedial legislation, should "[take] color from its surroundings . . . [in] the statute where it appears, and [derive] meaning from the context of that statute, which must be read in the light of the mischief to be corrected and the end to be attained."[45] The court concluded that an employment relationship should be analyzed in light of the "economic realities underlying the relationship between the individual and the so-called principal in an effort to determine whether that individual is likely to be susceptible to the discriminatory practices which the act was designed to eliminate."[46] In issuing *Armbruster*, the Sixth Circuit specifically repudiated the D.C. Circuit's holding in *Spirides*, stating that the *Spirides* court misinterpreted the relationship between Congress's action in amending the NLRA in favor of a common law agency test and Congress's intent in the enactment of Title VII. The Sixth Circuit maintained that the NLRA was amended before Title VII was enacted and that, therefore, no logical relationship exists between the language of the two statutes.[47]

The Common Law Agency Test

The third and final test the courts have used to determine the existence of an employment relationship is the "common law agency" test. Prior to 1992, no court had utilized the pure common law agency test to analyze the existence of an employment relationship since *Smith v. Dutra Trucking Company* was decided in 1976.[48]

The resurgence of the use of the common law agency test for Title VII and the ADEA purposes has its origins in an Employee Retirement Income Security Act (ERISA) case, *Nationwide Mutual Insurance Company v. Darden*,[49] the U.S. Supreme Court decided in 1992. The issue in *Darden* was whether an insurance agent for Nationwide was an "employee" within the meaning of ERISA. In *Darden* the Court stated that the definition of employee under ERISA was nominal and "completely circular and

---

45. *Id.* at 1340.
46. *Id.*
47. *Id.* at 1341. It should be noted that in *Eyerman v. Mary Kay Cosmetics, Inc.*, 967 F.2d 213 (6th Cir. 1992), the Sixth Circuit again considered the economic realities test, and interpreted, in *dictum*, that the holding in *Armbruster* could extend protection to independent contractors under Title VII, if under the economic realities test they were "susceptible to the types of discrimination Title VII meant to prohibit." *Id.* at 218.
48. 410 F.Supp. 513 (N.D.Cal. 1976).
49. 503 U.S. 318, 112 S.Ct. 1344, 177 L.Ed.2d 581 (1992).

explains nothing."[50] Instead of looking to case law that had interpreted similar statutory language for guidance, the Court, followed its analysis in *Community for Creative Non-Violence v. Reid*,[51] a case under the Copyright Act of 1976. In formally adopting the common law agency test as developed in *Reid* for determining who is an employee under ERISA, the *Darden* court stated:

> In determining whether a hired party is an employee under the general common law of agency, we consider the hiring party's right to control and the manner and means by which the product is accomplished. Among the other factors relevant to this inquiry are the skill required; the source of instrumentalities and tools; the location of the work; the duration of the relationship between the parties; whether the hiring party has the right to assign additional projects to the hired party; the extent of the hired party's discretion over when and how long to work; the method of payment; the hired party's role in hiring and paying assistants; whether the work is a part of the regular business of the hiring party; whether the hiring party is in business; the provision of employee benefits; and the tax treatment of the hired party.[52]

In its reasoning, the Supreme Court rejected the U.S. Court of Appeals for the Fourth Circuit's application of the pure "economic realities" test, which construed the term employee "in the light of the mischief to be corrected and the end to be attained."[53] The Court chose not to follow this course because "ERISA and the FLSA are distinguishable and that the textual asymmetry between the two statutes precludes reliance on FLSA cases when construing ERISA's concept of 'employee.'"[54]

The Supreme Court's interpretations in both *Darden* and *Reid* have had ramifications in lower court Title VII and ADEA decisions. In *Frankel v. Bally, Inc.*,[55] the plaintiff, Frankel, who had worked as a shoes salesman for Bally for thirteen years pursuant to an employment contract, was terminated. Frankel filed suit under the ADEA claiming that his termination was the product of age discrimination. The issue for the court was whether Frankel was an employee or an independent con-

---

50. *Id.* at 323, 112 S.Ct. at 1348.
51. 490 U.S. 730, 109 S.Ct. 2166, 104 L.Ed.2d 811 (1989).
52. *Darden, supra* note 49, at 324, 112 S.Ct. at 1348 (citing *Reid, supra* note 51, at 751–752, 109 S.Ct. at 2178–2179).
53. *Id.*, 112 S.Ct. 1349.
54. *Id.* at 325–326, 112 S.Ct. at 1350.
55. 987 F.2d 86 (2d Cir. 1993). See also *Cox v. Master Lock Co.*, 815 F.Supp. 844 (E.D.Pa.), *aff'd* without opinion, 14 F.3d 46 (3d Cir. 1993) (holding that the common law agency test applies in the ADEA context).

tractor. In deciding whether Frankel was an employee, the U.S. Court of Appeals for the Second Circuit followed the Supreme Court's reasoning in *Darden* for two reasons. First, the chief rationale to employ a broader test had been eliminated. The Supreme Court, in *Darden*, specifically chose to reject its prior decisions holding that these terms should be interpreted "in the light of the mischief to be corrected and the end to be attained."[56] Second, in *Darden*, the Supreme Court specifically excepted the FLSA on the basis that it gives the term "employ" a much more expansive definition than any other statute, including the ADEA.[57]

The impact of the *Darden* decision cannot be understated. Although the case does settle the question of which test is to be used, it fails to reflect the economic realities of today's marketplace. Many discrimination cases that have come before the lower federal courts have adopted the rule promulgated in *Darden*. The only way to reverse the present trend is for Congress to amend the laws and state explicitly which individuals are to be protected by antidiscrimination statutes.

Numerical Threshold

Both Title VII and the ADEA require that an employer have a minimum number of employees to meet the definition of an "employer" under the acts. This requirement is designed to avoid bringing comparatively small employers within the statutes' coverage.[58] Title VII has a threshold of fifteen employees[59] and the ADEA has a twenty employee threshold.[60] Significantly, if an employer does not have the requisite number of employees to called an "employer" under Title VII or the ADEA, then those employees will not be covered by the acts. Until recently, the method of counting employees had presented some difficulties and a split among the circuit courts. However, the Supreme Court recently resolved the conflict among circuit courts in *Walters v. Metropolitan Educational Enterprises, Inc.*[61]

56. *Id.* at 90, (quoting *Silk, supra* note 12, at 713, 67 S.Ct. at 1468).

57. *Id.*; see also *Lattanzio v. Security National Bank*, 825 F.Supp. 86 (E.D.Pa. 1993); *Simpson v. Ernst & Young*, 850 F.Supp. 648 (S.D.Ohio 1994); *Thomason v. Prudential Insurance Co. of America*, 866 F.Supp. 1329 (D.Kan. 1994); and *Stouch v. Brothers of the Order of Hermits of St. Augustine*, 836 F.Supp. 1134 (E.D.Pa. 1993).

58. *Wright v. Kosciusko Medical Clinic, Inc.*, 791 F.Supp. 1327 (N.D.Ind. 1992).

59. The 1972 Amendment to the Civil Rights Act of 1964 served to broaden its reach by subjecting more employers to the Act as a result in the reduction in the statutory minimum number of employees from twenty-five to fifteen. *Id.* at 1329, n. 4.

60. 29 U.S.C. § 630(b).

61. 117 S.Ct. 660, 1997.

Prior to *Walters*, the courts had fashioned two separate approaches to counting employees. The first method—commonly referred to as the payroll method—provides that all employees who worked for a given week be counted. The second method dictates that employees on each working day (rather than a work week) be counted. The case of *Thurber v. Jack Reilly's Inc.*[62] illustrates the first method. In *Thurber*, the plaintiff, a waitress who worked at Jack's Bar and Restaurant, filed a Title VII suit alleging that Jack's refused to train her to become a bartender because Jack's only hired males to be bartenders. The court determined that in order to stay open seven days a week, Jack's maintained more than fifteen employees on the payroll for more than twenty weeks during the relevant time—even though no more than eleven employees ever reported for work on any one day.[63] The *Thurber* court also held that part-time workers are to be counted in ascertaining whether a "person" is an employer under Title VII.[64]

The alternative approach was stated in *Zimmerman v. North American Signal Co.*,[65] in which the U.S. Court of Appeals for the Seventh Circuit focused not on the number of employees on the payroll for each week but rather on the number of employees for each day of the week. In *Zimmerman*, the plaintiff brought suit against North American Signal, alleging an ADEA violation when he was fired as vice president of North American Signal in 1979.[66] North American moved to dismiss Zimmerman's case on the grounds that it was not an employer within the meaning of the ADEA because it did not have the requisite number of employees The court, which agreed with the employer's theory, held that "salaried workers are counted as employees for every day of the week they are on the payroll, whether or not they were actually at work on a particular day. Its hourly paid workers are counted as employees only on days when they are actually at work and on days of paid leave."[67] In reaching its conclusion, the Seventh Circuit consulted the language and legislative history of the ADEA and focused on the word-

---

62. 717 F.2d 633 (1st Cir. 1983), *cert. denied*, 466 U.S. 904, 104 S.Ct. 1678, 80 L.Ed.2d 153 (1984).

63. *Id.* at 634.

64. *Perry v. City of Country Club Hills*, 607 F.Supp. 771, 775–776, n. 4 (E.D..Mo. 1983) (citing *Hornick v. Borough of Duryea*, 507 F.Supp. 1091, 1098 (M.D.Pa. 1980); *Pedreyra v. Cornell Prescription Pharmacists*, 465 F.Supp. 936, 941 (D.Colo. 1979); *Pascatoi v. Washburn-McReavy Mortuary*, 11 F.E.P. Cases 1325, 1327 (D.Minn. 1975). *aff'd* 566 F.2d 1178 (8th Cir. 1977).

65. 704 F.2d 347 (7th Cir. 1983).

66. *Id.* at 350.

67. *Id.* at 353.

ing that "an employer must have twenty or more employees for *each working day* of a week before a week can be counted toward the jurisdictional minimum."[68]

In *Walters*, the Supreme Court expressly rejected the conclusion in *Zimmerman*. The court held that the payroll method "represents the fair reading of the statutory language"[69] and is therefore the best means to count employees. It reasoned that the Zimmerman approach would be "improbable and . . . impossible to administer (few employers keep daily attendance records of all their salaried employees).[70]

To conclude, the existence of an employment relationship under Title VII and the ADEA is often difficult to determine. The Supreme Court in *Darden* has only exacerbated the problem. Congressional guidance is needed to clarify and give life to the original remedial purpose of this antidiscrimination legislation. Congress should consider expanding coverage to independent contractors as well as other contingent workers and codifying the economic realities test to ensure that the greatest number of workers are provided workplace protections against discrimination.

The Family and Medical Leave Act of 1993

The Family and Medical Leave Act of 1993 ("FMLA") was enacted in order to "balance the demands of the workplace with needs of families, to promote stability and economic security of families, and to promote national interests in preserving family integrity."[71] In short, the FMLA allows "eligible employees" of a covered employer to take unpaid leave for up to a total of twelve workweeks in any twelve-month period to give birth and care for a newborn child, to adopt a child or receive a child for foster care, to care for a family member with a serious health condition, or to care for the employee's own serious health condition that renders the employee unable to perform the functions of his/her job.[72] In addition, eligible employees are entitled to return to their job or an equivalent one upon return from FMLA leave.[73] Because only "eligible employees" are entitled to the rights, benefits, and protections

68. *Id.* (emphasis in the original).
69. 117 S.Ct., 664.
70. *Cohen v. S.U.P.A.*, 814 F.Supp. 251, 254 (N.D.N.Y. 1993) (E.E.O.C. Policy Statement No. 915-052, at 6 (April 20, 1990)).
71. 29 U.S.C. § 2601(b)(1).
72. 29 U.S.C. § 2612(a); 29 C.F.R. § 825.100(a).
73. 29 U.S.C. § 2614(a)(1); 29 C.F.R. § 825.214.

afforded by the FMLA, it is important to understand which workers are "eligible employees" under the FMLA.

The FMLA defines "eligible employee" as an employee who has been employed (1) for at least twelve months by the employer, (2) for at least 1,250 hours of service with such an employer during the previous twelve-month period, and (3) at a work site where there are at least fifty or more employees within a seventy-five-mile radius.[74]

Regarding the first requirement—employed for at least twelve months—the regulations issued by the Department of Labor state that the twelve months an employee must have worked for the employer need not be consecutive months.[75] Indeed, the Labor Department regulations provide that so long as an employee is "maintained on the payroll" for any part of a week, even if it is for periods of "paid or unpaid leave," then that week counts as a week of employment for purposes of calculating the twelve months worked.[76]

With respect to the second requirement—1,250 hours of service—the FMLA and the regulations provide some clarification. The statute states that in determining whether an employee meets the hours requirement, the "legal standards established under section 207 of this title [29 U.S.C. § 207, the Fair Labor Standards Act] shall apply."[77] Further, the Labor Department's regulations provide that the "determining factor" is the "number of hours worked for the employer within the meaning of the FLSA."[78] In *Robbins v. The Bureau of National Affairs, Inc.*, the plaintiff brought suit alleging that the defendant violated the FMLA by denying her right to be restored to her position upon returning from leave.[79] The defendant in *Robbins* argued that the plaintiff was not an "eligible employee" because she only worked 875.5 hours in the preceding twelve months.[80] In response, the plaintiff asserted that paid holiday time, vacation time, sick leave, and unpaid maternity leave should be included in the calculation of her hours worked.[81] The U.S. District Court agreed with the defendant.[82] In dismissing the plaintiff's case, the court held that be-

74. 29 U.S.C. § § 2611(2)(A) and (B); 29 C.F.R. § 825.110(a); see also *Rich v. Delta Airlines, Inc.*, 921 F.Supp. 767 (N.D.Ga. 1996).
75. 29 C.F.R. § 825.110(b).
76. *Id.* See also *Jessie v. Carter Health Care Center, Inc.*, 926 F.Supp. 613 (E.D.Ky. 1996).
77. 29 U.S.C. § 2611(3); 29 C.F.R. § 825.110(c).
78. 29 C.F.R. § 825.110(c).
79. *Robbins v. The Bureau of National Affairs, Inc.*, 896 F.Supp. 18 (D.D.C. 1995).
80. *Id.* at 21.
81. *Id.*
82. *Id.*

cause the FLSA standards are used for determining "hours of service" under the FMLA, and because under the FLSA neither paid leave nor unpaid leave are included in the calculation of "hours of service," only hours actually worked, and not holiday pay, sick leave, etc., are included in the calculation of hours of service under the FMLA.[83] Therefore, the court held that the plaintiff was not an "eligible employee" under the FMLA.[84] In *Rich v. Delta Airlines, Inc.,* the U.S. District Court for the Northern District of Georgia found that the plaintiff met the 1,250 hours of service criteria despite the fact that there were no accurate records of her actual time worked.[85] The court in *Rich* held that under the Department of Labor's regulations, because the defendant did not keep accurate records of the plaintiff's actual time worked, the plaintiff is presumed to have worked 1,250 hours during the preceding twelve months.[86] It should be noted that whether the first two criteria have been met is determined by using the date the employee's leave commences.[87]

With respect to the third criteria—the work site must have at least fifty employees employed within seventy-five miles—the calculation is made at the time the employee provides notice of the need for leave.[88] The Department of Labor's regulations provide that a work site can refer to either a single location or a group of locations.[89] Notably, employees who have no fixed work site, such as construction workers, salespersons, etc., their "work site" is the "site to which they are assigned as their home base, from which their work is assigned, or to which they report."[90] Finally, the determination of how many employees are employed with the seventy-five miles of the work site is based on the number of employees maintained on the payroll.[91] In *Figueria v. Black Entertainment Television, Inc.,* the plaintiff/worker claimed that the defendant employed more than fifty employees within seventy-five miles of her work site.[92] However, the defendant argued that it employed only thirty employees within the seventy-five miles and that the other workers were independent contractors and therefore not employees.[93] In ruling on the

83. *Id.*
84. *Id.*
85. *Rich v. Delta Airlines, Inc.,* 921 F.Supp. 767 (N.D.Ga. 1996).
86. *Id.* at 773.
87. 29 C.F.R. § 825.110(d).
88. 29 C.F.R. § 825.110(f).
89. 29 C.F.R. § 825.111(a).
90. 29 C.F.R. § 825.111(a)(1).
91. 29 C.F.R. § 825.111(c).
92. *Figueria v. Black Entertainment Television, Inc,* 944 F.Supp. 299 (S.D.N.Y. 1996).
93. *Id.* at 308.

defendant's motion to dismiss the plaintiff's FMLA claim, the U.S. District Court held that there was insufficient evidence in the record to determine the number of employees the defendant employed within the seventy-five-mile radius.[94] The court noted that if the persons working within the seventy-five miles were "employees" (not independent contractors), then the plaintiff would be an eligible employee and have a valid claim under the FMLA.[95]

The Department of Labor's regulations also provide that, in some circumstances, even if an employee falls short of meeting the eligibility requirements, the employee may nonetheless qualify as an eligible employee. Specifically, the regulations provide that if an employee notifies an employer of the need for FMLA leave before the employee meets the eligibility requirements, the employer must either confirm that the employee will be eligible on the date the leave commences or advise the employee when the eligibility requirement will be met.[96] Significantly, if the employer "fails to advise the employee whether the employee is eligible prior to the date the requested leave is to commence, the employee will be deemed eligible."[97] Further, the employer "may not, then, deny the leave."[98] Notably, at least one court has determined that these provisions of the Department of Labor's regulations are inconsistent with the statute and therefore unconstitutional. In *Wolke v. Dreadnought Marine, Inc.,* the U.S. District Court for the Eastern District of Virginia held that "under a literal application of the regulation, an employee could work for one day, then inform her employer that she is sick and is leaving. If the employer fails to tell the employee she is ineligible for FMLA leave, the regulation at issue ostensibly would deem her eligible, even though she has worked for merely one day."[99] In declaring this provision of the regulations unconstitutional, the *Wolke* court held that § 825.110 "directly contradicts Congress's expressed intent regarding employee eligibility under the FMLA."[100]

In conclusion, the definition of "eligible employees" under the FMLA makes it impossible for part-time employees—barring overtime hours worked to carry the employee to the threshold of 1,250 hours—to meet

---

94. *Id.*
95. *Id.* at 308–309; see also *Muller v. The Hotsy Corp.*, 917 F.Supp. 1389 (N.D. Iowa 1996).
96. 29 C.F.R. § 825.110(d).
97. *Id.*
98. *Id.*
99. *Wolke v. Dreadnought Marine, Inc.*, 954 F.Supp. 1133, 1137 (E.D.Va. 1997).
100. *Id.*

the eligibility requirements under the FMLA. Furthermore, it is just as impossible for temporary workers and independent contractors to be covered by the FMLA due to the nature of their employment and the definition of "eligible employees." In order to bring all workers—temporary and part-time employees and independent contractors—within the ambit of the FMLA, Congress would need to amend the law and redefine "eligible employees" by deleting the criteria of twelve months and 1,250 hours of service. Until Congress amends the definition of "eligible employees," part-time and temporary employees and independent contractors will be ineligible to enjoy the rights and protections of the FMLA.

The Occupational Safety and Health Act

Congress enacted the Occupational Safety and Health Act[101] (OSHA) in 1970 with the intent to provide "so far as possible every working man and woman in the Nation safe and healthful working conditions."[102] OSHA was designed to prevent death and disability in the workplace by encouraging employers and employees to become aware of, and warn against, possible hazards.[103] Thus, OSHA imposes on the employer the duty to "furnish to each of his employees a place of employment which is free from recognized hazards that are causing or likely to cause death or serious physical harm to his employees."[104] Employees have the duty to "comply with occupational safety and health standards and all rules, regulations, and orders."[105] In order for OSHA liability to be found, an employment relationship must be established.

For purposes of the Act, the term "employer" is defined as "a person engaged in a business affecting commerce who has employees."[106] Pursuant to OSHA, an "employee" is defined as "an employee of an employer who is employed in a business of his employer which affects commerce."[107]

Brennan v. Gilles & Cotting, Inc.,[108] is the seminal case regarding which test to apply in analyzing the existence of an employment relationship

101. 29 U.S.C. § 651.
102. 29 U.S.C. § 651(b).
103. *Brennan v. Occupational Safety & Health Review Commission*, 513 F.2d 1032, 1039 (2d Cir. 1975).
104. 29 U.S.C. § 654(a).
105. 29 U.S.C. § 654(b).
106. 29 U.S.C. § 652(5).
107. 29 U.S.C. § 652(6).
108. 504 F.2d 1255 (4th Cir. 1974).

under OSHA. In *Gilles*, the matter before the U.S. Court of Appeals for the Fourth Circuit was whether a general contractor should be considered a joint employer, along with one of its subcontractors, in deciding the liability for the death of two workers on a job site. Gilles was the general contractor for a construction project and Southern Plate Glass was a subcontractor. Two of Southern's employees died following the collapse of a scaffold. As a general contractor, Gilles's responsibilities included overall safety and accident prevention on the project site.[109] The defective scaffolding was built by Southern, which used the scaffolding exclusively. After the accident, OSHA investigators determined that there had been a violation for which Gilles was held to be responsible. An Administrative Law Judge (ALJ) concurred with the OSHA investigator's conclusion. On appeal, the Occupational Safety and Health Review Commission (OSHRC) reviewed the case and reversed the ALJ's finding: Gilles was not responsible for safety violations hazardous to Southern's workers because Gilles, as the general contractor, was not an "'employer' of the subcontractor's workers."[110] The Secretary of Labor appealed the OSHRC's decision to the Fourth Circuit.

On appeal, the Fourth Circuit found very little guidance from OSHA's definitions of "employer" and "employee" and specifically rejected any reliance on common law in the determination of the existence of an employment relationship. The court reasoned that the evolution of the common law definition of "employer" had been decided primarily in the context of tort law, which is inapplicable in an OSHA situation.[111] Rather, the court held that the "economic realities" test developed under the FLSA was applicable because it provides a uniform approach to interpreting OSHA cases and effectuates the remedial purposes of the OSHA statute by providing a liberal interpretation of the employment relationship. In its conclusion, the *Gilles* court deferred to the decision of the OSHRC because it had been intimately familiar with the "economic realities . . . [of] the working relationships between general contractors and subcontractor's workmen."[112]

The "economic realities" test, enunciated in *Gilles*, was honed by the OSHRC in *Griffin & Brand of McAllen, Inc.*[113] In applying the "eco-

109. *Id.* at 1257.
110. *Id.* at 1259.
111. *Id.* at 1261.
112. *Id.* at 1262.
113. 6 O.S.H. Cas. (BNA) 1702 (1978). See also *S & S Diving Company*, 8 O.S.H. Cas. (BNA) 2041, OSAHRC Docket No. 77-4234 (1980).

nomic realities" test outlined in *Gilles*, the OSHRC, stated that there was no single criterion to apply when making its decision, but that the following factors would provide some guidance:

1. Whom do the workers consider their employer?
2. Who pays the workers' wages?
3. Who has the responsibility to control the workers?
4. Does the alleged employer have the power to control the worker?
5. Does the alleged employer have the power to hire, fire, or modify the employment condition of workers?
6. Does the workers' ability to increase their income depend on efficiency rather than initiative, judgment, and foresight?
7. How are the workers' wages established?[114]

One of the most difficult tasks in interpreting OSHA is assessing liability in a multiemployer situation. The multiemployer issue arises, most commonly, in the construction industry where the norm is to have a general contractor and several subcontractors. As a general rule, a general contractor will not be liable for an OSHA violation unless one of its employees is exposed to an OSHA hazard. *Brennan v. Gilles & Cotting, Inc.,*[115] and *Southeast Contractors, Inc., v. Dunlop*[116] are cases that have refused to extend liability to general contractors for violations at the work site involving only employees of subcontractors.[117]

Over time, the liability of general contractors has been expanded. *In Grossman Steel & Aluminum Corporation,*[118] the OSHRC considered whether a subcontractor could be held liable for the exposure of its employees to a hazard despite the fact that the subcontractor did not create or control the hazard. In its discussion, the OSHRC stated that general contractors have the duty to assure that other contractors are in compliance with OSHA. Moreover, it found that general contractors are "well situated to obtain abatement of hazards, either through its

114. *Id.* at 1703, citing *Weicker Transfer and Storage Co.,* 75 OSAHRC 29/A2, 2 BNA O.S.H. Cas. 1493, 1974–1975, CCH OSHD ¶ 19,215 (Nos. 1362 & 1372, 1975); *Hodgson v. Griffin and Brand of McAllen,* 471 F.2d 235 (5th Cir. 1973), *cert. denied,* 414 U.S. 819 (1973); see also *Frohlick Crane Service, Inc., v. Occupational Health & Safety Review Commission,* 521 F.2d 628 (10th Cir. 1975).
115. *Supra* note 108.
116. 512 F.2d 675 (5th Cir. 1975).
117. *Dore Wrecking Company,* 1 O.S.H. Cas. (BNA) 1555 (1974); *Humphreys & Harding, Inc.,* 1 O.S.H. Cas. (BNA) 1700 (1974).
118. 4 O.S.H. Cas. (BNA) 1185 (1975).

own resources or through its supervisory role with respect to other contractors."[119] Furthermore, in *dictum*, the OSHRC extended responsibility to general contractors for violations "it could reasonably have been expected to prevent or abate by reason of its supervisory capacity."[120] The U.S. Court of Appeals for the Eighth Circuit adopted this standard in *Marshall v. Knutson Construction Co.*,[121] where the issue before the court was to determine whether Knutson, a general contractor committed a serious violation of OSHA when a scaffold used by one of its subcontractors failed to comply with the relevant safety standards. The Eighth Circuit, citing *Grossman*, held that Knutson had a duty to assure that the other contractors were fulfilling their safety obligations, and to abate any hazards that it found. In determining if a general contractor has violated its duty under section 654(a)(2) of OSHA in regard to safety standard violations of its subcontractors, the court applied the following factors: (1) degree of supervisory capacity; (2) nature of the safety standard violation; and (3) nature and extent of the precautionary measures taken.[122] Concluding its analysis, the court affirmed the OSHRC's decision that Knutson was not liable for the serious violations because it had been diligent in making inspections of the site.

The courts and the OSHRC have also considered the matter of subcontractor liability but are split on the issue of when a subcontractor is liable to its employees for a hazard it did not create or control. In *R. H. Bishop Company*,[123] the OSHRC decided that exposure of a subcontractor's employees to a lighting hazard violated OSHA, despite the fact that the subcontractor did not create or control the violative conditions. Bishop argued that another subcontractor had been responsible for temporary lighting on the site. Nevertheless, the OSHRC refused to accept the defense that others had created and controlled the hazard, and it found Bishop to be liable because Section (5)(a)(2) of the Act mandates employer compliance with safety and health standards promulgated by the Department of Labor.[124]

Conversely, the federal courts have fashioned a different approach to the issue of subcontractor liability. The U.S. Court of Appeals for the

119. *Id.* at 1188.
120. *Id.*
121. 566 F.2d at 596 (1977).
122. *Id.* at 601.
123. 1 O.S.H. Cas. (BNA) 1767 (1974). See also *Alcap Electrical Corporation*, 3 O.S.H. Cas. (BNA) 1203 (1975); *California Stevedore & Ballast Co.*, 1 O.S.H. Cas. 1767 (1974); *Robert E. Lee Plumbers, Inc.*, 3 O.S.H. Cas. (BNA) 1150 (1975).
124. *Id.* at 1768.

Seventh Circuit confronted the question of subcontractor liability in *Anning-Johnson Co. v. Occupational Safety and Health Review Commission*.[125] Wright Construction Company, the general contractor, hired Anning-Johnson as a subcontractor on a construction site to install fireproofing. When an OSHA inspector arrived on the job site, he found that some guardrails had not been put in place and that openings in the floor had not been not covered and assessed a few "non-serious violations" against Anning-Johnson. Anning-Johnson contested the citations on the grounds that it did not create nor did it control the hazards. The Seventh Circuit consulted the legislative history of the Act for guidance. Specifically, it looked to Congress's goal of trying to strike a balance to have a healthy workforce without exerting undue influence in industry. The court concluded that Congress did not intend to adopt a broad mandatory ruling that all employees subject to exposure would result in employer liability.[126] The court held that because the subcontractor did not create or control the violation, the subcontractor could not be held responsible, even though its employees were exposed to the hazard. However, the court found that the subcontractor did have a duty to exert reasonable efforts to protect its own employees from the safety standard violations of others.[127] The court specifically limited liability to "non-serious" violations only.[128]

The requirement to establish an employment relationship between the creator and controller of the hazard and the exposed worker is too onerous a burden in light of the remedial purpose of the legislation. Policy makers should consider expressly expanding the liability of general contractors to all of the workers of a job site.

Worker Adjustment and Retraining Notification Act

Enacted in 1988, the Worker Adjustment and Retraining Notification Act[129] (WARN) was intended to provide further protection to workers, their families, and communities by "prohibiting certain employers from ordering a plant closing or mass layoff until 60 days notice of the layoff is given to the employees and/or their union."[130] The Act provides in relevant

125. 516 F.2d 1081 (7th Cir. 1975). See also *Grossman Steel*, *supra* note 118.
126. *Id.* at 1088.
127. *Id.* at 1086–1089.
128. *Electric Smith, Inc., v. Secretary of Labor*, 686 F.2d 1267 (9th Cir. 1982).
129. 29 U.S.C. § 2101.
130. 20 C.F.R. § 639.1.

part: "An employer shall not order a plant closing or mass layoff until the end of a 60 day period after the employer serves written notice of such an order—(1) to each representative of the affected employees as of the time of the notice or, if there is no such representative at that time, to each affected employee; and (2) to the State dislocated worker unit . . . and the chief elected official of the unit of local government within which such closing or layoff is to occur."[131]

WARN defines an "employer" as any business enterprise that employs "(A) 100 or more employees, excluding part time employees; or (B) 100 or more employees who in the aggregate work at least 4000 hours per week (exclusive of hours of overtime)."[132] The Act defines "affected employees" as "employees who may reasonably be expected to experience an employment loss as a consequence of a proposed plant closing or a mass lay-off by their employer."[133] Further, "part-time employee" is defined as "an employee who is employed for an average of fewer than 20 hours per week or who has been employed for fewer than 6 of the 12 months preceding the date on which the notice is required."[134] Pursuant to the Act, a "plant closing" is defined as the permanent or temporary shutdown of a single site of employment, or one or more facilities or operating units within a single site of employment, if the shutdown results in an employment loss during any thirty-day period for fifty or more employees excluding any part time employees.[135] Issues of litigation under WARN have varied. Some cases deal with the question of who is an employer pursuant to the statute, others have dealt with the status of laid-off employees, and still others have considered the personal liability of directors and officers who have called for the plant closings or mass layoffs.

In *Carpenters District Council of New Orleans and Vicinity v. Dillard Department Stores, Inc.*,[136] the former employees of D. H. Holmes Co. Ltd. (Holmes) brought a class action suit against Holmes and Dillard Department Stores (Dillard) because they were "involuntarily terminated from employment between May 8, 1989 and August 9, 1989 as a result of the acquisition of Holmes by Dillard and who did not receive 60 days notice of said termination."[137] In order to solve its financial dif-

131. 29 U.S.C. § 2102(a).
132. 29 U.S.C. § 2101(a)(1).
133. 29 U.S.C. § 2101(a)(5).
134. 29 U.S.C. § 2101 (a)(8).
135. 29 U.S.C. § 2101(a)(2).
136. *Carpenters District Council of New Orleans and Vicinity v. Dillard*, 778 F.Supp. 297 (E.D.L.A. 1991).
137. *Id.* at 300.

ficulties, Holmes and Dillard entered into a merger agreement which was approved by the U.S. Securities and Exchange Commission on April 10, 1989, and became effective on May 9, 1989. Thereafter, Dillard directed that initial layoff notices were to be issued on April 19, 1989. The notices, which were sent to Holmes's Corporate Planning Division and its warehouse facilities, stated that workers at those locations would be terminated effective May 9, 1989, and provided less than the sixty days required by WARN.[138] On May 12, 1989, additional notification was sent to the employees of the Canal Street store that they would be laid off between June 10 and July 8, 1989.

One issue before the U.S. District Court for the Eastern District of Louisiana was whether full-time and part-time employees received adequate notice. The defendants in the case admitted that they were employers within the meaning of the statute and that the several closings of Holmes's stores and warehouses constituted a plant closing. Defendants argued that of the employees terminated at the Canal Street Store, sixty-seven were part-time employees who worked less than twenty hours per week and that twelve were on-call employees, who did not work a regular schedule and would be called to work less than twenty hours a week on an as-needed basis. These employees, defendants maintained, were not entitled to notice because they were not "affected employees" and were not employed by Dillard.[139] The court held that the defendants were correct in asserting that the Canal Street employees were part-time employees under the statute. However, the court held that these part-time employees were "affected employees" as defined by WARN and were thus entitled to proper and timely notification of termination.[140] The court reasoned that since Congress had explicitly referred to part-time employees in its definition of employer, it could have just as easily excluded the part-time employees in its definition of "affected employee."[141]

Laid-Off Employees

A question that has been frequently litigated under WARN is whether workers who have been laid off prior to the time of a particular plant closing covered by WARN can be considered employees for the purpose of determining whether a business constitutes an "employer" under

138. *Id.* at 301.
139. *Id.* at 313.
140. *Supra* note 136, at 313–314.
141. *Id.* at 314.

WARN. Department of Labor regulations provide that "[w]orkers on temporary layoff or on leave who have a reasonable expectation of recall should be counted as employees. An employee has a 'reasonable expectation of recall' when he/she understands, through notification or industry practice that his/her employment has been temporarily interrupted and that he/she will be recalled to the same or to a similar job."[142] Therefore, in order to be counted as an employee an individual must prove that he/she is an "affected employee," which is defined as those persons "who may reasonably be expected to experience an employment loss as a consequence of a proposed plant closing or mass layoff by their employer."[143] In *Damron v. Rob Fork Mining Corp.*,[144] four former employees of the defendant brought suit against Fork Mining for failure to notify them of the closing of Mine 29. The defendants argued that they were not employers under the Act because they no longer had the requisite number of employees. The former miners claimed that they could be counted even though they had been laid off eight to ten years.[145]

In the instant case, the plaintiffs claimed that Mine 29 had a total of seventy-three persons working as of October 2, 1989. To reach the requisite level of one hundred employees, the plaintiffs alleged that the company had planned to recall sixty hourly workers to open two new sections of the mine.[146] However, the U.S. Court of Appeals for the Sixth Circuit rejected the plaintiffs' argument. The Sixth Circuit, relying on the Department of Labor's regulations, focused upon the term "temporary layoff." The *Damron* court stated that a "reasonable expectation of recall" should be determined by considering the following factors: (1) past experience of the employer; (2) the employer's future plans; (3) the circumstances of the layoff; (4) expected length of the layoff; (5) industry practice.[147] Applying these factors to the miners in *Damron*, the court held that the miners had not received a recall notice; nor did they anticipate receiving one; plaintiffs failed to demonstrate that such long-term layoffs were industry practice; and they failed to present any cases that an eight-to ten-year layoff is a reasonable practice.[148] The court held that due to the extended length of time they had been laid off (eight to ten years), it

142. 20 C.F.R. § 639.3(a)(ii).
143. *Supra* note 133.
144. 945 F.2d 121 (6th Cir. 1991). See also *Damron v. Rob Fork Mining Corp.*, 739 F.Supp. 341 (E.D.Ky. 1990).
145. *Id.*, 739 F.Supp. at 342.
146. *Id.* at 343.
147. *Id.*, 945 F.2d at 124.
148. *Id.*

was impossible to say that they were persons in "reasonable expectation of being recalled."[149] The plaintiffs, therefore, did not have to be counted as employees for the purpose of WARN notices.

In summary, WARN is a relatively new statute that has been rarely litigated. Although remedial in nature, WARN is purposefully designed to cover only larger employers. An immediate way to expand coverage would be to reduce the requisite number of employees needed to define the term "employer" as well as to eliminate the exclusion of part-time workers in the accounting of that requisite number.

As the foregoing analysis of employment laws illustrates, American employment law and the definitions of those who are covered by them have not kept pace with evolving labor market trends. As the definitions of employee and employer under the foregoing statutes indicate, not all workers who experience discrimination or other unfair treatment in the workplace enjoy the rights and protections of those laws. In addition, not only do the disparate definitions of these terms within the statutes leave many workers outside their scope, the inconsistent interpretation of these definitions by the federal courts has further exacerbated the problem. Given the continuing change in the nature of the American workforce—from permanent employment to temporary and/or contingent workers—Congress, analysts, and policy makers need to review these laws to develop a unified approach that furnishes a much greater number of workers with workplace rights and remedies. Furthermore, analysts and policy makers should balance the need and desire of businesses that wish to maximize the exploitation of a "flexible" workforce against the individual worker's aspirations to be employed on a full-time, permanent basis with full benefits and a pension. As the traditional lines continue to blur, it is important to adapt to these changes in order to devise new strategies so that this contingent workforce can be accommodated. The overriding goal should be to provide all workers with the same level of protection. Finally, it is necessary that Congress and policy makers initiate and maintain a dialogue regarding how these employment laws can be amended to adapt to an evolving workforce.

---

149. *Id.* See also *Kildea v. Electro Wire Products, Inc.*, 775 F.Supp. 1014 (E.D.Mich. 1991). The issue of "affected employees" was enunciated by the court in *Kildea v. Electro Wire Products, Inc.*, 792 F.Supp. 1046 (E.D. Mich. 1992); *Jones v. Kayser-Roth Hosiery, Inc.*, 748 F.Supp. 1276 (E.D.Tenn. 1990).

CHAPTER THIRTEEN

Charting Future Research

Kathleen Barker
Kathleen Christensen

A s the chapters in this book attest, contingent work defies easy conceptualization and understanding. However, at the heart of this
book are three fundamental questions:

- Who are the contingent workers?
- How are American businesses using contingent staffing?
- What are the human experiences of working contingently?

These paramount questions will determine the direction of future research on contingent work arrangements and contingent workers.

Who Are the Contingent Workers?

There are no simple answers to this question. Any answer hinges on definition. No universally accepted definition of contingency exists. According to the Bureau of Labor Statistics (BLS), contingency is defined
primarily in terms of *perceived* job security. Contingent workers are
defined as *individuals who do not perceive themselves as having an explicit or implicit contract for continuing employment*. In their 1995 survey, the BLS relied on three factors to determine whether workers
perceived themselves as contingent: whether they considered their present jobs to be temporary or unlikely to continue, how long they expected to hold their jobs, and how long they had held them.

No authors in this volume define contingent workers according to
the BLS definition. Many, in fact, define contingency in terms of what
the BLS would call alternative or nonstandard work arrangements.
According to the BLS, nonstandard workers are hired in ways that devi-
ate from full-time regular employment, and they include independent

contractors, on-call workers, workers paid by temporary help agencies, and workers whose services are provided through contract firms (Chapter 2, this volume).

The BLS maintains that nonstandard workers may or may not be contingent, since contingency is a function of *perceived* job insecurity, whereas nonstandard work is a function of specific *employment arrangements*. According to the BLS, for example, some contract company employees may perceive their jobs as temporary and therefore should be classified as contingent, while many expect their jobs to be ongoing and therefore are not to be classified as contingent. This distinction between contingent and nonstandard may eventually provide clarity, but it complicates the popular understanding of the term "contingent," which is often equated with nonstandard arrangements that are inherently insecure, such as being an employee of a temporary help agency or working on an on-call basis. Furthermore, "contingent," as defined by the BLS, cannot be used to describe business hiring practices because a firm does not hire a person based on his or her perceived job security. A firm hires on the basis of an employment arrangement.

Using neither perceived job insecurity nor categories of employment arrangements, Roberta Spalter-Roth and Heidi Hartmann define contingent workers as "workers with multiple employers who work less than full-time/full-year"(Chapter 3). By using actual time spent in employment during the year and the actual number of different jobs a worker held during a year as an indicator of a worker's tentative connection to the workplace, these researchers propose a broader definition of contingent work that is sensitive to workers actual work patterns and job attachments.

How Many Are There?

Based on the results of their 1995 survey, the Bureau of Labor Statistics calculated that there are between 2.7 and 6.0 million contingent workers. These estimates ranged from 2.2 percent of the total employed, which covers only wage and salary workers who expect to be with their employer for two years or less (Estimate 1, the narrowest), to 2.8 percent when the self-employed are included in (Estimate 2), and finally to 4.9 percent when the assumptions about tenure are relaxed (Estimate 3, the broadest).

Using longitudinal data from the U.S. Bureau of the Census Survey of Income and Program Participation (SIPP), Spalter-Roth and Hartmann distinguished full-time/full-year workers with only one job from those who work full-time and full-year but only by packaging several jobs. According to their definition, individuals working contingently amount to 16 percent of all employed, and an additional 13 percent work under conditions that could arguably be called contingent—figures significantly higher than the broadest BLS estimate of 4.9 percent of the workforce.

According to the BLS, nonstandard workers, who may or may not view themselves as contingent, numbered 12.2 million in February 1995, representing nearly 10 percent of the workforce. At that time, 8.3 million (6.7 percent of the total employed) identified themselves as independent contractors, 2.0 million (1.6 percent) worked on-call, 1.2 million (1.0 percent) worked for temporary help agencies, and 652,000 (.5 percent) worked for contract firms.

What Are the Demographics of the Contingent Workforce?

According to Dean Morse, since the late 1800s the peripheral workforce has been segregated by race, ethnicity, and gender, marked first by the dominance of blacks and later by newly arrived immigrants, women, and other marginalized groups such as older workers (see Chapter 1). The pattern continues, in large measure, today. Regardless of which of the current data sets is used, BLS or SIPP, minorities and marginalized workers are overrepresented in the contingent workforce and among most types of nonstandard workers. According to BLS figures, blacks comprise 13.3 percent of the contingent workforce and only 10 percent of the "permanent," noncontingent workforce, while Hispanics make up 11.3 percent of the contingent workforce and only 8.3 percent of the "permanent" one (BLS Estimate 3). With few exceptions, this pattern of racial and ethnic segregation in contingent work arrangements is again observed in the BLS data regarding most of the nonstandard workers, including on-call workers and employees of temporary agencies and subcontracted firms. The exception is seen among independent contractors, among whom blacks and Hispanics are underrepresented.

Unlike blacks and Hispanics, whites are underrepresented in the contingent workforce. Whites account for 80.5 percent of the contingent workforce and 85.6 percent of the permanent one. In addition, if we look at the racial and ethnic profile of nonstandard workers, whites account for the overwhelming majority (92.3 percent) of the most privileged nonstandard workers, the independent contractors. According to the BLS, independent contractors, when compared to temporary and on-call workers, are most likely to be white, male, and college educated and the least likely to report working on an involuntary basis. Of all of the nonstandard workers, the independent contractors are most likely to prefer their nontraditional arrangements. Compared to these other nonstandard workers, contractors also earn more, are more likely to have health insurance, and are more likely to be male. Just as there appears to be a pattern of racial and ethnic segregation within the contingent and alternative workforce, there also is a distinct pattern of gender segregation in contingent and alternative work arrangements.

According to BLS figures, younger and older women are more likely to be contingent workers than noncontingent ones. (This pattern did not hold, however, for women aged 35–64, who were more likely to work noncontingently) According to Spalter-Roth and Hartmann's analyses of SIPP data, the gender segregation of the contingent workforce is even more striking. They found that women held 61 percent of the contingent jobs while holding only 39 percent of the permanent jobs, many of the latter being part-time. Gender and race also co-vary in distinct ways. In the BLS data set, young black women were highly visible in the temporary help industry (THI). Those working in the THI were also the least educated, and the industry had an overrepresentation of single mothers.

Any research agenda developed around contingent workers must recognize that minorities and women participate disproportionately in the contingent workforce (Tables 2.2 and 2.9). Yet, as has been made clear in earlier chapters, much of our current employment and labor law fails to address issues faced by contingent workers, including whether there are discriminatory hiring practices.

What Definition Should Be Used in the Future?

There is no doubt that the BLS definition of contingent work will provide an important starting point for many researchers. Many will find themselves working within or extending the boundaries of this definition. Although the BLS should be commended for pursuing this thorny and contentious issue and for seeking commentary from experts at the start of its research project, it is not surprising that disagreement emerge over aspects of its definition or protocols.

We feel that there are three inherent problems with the BLS definition that must be resolved prior to its widespread adoption. First, the BLS's reliance on *perceived* job security may result in a distortion of the number of people actually working in insecure job arrangements. Second, allowing proxies to respond to the question of perceived job security has inherent problems. Third, by using a range of estimates, an impression is created of providing a more inclusive definition of contingency than actually exists.

Relying on respondents' perceptions of job security, as the BLS does, may or may not be predictive of what a person's actual job security will be over the course of specified time. In some instances, the perception will match the subsequent reality, in others it will not. Rather than relying on perception, Spalter-Roth and Hartmann used a complex set of actual workplace attachments and came up with a much larger percentage of the workforce working insecurely (16 percent) than did the BLS (2.2 percent to 4.9 percent).

If one accepts the validity of psychological perception as a basis for determining contingency, then other psychological dimensions of contingency should also be included. Kathleen Barker proposes a social-psychological definition of contingent relations (Chapter 8). In addition to *perceived insecurity*, she argues, contingency also involves *exclusion from organizational, social, and skill-related opportunities available to permanent employees in that work setting*. Therefore, a social-psychological approach to contingent work status would entail conceptualizing it as a series of status and opportunity structures that are distinct from what is available to comparable workers who are permanent employees.

In conducting the BLS survey, household respondents were allowed to serve as proxies for other adults in the household. In effect, one adult reported another's perceived job insecurity. Proxies may not be suitable replacements for respondents when questions shade toward personal information about the future. Ethnographic studies of employees show that individuals who are laid off or fired often hide the fact of their unemployment for long periods of time from their spouses and children (Newman, 1988). If they can hide their unemployment, it is not unwarranted to believe that they may be able to hide their perceived fear of unemployment, that is, their perceived job insecurity. It is an inferential leap, therefore, to act on the assumption that two groups, respondents and proxies, are equivalent, and that their responses should be treated equally.

By providing a range of estimates, as the BLS does, the impression is given that there is more inclusiveness in their definition of contingency than actually there is. This impression is achieved through the contrast of Estimate 1, the most restrictive definition, with the two subsequent estimates. Estimate 1 requires workers to meet very strict criteria in order to be classified as contingent. For example, under Definition 1, any individual who was self-employed does not count, and neither does a temporary worker who expects her employment with a temp agency to end within a year *but* who has worked for the current temp employer for more than a year. In essence, Estimate 1 creates a *perceptual contrast* for any estimate presented after it. In human perception, the contrast principle exerts social influence because it "affects the way we see the difference between two [or more] things that are presented one after another. Simply put, if the second item is fairly different from the first, we will tend to see it as more different than it actually is. . . . The contrast principle is well established in the field of psychophysics and applies to all sorts of perceptions" (Cialdini, 1988:12–13).

If we start with a stringent estimate that is based on an extremely exclusive set of conditions regarding contingency, perceptual contrast could result in the two subsequent definitions being viewed as more inclusive than actually they are. What concerns us is whether the discussion and subsequent empirical examination of contingent work will be advanced if these three estimates and sets of conditions upon which they rest are seen as providing the widest range possible. If researchers are to use the BLS data, it is important that they challenge the assumptions underlying the estimates.[1]

What Research Designs Will Be Critical in the Future?

In addition to extending the BLS assumptions and testing them on the BLS data set, researchers can develop other assumptions regarding contingency and test them on different sets of data. In looking toward future research efforts, it is important to conduct longitudinal as well as ethnographic studies to complement cross-sectional survey work. Longitudinal

---

1. In that vein, three sociologists—A. L. Kalleberg, K. Hudson, and B. F. Reskin—argue that a worker is contingent if she or he meets the following conditions: "(1) reports their job as temporary; *or* (2) reports they cannot work for their employer as long as they wish; *or* (3) is not sure about criteria '1' or '2'; *or* (4) expects their job to last for only one year or less" (1997:13). These researchers maintain that defining a contingent worker based on the BLS criteria of current time spent with an employer as one year or less and a job's expected duration of one year or less results in a BLS definition that is overly restrictive. In Estimate 3, these criteria are maintained only for the self-employed, but Kalleberg and his colleagues argue that even there the criteria are never qualitatively meaningful and should be abandoned for all categories of contingent workers. For example, they point out that whether or not one has worked in a job for one year or less has little to do with whether that job is currently secure and will continue. Using their expanded criteria for contingency, Kalleberg and his colleagues have provided a new estimate, Estimate 4, of the number of contingent workers. According to this estimate, 11 percent of female workers and 9.5 percent of male workers are employed contingently, as compared with BLS estimates of 5.3 percent and 4.5 percent. In Estimate 4, we observe a near doubling of the BLS estimate of the number of workers who say they have a job of uncertain duration.

data sets can provide the ability to look at actual workplace behaviors and can, therefore, be useful in charting new workplace attachments. Yet, not all national longitudinal surveys, or even many cross-sectional ones, are currently equipped to deal with the changing conditions of work. The survey developers of some of the major survey organizations, such as the National Opinion Research Organization (NORC), General Social Survey (GSS), and National Longitudinal Surveys of Labor Mark Experience (NLS), need to be brought together with contingent work researchers.

It is also methodologically important that ethnographic studies balance large-scale data collection efforts. While survey data, collected either through longitudinal or cross-sectional efforts, provide important clues regarding the demographics of contingent workers, such research needs to be balanced by qualitative small-scale studies. Qualitative approaches provide researchers with findings that are subtle and nuanced and that can often challenge suppositions made by large-scale studies.

How Are Businesses Using Contingent Workers?

Contingent staffing represents a critical element in the changing relationship between the employer and the worker. By relying on contingent workers such as independent contractors, agency temps, on-call workers, and employees of subcontracted firms, a firm legally distances itself from these workers; it can thereby—it is assumed—reduce its labor costs, enhance its workforce flexibility, and simultaneously increase job security for its core employees. Critical questions remain as to how American businesses are actually using their contingent workers.

According to a 1995 Conference Board study, almost half of the U.S. corporations surveyed indicated that the use of contingent workers was not part of any strategic plan; between 40 and 60 percent (depending on the type of contingent arrangement) had no policies or guidelines for using these workers; and close to 40 percent admitted that no cost controls were imposed upon their use (Nollen & Axel, Chapter 5). More often than not, contingent staffing decisions are made on ad hoc or incremental bases.

What Do Firms Know about Their Own Contingent Workers?

Corporations generally do not collect data or keep records on their contingent workers or on those who hold temporary, on-call, or contract jobs (see Nollen & Axel, Chapter 5; Christensen, Chapter 4). Few if any firms can provide comprehensive or accurate data on their contingent workers in terms of their numbers, their demographics, their average tenure, their compensation, their rates of turnover, or their performances. Without a clear mandate from the firm, managers in human relations departments or elsewhere have little to no authority or rationale for collecting accurate or comprehensive information about how many contingent workers they have at any point in time. As a result, firm-specific data on contingent workers are very uneven. Temporary help agencies and subcontracted firms will have data on the employees assigned to the client firm, but the client firm itself will likely have no data. No firm studied by authors in this book collected any centralized data on independent contractors.

The reasons why firms keep such poor records are multiple. First, under law, they are under no requirement to keep detailed records on workers who are not direct employees. Other than on-call workers, none of the nonstandard workers are direct employees. Independent contractors are self-employed, and the employees of the temporary or subcontracting firms are technically employees of those firms, not of the client firm at whose site those workers actually work.

The second reason for poor record keeping is organizational. While human resource departments are responsible for their permanent employees and direct-hire on-call workers, they typically assume little to no responsibility for the self-employed contractors or the employees of the temp or subcontracting firms. In fact, as Kathleen Christensen notes (Chapter 4), large sole-source contracts with national temporary help firms are often negotiated through purchasing rather than human re source departments.

The final reason is likely that the entire rationale behind contingent staffing is to distance the client firm from workers who are not part of their permanent workforce. If the rationale is to seek distance, why would a firm want to bring these workers into closer focus by documenting in any detail the extent of their contingent staffing arrangements or the nature of these contingent workers?

There could be several reasons why firms might want to bring these nonstandard work arrangements into closer focus. First, they could determine the actual percentage of jobs central to the organization that are being done by nonpermanent employees. Second, they could calculate the actual costs and benefits of this staffing strategy. Third, they could evaluate whether and to what extent these staffing arrangements really allow a firm to achieve its goals, one of which is to enhance job security for core employees.

Although firm-specific data on contingent staffing are limited, they do shed light on how businesses actually use contingent staffing, and they raise important questions for future research.

Do Contingent Workers Lower Labor Costs?

The conventional wisdom is that because contingent workers frequently receive lower wages and benefits, they are cheaper. According to Stanley Nollen and Helen Axel (Chapter 5), however, the actual costs of contingent workers have to include other factors such as training costs, rates of turnover, and performance and productivity levels. In addition, firms typically do not add in the costs of their legal responsibilities to contingent workers, which are most likely to be incurred in the instances of joint employer relationships, such as with a temp agency, or in the case of misclassified independent contractors. When all of these costs were taken into account and weighed against productivity measures, Nollen and Axel found that contingent workers were not cost-effective in two of the three companies they studied. This finding argues for more detailed case studies which calculate the actual costs and benefits of using contingent workers.

Does Contingent Staffing Increase Job Security for Core Employees?

Two parallel trends are being played out within American business: a move toward high-performance workplaces in which there is high employee involvement; and a trend toward contingent staffing, in which there are weakened and insecure attachments between the employer and the worker. Although quite different at first glance, these two trends might in fact intersect in important ways. While the high-performance workplace purports to value core employees, the contingent staffing model devalues contingent workers. Yet it may be through contingent staffing that a firm can achieve workforce flexibility, thereby ensuring job security for the firm's valued core employees.

According to labor economist Robert Drago (Chapter 6), there are three possible linkages between high-performance workplaces and contingent staffing arrangements: (1) as noted above, contingent workers may function as a cheap and flexible periphery, supporting core-worker job security and wages, and hence promoting high-performance workplaces; (2) contingent workers may be anathema to high-performance workplaces, undercutting the trust and long-term relationships required for success; or (3) certain types of high-performance workplaces may be associated with collective threats to employee job security, thereby making all workers appear contingent. It is difficult, if not impossible, to examine Drago's three hypotheses in U.S. workplaces, given the lack of firm-specific data on contingent workers.

By using an Australian workplace data set, however, Drago was able to investigate the three linkages. In Australia, workers are distinguished as casual or permanent. Casual workers have no job security and very limited rights on the job, while permanent employees cannot be terminated at will by managers. Casual workers are clearly the equivalent of the BLS's contingent workers.

Drago's analyses conclude that linkage 3 best represents the Australian experience with contingent labor. When contingent workers are used in Australian firms, they signal job insecurity for all employees and do not serve as a buffer for any employee's job security. In other words, at least in Australia, contingent workers do not achieve the goal stated as important to American firms—to hire contingent workers in order to ensure job security for core employees. In fact the opposite occurs—the use of contingent work is associated with creating a collective climate of insecurity and making all workers appear to be contingent.

Enough similarities exist between the U.S. and Australian economy to warrant further study of how contingent staffing affects the job security of core employees in U.S. firms.

What Drives the Use of Contingent Staffing?

Most of the chapters in this volume assume that market forces are the critical drivers behind the use and reputed increases in contingent staffing. George Gonos argues that the macroeconomic and political environments within which the individual firm operates must also be analyzed (Chapter 7). He points out that federal case law played a major role, beginning in the 1950s, in creating a legal environment conducive to the development of the temporary help services industry, which raises the question: How do the courts facilitate or impede further development of other types of contingent work arrangements?

What Are the Human Experiences of Working Contingently?

There are important questions to address regarding the consequences of working contingently on the worker and on his or her career and family. At this point we can only point to some of the answers.

Social-Psychological Consequences

According to Barker, many workers place a high premium on job tenure and occupational growth and look forward to working in jobs that will prepare them for increasing amounts of responsibility and status (Chapter 8). Yet contingent workers have tenuous attachments to their employers and insecure futures within the organization. For some contingent workers in some industries and organizational settings, there are very real social and psychological consequences of being weakly tethered to the organization. Based on a study of adjunct faculty in higher education, Barker identified several such consequences: being excluded from the normal rules and social expectations of how people are to be treated and dealt with; experiencing a stigmatized professional identity as a second-class citizen within the organization; finding no socially legitimate avenues for protesting; and feeling increasing despair about meritocracy in the workplace. To test whether these perceived consequences were actual risks, Barker conducted a study to determine the chances of an adjunct being recommended for hiring in a full-time, tenure-track position. The results were unequivocal: even though working on an adjunct basis provides one with job-relevant training, the more adjunct experience one has, the lower the chance of being recommended for hiring.

Other industries and occupations, both high- and low-skilled, should be studied to determine the long-term effects of contingent work on career trajectories. As firms acquire flexibility through contingent staffing, are individuals losing ground? It would be valuable to understand the consequences of contingent work on the currency of one's job-relevant knowledge and skills, on one's self-identification with a job or profession, and on one's employability at different points in time.

Parallel studies of employers should be undertaken to determine how they evaluate contingent work experience when they make hiring decisions for permanent positions. What specific heuristics do employers use in evaluating the potential employability of contingent workers? If contingency is viewed negatively, how important is the fact that the person has not "landed" a permanent position, as compared for example, to the sense that the contingent has not contributed enough to the field or stayed as current as he or she should have? If contingency is viewed positively, what are the contributing factors?

Economic Effects

On the average, contingent workers experience an earnings penalty. According to BLS figures, contingent workers earn 80 percent of what noncontingent workers earn, whereas according to SIPP data they earn 52 percent ($5.15 an hour compared to $9.97 an hour).

The contingent workers described through the SIPP data are at particular economic risk. According to Spalter-Roth and Hartmann one out of seven of the women working contingently were able to meet their families needs only through the receipt of means-tested welfare benefits, such as Aid to Families with Dependent Children, Food Stamps, or WIC. These women were likely to have children under the age of six and to be the single support for these children.

The economic consequences of nonstandard work arrangements vary. According to the BLS, independent contractors, who are likely to be white, male, and educated, do not suffer a penalty and may, in fact, experience an earnings premium (at least before they have to pay their social security contribution and buy health care insurance). Yet the employees of temporary agency firms are more likely to be black, female, poorly educated, and single mothers and to suffer earnings penalties. As Jean McAllister graphically illustrates, the single mothers who temp experience real economic hardships.

For those contingent and nonstandard workers who do experience an earnings penalty, it is important in future research to determine what happens to their earnings over time. The only way to interpret changes in earnings is to have a clear understanding of the job trajectories for contingent and nonstandard workers: what jobs did they have prior to their first contingent or nonstandard job, and what jobs did they have subsequently? Where, in fact, does working contingently fit in the entire arc of one's job history? Is it a platform for more regular or permanent employment or is it a dead-end, and for whom and under what conditions?

Besides the earnings penalties incurred from working contingently, many contingent workers experience other costs which will have direct monetary consequences. One of these costs involves the exclusion of many of contingent workers from the kinds of skill and training opportunities afforded their peers in "permanent" jobs. Although training is not a palliative to the loss of job security, it is increasingly important to basic skill development and currency. Contingent workers, consistently passed over for training, promotion, and advancement, can become anachronistic to themselves and to their employers in many industries. More important, many contingent workers are personally assuming the cost of training or skill upgrades.

Future research efforts should examine how tax law could be changed to enable contingent workers to afford the costs of training, both the direct cost of the training itself and the indirect costs incurred by forgoing earning during the training period. Individuals could benefit by being able to deduct training costs from their personal income taxes, regardless of whether the training or education is related to their current job (IRS allowed) or to making a transition to a different career path (IRS not allowed). Future actions could be directed to developing new training models or opportunities through unions or private sector initiatives. Union-based training for nonmembers could lead to new models for organizing based on occupation and geography (Cobble, 1991; Wial, 1993; in duRivage, Carré, & Tilly, Chapter 11).

Unique Health and Safety Risks

Many of the workers on nonstandard arrangements fall outside the legal safety network put forth both in labor law and employment law (Chapters 11 and 12). For example, James Rebitizer (Chapter 10) documents the high accident rates of contractors compared to permanent employees. As he notes, firms in the petrochemical industry have a disincentive to collect safety information on contract workers, because to do so can make them legally liable for these workers. Due to existing liability law, it makes no sense for a firm to train contractors to the same skill and safety levels as permanent employees. What we do not know, however, is whether contingent workers in other industries are as "at risk" as were the contractors in the petrochemical industry.

What Happens within Families?

Permanent employees face conflicts in managing home and work demands but do so in a context in which the employer may provide benefits meant to ameliorate such conflict. Contingent workers typically labor in a context that provides minimal to no formal support for work-family issues (Chapter 4). Yet the costs of working contingently can be devastating to the workers themselves and to their families, especially if no one in their family has a stable or "killer" job (Chapter 9).

Many contingent nonstandard workers with the exception of independent contractors receive poor wages, are intermittently employed, and lack the employment scaffolding that most workers in the permanent workforce take for granted: a functional car, cash and credit to finance living expenses on a regular basis, and phone service, to name a few. Some women supplement their contingent wages with benefits provided under welfare (Spalter-Roth & Hartmann, Chapter 3). With changes to income entitlements such as welfare and many of its associated benefits, what survival strategies will these women use?

Conventional wisdom holds that women "choose" contingent work because of its inherent flexibility. Yet research findings on satisfaction with flexibility are mixed. Industry-sponsored surveys conducted by the National Association of Temporary Service (NATS) produced findings that support that claim. But independent case-study research does not support it (Chapter 9; Martella, 1990). This disparity in findings raises questions about how flexibility is defined and how the value of flexibility is determined by workers. For example, most temporary assignments are full-time for set periods. This provides for only an annual flexibility by which someone over the course of a year can go in and out of the labor market. Rarely do temporary assignments provide a type of flexibility that allows someone to work a shortened workday or workweek. In future research, researchers' and respondents' definitions of flexibility must be clearly laid out.

In addition, the value of flexibility must be examined in light of a person's set of needs. Since many temporary workers are single mothers, it is unlikely that flexibility is the main reason they are working under these conditions. While flexibility may provide some benefits, it does not always offset other needs, such as for a steady paycheck or a health benefits package. The fact that the BLS reports broad dissatisfaction among many temp workers indicates that the tradeoffs they make between flexibility and compensation may not be inherently satisfying. Since 80 percent of temporaries report that they want permanent jobs, it is clear that flexibility, although valued, is not likely to be their driving motivation. They are hoping to use contingency as a way to audition for more permanent positions. This leads us to pose the question, What do we know about temps' placement rates into permanent jobs?

In suggesting that scholars and activists study the transformation of employment relations, we acknowledge that there may be little, if any, incentive for the private sector to correct some of the problems that may be uncovered, such as the restriction of benefits to contingent workers. Therefore, one suggestion is that future workplace reforms should focus on the various ways in which federal and state laws could be amended to include these workers.

It may also be time for states to consider a certification process for temporary and contract firms that would have as one of its aims ensuring compensation and training parity between client firm practices and temporary or contract firm practices. Temporary agencies and contract firms could be regulated in a certification process that would grant them particular status based on their benefits packages and safety records. Client firms would be required to hire workers from temporary agencies and contract firms that provide benefits commensurate to those offered to their own permanent employees. Although one could argue that this could drive up the costs of temps for the client firms, Spalter-Roth and Hartmann's analysis demonstrate that the public costs incurred by taxpayers are already driven up through the contingent workers' use of means-tested welfare benefits.

Finally, it may be appropriate for unions to look at innovative ways to meet the needs of nonmember contingent workers. For example, they could more aggressively open their affiliate memberships to contingent workers to enable them to purchase lower-cost health or pension coverage.

People need jobs, health care, and training. The dominant twentieth-century employment relations model traditionally linked all three together. Increasingly, each is being severed from the others, perhaps nowhere as dramatically as in the case of contingent workers. In the coming decades, either government or unions will need to step in to meet the needs of contingent workers. In the interim, businesses would be well served to take a hard look at whether the benefits of flexibility that they seek through contingent staffing arrangements truly offset the costs of relying on this loosely tethered workforce.

References

9 to 5, National Organization of Working Women (1994, October 7). Statement presented to the Commission on the Future of Worker-Management Relations (Dunlop Commission), U.S. Department of Labor, Washington, D.C.

Abel, E. K. (1984). *Terminal degrees: The job crisis in higher education.* New York: Praeger.

Abraham, K. G. (1990). Restructuring the employment relationship. In K. Abraham and R. McKersie, eds., *New developments in the labor market: Toward a new institutional paradigm*, 85–118. Cambridge: MIT Press.

Alito, R. (1992). *New Jersey employment law.* Newark, N.J.: New Jersey Law Journal Books.

Allport, G. W. (1954). *The nature of prejudice.* Reading, Mass.: Addison-Wesley.

Apfelbaum, E. (1979). Relations of domination and movements for liberation: An analysis of power between groups. In W. G. Austin and S. Worchel, eds., *The social psychology of intergroup relations*, 188–204. Monterey, Calif.: Brooks/Cole.

Appelbaum, E. (1987). Restructuring work: Temporary, part-time and at-home employment. In H. Hartmann, ed., *Computer chips and paper clips.* Vol. 2, *Technology and women's employment*, 268–310. Washington, D.C.: National Academy Press.

—— (1992). Structural change and the growth of part-time and temporary employment. In V. L. duRivage, ed., *New policies for the part-time and contingent workforce*, 1–14. Armonk, N.Y.: Sharpe.

—— (1993, June 15). Management strategies for competitiveness: Contingent workforce or high performance work systems. Statement to the Committee on Labor and Human Resources, U.S. Senate.

Appelbaum, E., and R. Batt (1994). *The new American workplace.* Ithaca, N.Y.: ILR Press.

Appelbaum, E., and J. Gregory (1988). Union responses to contingent work: Are win-win outcomes possible? In *Flexible workstyles: A look at contingent labor*, 69–75. Washington, D.C.: U.S. Department of Labor, Women's Bureau.

Asian Law Caucus, California Rural Legal Assistance, Carolina Alliance for Fair Employment, Farm Worker Justice Fund, Inc., Korean Immigrant Workers Advocates, National Employment Law Project, 9 to 5 (National Organizational of Working Women), S.E.I.U. (Service Employees International Union), Southerners for Economic Justice (1994, October 7). *Statement on changes to current labor laws necessary to address the critical needs of the contingent labor force.* Statement presented to the Commission on the Future of Worker-Management Relations, United States Department of Labor, Washington, D.C.

Axel, Helen (1993). Downsizing. *HR Executive Review* 1 (1).

—— (1995). Contingent employment. *HR Executive Review* 3 (2).

Axelrod, J. G. (1987). Who's the boss? Employee leasing and the joint employer relationship. *Labor Lawyer* 3, 853–872.

Barker, K. (1993). Changing assumptions and contingent solutions: The costs and benefits of women working full and part-time. *Sex Roles* 28, 47–71.

—— (1995). Contingent work: Research issues and the lens of moral exclusion. In Tetrick, L., and J. Barling, eds., *Changing employment relations: Behavioral and social perspectives*, 31–60. Washington, D.C.: American Psychological Society.

—— (1997, August). Where's the payoff? The evaluation of contingent work experience. Paper presented at the meeting of the American Psychological Association, Chicago, Ill.

Barrett, G. J. (1993). Job satisfaction in the temporary workforce. Ph.D. diss., George Washington University.

Becker, G. (1991). *A treatise on the family*. 2d ed. Cambridge: Harvard University Press.

Becker, G. S. (1975). *Human capital*. 2d ed. Cambridge, Mass.: National Bureau of Economic Research.

Belous, R. (1989). *The contingent economy: The growth of the temporary, part-time and subcontracted workforce*. NPA Rep. No. 239. Washington, D.C.: National Planning Association.

Benjamin, E. (1995). A faculty response to the fiscal crisis: From defense to offense. In M. Bérubé and C. Nelson, eds., *Higher education under fire*, 52–72. New York: Routledge.

Bennett, A. (1989). Death of the organization man. New York: William Morrow.

Berets, D. (1989, April–June). Professional temporaries. *Business and Economic Review* 35 (3), 10–13.

Bérubé, M., and C. Nelson (1995). *Higher education under fire: Politics, economics, and the crisis of the humanities*. New York: Routledge.

Binning, J. F., M. A. Goldstein, M. F. Garcia, J. L. Harding, and J. H. Scataregia (1988). Effects of pre-interview impressions on questioning strategies in same- and opposite-sex employment interviews. *Journal of Applied Psychology* 73, 30–37.

Bluestone, B., and I. Bluestone (1992). *Negotiating the future*. New York: Basic.

Boroughs, D. (1994, July 4). Business gives in to temptation. *U.S. News and World Report* 117 (1), 56–58.

Bourdieu, P. (1987). The force of law: Toward a sociology of the juridical field. *Hastings Law Journal* 38, 805–853.

Bronfenbrenner, K. (1988). Legal status of contingency workers. Paper presented at a meeting of the AFL-CIO Executive Board, Washington, D.C.

Bronfenbrenner, K., and V. L. duRivage (1994). *The labor law rights of contingent workers: Organization and representation issues*. University Park, Pa.: Department of Labor Studies and Industrial Relations, Pennsylvania State University.

Brophy, B. (1987, November 23). The "just in time" worker. *U.S. News and World Report* 103 (21), 45–46.

Brown, C., M. Reich, and D. Stern (1992). *Becoming a high-performance work organization: The role of security, employee involvement, and training*. Berkeley: Institute of Industrial Relations, University of California at Berkeley.

Brown, C., M. Reich, D. Stern, and L. Ulman (1993). Conflict and cooperation in labor-management relations in Japan and the United States. In *Proceedings of the Forty-Fifth Annual Meeting*, Forty-Fifth Annual Meeting, Industrial Relations Research Association, 426–436.

Burch, P. (1975). Interest groups. In A. Rosenthal and J. Blydenburgh, eds., *Politics in New Jersey*, 81–109. New Brunswick, N.J.: Eagleton Institute.

Burgan, M. (1997). Ratcheting up. *Academe* 83 (3), 5.

Callaghan, P., and H. Hartmann (1992). *Contingent work: A chartbook on part-time and temporary employment*. Washington, D.C.: Institute for Women's Policy Research, Economic Policy Institute.

Callus, R., A. Morehead, M. Cully, and J. Buchanan (1991). *Industrial relations at work: The Australian workplace Industrial Relations Survey*. Canberra: Australian Government Printing Service.

Canter, S. (1988). The temporary help industry: Filling the needs of workers and business. In *Flexible workstyles: A look at contingent labor*, 46–49. Washington, D.C.: U.S. Department of Labor, Women's Bureau.

Carnevale, A. P. (1994, February 8). The growing contingent workforce: Flexibility at the price of fairness. Labor and Human Resources Conference: Testimony before U.S. Senate Subcommittee on Labor.

Carolina Alliance for Fair Employment (1995, June). *Report on the Carolina Alliance for Fair Employment Greenville Temp School, 7–11 Nov 1994*. Greenville, S.C.: Carolina Alliance for Fair Employment.

Carré, F. J. (1992). Temporary employment in the eighties. In V. L. duRivage, ed., *New policies for part-time and contingent workers*, 45–87. Armonk, N.Y.: M. E. Sharpe

Carré, F.J., and L. Dougherty (1995, May). *Improving employment conditions for contingent workers: The Massachusetts Community Care Workers campaign by SEIO Local 509*. Unpublished paper presented at the meeting, Workplace 2000: Women's Rights, Worker Rights, New York.

Carré, F. J., V. L. duRivage, and C. Tilly (1994). Representing the part-time and contingent workforce: Challenges for unions and public policy. In S. Friedman, R. W. Hurd, R A, Oswald, and R.L. Seeber, eds., *Restoring the promise of American labor law*. Ithaca, N.Y.: ILR Press.

—— (1995). Piecing together the fragmented workplace· Unions and public policy on flexible employment. In L. G. Flood, ed., *Unions and public policy*, 13 34. Westport, Conn.: GreenwoodPress.

Cascio, W. (1993). Downsizing: What do we know? What have we learned? *Academy of Management Executives* 7 (1), 95–104.

Castro, J. (1993, March 29). Disposable workers. *Time* 140 (1), 43–47.

Chambers, R. (1983). *Rural development: Putting the last first*. New York: John Wiley & Sons.

Christensen, K. (1988a). *Independent contracting*. In K. Christensen and M. Murphree, eds., *Flexible workstyles: A look at contingent labor*. Conference Summary, 54–58. Washington, D.C.: U.S. Department of Labor, Women's Bureau.

—— (1988b). *Women and home-based work: The unspoken contract*. New York: Henry Holt.

—— (1989). *Flexible scheduling and staffing in U.S. corporations*. Conference Board Report No. 240. New York: The Conference Board.

—— (1993). Eliminating the journey to work: Home-based work across the life course of women in the United States. In C. Katz and J. Monk, eds., *Full circles: Geographies of women over the life course*. New York: Routledge.

—— (1995). *Contingent work arrangements in family-sensitive corporations*. Boston: Center on Work and Family, The Work and Family Institute, Boston College.

Christensen, K., and M. Murphree (1988). Introduction to Conference Proceedings. In K. Christensen and M. Murphree, eds., *Flexible Workstyles: A look at contingent labor*. Conference Summary, 1–4. Washington, D.C.: U.S. Department of Labor, Women's Bureau.

Cialdini, R. B. (1988). *Influence: Science and practice.* Glenview, Ill.: Scott, Foresman.

Cobble, D. S. (1991). Organizing the postindustrial workforce: Lessons from the history of waitress unionism. *Industrial and Labor Relations Review* 44 (3), 419–436.

Cohany, S. R. (1996, October). Workers in alternative employment arrangements. *Monthly Labor Review* 119, 31–45.

Collins, S. (1994, July 4). The new migrant workers. *U.S. News and World Report* 117 (1), 53–55.

Co-mingling (Fall, 1982). *Contemporary Times,* 20–21.

Committee G (1992). Report on part-time and non-tenure appointments. *Academe* 78, 39–48.

Cooke, W. N. (1992). Product quality improvement through employee participation: The effects of unionization and joint union-management administration. *Industrial and Labor Relations Review* 46, 119–134.

Coopers and Lybrand (1994, June). *Projection of the loss in federal tax revenues due to misclassification of workers.* New York.

Cordova, E. (1986). From full-time wage employment to atypical employment: A major shift in the evolution of labour relations? *International Labour Review* 125, 641–657.

Cutcher-Gershenfeld, J. (1991). The impact on economic performance of a transformation in workplace relations. *Industrial and Labor Relations Review* 44, 241–260.

Dantico, M. (1987). The impact of contracting-out on women and minorities. In *When public services go private,* 18–20. Washington, D.C.: AFSCME.

Deutsch, M. (1985). *Distributive justice: A social psychological perspective.* New Haven: Yale University Press.

Diebold, F., D. Neumark, and D. Polsky (1994). Job stability in the United States. National Bureau of Economic Research Working Paper No. 4859. Cambridge, Mass.: National Bureau of Economic Research.

Dipboye, R. L. (1982). Self-fulfilling prophecies in the selection-recruitment interview. *Academy of Management Review* 7, 579–586.

Doeringer, P., K. Christensen, P. Flynn, D. Hall, H. Katz, J. Keefe, C. Ruhm, A. Sum, and M. Useem (1991). *Turbulence in the American workplace.* New York: Oxford University Press.

Dougherty, T., D. Turban, and J. Callender (1994). Confirming first impressions in the employment interview: A field study of interviewer behavior. *Journal of Applied Psychology* 79, 659–665.

Drago, R. (1988). Quality circle survival: An exploratory analysis. *Industrial Relations* 27, 336–351.

—— (1995). Employee involvement in Australia: Workplace transformation and the disposable workplace. *Industrial Relations* 27, 336–351.

—— (1996). Workplace transformation and the disposable workplace: Employee involvement in Australia. *Industrial Relations* 35, 526–543.

—— (1997). Employee involvement in America: The 1930's and the 1980's. In M. Dobkowski, eds., *Research in Social Movements, Conflict and Change* 20, 61–101. Greenwich, Conn.: JAI Press.

Drago, R., G. T. Garvey, and G. K. Turnbull (1996). A collective tournament. *Economics Letters* 50, 223–227.

Drago, R., and G. K. Turnbull (1991). Competition and cooperation in the workplace. *Journal of Economic Behavior and Organization* 15, 347–364.

Drago, R., M. Wooden, and J. Sloan (1992). *Productive relations? Australian industrial relations and workplace performance.* Sydney: Allen & Unwin.

Durity, A. (May, 1991). Downsized HR executives join ranks of temps who enjoy an alternative lifestyle. *Personnel* 68 (8), 8.

duRivage, V. L. (1992a). New policies for the part-time and contingent workforce. In V. L. duRivage, ed., *New policies for the part-time and contingent workforce*, 89–122. Armonk, N.Y.: M. E. Sharpe.

—— (1992b, Spring). Flexibility trap: The proliferation of marginal jobs. *American Prospect* 9, 84–93.

Eaton, A. E. (1994). Factors contributing to the survival of employee participation programs in unionized settings. *Industrial and Labor Relations Review* 47, 371–389.

Eaton, A. E., and P. B. Voos (1992). Unions and contemporary innovations in work organization, compensation, and employee participation. In L. Mishel and P. B. Voos, eds., *Unions and Economic Competitiveness*, 173–215. Armonk, N.Y.: M. E. Sharpe.

Edsall, T. B. (1984). *The new politics of inequality*. New York: W. W. Norton.

Employee Benefit Research Institute (1990). *EBRI databook on employee benefits*. Washington, D.C.: Employee Benefit Research Institute.

Engelstein, L. (1996). Labor law for contract employees: A modest reform agenda. In B. Stein, ed., *Proceedings of the New York University 48th Annual National Conference on Labor and Employment Law*, 319–342. Boston: Little, Brown.

Epstein, E., and J. Monat (1973). Labor contracting and its regulation: I. *International Labour Review* 107, 451–470.

Ernst, B. (1995). A faculty response to the fiscal crisis: From defense to offense. In M. Bérubé and C. Nelson, eds., *Higher education under fire: Politics, economics, and the crisis of the humanities*. New York: Routledge.

Farber, H. (1995). Are life-time jobs disappearing? Job duration in the United States: 1973–1993. National Bureau of Economic Research Working Paper No. 5014. Cambridge, Mass.: National Bureau of Economic Research.

Fierman, J. (1994, January 24). The contingency workforce. *Fortune* 129 (2), 30–36.

Fine, M. (1997). Witnessing whiteness. In M. L. Fine et al., *Off white: Readings on race, power, and society*, 57–65. New York: Routledge.

Fine, M., L. Weis, C. Powell, and L. M. Wong (1997). *Off white: Readings on race, power, and society*. New York: Routledge.

Finney, M. I., and D. A. Dasch (1991). A heritage of service: The history of temporary help in America. Alexandria, Va.: National Association of Temporary Services.

Foust, D., and M. Mallory (1993, September 27). The boom belt: There's no speed limit on growth along the South's I-85. *Business Week* 3338, 98–104.

Frankenberg, R. (1993). *White women, race matters*. Minneapolis: University of Minnesota Press.

Freedman, A. (1985). *The new look in wage policy and employee relations*. Conference Board Rep. No. 865. New York: The Conference Board.

—— (1988). Rising use of part-time and temporary workers. Testimony before the Committee on Government Operations, U.S. House of Representatives. In *Rising use of part-time and temporary workers: Who benefits and who loses?* Washington, D.C.: U.S. Government Printing Office.

Freeman, R. B., and J. L. Medoff (1984). *What do unions do?* New York: Basic.

Friedman, M. (1969). *The process of work establishment*. New York: Columbia University Press.

Friedman, M., R. W. Hurd, R. A. Oswald, and R. L. Seeber, eds. (1994). *Restoring the promise of American labor law*. Ithaca, N.Y.: ILR Press.

Fuchs, V. R. (1988). *Women's quest for economic equality*. Cambridge: Harvard University Press.

Fusilier, M. R., and M. A. Hitt (1983). Effects of age, race, sex, and employment experience on students' perceptions of job applicants. *Perceptual and Motor Skills* 57, 1127–1134.

Galambos, L., and J. Pratt (1988). *The rise of the corporate commonwealth: United States business and public policy in the 20th century*. New York: Basic.

Gappa, J.M., and D. W. Leslie (1993). *The invisible faculty: Improving the status of part-timers in higher education*. San Francisco: Jossey-Bass.

—— (1997). *Two faculties or one? The conundrum of part-timers in a bifurcated work force*. Washington, D.C.: American Association for Higher Education.

General Accounting Office (1989, September). *Tax administration information returns can be used to identify employers who misclassify employees*. Report to Congress. Washington, D.C.: GAO.

Ginzberg, E. (1971). *Career guidance: Who needs it, who provides it, who can improve it*. New York: McGraw-Hill.

Giroux, H. A. (1983). Theories of reproduction and resistance in the new sociology of education: A critical analysis. *Harvard Educational Review* 53, 257–293.

Golden, L., and E. Appelbaum (1992). What is driving the boom in temporary employment? *American journal of economics and sociology* 51, 473–492.

Gonos, G. (1994). A sociology of the temporary employment relationship. Ph.D. diss., Rutgers University. Abstract in *Dissertation Abstracts International* 55 (June 1995), 4008-A. (University Microfilms No. DA9511473.)

Greller, M. M., and D. M. Nee (1989). *From baby boom to baby bust: How business can meet the demographic challenge*. New York: Addison-Wesley.

Harrison, B., and B. Bluestone (1987). *The dark side of labour market "flexibility": Falling wages and growing income inequality in America*. Working Paper No. 17. Geneva: International Labour Organization.

—— (1988). *The great U-turn: Corporate restructuring and the polarizing of America*. New York: Basic Books.

Hartmann, H., and J. Lapidus (1989). *Temporary work*. Report No. C302. Washington, D.C.: Institute for Women's Policy Research.

Hartmann, H., and R. Spalter-Roth (1992). *The labor market, the working poor, and welfare reform: Policy suggestions for the Clinton administration*. Report No. I902. Washington, D.C.: Institute for Women's Policy Research.

—— (1994). Reducing welfare's stigma: Policies that build upon commonalities among women. *Connecticut Law Review* 26, 901–911.

Hartmann, H., R. Spalter-Roth, and J. Chu (1996). Poverty alleviation and single mother families. *National Forum: The Phi Kappa Phi Journal* 76 (3): 24–27.

Hayghe, H. (1990). Family members in the workforce. *Monthly Labor Review* 113, 14–19.

Heckman, J., R. Roselius, and J. Smith (1994). U.S. education and training policy: A reevaluation of the underlying assumptions behind the new consensus. In A. Levenson and L.C. Solmon, eds., *Labor markets, employment policy and job creation*, 83–121. Santa Monica, Calif.: Milken Institute for Job and Capital Formation.

Helper, S. R., and D. Levine (1994). Supplier/customer participation and worker participation: Is there a linkage? *Proceedings of the Thirty-Fourth Annual Meetings*, 153–176. Madison, Wis.: Industrial Relations Research Association.

Henson, K. (1993). "Just a temp": The disenfranchised worker. Ph.D. diss., Northwestern University.

Hiatt, J. P., and L. Rhinehart (1993, August 10). The growing contingent workforce: A challenge for the future. Paper presented to the American Bar Association Section on Employment and Labor Law.

Hipple, S., and J. Stewart (1996a, October). Earnings and benefits of contingent and non-contingent workers. *Monthly Labor Review* 119, 22–30.

—— (1996b, October). Earnings and benefits of workers in alternative work arrangements. *Monthly Labor Review* 119, 46–54.

Hirschman, A. O. (1970). *Exit, voice, and loyalty: Responses to decline in firms, organizations, and states.* Cambridge: Harvard University Press.

Hitt, M. A., and S. H. Barr (1989). Managerial selection decision models: Examination of configural cue processing. *Journal of Applied Psychology* 74, 53–61.

Hood, J. B., B. A. Hardy, and H. S. Lewis (1990). *Workers' compensation and employee protection laws in a nutshell.* St. Paul, Minn.: West Publishing.

Howell, D. R. (1993). *Technological change and the demand for skills in the 1980s: Does skill mismatch explain the growth of low earnings?* Working Paper No. 101. Annandale-on-Hudson, N.Y.: The Jerome Levy Economics Institute.

International Labour Organization (1966, July). Interpretation of decisions of the International Labor Conference. *Official Bulletin* 49, 389–396.

Janoski, T. (1990). *The political economy of unemployment: Active labor market policy in West Germany and the U.S.* Berkeley: University of California.

Jones, E. E., and K. E. Davis (1965). From acts to dispositions: The attribution process in person perception. In L. Berkowitz, ed., *Advances in experimental social psychology* 7, 219–266. New York: Academic Press.

Kahn, S. (1987). Occupational safety and worker preferences: Is there a marginal worker? *Review of Economics and Statistics* 69 (2), 262–267.

Kahne, H. (1985). *Reconceiving part-time work: New perspectives for older workers and women.* Totowa, N.J.: Rowman & Allanheld.

—— (1992). Part-time work: A hope and a peril. In B. D. Warme, K. Lundy, and L. A. Lundy, eds., *Working part-time: Risks and opportunities,* 295–309. New York: Praeger.

Kalleberg, A. L., K. Hudson, and B. F. Reskin (1997). Bad jobs in America: Non-standard, contingent, and secondary employment relations in the United States. Paper presented at the 92d Annual Meetings of the American Sociological Association, Toronto.

Kalleberg, A. L., E. Rasell, K. Hudson, D. Webster, B. Reskin, N. Cassirer, and E. Appelbaum (1997). Nonstandard work, substandard jobs: Flexible work arrangements in the U.S. Washington, D.C.: Economic Policy Institute; Women's Research and Education Institute.

Kanter, R. M. (1995). Nice work if you can get it: The software industry as a model for tomorrow's jobs. *American Prospect* 23 (Fall), 52–59.

Keeton, W. P., ed. (1984). *Prosser and Keeton on the law of torts.* 5th ed. St. Paul, Minn.: West Publishing.

Kilborn, P. T. (1991, June 17). Part-time hirings bring deep change in U.S. workplaces. *New York Times,* A1.

Kinicki, A. J., and C. A. Lockwood (1985). The interview process: An examination of factors recruiters use in evaluating job applicants. *Journal of Vocational Behavior* 26, 117–125.

Klare, K. E. (1981). Labor law as ideology: Toward a new historiography of collective bargaining law. *Industrial Relations Law Journal* 4, 450–482.

Klein, E. (1991, September–October). Rent-a-boss. *D & B Reports* 39 (5), 38–40.

Klein, K. J., and T. A. D'Aunno (1986). Psychological sense of community in the work-place. *Journal of Community Psychology* 14, 365–377.

Kleingartner, A., and A. Paul (1992, January 3). Member attachment and union effective-ness in arts and entertainment. Paper presented at the 44th Annual Meeting of the Industrial Relations Research Association, New Orleans.

Knouse, S. B. (1994). Impressions of the resume: The effects of applicant education, expe-rience, and impression management. *Journal of Business and Psychology* 9, 33–45.

Kochan, T. A., H. C. Katz, and R. B. McKersie (1986). *The transformation of American industrial relations.* New York: Basic.

Kochan, T. A., M. Smith, J. C. Wells, and J. B. Rebitzer (1994, Spring). Human resource strategies and contingent workers: The case of safety and health in the petrochem-ical industry. *Human Resource Management* 33 (1), 55–77.

Kochan, T.A., J. C. Wells, and M. Smith (1992, Summer). Consequences of a failed I.R. system: Contract workers in the petrochemical industry. *Sloan Management Review* 33 (4), 79–89.

Kornbluh, J. L. (1988). *Historical perspectives on part-time and temporary workers. Flex-ible workstyles: A look at contingent labor.* Conference summary, 54–58. Washing-ton, D.C.: U.S. Department of Labor, Women's Bureau.

Krecker, M. L. (1994). Work careers and organizational careers: The effects of age and tenure on worker attachment to the employment relationship. *Work and occupa-tions* 21, 251–283.

Labor-for-rent war (1966, November 5). *Business Week*, 160–162.

Laird, K., and N. Williams (1996). Employment growth in the temporary help supply industry. *Journal of Labor Research* 17, 663–681.

Lawler, E. E., III., S. Mohrman, and G. E. Ledford (1992). *Employee involvement and total quality management.* San Francisco: Jossey-Bass.

Lazear, E. P., and S. Rosen (1981). Rank-order tournaments as optimum labor contracts. *Journal of Political Economy* 89, 841–864.

Leatherman, C. (1997, March 28). Heavy reliance on low-paid lecturers said to produce "faceless departments." *Chronicle of Higher Education*, A12–A13.

Lee, S., and S. Flack (1987, March 9). Hi-ho silver. *Forbes* 139 (5), 90.

Legislative monitoring—an association necessity (1982, Winter). *Contemporary Times*, 15.

Lenz, E. A. (1985a, Summer). The status of temporary help companies as employers: A legal update. *Contemporary Times*, 8–10.

—— (1985b, Winter). Getting involved: Why grass roots political relationships are the key to effective legislative advocacy. *Contemporary Times*, 4–5.

—— (1990, Summer). Temporary help customers risk liability using "independent con-tractors." *Contemporary Times*, 50.

—— (1991, Spring). Law notes. *Contemporary Times*, 37–42.

Levin, M. (1994, August). Appealing to investors. *Asian Business* 30, 46–48.

Levine, D. I., and S. Helper (1993, April). *A quality policy for America.* OBIR Working Paper 61. Berkeley: Organizational Behavior and Industrial Relations, University of California.

Levine, D. I., and L. D. Tyson (1990). Participation, productivity and the firm's external environment. In A. S. Blinder, ed., *Paying for productivity*, 183–243. Washington, D.C.: Brookings Institution.

Lewis, W., and N. Schuman (1988). *The temp worker's handbook.* New York: American Management Association.

Lewis, W. M., and N. H. Molloy (1991). *How to choose and use temporary services.* New York: American Management Association.

Liebow, E. (1968). *Tally's corner: A study of Negro street-corner men*. Boston: Little, Brown.

Macan, T., J. Detjen, and K. L. Dickey (1994). Measures of job perceptions: Gender and age of current incumbents, suitability, and job attributes. *Sex Roles* 30, 55–67.

Macan, T. M., and R. L. Dipboye (1988). The relationship of pre-interview impressions to selection and recruitment outcomes. *Personnel Psychology* 43, 745–768.

Machan, D. (1990, January). Rent-an-executive. *Forbes* 145 (1), 132–133.

Mackail, L. (1988, Winter). OPM opens doors to private sector temporaries. *Contemporary Times*, 46–47.

Mangan, K. S. (1991, August 7). Many colleges fill vacancies with part-time professors. *Chronicle of Higher Education*, A9–10.

Mangum, G., D. Mayall and K. Nelson (1985). The temporary help industry: A response to the dual internal labor market. *Industrial and Labor Relations Review* 38 (4), 599–611.

Maniscalco, R. (1992, March). High-tech temps in supply and demand. *HR Magazine* 37 (3), 66–67.

Martella, M. (1990). *Just a temp: Expectations and experiences of women clerical temporary workers*. Washington, D.C.: U.S. Department of Labor, Women's Bureau.

—— (1992). The rhetoric and realities of contingent work: The case of women in clerical temporary work. Ph.D. diss., Temple University.

McDonald, T., and M. D. Hakel (1985). Effects of applicant race, sex, suitability, and answers on interviewer's questioning strategy and ratings. *Personnel Psychology* 38, 321–334.

McKinney, S. (1992, February). Interim managers: Stop-gap staffing. *Personnel Journal* 71 (2), 88–89, 91–92.

Messmer, M. (1992, June). Strategic staffing. *Management accounting* 73 (12), 28–30.

Mincer, J. (1962, October). On-the-job training costs, returns, and some implications. *Journal of Political Economy* 70 (5, pt. 2), 50-79.

Moberly, R. B. (1987). Temporary, part-time, and other atypical employment relationships in the U.S. *Labor Law Journal* 16, 620–634.

Moore, M. A. (1965a). The legal status of temporary help services. *Labor Law Journal* 16, 620–634.

——. (1965b). The temporary help service industry: Historical development, operation and scope. *Industrial and Labor Relations Review* 18, 554–569.

——. (1975). Proposed federal legislation for temporary labor services. *Labor Law Journal* 26, 767–781.

Morse, D. (1969). *The peripheral worker*. New York: Columbia University Press.

Nardone, T. (1994). *Contingent workers: Characteristics and trends*. Working paper. Washington, D.C.: U.S. Department of Labor, Bureau of Labor Statistics, Office of Employment and Unemployment Statistics.

National Association of Temporary Services (1994a). *1994 profile of the temporary workforce*. Alexandria, Va.: National Association of Temporary and Staffing Services.

—— (1994b, July 18). Statement presented by Edward A. Lenz, senior vice president, legal and governmental affairs, National Association of Temporary Services, Alexandria, Va., to the Commission on the Future of Worker-Management Relations (Dunlop Commission), U.S. Department of Labor.

Negrey, C. (1993). *Gender, time, and reduced work*. Albany, N.Y.: State University of New York Press.

Newman, K. S. (1988). *Falling from grace: The experience of downward mobility in the American middle class*. New York: Vintage.

—— (1994). *Declining fortunes: The withering of the American dream.* New York: Basic.

New Ways to Work (1992). *New policies for part-time and contingent workers.* San Francisco.

New York Times (1996). *The downsizing of America: Special report.* New York: Times Books, Random House.

Nilles, J. (1994). *Making telecommuting happen: A guide for telemanagers and telecommuters.* New York: Van Nostrand Reinhold.

Nollen, S. (1982). *New work schedules in practice: Managing time in a changing society.* New York: Van Nostrand, Reinhold.

—— (1993, June 16–17). Exploring the myth: is contingent labor cost effective? A Report from *New Ways to Work.* Presented at The Conference Board meeting, "Reinventing the workplace: New prespectives on flexibility in tomorrow's competitive company," New York.

Nollen, S. D., and H. Axel (1996). *Managing contingent workers: How to reap the benefits and reduce the risks.* New York: AMACOM.

Office of Personnel Management (1989, Jan 25). Government use of private sector temporaries. *Fed. Reg.* 54, 3762-01.

—— (1991). Use of private sector temporaries. *Federal Personnel Manual,* chap. 300, subchapter 13.

Olian, J. D., D. O. Schwab, and Y. Haberfeld (1988). The impact of applicant gender compared to qualifications on hiring recommendations: A meta-analysis of experimental studies. *Organizational Behavior and Human Decision Processes* 41, 180–195.

Opotow, S. (1990). Moral exclusion and injustice: An introduction. *Journal of Social Issues* 46 (1), 1–20.

Ors, R. (1991, November–December). Flexible attorney staffing-project attorneys. *Law Practice Management* 17 (8), 52–55.

Osterman, P. (1988). *Employment futures: Reorganization, dislocation and public policy.* New York: Oxford University Press.

—— (1994). How common is workplace transformation and who adopts it? *Industrial and Labor Relations Review* 47, 173–188.

Parker, M., and J. Slaughter (1994). *Working smart: A union guide to participation programs and reengineering.* Detroit: Labor Notes.

Parker, R. E. (1994). *Flesh peddlers and warm bodies: The temporary help industry and its workers.* New Brunswick, N.J.: Rutgers University Press.

Part-time concerns are a full-time issue (1992, May). *United University Professions Voice* 3, 3.

Perrow, C. (1984). *Normal accidents: Living with high-risk technologies,* New York: Basic.

Pfeffer, J., and J. Baron (1988). Taking the workers back out: Recent trends in the structuring of employment. In B. Staw and L. Cummings, eds., *Research in organizational behavior* 10, 257–303. Greenwich, Conn.: JAI Press.

Pierce, J. L. (1989). *Alternative work schedules.* Boston: Allyn and Bacon.

Pierson, T. (1994, February 8). The growing contingent workforce: Flexibility at the price of fairness. Testimony. Washington, D.C.: Subcommittee on Labor of the Committee on Labor and Human Resources, United States Senate.

Polivka, A. E. (1996a, October). Contingent and alternative work arrangements defined. *Monthly Labor Review* 119, 3–9.

—— (1996b, October). A profile of contingent workers. *Monthly Labor Review* 119, 10–21.

—— (1996c, October). Into contingent and alternative employment: By choice? *Monthly Labor Review* 119, 55–74.

Polivka, A. E., and T. Nardone (1989, December). On the definition of "contingent work." *Monthly Labor Review* 112, 9–16.

Pretty, G. M. H., and M. McCarthy (1991). Exploring psychological sense of community among women and men of the corporation. *Journal of Community Psychology* 19, 351–361.

Rebitzer, J. B. (1995, January). Job safety and contract workers in the petrochemical industry. *Industrial Relations* 34 (1), 40–57.

Rebitzer, J. B., and L. Taylor (1991). A model of dual labor markets when product demand is uncertain. *Quarterly Journal of Economics* 106 (4), 1373–1383.

Reichheld, F. F. (1996). *The loyalty effect: The hidden force behind growth, profits, and lasting value*. Boston: Harvard Business School Press.

Reskin, B. F., and P. A. Roos (1990). *Job queues, gender queues: Explaining women's inroads into male occupations*. Philadelphia: Temple University Press.

Ricca, S. (1982). Private temporary work organizations and public employment services: effects and problems of coexistence. *International Labour Review* 121, 141–153.

Rogers, J. K. (1995). Just a temp: Experience and structure of alienation in temporary clerical employment. *Work and Occupations* 22, 137–166.

Rose, S. J. (1995). *Declining job security and the professionalization of opportunity*. Research Report No. 95-04. Washington, D.C.: National Commission for Employment Policy.

Rosenberg, S. (1989). *The state and the labor market*. New York: Plenum.

Rosenfeld, R. A. (1992). Job mobility and career processes. *Annual Review of Sociology* 18, 39–61.

Rosenthal, A. (1975). The governor, the legislature, and state policy making. In A. Rosenthal and J. Blydenburgh, eds., *Politics in New Jersey*, 141–174. New Brunswick, N.J.: Rutgers.

Rowland, M. (1993, September 12). Temporary work: The new career. *New York Times*, 15.

Rubenstein, S., M. Bennett, and T. Kochan (1993). The Saturn partnership: Co-management and the reinvention of the local union. In B. E. Kaufman and M. M. Kleiner, eds. *Employee representation: Alternatives and future directions*, 339–370. Madison, Wis.: IRRA Press.

Rusin, M., and L. A. Hofmann (1991). *Serious incidents in the U.S. petroleum refining industry: 1985–1989*. American Petroleum Institute.

Ryan, W. (1971). *Blaming the victim*. New York: Vintage.

S. 3259 (1962). Regulation of private employment agencies in District of Columbia, 87th Cong., 2d Sess.

Sackett, P. R. (1982). The interviewer as hypothesis tester: The effects of impressions of an applicant on interviewer questioning strategy. *Personnel Psychology* 35, 789–804.

Sales, E., and I. H. Frieze (1984). Women and work: Implications for mental health. In L. E. Walker, ed., *Women and mental health policy*, 229–246. Beverly Hills, Calif.: Sage.

Schellenbarger, S. (1995, February 1). When workers' lives are contingent on employers' whims. *Wall Street Journal*, 4.

Schmidt, F. L., J. E. Hunter, and A. M. Outerbridge (1986). Impact of job and supervisory ratings of job performance. *Journal of Applied Psychology* 71, 432–439.

Segal, L. M., and D. G. Sullivan (1995, March/April). The temporary labor force. *Economic Perspectives* 19, 2–19.

—— (1997). The growth of temporary services work. *Journal of Economic Perspectives* 11, 117–136.

Seigel, S. (1956). *Nonparametric statistics for the behavioral sciences*. New York: McGraw-Hill.

Selcraig, B. (1992, April). Bad chemistry: How reaganomics has fueled Texas plant explosions. *Harpers Magazine*, 62–73.

Selznick, P. (1969). *Law, society and industrial justice*. New York: Russell Sage Foundation.

Service Employees International Union (1993). *Part-time, temporary, and contracted work: coping with the growing contingent workforce*. Washington, D.C.: SEIU.

—— (1994, October 19). Regulatory and administrative changes that may be implemented under current law to protect and extend rights available to contingent workers. Paper presented to the Commission on the Future of Worker-Management Relations.

Shell, A. (1991, September). Recruiters enter "temp" business: Death of full-time jobs spurs change. *Public Relations Journal* 47, 7–8.

Shockey, M. L., and C. W. Mueller (1994). At-entry differences in part-time and full-time employees. *Journal of Business and Psychology* 8, 355–364.

Singer, M. S., and C. Bruhns (1991). Relative effect of applicant work experience and academic qualification on selection interview decisions: A study of between-sample generalizability. *Journal of Applied Psychology* 76, 550–559.

Smith, M. (1990). *Managing work place safety and health: The case of contract labor in the U.S. Petrochemical industry: Case studies*. Beaumont, Tex.: John Gray Institute, Lamar University.

Snyder, M., and W. Swann (1978). Hypothesis-testing processes in social interactions. *Journal of Personality and Social Psychology* 36, 1202–1212.

Southeast Regional Economic Justice Network (1994, July 18). Statement presented to the Commission on the Future of Worker-Management Relations (Dunlop Commission), U.S. Department of Labor, Washington, D.C.

Spalter-Roth, R. (1996). Dependency and the economic well-being among low-income mothers and their families. Paper presented at Women, Welfare and Work: 1996 Annual Workshop, National Association for Welfare Research and Statistics, San Francisco.

Spalter-Roth, R., B. Burr, H. Hartmann, and L. Shaw (1995). *Welfare that works: The working lives of AFDC recipients*. Report No. D422. Washington, D.C.: Institute for Women's Policy Research.

Spalter-Roth, R., and H. Hartmann (1994). Dependence on men, the market, or the state: The rhetoric and reality of welfare reform. *Journal of Applied Social Sciences* 18, 55–70.

Spalter-Roth, R., H. Hartmann, and L. Andrews (1992). *Combining work and welfare: An alternative anti-poverty strategy*. Report No. D406. Washington, D.C: Institute for Women's Policy Research.

Spalter-Roth, R., H. Hartmann, and L. Shaw (1993). *Exploring the characteristics of self-employment and part-time work among women*. Report No. C323. Washington, D.C.: Institute for Women's Policy Research.

Spalter-Roth, R. M., A. L. Kalleberg, M. E. Rasell, N. Cassirer, B. F. Reskin, K. Hudson, D. Webster, E. Appelbaum, and B. Dooley (1997). Managing Work and Family: Non-standard Work Arrangements among Managers and Professionals. Washington, D.C.: Economic Policy Institute; Women's Research and Education Institute.

Spragins, E., ed. (1991, June). Art of hiring professional temps. *Inc.* 13, 133–135.

Staub, E. (1987, August). Moral exclusion and extreme destructiveness: Personal goal theory, differential evaluation, moral equilibration and steps along the continuum of destruction. Paper presented at the meeting of the American Psychological Association, New York.

Steinberg, B. (1995, Spring). Temporary help services: An annual update for 1994. *Contemporary Times*, 11–16.

Stevens, A. (1994, September 23). Big companies hire more lawyer-temps. *Wall Street Journal*, 1.

Stinchcombe, A. L. (1983). *Economic sociology*. New York: Academic Press.

Stinson, J. F. (1990). Multiple jobholding up sharply in the 1980s. *Monthly Labor Review* 113, 3–10.

Stone, C. I., and B. Sawatzki (1980). Hiring bias and the disabled interviewee: Effects of manipulating work history and disability information of the disabled job applicant. *Journal of Vocational Behavior* 16, 96–104.

Strauss, G. (1988). Australian labor relations through American eyes. *Industrial Relations* 27, 131–148.

Struve, J. (1991, November). Making the most of temporary workers. *Personnel Journal* 70 (11), 43–46.

Tilly, C. (1991a). Reasons for the growth of continuing growth of part-time employment. *Monthly Labor Review* 114, 10–18.

—— (1991b). *Short hours, short shrift*. Washington, D.C.: Economic Policy Institute.

—— (1991c, May 7). Testimony on part-time and temporary work, Arbitration Proceedings, U.S. Postal Service, National Association of Letter Carriers, AFL-CIO, and American Postal Workers Union. Washington, D.C.: AFL-CIO.

—— (1992a, Spring). Dualism in part-time employment. *Industrial Relations* 31 (2), 330–347.

—— (1992b). Short hours, short shrift: Causes and consequences of part-time work. In V. L. duRivage, ed., *New policies for part-time and contingent workers*, 15–44. Armonk, N.Y.: Sharpe.

—— (1992c). Two faces of part-time work: Good and bad part-time jobs in the U.S. service industries. In B. D. Warme, K. Lundy, and L. A. Lundy, eds., *Working part-time: Risks and opportunities*, 227–238. New York: Praeger.

—— (1996). *Half a job: Bad and good part-time jobs in a changing labor market*. Philadelphia: Temple University Press.

Tucker, J. (1993). Everyday forms of employee resistance. *Sociological Forum* 8, 25–45.

Uchitelle, L. (1996, August 23). Despite drop, rate of layoffs remain high. *New York Times*, A1.

U.S.A. snapshots: rising market for temps (1995, May 8). *U.S.A. Today*, A1.

U.S. Bureau of Labor Statistics (1990, June). *Employee benefits in medium and large firms, 1989*. Bulletin No. 2363.

—— (1991, January). *Employment and earnings*. Washington, D.C.: U.S. Government Printing Office.

—— (1993). *Industry wage survey: Help supply services, 1989*. Bulletin No. 2430.

—— (1995a). *Employment and earnings*. Washington, D.C.: U.S. Government Printing Office.

—— (1995b). *Contingent and alternative employment arrangements*. Report No. 900.

—— (1997). Table 1. Work experience of the population during the year by sex and extent of employment, 1994–1995 (Data from the Current Population Survey posted on the World Wide Web). Retrieved April 1, 1997, from the World Wide Web: http://stats.bls.gov/news.release/work.t01.html.

U.S. Congress (1971). Hearings before the special subcommittee on labor of the committee on education and labor on H.R. 10349, A bill to establish and protect the rights of day laborers (92d Congress). Washington, D.C.: U.S. Government Printing Office.

U.S. Department of Education, National Center for Education Statistics (1993). *The condition of education, 1993*. Rep., NCES. Washington, D.C.: Government Printing Office.

—— (1995). *The condition of education, 1995*. Rep. No. NCES 96-793. Washington, D.C.: Government Printing Office.

—— (1996). *1993 National study of postsecondary faculty (NSOPF-93), Institutional policies and practices regarding faculty in higher education*. Report No. NCES 97-080. Washington, D.C.: Government Printing Office.

U.S. Department of Labor (1960, January). *State laws regulating private employment agencies*. Bulletin No. 209. Washington, D.C.: Bureau of Labor Standards.

—— (1962, December). *State laws regulating private employment agencies*. Bulletin No. 252. Washington, D.C.: Bureau of Labor Standards.

—— (1994). *Report on the American Workforce*. Washington, D.C.: U.S. Government Printing Office.

U.S. Department of Labor and U.S. Department of Commerce (1994a, May). *Commission on the Future of Worker-Management Relations*. Fact Finding Report.

—— (1994b, December). *Commission on the Future of Worker-Management Relations*. Final Report.

U.S. General Accounting Office (1986, March). *Employment service: More jobseekers should be referred to private employment agencies*. Washington, D.C.: Report to the chairman, Committee on Governmental Affairs, U.S. Senate.

—— (1991). *Workers at risk: Increased numbers in contingent employment lack insurance, other benefits*. Report to the Chairman, Subcommittee on Employment and Housing, Committee on Government Operations, House of Representatives, Washington, D.C.: GAO.

U.S. House of Representatives (1988). Rising Use of Part-Time and Temporary Workers: Who Benefits and Who Loses? Hearings held by Employment and Housing Subcommittee, Committee on Government Operations, May 1988. Washington, D.C.: GPO.

U.S. Senate Committee on Labor and Human Resources, 103d Congress (1993). *Toward a disposable workforce: The increasing use of "contingent labor."* Washington, D.C.: Government Printing Office.

Valticos, N. (1973). Temporary work agencies and international labour standards. *International Labour Review* 107, 43–56.

Veldkamp, G. M. J., and M. J. E. H. Raetsen (1973). Temporary work agencies and Western European social legislation. *International Labour Review* 107, 117–131.

Warme, B., and K. Lundy (1988). Erosion of an ideal: The "presence" of part-time faculty. *Studies in Higher Education* 13, 202–213.

Warner, J. (1991, February 11). How to temp your way to the top. *Business Week* 119, 89.

Weiler, P. C. (1990). *Governing the workplace: The future of labor and employment law*. Cambridge: Harvard University Press.

Wells, J. C., T. A. Kochan, and M. Smith (1991). *Managing work place safety and health: The case of contract labor in the U.S. petrochemical industry*, Beaumont, Tex.: John Gray Institute, Lamar University.

Whalen, B., and S. Dennis (1991, Spring). The temporary help industry: An annual update. *Contemporary Times*, 10–14.

Whyte, W. (1956). *The organization man*. New York: Simon & Schuster.

Wial, H. (1993). The emerging organizational structure of unionism in low-wage services. *Rutgers Law Review* 45 (3), 671–738.

—— (1994). New bargaining structures for new forms of business organization. In S. Friedman, R. W. Hurd, R. A. Oswald, and R. L. Seeber, eds., *Restoring the promise of American labor law*, 303–313. Ithaca, N.Y.: ILR Press.

Williams, H. (1989, March). What temporary workers earn: Findings from new BLS survey. *Monthly Labor Review* 112 (3), 3–6.

Withey, M. J., and W. H. Cooper (1989). Predicting exit, voice, loyalty, and neglect. *Administrative Science Quarterly* 34, 521–539.

Women's Bureau, U.S. Department of Labor. *Flexible workstyles: A look at contingent labor*. Conference Summary. Washington, D.C.: U.S. Department of Labor, Women's Bureau.

Wood, S. (1989). *The transformation of work? Skill, flexibility and the labour process*. London: Unwin Hyman.

Yoon, Y. H., S. Aaronson, H. Hartmann, L. Shaw, and R. Spalter-Roth (1994). *Women's access to health insurance*. Report No. A114. Washington, D.C.: Institute for Women's Policy Research.

Yoon, Y. H., R. Spalter-Roth, and M. Baldwin (1995). *Unemployment insurance: Barriers to access for women and part-time workers*. Report No. D425. Washington, D.C.: Institute for Women's Policy Research.

Young, M. D. (1958). *The rise of meritocracy, 1870–2033: The new elite of our social revolution*. New York: Random House.

Zemsky, R., and W. F. Massey (1990). Cost containment. *Change* 22, 16–22.

Contributors

Helen Axel, a management research consultant, is also a senior research fellow and former research director at The Conference Board. She has a master's degree from Columbia University. She is coauthor (with Stanley D. Nollen) of *Managing Contingent Workers: How to Reap the Benefits and Reduce the Risks*, published by AMACOM in 1996. Conference Board publications include *HR Executive Review: Contingent Employment* (1995) and *HR Executive Review: Downsizing* (1993). In addition, her chapter "Part-Time Employment: Crosscurrents of Change" appears in *Flexible Workstyles: A Look at Contingent Labor*, published by The Women's Bureau, U.S. Department of Labor, in 1988.

Kathleen Barker is a social psychologist who received her Ph.D. in Social-Personality Psychology from the Graduate School, City University of New York. She has published a number of articles on part-time and contingent work including "Changing Assumptions and Contingent Solutions: The Costs and Benefits of Women Working Full- and Part-Time," published by the journal *Sex Roles*; "Contingent Employment: Research Issues and the Lens of Moral Exclusion," in *Changing Employment Relations*, published by the American Psychological Association; and "Where's the Payoff? The Evaluation of Contingent Work Experience." Dr. Barker has also published a number of articles on research methodology and social issues. She has served as an Alfred P. Sloan Research Network Member on Work and Family. She is currently on faculty in the Psychology Department, Pace University, and is the associate director of VIA PACE, the University's program in social responsibility and service learning.

Anthony J. Carnevale is vice president for public leadership at Educational Testing Service (ETS). Before coming to ETS, Carnevale served as vice president and director of human resource studies at the Committee for Economic Development. In August 1993 President Clinton appointed Carnevale as chair of the National Commission for Employment Policy. Carnevale received his Ph.D., with a concentration in public finance economics, from the Maxwell School at Syracuse University.

Françoise J. Carré is research program director at the Radcliffe Public Policy Institute. She holds a B.A. from Wellesley College (1979) and a Ph.D. from the Department of Urban Studies at MIT (1993). She writes about employment transformation and its implications for workers in the United States, France, and Canada. Recent publications include "Temporary Employment in the Eighties," in V. duRivage, ed., *New Policies for the Part-Time and Contingent*; "Policy Responses to the Growth of Unstable Employment Arrangements: The French and Canadian Experiences," in Proceedings of the Forty-Seventh Annual Meeting of the IRRA; and "Piecing Together the Fragmented Workplace," with V. duRivage and C. Tilly.

Kathleen Christensen is a program officer at the Alfred P. Sloan Foundation, where she directs their Family and Work Research Program. She is on leave from the Graduate School, City University of New York, where she is a professor of environmental psychology. She has authored or coauthored a number of books on the changing nature of the workplace including *Women and Home-Based Work: The Unspoken Contract*; *The New Era of Home-Based Work: Directions and Policies*; and *Turbulence in the American Workplace*. She also published the Conference Board report *Flexible Staffing and Scheduling in the American Workplace*. Working with Mary Murphree of the U.S. Women's Bureau of the Department of Labor, she was a co-organizer of the first national conference on contingent work in 1987. She received her Ph.D. from Pennsylvania State University.

Sharon R. Cohany is an economist in the Office of Employment and Unemployment Statistics of the Bureau of Labor Statistics. Her articles on employment trends and survey redesign have been published in the *Monthly Labor Review* and other periodicals. She is a graduate of the University of Pennsylvania.

Robert W. Drago received a Ph.D. in economics from the University of Massachusetts, Amherst, in 1983 and is professor of economics and director of the Masters in Industrial and Labor Relations Program at the

University of Wisconsin–Milwaukee. He has coauthored *Productive Relations? Workplace Performance and Industrial Relations in Australia* with M. Wooden and J. Sloan (1992) and *Unlevel Playing Fields: Understanding Wage Inequality and Discrimination* with R. Albelda and S. Shulman (1997).

Virginia L. duRivage teaches labor education for the Communications Workers of America and is a research fellow with the Economic Policy Institute. She writes about organizing and representing part-time and contingent workers. DuRivage is the editor of the EPI volume *New Policies for the Part-Time and Contingent Workforce*. Recent publications include "Piecing Together the Fragmented Workplace, with F. Carré and C. Tilly, in L. Flood, ed., *Unions and Public Policy*, and *The Labor Law Rights of Contingent Workers: Organization and Representation Issues* (Publication Series, Department of Labor Studies, Pennsylvania State University, 1994).

James M. Eisenmann is a principal in the Washington, D.C.–based labor and employment law firm of Passman & Kaplan, P.C. Eisenmann received his bachelor of arts degree in political science from West Virginia University in 1986 and his J.D. in 1991 from the Catholic University of America. Eisenmann has represented Passman & Kaplan's clients in many federal trial and appellate courts and administrative agencies in cases concerning employment discrimination and labor law. Eisenmann has been published in the *Employment Discrimination Report* and *The Federal Merit Systems Reporter* regarding the Family and Medical Leave Act and other federal civil service law issues.

George Gonos received a Ph.D. from Rutgers University and is assistant professor of sociology at Centenary College, N.J. His publications include articles in the *American Sociological Review* and the *Journal of American Folklore*. His chapter in this volume is based both on scholarly research and on years of personal involvement in community-based efforts as an advocate for temporary and other underrepresented workers. He is currently writing a book on temporary help and the restructuring of U.S. employment relations.

Heidi Hartmann holds a Ph.D. in economics from Yale University and is the director and president of the Institute for Women's Policy Research (IWPR). She is a 1994 recipient of the MacArthur "genius" award. She has authored or coauthored many IWPR reports, such as "Welfare That Works: The Working Lives of AFDC Recipients"; "What Do Unions Do for Women?"; "Low-Wage Jobs and Workers: New Findings on Race, Ethnicity, and Gender"; "Women's Access to Health Care"; and "Unnecessary Losses: The Costs to Americans of the Lack of Family and Medical Leave." She has also directed several specific projects on such topics as pay equity, affirmative action, contingent work, and tax and budget analysis.

Steven F. Hipple is an economist in the Office of Employment and Unemployment Statistics of the Bureau of Labor Statistics. His analyses of the labor market have appeared in the *Monthly Labor Review*. He received his bachelor's and master's degrees from Vanderbilt University.

Lynn A. Jennings is an attorney who was counsel and policy analyst to the National Commission for Employment Policy when she coauthored Chapter 12 with Dr. Carnevale. Currently, Ms. Jennings works in the Office of the Secretary of the Department of Labor. She previously served as the chief of staff in the Management Bureau of the U.S. Agency for International Development. Ms. Jennings has a bachelor of arts degree in political science from the University of Rochester and a J.D. from the Catholic University of America.

Jean McAllister is a doctoral student in the Department of Anthropology of Columbia University. She has received master's degrees in anthropology and international relations from Columbia. Previously, she worked as a research assistant at the National Service for National Agricultural Research, The Hague, Netherlands. Her current research explores the experience and strategies of women in the United States who subsist on insecure, low-wage employment.

Dean Morse received his Ph.D. from Columbia University and is an economics consultant living in New York City. For many years he was a senior research associate at the Eisenhower Center for the Conservation of Human Resources (Eli Ginzberg, director), Columbia University.

Thomas J. Nardone is the author of numerous labor market analyses, including "On the Definition of Contingent Work," which appeared in the December 1989 issue of the *Monthly Labor Review* (coauthored with Anne E. Polivka). He is a senior economist in the Office of Employment and Unemployment Statistics of the Bureau of Labor Statistics and a graduate of King's College.

Stanley D. Nollen received a Ph.D. from the University of Chicago and is a professor of management in the School of Business at Georgetown University. His publications in the field include three books, the most recent of which is *Managing Contingent Workers: How to Reap the Benefits and Reduce the Risks* (with Helen Axel), published by AMACOM in 1996; and several articles and book chapters including "Negative Aspects of Temporary Employment," *Journal of Labor Research* (Fall 1996), and "Managing without a Complete Full-Time Workforce" (with Martin Gannon), in P. Flood et al., eds., *Managing without Traditional Methods* (1995).

Anne E. Polivka is a research economist at the Bureau of Labor Statistics, Office of Employment Research and Program Development. She has a Ph.D. in economics from the University of Wisconsin. Related publications include "On the Definition of Contingent Work" (with Thomas J. Nardone) and articles in *Public Opinion Quarterly*, the *Journal of Economic Perspectives*, and a National Bureau of Economic Research conference volume.

James B. Rebitzer received a Ph.D. in economics from the University of Massachusetts, Amherst, in 1985. His research concerns the economics of employment relationships and labor markets. His chapter in this volume is part of a larger effort to study the incentive structures embedded in human resource systems. Other research in this project concerns the determination of hours in professional service firms and the effect of group norms on incentive pay in medical groups. Rebitzer's current work examines the behavioral foundations of the economic analysis of incentives.

Roberta M. Spalter-Roth obtained her Ph.D. in sociology in 1984. Dr. Spalter-Roth is currently working on a major study of the impact of downsizing and displacement on women workers for the U.S. Department of Labor, Women's Bureau. She holds an adjunct professorship at the American University. From 1987 through 1996 she was director of research at the Institute for Women's Policy Research, where she set the institute's research agenda and directed specific projects. These included "Welfare That Works: The Working Lives of AFDC Recipients"; "Contingent Work: Its Consequences for Economic Well-Being"; "What Do Unions Do for Women?"; "Low-Wage Jobs and Workers: New Findings on Race, Ethnicity, and Gender"; "Women's Access to Health Care"; "Unemployment Insurance: Barriers for Women and Part-Time Workers"; and "Unnecessary Losses: The Costs to Americans of the Lack of Family and Medical Leave."

Jay C. Stewart is a research economist in the Office of Employment Research and Program Development at the Bureau of Labor Statistics. He has a Ph.D. in economics from the University of California, Los Angeles. He has coauthored articles in a National Bureau of Economic Research conference volume and in the *Monthly Labor Review*.

Chris Tilly received a joint Ph.D. in economics and in urban studies and planning from the Massachusetts Institute of Technology. He is currently associate professor of policy and planning at the University of Massachusetts, Lowell. His research interests focus on low-wage labor markets, racial discrimination in employment, and earnings inequality. Tilly's' recent work includes *Half a Job: Bad and Good Part-Time Jobs in a Changing Labor Market* and *Glass Ceilings and Bottomless Pits: Women, Poverty and Welfare*.

Index